Pierce Bounds

Wendy Moffat is a professor of English at Dickinson College in Carlisle, Pennsylvania. This is her first book.

A Great Unrecorded History

A NEW LIFE OF E. M. FORSTER

Wendy Moffat

PICADOR

FARRAR, STRAUS AND GIROUX

NEW YORK

www.picadorusa.com

Picador® is a U.S. registered trademark and is used by Farrar, Straus and Giroux under license from Pan Books Limited.

For information on Picador Reading Group Guides, please contact Picador. E-mail: readinggroupguides@picadorusa.com

Owing to limitations of space, all acknowledgments for permission to reprint previously published material appear on pages 405–408.

Designed by Jonathan D. Lippincott

The Library of Congress has cataloged the Farrar, Straus and Giroux edition as follows:

Moffat, Wendy, 1955–
    A great unrecorded history : a new life of E. M. Forster / Wendy Moffat.—1st ed.
       p. cm.
    Includes bibliographical references and index.

    1. Forster, E. M. (Edward Morgan), 1879–1970. 2. Forster, E. M. (Edward Morgan), 1879–1970—Relations with men. 3. Forster, E. M. (Edward Morgan), 1879–1970—Friends and associates. 4. Authors, English—20th century—Biography. 5. Gay authors—Great Britain—Biography. I. Title.

PR6011.O58Z8228 2010
823'.912—dc22
[B]
                                                                    2009029504
Picador ISBN 978-0-312-57289-1

First published in the United States by Farrar, Straus and Giroux

First Picador Edition: May 2011

P1

For Donald, *who listened,*
and for Lucy and Emma

Contents

A Great Unrecorded History

Prologue: "Start with the Fact That He Was Homosexual"

The wooden gate snapped shut behind him, and John Lehmann descended the steps carved into the canyon wall. Twenty feet below the road a small modern house nestled in the hillside. Entering the living room gave an uncanny feeling of going outdoors—the small house was bright and expansive, even on a misty November morning. Here at the north end of Santa Monica it was still possible to believe in the wildness and innocence of California. The room offered an extravagant, improbable view. Hardtop twisting below, a little house with a peaked Tudor roof almost hidden among the green of eucalyptus, live oak and pines, flat boxy roofs, down down down a cascade of curves and rectangles like a Cezanne landscape. Far off, a mirror image in the steep face of the opposite canyon. Over Lehmann's left shoulder the gray glint of the Pacific Ocean shimmered in the mist. It was just before Thanksgiving 1970.

Christopher Isherwood had summoned him. He and Lehmann had been friends for almost forty years. They first met in the early 1930s, in the damp Bloomsbury office of Virginia and Leonard Woolf's Hogarth Press. Lehmann, then the Woolfs' assistant, had persuaded them to publish Isherwood's novel *The Memorial*. Isherwood and Lehmann made a striking pair—two gay British expatriates of distinctly opposite types. Small and still boyish though he was over sixty, Isherwood retained the seductive, irreverent charm that made it "impossible not to be drawn to him." He had bright blue sparkling eyes, a flop of brown hair raked across his forehead, and a shelf of eyebrow that had grown wild and white with age. Lehmann was a different kind of attractive, a full head taller, leonine. He was three years younger than Isherwood, but seemed a generation older. Since his youth, he had projected an air of authority verging on pomposity. His mane had gone gray before he was thirty, and he spoke slowly in a commanding, precise baritone that "might have belonged to a Foreign Office expert."

Lehmann's "pale narrowed quizzing eyes" had discovered most of the crop of young political writers who revolutionized writing in the thirties. He brought Brecht and García Lorca to British audiences. Stephen Spender and C. Day Lewis became household names because of Lehmann's promotion of their work. Auden's poem "Lay Your Sleeping Head My Love" and George Orwell's essay "Shooting an Elephant" debuted in Lehmann's anthology *New Writing*. And he nurtured adaptations of Isherwood's Berlin stories from *I Am a Camera* to *Cabaret*. He had done more than anyone alive to capture the vitality and range of the British writers born in the first years of the twentieth century.

But his sway had diminished. Lehmann had been a major force in publishing fiction and poetry, but the newest generation of angry writers were playwrights. Osborne, Pinter, and Orton owed nothing to Lehmann. Eventually even his eponymous imprint—once the arbiter of the best of the new—lost its cachet and the backing of the moneymen. When his publishing career collapsed, Lehmann turned to America by necessity. He began an itinerant life lecturing on campuses where he could hold forth on his long-lived and impressive literary connections. Each term, he embarked on a new tragic romance with a much younger American man who adored him for the few months it took for the patina to wear off. Despite living in Austin, San Diego, and Berkeley, he remained British to the core.

Christopher Isherwood had given up on England long ago. With his friend and sometime lover W. H. Auden he emigrated to America in January 1939. Isherwood, the man who held "the future of the English novel in his hands," was excoriated for abandoning his country in time of war. Auden stayed in New York but Isherwood pressed westward, settling in Los Angeles, his "sexual homeland." He became a U.S. citizen in 1946. For three decades he had been happily ensconced in Southern California. On the beach below—within sight of the canyon house—he had met the great love of his life, the young artist Don Bachardy. He and Bachardy had lived together for almost twenty years. But this afternoon he consulted the old friend who had known him forever, a friend from the old world. Though sometimes he found Lehmann's self-importance boring, Christopher valued his editorial instinct. He had a secret, and he wanted John's advice.

A packet had arrived from King's College, Cambridge. In death, Morgan Forster had brought them together again. The great architect of narrative surprise had unveiled a final turn of plot.

E. M. Forster, the "master" whom they called by his intimate name, Morgan, was the only writer of the previous generation they admired without reservation. On the face of it, he seemed like an odd literary mentor. Born in 1879, Forster was more than twenty years their senior. He made his name before the First World War. By the time he was thirty, he had published a collection of short stories and four well-received novels: *Where Angels Fear to Tread, The Longest Journey, A Room with a View,* and *Howards End.* Compared to the great experimenters Joyce or Woolf, Forster's early novels seemed sedate. But to John and Christopher, these subtle satires of buttoned-up English life were revelatory and unpredictable. Christopher admired Morgan's light touch, his razor balance of humor and wryness, insight and idealism. "Instead of trying to screw all his scenes up to the highest possible pitch, he tones them down until they sound like mothers' meeting gossip . . . There's actually *less* emphasis laid on the big scenes than on the unimportant ones." The novels looked at life from a complicated position—finding a dark vein of social comedy in the tragic blindness of British self-satisfaction. In spite of their sensitivity, they had a sinewy wit.

After the first four novels, there was silence. Morgan struggled for more than a decade to produce his last novel. *A Passage to India* came out in 1924. It had all the hallmarks of his earlier novels, but Morgan's insight was burnished into a tragic wisdom. Now he asked, in the voice of an Indian man, if it was "possible to be friends with an Englishman." Despite their intentions to connect in spite of barriers of race and culture, Forster's complex and enlightened characters—Mrs. Moore and Fielding, Dr. Aziz and Professor Godbole—faced a world that seemed destined to break their wills and their hearts. But after *A Passage to India,* a curious silence. One of the most prominent novelists of his time appeared to simply cease writing fiction at the relatively young age of forty-five. Though he had almost fifty more years to live, there would be no more novels from Morgan.

But Forster forged on as a journalist, reviewer, and advocate for writers' freedom. Despite being "so shy it makes one feel embarrassed," he became a pungent social critic. He argued that Western democracies deeply misunderstand the third world. And he believed that democracy can be sustained only through tolerance and openness, *especially* when these qualities seem to threaten national security. More than anyone Christopher knew, Morgan lived by his personal beliefs. Christopher admired Morgan's integrity, his ability to apply his liberal beliefs in day-to-day ethical practice. He pronounced Morgan "saner than anyone else I know . . . He's strong because he doesn't try to be a stiff-lipped stoic like the rest of us, and so he'll never crack."

For more than fifty years Forster entered political fights from the position of the underdog. Almost every week one could read a pithy and pointed letter to the editor in his inimitable voice. He protested against fascism, against censorship, against communism, against "Jew-Consciousness," against the British occupation of Egypt and India, against racism and jingoism and anything that smelled of John Bull. Morgan's public voice wasn't stentorian. He raised it, tremulously, often alone, against the edifice of conformity.

As self-proclaimed gay men, Isherwood and Lehmann adopted the American neologism adopted by the men who resisted police harassment at the Stonewall Inn in Sheridan Square, the men who embraced gay liberation, who eschewed the medical term *homosexual*, which had marked them for decades as a "species." That they had lived through a sea change in attitudes and argot gave them fierce insight into the mystery of Morgan's strange broken-backed career. They knew—or suspected—that by the time he published *Howards End* in 1910, Morgan had grown tired of the masquerade of propriety—the unspoiled-countryside settings, the oh-so-English people in their white linen suits, the clever repartée—that generated his plots. As early as June 1911, he confided in his diary his "weariness of the only subject that I both can and may treat—the love of men for women & vice versa." After *A Passage to India*, published in 1924, he simply gave that task up.

Five months had passed since Morgan died in early June. The great old man was ninety-one. He had been a beacon to them both—a confidant, and a cultural father figure.

The brightness of the November day was transitory. With the mysterious package lurking in the book-lined study at the end of the hall, Lehmann allowed himself to be "dragged . . . off" to sit for a portrait. Isherwood's partner, Don Bachardy, was a skilled draftsman with a distinctive, intimate style: he drew only from life, in real time and natural light, finishing the work in a single session as he sat close enough to his subject to feel his breath. When they had met almost twenty years before, Bachardy was barely eighteen and Isherwood forty-nine. It was a romance as dramatic and impossible— seemingly as sure to collapse—as Bachardy's little studio perched on the hillside. But the couple, gay, out, defiant, had rewritten the familiar story in their long partnership. Looking back on their long life together, Bachardy couldn't repress a mischievous gap-toothed grin. Isherwood, he said with glee, "took [a] young boy and warped him to his mold. It was exactly what the boy wanted, and he *flourished*."

The light fading, the portrait still wet with wash, Bachardy discreetly slipped away to have dinner with friends. Lehmann and Isherwood settled into the two chairs in the living room, where David Hockney had famously posed Don and Christopher for a double portrait the year before. Before they could dig in to conversation, the Bride of Frankenstein appeared. Literally. The actress Elsa Lanchester, another British transplant in Hollywood, was Christopher's nearest neighbor in the canyon. The lonely widow of Charles Laughton, she had an "unnerving habit of appearing uninvited through hedges." Hearing of Lehmann's visit, she had decided to pay a call.

Lanchester had lived alone for a decade. She was capable of drinking too much. Her large brown eyes could grow pathetic with storms of emotion. But that night, "very affectionate and gentle," she reminisced about John's sister Beatrix, a friend and fellow actress with whom she had worked in England long ago. The men delicately escorted Lanchester home, and finally settled in Isherwood's study. The windows overlooking the ocean began to darken.

Christopher had designed a massive blond wood worktable to stretch along the full window wall. Spread out upon it was a treasure. Pages and pages and pages. For hours, the two men sifted through them in stunned silence as the flat autumn light dimmed, then failed. The final typescript of *Maurice*, the homosexual novel Forster had suppressed for almost sixty years, lay before them.

Maurice was a revolutionary new genre—a gay love story that ended happily. It was Morgan's cri de coeur. For him, "a happy ending was imperative. I shouldn't have bothered to write otherwise. I was determined that in fiction anyway two men should fall in love and remain in it for the ever and ever that fiction allows." Like its predecessor *Howards End*, *Maurice* was about the stranglehold of social class. Like *Howards End*, it was a plea to "only connect," to find the courage to understand and to love people different from ourselves. The emotional power of the story was a reflection of Morgan's sexual awakening, but the novel itself was a utopian fantasy. Maurice Hall is a stockbroker, as different in character from Morgan as he could possibly be: "handsome, healthy, bodily attractive, mentally torpid, not a bad business man and rather a snob." And Alec Scudder, the gamekeeper "senior in date to the prickly gamekeepers of D. H. Lawrence," is bright, earthy, irreverent, and utterly stifled by his place in prewar England. Alec dispels the suburban nonsense that clouds Maurice's heart and mind—the talk of platonic love from Maurice's "former faithless lover" Clive Durham, all dutiful sacrifice and stiff upper lip. He grabs hold of Maurice, and makes him believe in a future together. "He knew what the call was, and what his answer must be. They must live outside class, without relations or money; they must work and stick to each other till death. But England belonged to them . . . Her air and sky were theirs, not the timorous millions' who own stuffy little boxes, but never their own souls."

Christopher and John pawed through the masses of new typescript. Throughout were new emendations, and marginal notes in Forster's spidery hand. This version of *Maurice* was much more forthright than the draft Christopher had seen years before. Morgan had taken his advice: that gauzy, sexless version was invigorated with an entirely new, and frank, sex scene. And the resolution was firmer, too. In the draft Morgan showed Christopher years before, Alec emigrated to South America, leaving Maurice only to hope for a reunion. But in the new draft the lovers end up in each other's arms—in England, of all places and, of all times, before the First World War. In this final draft, Alec tells Maurice decisively. "Now we shan't be parted no more, and that's finished."

Looking down at the jumble of pages, Lehmann was "stunned" to see that the revised *Maurice* typescript was just the beginning. There were masses of new stories "on a homosexual theme, of quite extraordinary power and depth." One—a terrifying love affair between a colonial master and his subaltern lover—could be read as a darker, sexier iteration of the unrealized friendship between Dr. Aziz and Mr. Fielding in *A Passage to India*. So Morgan had not stopped writing fiction. Indeed, he had composed stories into extreme old age. Christopher was gleeful; John "overwhelmed." Morgan had kept his promise. Christopher felt the future of fiction, and the true meaning of Morgan's life, was in his hands.

Only weeks before Morgan died, Christopher made a pilgrimage to see him at King's College. Not that it seemed he would ever die. To be sure, he was over ninety, but he had been chugging along. The March visit began with a characteristic comic muddle. On the way up to Forster's rooms, Christopher encountered him by chance in the stairwell. Morgan exclaimed, "That's most extraordinary!" as if he had seen an apparition. Isherwood asked, "Have I changed so much?" to which Forster, recovering himself, replied firmly, "Thicker!" To prove his point, when they reached his rooms, Morgan made a studious examination of Christopher's body, discerning special "thickness" in his neck.

Settled in front of the coal fire, with the pale spring light pouring through the Gothic windows, Morgan seemed to have retrenched into an Edwardian world. The enormous dark mantelpiece had been pried from the dining room of the house where he had lived with his mother until her death in 1945. The walls were hung with "portraits of ladies in bonnets and gentlemen in cravats"—to the left of the mantel, a faux Constable landscape painted by a distant cousin. A mahogany bookshelf wheezed under its load of leather-bound books. Threadbare rugs from India and Egypt were scattered on the floor. An adjustable chair, surrounded by a penumbra of books and papers on the carpet, formed the epicenter of his little universe. It was eons from California.

Though his spirit and sense of humor were intact, for the first time Morgan looked "stooped and feeble" to Christopher. He seemed to be imploding. When the two men ventured out into the forecourt near the chapel, Morgan stopped for a moment. Bent almost in two, sitting on a bench, he was a caricature—just a tweed cap, walking stick, brown shoes. But his rosy face still lit up when he heard a good piece of gossip. He remained cheerful, sensitive, and wily as a "raccoon."

Christopher and Morgan accepted an invitation from the artist Mark Lancaster to come and see his studio in the great rotunda atop the eighteenth-century Gibbs Building across the courtyard. Mark recalled being "as 'openly gay' as people were in 1968." In Britain, it was the first year that consensual homosexual acts were no longer a crime: the Labouchère Amendment, under which Oscar Wilde had been convicted of "gross indecency," had finally been repealed. As the college's first ever artist-in-residence, he brought a whiff of spice into the settled "half-in and half-out of the closet" tradition of homosexuality at King's. In college, it was a semisecret that Forster was homosexual. There were even rumors of a secret manuscript. But week after week at High Table, Mark never breathed a word, never asked a question. And Morgan, ever courteous, kept to himself.

Not quite thirty, Lancaster was painting a series of big green-and-blue abstract canvases. He had come back to England from New York, where he had worked at the Factory with Andy Warhol. *Work* actually seemed the wrong word for entering that creative vortex. Andy was equally curious about everything. His detachment was liberating. Under his odd, watchful gaze experiences shook free from the strictures and stigmas that extrinsically accrued to them in the world outside the Factory. His gentle manner encouraged things to *be* without being labeled. In 1964 he filmed Lancaster and Gerard Malanga in a single endlessly long kiss. He called the movie *Kiss*. Warhol spliced it together with film of other couples kissing, couples of all configurations and stripes, eyes open, eyes closed, curious, passive, unerotic. The effect of this moral flatness was strange. It held a mirror up to the audience. The only thing pornographic about this depiction of sex on screen was the discomfiture of those in the audience who singled out—and reviled—the homosexual kissing scene. "In the atmosphere of the Warhol Factory" for the first time, Lancaster felt it was "normal," even "superior, to be gay." Compared to the Factory, Lancaster found English life class-bound and rigid, and English gay life "(necessarily) furtive and unspoken."

Warhol radiated stillness and equanimity. Like an anthropologist from Mars, he watched impassively. Sometimes this unflappable manner revealed just how violent and atavistic the homophobia he and his friends faced actually was. Once, when Norman Mailer punched Mark in the stomach for wearing a pink shirt—"pansy, effete Englishman"—Andy acted out a little charade of plaintive envy. In his breathy voice he asked, "What do *I* have to do to get punched in the stomach by Norman Mailer?" Lancaster, too, was semicomically incensed. There was nothing un-American about the shirt. He had bought it at Bloomingdale's.

Lancaster had transformed the aerie atop King's. His door was open whenever he was not "sporting the oak"—shutting the public outer door to his rooms to signal he was at work. The walls that had divided the room into a set had been dismantled to form a real studio, exposing an immense half-moon window that dominated the courtyard wall, opening onto a view of the green carpet of lawn and the lacy Gothic screen that cut off the college from the town. A painted mantel remained incongruously anchored to the wall. Christopher patiently walked beside Morgan as he teetered his way up the four flights of stairs to Lancaster's studio. Dazzling light, somehow unfamiliar. Yes, for decades this room had housed one of Morgan's dearest friends, the political philosopher Goldsworthy Lowes Dickinson. But Morgan hadn't been here since Goldie died in 1932. When Lancaster expressed surprise, Morgan replied that the historian F. E. Adcock, the room's subsequent occupant, "was such a bore."

Seated side by side, the grand old men of letters jovially reminisced for Lancaster's benefit. Laughing and chatting amiably, they took tea and biscuits while he stole a quick snapshot to record the occasion. Morgan folded himself into a zigzag, his hands clasped awkwardly, his hair a cloud of white fuzz as delicate as a dandelion. Later, when the two had gone, Lancaster rested the picture on the mantel beside another informal photograph of a visitor sitting in the same chair that Morgan chose—a slender young man with huge blue eyes precisely matching the color of his denim shirt. Framed by dark hair, the melancholy face of Pete Townshend, the guitarist for the Who, looked like a Modigliani portrait.

On that spring morning, as always, Morgan looked impeccably ordinary, like "the man who comes to wind the clocks." It was a canny disguise. In the 1920s, his college friend Lytton Strachey had nicknamed him the "Taupe," the French word for "mole." Though he was one of the great living men of letters, in a loose-fitting tweed suit and a cloth cap he slipped unnoticed into the crowd or sat quietly at the edge of the conversational circle. This mousy self-presentation was no accident. Forster came of age sexually in the shadow of the 1895 Wilde trials, and he learned their lessons well. Naturally quite shy, he consciously inverted Wilde's boldly effeminate persona. Where Wilde—and Strachey after him—cut flamboyant and dandified figures, Forster disappeared into the woodwork. Wilde's bons mots became famous epigrams, but Forster instead chose to draw people inward, to reveal themselves to him as he remained enigmatic. To speak with him was to be seduced by an inverse charisma, a sense of being listened to with such intensity that you had to be your most honest, sharpest, and best self. Morgan's steadfast scrutiny tested his friends' nerves. Siegfried Sassoon found it "always makes me into a chatterbox." The attention made Christopher feel "false and tricky and embarrassed." He always had to suppress an urge to act the clown, to "amuse" Morgan to dispel the moral weight of his stillness and empathy.

All his life Morgan's friends struggled to put their finger on the ineffable quality that made him such an exceptional man. His pale blue eyes were terribly nearsighted, but everyone close to him noticed that they missed nothing. He had a "startlingly shrewd look of appraisal . . . behind the steel-framed spectacles . . . It was a curious feeling to be welcomed and judged at the same time." To Christopher, Morgan's eyes made him look like "a baby who remembers his previous incarnation and is more amused than dismayed to find himself reborn in new surroundings." In life and in writing, Morgan preferred to plumb the depths and to leave himself open to surprise. Even the most ordinary conversation could "tip a sentence into an unexpected direction and deliver a jolt."

Forster conducted his life as if everyone lived in a novel, with the rich inner life of characters' motives and feelings operating as the rules of the world. Every occasion was carefully observed, and even the most clear-cut matters subject to interpretation. His excessive insight made him seem hopeless about practicalities. One friend called him a "dreamer" and counseled that he should "face facts." Morgan responded precisely: "It's impossible to face facts. They're like the walls of a room, all round you. If you face one wall, you must have your back to the other three." His hyperprecision sometimes savored of the absurd: once when asked if it was raining, Forster slowly walked to the window and replied, "I will try to decide."

The previous July, just after he arrived at King's for his residency, Lancaster found himself alone in an octagonal room where a tiny black-and-white television had been installed on a tea cart before the fireplace as a begrudging acknowledgment of the wider world. Next door was the Fellows' Senior Combination Room, on whose claret-colored walls the portraits of great Kingsmen—all friends of Morgan, all dead—gazed down: Rupert Brooke, a Roger Fry self-portrait, Duncan Grant's painting of Maynard Keynes. In contrast, the little room had barely enough room for two armchairs and a couple of vitrines stuffed with ancient pottery that flanked the Gothic window. It was a nondescript time in the midmorning, and the BBC was broadcasting coverage of the first moon landing. Decades later, Lancaster still remembered the scene clearly. Morgan "shuffled in, asked me what it was, settled down to watch" on the armchair beside him. He leaned forward conspiratorially toward Mark. "I'm not sure they should be doing that," he said quietly.

When Christopher first met Morgan in September 1932, he was already yearning to be his "disciple." Here was a gay mentor, a novelist who had found "the key to the whole art of writing." Christopher admired Morgan's technical skill, but he was awed by his humility. He reminded Christopher of a Zen master. For his part, Forster was attracted to the courage and clarity of the young man's writing. *The Memorial* had caught his eye. It was published by his old friends the Woolfs, and came recommended by a congenial new friend, William Plomer, whose novel *Sado* centered on a homoerotic affair between an expatriate (much like Plomer) and a Japanese boy. The Woolfs had published *Sado*, too.

The Memorial was subtitled "Portrait of a Family" but Christopher's working title had been "War and Peace." Charting the wreckage of the Great War through the story of an upper-middle-class English family was precariously close to autobiography for Christopher. His father had been killed at Ypres in 1915 when the boy was only ten. All his life Christopher deeply resented his widowed mother's psychic sway over him. But the dark character at the center of the novel resembled Christopher only slightly. Edward Blake was a galvanic creation: homosexual, bitterly funny, miserable, shell-shocked, a veteran of the war. In one scene, told from Edward's point of view, he puts the muzzle of a gun into his mouth, pulls the trigger—and botches the suicide. The novel's voice was a perfect blend of the attitude of the postwar generation: arresting, grim, and sardonic. Christopher's writing was so lucid and matter-of-fact that people mistook it for journalism all his life.

He was masterful at writing about sex. The young people are refreshingly irreverent about this solemn subject. Edward proposes to sleep with Margaret, his putative girlfriend, by invoking "our duty to our neighbours." Margaret complies, laughingly threatening him: "To think, Edward—I might cure you."

And so, one evening at the studio, after a particularly hectic party, they'd started—and it had been really very funny and not the least disgusting—but quite hopeless. They sat up in bed and laughed and laughed. "Oh Edward!" laughed Margaret—for she was pretty tight, too—"I shall never be able to sleep with a man again. At the critical moment I shall always think of you." . . . "I might return the compliment," said Edward.

In the final scene of the novel, Edward Blake finds the place where he belongs: in Berlin, in bed with a venal if seductive German boy.

Anticipating his first meeting with Morgan, Christopher wrote Stephen Spender half-jokingly, "I shall spend the entire morning making up." Not that he put on mascara. Rather, he polished his most precious currency: tantalizing tales of the boy bars in Berlin. And he had stories to tell of Dr. Magnus Hirschfeld and his Institute for Sexual Science, with its museum crammed with sex toys and fantasy pictures. Hirschfeld came straight out of Central Casting for the figure of a German scientist; he was a "silly solemn old professor with [a] doggy mustache" and thick glasses. He lived over the shop with Karl Giese, his secretary and lover. There was something poignant and defiant about Hirschfeld's resolute belief that sex was a legitimate object of study, and he had paid a price for his public campaign to decriminalize consensual sex between men. Twice he had been badly beaten in the street by Nazi thugs. To Christopher, Berlin was a place where there was no pretense to the "duty" of heterosexual affections. By going to Germany he thought he had escaped the hypocrisy, the puritanism, the portentous respectability of the prison he called England.

They met in the Brunswick Square flat that Morgan had rented a few years before as an occasional escape from the suburban surveillance of his mother. It was a plain set of rooms in a rather shabby Victorian row house. On the sitting-room wall hung a talisman of Morgan's friendship with the exotic and dashing T. E. Lawrence—an original illustration of an Arab boy, knife unsheathed, which had been commissioned for the privately printed edition of *The Seven Pillars of Wisdom*. Christopher was so bowled over that he barely recalled their conversation. But the pleasurable sense of being invited into the circle of the elect was palpable. In a special token of intimacy, Forster lent Isherwood the precious copy of *The Seven Pillars of Wisdom* given to him by Lawrence himself. The book was a brilliant record of Lawrence's campaign in the Middle East just after the war. The story of his disguising himself to fight alongside the Arabs was so colorful that some readers thought it was an Orientalist fantasy. It was by turns heroic and harrowing. In one horrifying scene, Lawrence describes his rape and torture as a prisoner of the Turks in Deraa. Christopher left the flat "clasping this magic volume," aglow with excitement and awe.

If Christopher wanted to be a disciple, Morgan equally found himself in need of one just then. For him it was an especially vulnerable moment. His "lover and beloved," Bob Buckingham, had recently married, and Morgan was just beginning to reconcile himself painfully to the fact. Meeting these new young friends, these gay intellectuals and writers, was a partial salve. He needed companionship, frank talk, and laughter, not sex. Expanding the circle of confidants and friends was a characteristic means for him to move past an emotional bottleneck.

Six months after his first meeting with Morgan, Christopher returned to London as the world of Berlin collapsed in ruins around him. The recently elected Nazi government was making a show of cleaning up vice, shutting down the boy bars and arresting gay men in roundups. Virulent mobs smashed windows and set fire to Hirschfeld's institute, forcing him and Giese to flee. Christopher recognized that Germany was no longer the haven he once imagined it could be. Some homosexuals he knew had declared themselves Nazi sympathizers, believing it would protect them, but Christopher lamented the tragedy of "self-deceivers." His burning concern was how to find a way for his lover, Heinz Neddermeyer, whom he had left behind, to escape to some shared safety.

On this second visit, in a gesture that became a ritual of intimacy, Morgan showed Christopher the typescript of *Maurice*. Like John Lehmann and Christopher almost forty years later, Morgan and Christopher sat side by side in the Brunswick Square boîte with the precious draft between them. What did he think, Morgan wanted to know? The master appealed to the pupil, and the pupil was overwhelmed. The truth was that to the younger man's ear, Morgan's writing about sex sounded "antique" and prudish. The scene when Maurice announces that he's slept with Alec made him cringe with embarrassment. Morgan had concocted a ridiculous euphemism for making love—the word *sharing*.

"I have shared with Alec," [Maurice] said after deep thought.
   "Shared what?"
   "All I have. Which includes my body."

But the novel's occasional solecisms were almost beside the point. Morgan came from a different time. The man who had penned the word *sharing* could hardly be expected to call himself gay. Morgan's lifelong resistance to labeling had nothing to do with caution or cowardice. Whatever its locutions, *Maurice* was passionate and honest. Christopher was moved by the thought of Morgan so brave and alone, "imprisoned within the jungle of pre-war prejudice, putting these unthinkable thoughts into words." He understood that being shown the novel was Morgan's expression of a quasi-paternal connection with a gay man from the thirties generation. Morgan struck Christopher as immensely lonely, and Morgan was sensitive that the novel had lived in the hothouse for too long. Apprehensively, he asked Christopher: "Does it date?" Christopher's response was a perfect blend of compassion and honesty. "Why *shouldn't* it date?" he replied stoutly. "Eyes brimming with tears," the young acolyte told Morgan that he admired the novel profoundly, that it was pioneering work, that he thought it was wonderful and brave. Hearing this, Forster leaned forward and gently kissed Christopher on the cheek. The moment cemented their friendship for life.

But acquiescing to Christopher's desire that the novel should be *published* was another matter altogether. Here it was impossible to distinguish Morgan's self-protectiveness from timidity. Christopher hammered away all summer long, in letters from abroad. Heinz had tried unsuccessfully to enter England, ostensibly to work for Christopher as a domestic servant, but he was interrogated at Harwich and deported. Auden, who was a witness to the event, guessed that the malevolent customs officer, a "bright-eyed little rat," was "*one of us*." So Christopher left England, "committed to wandering the world until he found somewhere they could both settle, unharried by immigration checks and customs officials." For a time, that place was the Canary Islands.

Morgan's letters to Christopher in this warm paradise led Morgan to speculate on his fictional lovers as if they were real people living in the world. Confiding in the young man, Morgan ruminated on the question, still quite raw after Bob's marriage, of what he could expect in the way of fidelity and intimacy. He cast the discussion in terms of strategies to revise the novel, but the idea was clearly a proxy for his own emotional state.

> I think what might happen is a permanent relationship, but with all sorts of vagaries, fears, illnesses, distraction, fraying out at its edges, and this would take a long time to represent. One may shorten it, perhaps,

if one made them take a vow, and Maurice could take it, but I doubt about Alec, as about myself. We are, both of us, more likely to look back and realise that we have, after all, sacrificed enough to bring the thing off.

Despite the mess with Heinz, Christopher assured him that *Maurice* should be published, and that to do so would be inspiring to gay readers. But Forster wouldn't budge. He was not at all sure that attitudes toward homosexuality had progressed since his youth.

The younger man took the lead. Isherwood pressed Morgan to relent—in 1938, 1948, 1952. Morgan was flattered, but he did not budge. He told Christopher, "I am ashamed at shirking publication but the objections are formidable." He was chiefly concerned that the news of his homosexuality would hurt those he loved. As time passed, Morgan's younger friends joined Christopher in making the case to publish. One friend pointed to the example of André Gide, whom Forster admired, and who had published explicitly homosexual memoirs. Forster retorted: "But Gide hasn't got a mother!" Then, after the war, after his mother died, Morgan was worried that Bob Buckingham would be exposed to "bother or harm" if the book were published.

Two decades of importuning won Isherwood a persuasive victory. As he grew older Forster became more comfortable with the idea of frankness about his sexual life. He imagined a posthumous biography "briefly and blazingly written." By early 1952 he finally agreed that *Maurice* should be published after he died, and took steps to arrange that the cherished typescript should come into Isherwood's hands for safekeeping.

But Morgan's earlier skepticism about the progress of tolerance for homosexuality was well founded. In October 1952, Christopher's first copy was shepherded by hand, from Cambridge to London to New York to Chicago to Los Angeles, by trustworthy friends, all gay men. They chose this method of delivery to protect both the book and its author. On both sides of the Atlantic, the cold war fueled anxiety about the loyalty and patriotism of homosexuals, and the machinery of the state was being used to gather evidence and entrap gay men. In the United States, the House Un-American Activities Committee had begun a "lavender scare" to root out homosexual men in government, who were deemed a security risk because their sex lives made them vulnerable to blackmail. The U.S. postmaster general revived the eighty-year-old Comstock laws to prosecute gay men who used the mail to convey "obscene, lewd, lascivious or filthy" materials. In London, police sting operations against gay men were intensifying, and men who were arrested often found their personal papers confiscated without a warrant. Morgan jocularly called the packet enclosing the typescript "the main goods" to emphasize their clandestine machinations. He dotted every *i*, composing a contract that expressly permitted Christopher to have the American rights, and formally requesting a special waiver from his literary executor.

The men who arranged this pony express were not being paranoid. Even very eminent men who were homosexual were being prosecuted and humiliated. The actor Sir John Gielgud was caught up in a sting operation in a public lavatory when he was at the height of his career on the London stage. Just months before the *Maurice* manuscript was spirited to California, the famous mathematician Alan Turing, whose solution to the Nazi Enigma code machine had materially helped the Allies win the war, was caught in the net. He was forcibly given female hormones to "cure" him of his homosexual desires as part of a plea bargain to avoid imprisonment under the same laws used to convict Oscar Wilde in 1895. Two years later, Turing killed himself. None of Morgan's friends wished to risk the loss of *Maurice* or the liberty of its author in those perilous times. There were still plenty of "beasts and idiots who . . . prowl in the darkness, ready to gibber and devour."

In Christopher's study, late into the autumn night, Christopher and John Lehmann discussed the mechanics of publishing *Maurice* in America. The thought of Morgan's death evoked a bit of black humor: John drily called the pages Forster's "literary remains." But the men shared a reverence for the novel's place in gay patrimony. The typescript was weighed down by the care so many had taken to preserve it for so long. It was heavy with a history of stealth. For six decades Forster had nurtured it in secret, painstakingly revising and adding chapters. He commissioned two wondrously named lady typists— Mrs. Jones and Mrs. Snatchfold—to copy the contraband manuscript in pieces, to protect them from the novel's secrets. He carefully kept track of each copy of the typescript, requesting that the chosen reader return it to a safely neutral location—usually the Reform Club. Late in old age, when he was almost eighty-five, Forster reflected on the cost of this lifetime of effort: "How *annoyed* I am with Society for wasting my time by making homosexuality criminal. The subterfuges, the self-consciousness that might have been avoided."

There was great hope in *Maurice*. But even in 1960, when he penned an author's note to the novel, Morgan was unsentimental about its future. On the face of it, conditions for gay men looked to be improving in England at long last. Six years before, a government committee led by Sir John Wolfenden had begun to deliberate on whether to revise or repeal the laws against "homosexual offenses." In 1957, the Wolfenden Report recommended measures to partially decriminalize consensual sex between adult men. But while he had hoped as a young man that "knowledge would bring understanding" about homosexuality, late in life Forster realized that the change in public attitudes in his long lifetime had merely shifted from "ignorance and terror to familiarity and contempt . . ." Clear-eyed and somewhat bitter, too, Morgan could not imagine a world as utopian as his novel, even in the distant future. He lamented that homosexuality "can only be legalised by Parliament, and Members of Parliament are obliged to think or appear to think. Consequently the Wolfenden recommendations will be indefinitely rejected, police prosecutions will continue, and Clive on the bench will continue to sentence Alec in the dock. Maurice may get off."

He was right that the legal changes came painfully slowly. In July 1967, when Morgan was eighty-eight, the Sexual Offenses Act was finally passed. Sex between men who desired each other, were alone in a house, and over twenty-one was legalized—provided that neither of the men was in the armed forces or the merchant navy. And, in a final fillip, the new law applied only to men living in England and Wales.

Isherwood and Lehmann knew they were breaking a magic circle of private readership. Sharing the manuscript of *Maurice* had been a kind of covenant among Forster's closest friends for decades. Now this secret would be open for everyone. Like Prospero breaking his staff at the end of *The Tempest*, Isherwood hoped to shatter the spell that had kept the silence about Forster's homosexuality for so long.

They knew they risked offending, even exposing, some of Forster's surviving friends. But Isherwood also felt righteous, that his incautiousness was a badge of honor. He complained to Lehmann that Forster's British literary executors were stymieing his work by giving him shoddy copies and quavering about giving permission to print Forster's frank and reflective author's note in the American edition. He made much of the contrast between his sincerity and what he perceived to be the stuffiness and reticence of Forster's friends in England. For Isherwood, shepherding Forster's gay fiction posthumously into print was both a sacred trust and a political adventure. He believed that publication would give Forster a second life as a pioneer of gay writing. Publishing *Maurice* was part of his long campaign to celebrate sexual freedom and repudiate homophobia and hypocrisy.

That Forster's reputation as a giant of twentieth-century literature and the father of liberal humanism had accrued in part from decades of hiding his homosexuality was an irony not lost on Isherwood's circle. They were only too happy to use this goodwill to legitimize what one friend called "a kind of pro-homosexual strategy." The American writer Glenway Wescott—whose lover Monroe Wheeler carried the manuscript from London to New York—hoped that a "writer so socially acceptable" could lend "establishmentarian backing for the first homosexual love story with a happy ending."

This abjuring of their special status marked a completion of Isherwood's and Lehmann's own journeys as well. Decades before, they were young gay men galvanized by the passion and honesty of Morgan's declaration that "there can be real love, love without limits or excuse, between two men." Forster—a generation older—had always seemed irredeemably older than they were. Now they were sixty-six and sixty-four. They had caught up with him; they, too, had become old. Christopher rose from the desk and gazed across the room at the opposite wall crammed with books. There were dozens of books about Morgan. He was thinking about the future. His expression triumphant, he turned back to John. "Of course all those books have got to be re-written," he said. "Unless you start with the fact that he was homosexual, nothing's any good at all."

Even Christopher didn't know how many more secret manuscripts there were than the few he leafed through on that November day almost thirty-five years ago. Though he burned great bonfires of ephemera, Morgan carefully preserved the record of his gay life. Thousands of unpublished pages of letters, diaries, essays, and photographs tell the story of the life he hid from public view. Some of the pages are scattered in archives. Some have been coaxed out into the world from remarkable hiding places—a vast oak cupboard in a London sitting room, a shoebox humbly nestled among mouse turds in a New England barn. Many of Morgan's surviving friends have told their stories for the first time. Only in 2008 were the final entries in his private diary, restricted from view since his death, opened to readers. All his long life Morgan lived in a world imprisoned by prejudice against homosexuals. He was sixteen when Oscar Wilde was sent to prison, and he died the year after the Stonewall riots.

Almost a century ago, Forster dedicated *Maurice* to "a happier year." Perhaps that time is now.

PART ONE

Becoming a "Grown Up Man"

1

"A Queer Moment"

It was just Lily and Morgan. This had not been the plan.

Alice Clara Whichelo, known as Lily, married a marvelous young architect after an eight-week engagement when she was twenty-one. Edward Morgan Forster was the son of a clergyman. Lily and Eddie settled near Dorset Square in London, a few blocks from the rose gardens of Regents Park—a fine place for a young couple to start a family, and far enough away from Eddie's imposing relatives at Clapham to give them breathing space. It was January 1877. Eddie was twenty-nine, and a bit slow to get on his feet professionally. Coming down from Trinity College, Cambridge, he had taken a slightly crooked path, inching away from filial expectations that he become a vicar. He was just starting his career, and his family buoyed up the young people financially. His sister Laura, having inherited some money, commissioned him to draw up plans for a fine brick country house in Surrey.

Lily didn't know it, but her husband's commission of Laura Forster's West Hackhurst house would be the zenith of her happiness and security for a long time. She was pregnant within weeks of her wedding but their baby was stillborn. So ended the first year of her marriage. The next spring, almost before she had time to breathe, Lily was pregnant again. In the brief time before it would be unseemly for Lily to be seen traipsing about in public, Eddie took her to France to widen her horizons. His formidable "Aunt Monie"—the family matriarch who financed the trip—found the chaperoning arrangements rather unorthodox: "no Lady companion" for Lily unless one counted Eddie's university friend Ted Streatfeild, who accompanied the couple on their belated honeymoon. Streatfeild, Aunt Monie wrote acidly, was "very nearly" a lady companion, "I own, but not quite." While Lily rested at the hotel, the men walked and talked. For them Paris was familiar territory. Eddie was "very glib" at speaking French.

By the time they returned to London, Lily was heavily pregnant. On New Year's Day 1879 she and Edward celebrated the birth of a son, also called Edward Morgan. Naming him thus came from a mistake at the baptismal font—the alchemy of absentmindednesss and fear of social ostracism that would fuel Forster's first comic novels. In deference to Aunt Monie, the couple had settled on the family name Henry Morgan, the Henry honoring both Monie's father, Henry Thornton, and Eddie's brother Henry, a "shining light" who had died when Eddie was eighteen. So they had registered the baby's name in the official records, but when the verger read from the scrap of paper at the font, he found that Eddie—"distrait"—had written his own full name instead. To differentiate him from his father, they called him by his middle name. Soon after the baby was born, it was clear that Eddie was very ill. He developed a horrifying cough and all through the year he could not shake a cold. Through eighteen "months of languor and sickness" Lily "could not take her husband's illness seriously." She was focused on the baby, and "she was accustomed to young people remaining alive." Behind her back the Forsters and Eddie's maternal family, the Thorntons, were full of advice and recrimination.

Lily came by her obtuse optimism honestly, and it later served her well. Like her husband, she was one of ten children. But the Whichelos were a hearty family—all her siblings were humming along, "fond of pleasure, generous and improvident," full of "good looks . . . good taste and good spirits." The Forsters were a more delicate bunch. Eddie, the eighth born, had already seen the death of five siblings from tuberculosis. One after the other they had been struck down; John, the firstborn, had lived all the way to the age of thirty-four, but the rest died in their teens and twenties. By the late summer of 1880 Lily realized that she must take the illness in hand. She rented a large house with a view of the sea in Bournemouth, and moved Eddie and the baby there to breathe the brisk salty air. But it was already too late. On October 30, 1880, Eddie died of tuberculosis, just ten days before his thirty-third birthday. Before her son was two, Lily was a twenty-five-year-old widow. Morgan wrote later, "[S]he felt that her life had ended before it had begun." Her own words characterized her stupefying grief: "I wish tonight would never turn into day and that I could go on sleeping forever, it would be so nice." Morgan was all she had left.

. . .

There was no money on Lily's side of the family. Her father had been a draw-ing master—a big, dreamy man who cobbled together a living. He had died suddenly when she was twelve, leaving her mother, Louisa, indefatigable and resourceful, to find ways of pressing her children out into the world. As the third of ten children and the eldest girl, Lily had learned to be stout-hearted, uncomplaining, and to take care of herself. In 1872, she had bought a diary which she wryly dedicated to herself, "a great heroine . . . age 17, manners 71 years of age, from her infancy always very old for her age." Soon after, with an introduction from her family doctor, Lily became a companion to the neighboring Thorntons and a governess to the children of their friends. So she had met Eddie, and so she remained in the sway of his family after his death. Eddie had left a small inheritance. Seven thousand pounds would generate enough income for her to live a frugal middle-class life. By default Eddie had also left her to the redoubtable influence of his Aunt Monie, Mar-ianne Thornton.

The Thorntons, Morgan Forster later came to understand, had a genetic gift: they "always had known best—it was part of their moral integrity." And Aunt Monie "knew best better than ever" as she aged. She was eighty-two when Morgan was born, and she claimed not only the financial and moral power to determine her favored great-nephew's future but a formidable family history to guide him. The Thorntons had all the gravitas and social influence the Whichelos lacked. They had been among the first families in Clapham for generations. Marianne's father, Henry Thornton, was a founding member of the Clapham Sect, a group of Christian evangelists who proved to be effec-tive, if ornery, politicians in the early nineteenth century.

Henry Thornton's money came from banking. First he did well and then he did good. Family prayers were "a discipline and an institution," Morgan wrote later. "The Clapham Sect listened, rose from its knees, ate, and then made money—made as much as ever it could, and then gave as much as it could away. The activity in either direction was immense." Thorntons were great moralists, and despite all opposition they Stood Up for What Was Right. Year after year, Henry Thornton stood up in Parliament to support bills that would make this world a little more like the next: bills to establish asylums for the insane, bills for parliamentary reform against sinecures and corrup-tion, bills for peace with the Americas, bills to stabilize the banking system, which was hopelessly unregulated, always bubbling and bursting. Most famously, Thornton had been a great friend of William Wilberforce in the long campaign to end the British slave trade. Thornton was a moderate, humorless man who had not an ounce of whimsy in his bones. (His friend Hannah More had unironically named her two cats Non-resistance and Passive Obedience.) By the time of Eddie's death, in Marianne's hands the Thornton evangelical fervor had distilled to the essence of knowing what was right for Lily and the baby.

After a miserable and smothering year living in the gloom of Aunt Monie's large house in South London, Lily did something astonishing. She resisted her in-laws' desire to envelop her, and set off to establish a separate household for herself and Morgan. In the autumn of 1882 she found an eighteenth-century redbrick house to let on four acres of land *north* of the city. The house was an island, even an idyll, suspended in time and place. Neither country nor yet fully suburban, Rooksnest stood at the margin of the village of Stevenage.

Morgan and Lily would live at Rooksnest for the next decade. Once there had been a hamlet and farm called Rooksnest, but those had disappeared, and now the name attached like a ghost to a two-story gabled house with plain windows and broad chimneys in the center of the roof and at one end. There was nothing particularly grand or historical about the house. To Morgan, whose first proper piece of writing was a memoir of the house, composed when he was fifteen, its very ordinary Englishness made it seem mystical, tied as it was to a past that was rapidly being eroded by the growth of suburban London. The walk to the village was about a mile. In the meadow beside the house was an ancient wych-elm in which people of the distant past had pressed boars' fangs into the bark, little "votive offerings of people who had their toothache cured by chewing pieces of the bark." Next door was the Franklyn farm, where there were ponies and children to play with, and a barn full of sweet straw to hide in. The kitchen garden was big enough to be hard work. Lily adapted the lawn for tennis. She and Morgan lived with two domestic servants—one for indoors and one for out. There might have been a moat, so socially isolated was their little household. Years later Forster immortalized the house, and the feeling of the house, in a novel. He called it Howards End.

In *Howards End* the house is haunted not by a literal ghost but by a sort of genius loci. Eddie's ghost, if it walked at all, signified a lost world that might have supplanted or at least balanced out the "haze of elderly ladies"—the aunts and great-aunts, Victorian matrons who formed the only circle of friends with whom Lily felt comfortable. The lost world, Morgan came to understand, was an unspoken world, not only male but homoerotic. When he was in his mid-seventies, preparing a biography of Marianne Thornton, Morgan thought back on the oddities that he had stubbornly gleaned from Eddie's short life. There was the unusual interest in aesthetics, fashion, and the decorative arts, the kind of pursuit au courant with Oscar Wilde and his set at Oxford. In facing marriage, Eddie was described as "not wild like L[ily] but as befitted his seven more years all aglow with happiness and having looked 'things' steadily in the face . . ." *Things?* Why did the milk-livered Ted Streatfeild accompany the couple to Paris? Why had Aunt Monie worried that Eddie "won't be too old maidish to walk you down the Boulevard Italienne at night"? Then there was the strange companionship, akin to an informal adoption, between his dashing young uncle Percy Whichelo and an older military gentleman. In retrospect, Morgan thought "the implication was obvious." It was not merely wish fulfillment to see the root of his homosexuality in his family's past.

At Rooksnest, Lily Forster established the domestic pattern that would last the rest of her life: she and her boy against the world. She never remarried. Mother and son lived alone on a delicate reef of interdependence. A formal photograph taken when Morgan was five suggests the balance of power. The picture looks mid-Victorian though it was taken thirty years later. Wearing a little velvet suit with lace cuffs and collar, Mary Janes and stockings, his long hair cascading down his back, Morgan appears as an androgynous little Lord Fauntleroy. Though he is stout, Lily is shielding him as if he's delicate. She stands behind him, not yet thirty, still dressed in mourning, her long hair pulled back in an elegant coil of plaits. Steadying him with her right hand, his mother looks down at him adoringly. But Morgan—with wide blue eyes—faces the camera directly with the attitude of an odalisque.

Aunt Monie had given Morgan the "deplorable" nickname "The Important One," and it had grown less and less ironic over the years. He was accustomed to being the center of attention, but oddly this didn't translate into narcissism. Because he was intensely filial and intensely sensitive, Morgan felt the weight of his role as Lily's reason for living. He was a solemn little boy, often very still. He watched with interest the delicate dance women must adopt to be heard by men. He became in effect Lily's lady companion.

So close were he and Lily that their identities seemed to merge. He parroted her habit of cosseting and her intense interest in the exquisite proprieties of social standing and social etiquette. To his two dolls, Sailor Dollar and Sailor Duncan, he told long, complicated stories about what could and shouldn't be done. One afternoon when Morgan was five he and Lily settled down to play "our usual game at Bézique. M. had S. Duncan stuck under his arm, which a good deal interfered with his play. At last he said so gravely 'I am having such a miserable time with this doll. Do you think he would mind much not learning the game?'"

Learning the game seemed to be the key to living life. The whole of the world appeared as a set of rules, to be negotiated with care if you were not powerful. There seemed to be ways to earn a little safety. At the age of four, Morgan told his mother he "would much rather be a coward than brave because people hurt you when you are brave." At other times, it seemed that however much one tried, who you were was determined by whether you could adequately act a part. But both his anachronistic dress and his extremely sensitive manner made him seem "half a girl," Lily complained. "I wish he was more manly and did not cry so easily." Once, when he was mistaken for a girl by a servant, he was told to go back and correct the misapprehension. Dutifully, he returned and announced, "I'm a little boy." "Yes, miss," was the reply.

He was clever. By the age of four, he discovered that he could read. Thereafter he fiercely defended his interior life, commenting to Aunt Monie's maid that it was "[t]iresome to be interrupted in my reading when the light is so good." Learning to read opened a vista into a separate life—a life apart from Life, which he figured in a piece of juvenile fiction as a "secret place." Here it was possible to slow things down to consider them, to magnify feelings, to roll them around in the brain, to hone the strange interior truths of being and feeling. In later years, he crystallized these insights into a very funny, very sad essay he called "Notes on the English Character." "It is not," Morgan wrote there, "that the Englishman can't feel—it is that he is afraid to feel." The essence of English character is to "measure out emotions . . . as if they were potatoes." Even as a young boy, Morgan was both trapped in the English character and a connoisseur of its vagaries. When he was only four, he spent days earnestly studying an etiquette book for children. The book was titled *Don't!*

He became a keen pupil of different *kinds* of knowledge. There was the bilingualism of women, their private talk and their careful, vicious, oblique wielding of social power. And there was dream knowledge, a magical, incantatory way to discover what is already known to be true. In *Maurice*, he would write, "Maurice had two dreams at school; they will interpret him." The wishes that acted upon, or acted for, the passive Morgan were centered on affection for men. The warm, diffuse, disembodied yearning for connection and intimacy that appeared as a voice calling out in the dark, and the panicky, miserable jolt of fear when the yearning became embodied in any way. Thinking about things was relatively safe. Touching was not.

So Morgan persisted in trying to figure himself out in a kind of vacuum. His earliest self-knowledge was sexual and tinged with homoerotic hunger. At Rooksnest, this island where there were no men, he sought the company of Ansell, a neighboring garden boy, confiding in him and relishing his unknowing touch. Decades later, in his fifties, Morgan recorded the memory in his undated "Sex Diary." "We built a little house between a straw stack and hedge, and often lay in each other's arms, tickling and screaming." When he was eleven, the incantatory voice spoke to him at the scene of his father's death:

> [W]e all went to Bournemouth. There I remember a queer moment. I stood looking out of the sitting room at the deserted road and thought "It all depends on whether a man or a woman first passes." From the right came a gentleman with a brown moustache. I was much relieved . . . This is the first *conscious* preference that I recall.

The relief may have been conscious, but the queerness felt fateful. That he was attracted to men, Morgan had already known without knowing for some time.

At Rooksnest he soon outstripped Lily's capacity to tutor him and outlasted the patience of their housemaid, Emma, who turned in her notice after being imperiously instructed in botany, astronomy, cology—"about *shells*"— by a five-year-old. Lily turned to the village of Stevenage, where a pompous young Irishman named Mr. Hervey ran a mediocre day school he grandly called "The Grange." She commissioned Mr. Hervey not only to teach the boy, but to assist him in masculine activities like climbing. Morgan instead used the trees to masturbate:

> I used to hang on the branches, wind my legs about the curve and draw myself up and down. After a long time there would be a nice feeling between my legs, followed by tiredness, when I stopped and slid . . . Once I had the feeling when my tutor stood by—he was supposed to teach me climbing. He said laughing "How he kicks about!" I said to myself "You little know!"

Sometimes his secret life afforded a feeling of mastery over the adult world, but more often it engendered mysterious and startling surprises. Even the "fat dark" Mr. Hervey, with his hopeless little mustache, could summon powerful erotic thoughts in the boy. "Soon after Mr. Hervey came I had a dream which I perhaps added to in my waking hours: his prick, very long, filled the hall and the dining room like white macaroni and wound me up in it. I had never seen his prick, and indeed thought no one but myself had one, so the dream's odd."

The retreat into his imagination as a way to explore his desire safely became a lifelong pattern for Morgan. It would be decades before he found both the intimacy and the sexual contact he craved. He arrived at this blissful state, which he called *connection*, through his brain rather than his body, through listening to what he knew he felt before he actually felt it in the blood.

The world conspired with the Word to bewilder him. When he was four, Morgan faithfully told his mother he had discovered the "trick" of rubbing his prepuce "backwards and forwards." Lily told him that was called "Dirty," and "presently . . . 'help me get rid of the dirty trick' figured in my prayer." Lily did not know this, but her invocation of Christianity was the first step in the separation of mother and son. Encountering this boundary alerted him to things that could not be said, not even to his beloved mother. All his life Morgan kept his homosexuality a secret from her. One of his friends described their delicate dance: "Morgan never came out of the closet. He wanted to protect his mother. And by the time he could have come out, there wasn't any closet left."

He looked in books for ratification of his scanty sexual experience. But the "dirties" of others were sadly absent from *Smith's Classical Dictionary*, and "concealed by drapery in the illustrations to Kingsley's Heroes." Fiction, and the feelings it produced, were much more satisfying.

> Felt deeply about boys in books, especially about Ernest, the priggish second son in the *Swiss Family Robinson* . . . I could not bear that Ernest should grow up—he was 13 I think—so the end of the *Swiss Family Robinson*, which takes place 10 years later, was repellent to me, and I would pretend that Ernest and the others were magicked back into being boys.

When Lily misapprehended Morgan's thoughts, he did not correct her. "My mother said 'I believe Jack [third son—lively] is your favorite!'" He recognized that Lily, too, sought her consolations in literature. He would not be the man she wanted him to be, but she did not have to know.

Ironically, Sunday school stories became an excellent vehicle for homoerotic fantasies. The Christ omnipresent in Victorian stained glass—the genteel, compassionate figure in every Anglican parish church—is a grown-up Lord Fauntleroy. And this Christ was introduced into steamy narratives, "long serial stories. In one of them I was Christ and led my companions about." Morgan perfectly mirrored Edwardian preoccupations, neatly conflating imperial and Christian themes in his subsequent erotic fantasies: "sleeping with naked black man in a cave" and "converting the inhabitants of New Guinea to Christ."

There is no record of whether the era's sexual scandals—the Cleveland Street scandal, which implicated the Prince of Wales's son Albert in a homosexual brothel, or the discovery of a boy prostitution ring among British high officials in Dublin Castle—made their way to Morgan's ears or eyes. But his fantasies comprised a queer refashioning of cultural anxieties about male friendship that were very much in the news when he was a child. Sexual issues began to ossify into law: Parliament, which had been largely silent on these private matters, now began to make them public ones, encoding the age of consent, limiting traffic in "white slavery," and eventually criminalizing unspecified acts of "gross indecency" between men, in the Labouchère Amendment of 1885. This was the law that would send Oscar Wilde, the most famous and successful writer in London, to prison when Morgan was sixteen. Christian reformers, who had promoted laws to maintain social purity, now began to bewail some consequences of the public scrutiny of relations between men. All sorts of innocent actions now might be misconstrued. The new public consciousness about sexual behavior narrowed the terrain where social actions between men could be assumed to be innocent, meaningless, private, or ambiguous. One lamented, "A few more cases like Oscar Wilde's and we should find the freedom of companionship now possible to men seriously impaired to the permanent detriment of the race."

At about the same time that Mr. Hervey appeared, Aunt Monie finally died at the age of ninety. Morgan had been dutifully taken to visit her in her last illness, but he did not recall it. The "arrival of the news" came by the kind of circumlocution that he and Lily were beginning to develop:

> I knew that [Aunt Monie] was ill, and one gloomy afternoon I was walking with my mother towards our home . . . I asked her how Aunt Monie was, and she replied, in the strained tones then thought appropriate to the subject of death, "She is better."—"Is she well?" I asked. "She *is*" came the solemn answer and I burst into tears. They were composite tears . . . I cried because crying was easy and because my mother might like it, and because the subject was death.

At her death, Monie left him a bequest larger than Eddie had left for his young family, to be devoted to Morgan's education. And almost immediately, Lily sent him away to school. It was time he grew up and entered the world.

Going away to school meant both separation from Lily and harsh induction into a new world of uncompromising masculine conventions. He was supremely ill-suited to the public school ethos, with its hierarchies of power and its emphasis on manly sport, and he quickly came to hate it with a fervor he sustained into old age. The Kent House school in Eastbourne, to which he was sent in 1890, was small and relatively enlightened by the standards of the day. There were only thirty boys attending and the headmaster was a bit of an egghead, well-meaning but obtuse when faced with a very sensitive boy. Morgan was painfully homesick, and snubbed by most of the other boys, who called him "Mousie." They were immune to his intellectual charm. School subjected him to all sorts of indignities—the public bathing was a special humiliation. One of the boys announced, "Have you seen Forster's cock? A beastly little brown thing," and in one stroke he both learned the word and felt the sting of being thought repellent.

Most of all, going off to Kent schooled Morgan in the art of detachment. During his second term there, to his great relief, he was excused from playing games, and allowed to walk along the Downs for exercise. There he encountered a pedophile. It was a momentous event in the boy's education but not for the reasons one might expect. Morgan began his Sex Diary to trace his origins as a man and a writer, certain that his homosexuality was the central fact of his being. More than forty years later, the details of the encounter with the pedophile were etched in his mind.

It was March 1891, and patches of snow still clung to the hills. Setting out over the Downs, Morgan encountered a man of forty or fifty—"large moustache, pepper and salt knickerbockers suit, deer stalker cap, mackintosh on arm"—near the summit, ostentatiously pissing into a gorse bush.

> Having concluded he spoke to me, I forget how, then walked me aside and made me sit between some gorse bushes on the mackintosh. He sat on my left—then undid his flies, I forget how soon, and told me to take hold of his prick. "Dear little fellow . . . play with it . . . dear little fellow . . . pull it about." I obeyed with neither pleasure or reluctance. Had no emotion at the time, but was startled at the red lolling tip (my own prepuce covering the gland even at erection) and was startled when some thick white drops trickled out. He rapidly lost interest in me, asked me where I lived ("Hertfordshire") and offered me a shilling ("no thank you"). He didn't try to handle me and I went off quietly.

The encounter with the pedophile did not fundamentally damage Morgan. Nor did it have much "effect on [his] development" since he "connected it with no sensations of my own." But leaving the man raised the complex moral question of whether he should *tell* anyone about his experience, and here the tension began to mount in the young boy. "Going down hill I became upset and thought how if I had accepted the 1/- I would have hurled it into a patch of snow." He decided to write to Lily about it.

As the event became public property, it magnified and hardened in predictable ways. Lily consulted her rector's wife, and advised on the tone Morgan should take in reporting the circumstances to his headmaster, Mr.

Hutchinson. "By this time," Morgan wrote in his Sex Diary, "I was in another mood, hard and important." He decided to adopt a manly air, and to approximate a manly metaphor for what had occurred. "You know your bowels sir" [Morgan asked.] Mr. H said he did, and I described how this man's bowels were diseased. This conversation took place near a fireplace in the dining room. It was followed by another equally disconcerting for Mr. H, as we walked down to the Police Station to report the matter."

Mr. Hutchinson, too, sought refuge in allegory. He told Morgan haplessly,

"We know from the Bible about certain things, and there is the story of Adam and Eve . . . boys may do great harm to themselves." He asked if I could identify the man again. All for vengeance, I said that I should, but he warned me against accusing strangers—if I saw anyone whom I suspected, I was to tell one of the masters quietly. "But we shall know him Sir, by this disease." Mr. H did not reply, his long horse-shaped face was silent, he lost a great opportunity of enlightening me, for I was full of curiosity and quite cheerful . . .

The man was never identified and never found. Mr. Hutchinson even spared the boy the necessity of giving evidence to the police. But the encounter did bring home to Morgan important lessons about how shame and panic could be easily harnessed, even by a young boy, into full-blown hysteria. Forster's novels would be perspicacious in their examination of how the public voice— what he called in *A Passage to India* "the herd instinct"—could do savage and irreparable harm. He would become the master of depicting a particular kind of male obtuseness, from hapless cowardice to outright malignity. And he would specialize in placing his readers in complex positions of sympathy, as indeed he had been in even at the time. The lesson of the pedophile was the lesson of telling the story to ignorant people in power, and watching them unravel and strike out in predictable ways. And it offered the inexorable instruction of estrangement. Afterward, he could no longer speak to Lily, or to anyone, about the things that touched him most deeply. The sign that he had learned this came in writing a single word in a now-lost diary. "I made an entry in my Diary <<<Nothing>>> to remind me it had been something."

Only by inscribing such a concrete lie could Morgan articulate the complicated lessons of his strange encounter with panic and power. Writing the word showed that he understood how dangerous writing the truth could be, how even describing things honestly might enmesh him, too. The "<<<Nothing>>>" incident became a kind of parable in itself, a parable of both finding himself as a writer and losing his faith in social systems. It was like an expulsion from Eden, for he could no longer talk to or trust Lily. "Later in the term mother came to see me, and said how painful it had been to her to write the letter that Mr. H saw, also asked me whether I had cured myself of my 'dirty trick.' I said I hadn't and she was so distressed and worried that I decided not to mention it to her again. This ended my last chance of a confidant." At the same time he jettisoned his belief in Christianity. He concluded that he could not be a Christian, because there was no evidence in the Bible that Christ had a sense of humor.

The episode with the pedophile effectively ended Morgan's stint at the Eastbourne school. He came back home for an unsatisfactory resumption of his studies with Mr. Hervey at the Grange. But the lease on Rooksnest expired at the same time, and Lily decided to move to a place where she could live near a good school, and allow Morgan to go there as a day boy. So they moved to Tonbridge, where they joined many other families who took advantage of an obscure provision in the school's charter that made such an arrangement cheaper than it might have been. Tonbridge School was a relative latecomer to the public-school tradition; it had been converted in the nineteenth century from a kind of guild academy for middle-class boys, and it had all the pretensions of a latecomer trying to prove itself worthy. There were houses and prefects and an elaborate system of sucking up to the older boys. And the place attracted a certain kind of pompous schoolmaster who felt he had to prove himself.

The best depiction of Tonbridge School as Morgan saw it is his scathing sketch of Sawston in *The Longest Journey*, and it is impossible to separate the sense of what the school was like from his virulent active loathing of his two years there. In middle age, Morgan shaped a delicious fantasy that he had actually been invited to supervise the *destruction* of a boarding school, and he lit into the project with glee. Affecting a precious accent he associated with the would-be upper-class men who attended Tonbridge, Forster addresses the audience:

> Ladies and gentlemen, boys and bies: school was the unhappiest time of my life, and the worst trick it played on me was to pretend that it was the world in miniature. For it hindered me from discovering

how lovely and delightful the world can be, and how much of it is intelligible. From this platform of middle age, this throne of experience, this altar of wisdom, this scaffold of character, this beacon of hope, this threshold of decay, my last words to you are: "there's a better time coming."

At almost exactly the same time he wrote these cathartic words, Morgan settled down to compose his Sex Diary. The miseries were more comfortably in his past.

In the present moment, Morgan was subjected to the most crude bullying of his life. One Tonbridge alumnus, when asked about Morgan in the 1950s, recalled him with un-self-conscious spite: "Forster? The writer? Yes, I remember him. A little cissy. We took it out of him, I can tell you." There is very little concrete evidence of Morgan's own thoughts at the time. Edmund Gosse's letter might have applied to the young Forster: "The position of a young man so tormented is really that of a man buried alive and conscious, but deprived of speech."

Morgan survived Tonbridge, though he felt it prepared him neither for Cambridge nor for life. He took school prizes in Latin and geography, and though he did not distinguish himself enough to earn a scholarship, he was offered entrance to King's College in October 1897, when he was eighteen.

The young man who went off to university was not nearly so physically ugly as he imagined himself. He had reached almost six feet in height, and had long, slender hands, musical hands. He played piano with intense passion and quite well. He already had learned to use his diffidence to advantage, devising creative ways to hide in plain sight. Shy and nondescript in his habits of dress, the young Morgan fashioned a caricature of an ordinary middle-class Englishman. He looked both completely unassuming and completely correct. He was gangly, a bit stooped even in his youth, and almost chinless. As a friend, Forster was funny, whimsical, emotionally urgent, and unpredictable. Like his great creation in *Howards End* Mrs. Wilcox, he seemed perfectly ordinary, and yet appeared to live on a deeper plane than other mortals.

He was still almost incomprehensibly naïve about sexual matters. After the debacle at the school in Eastbourne, Morgan had tried one last time to communicate with Lily about the strange conflation of biblical and sexual knowledge he had gleaned from Mr. Hutchinson.

Learnt that there was queer stuff in Bible, and thought that "lying together" meant that a man placed his stomach against a woman's and that it was a crisis when he warmed her—perhaps that a child was born, but of this I cannot be sure. Told my mother in the holidays that now I knew what committing adultery was. She looked worried, and said "So you understand now how dreadful it would be to mention it, especially if a gentleman was there." Never connected warming operation with my sexual premonitions. This chance guess, that came so near to the truth, never developed and not till I was 30 did I know exactly how male and female joined.

He began to apply the lessons of his bifurcated life to his conduct in the world, at first unconsciously. A real innocence was at the heart of this sensibility. It consisted of bringing himself, and eventually his friends and his readers, into an imagined world where the limitations of behavior and the possibilities of expression were wider, more honest, and more recondite than those of the material world. Morgan taught himself how to feel by force of a fierce, obtuse innocence.

He went up to King's green as a reed.

2

Kings and Apostles

Morgan came to Cambridge at a moment of transition for the university. Even a generation before, a boy like him would probably not have been admitted to King's. At that time the college favored the kind of confident young man who transformed the word *university* into the languid drawl of *varsity*. The sort of "silly and idle" fellow who "takes pass-degrees, roars round football fields," the sort of young man who in drunken oblivion "sits down in the middle of Hammersmith Broadway after the boat race . . ." At King's, this kind of chap breezed in, with no questions asked, directly and almost exclusively from Eton.

For more than four hundred years Eton College had been the wellspring for King's students. But the luster of the founder's pious intentions had dulled over the centuries. In 1441 the king in question—Henry VI, the young son of the victor of Agincourt—established a fund to educate young men training for holy orders. The whole of the college comprised seventy souls: the number of Jesus' disciples, according to St. Luke. Like the kneeling figures carved in stone in the college's wondrous Gothic chapel, Henry's acolytes proceeded in a "steady pilgrimage" from Eton, the king's charitable school near Windsor palace, to King's, where they remained until they married or died, then presumably on to heaven above.

But by the mid-eighteenth century this design had devolved into a system of "automatic and effortless advancement" for privileged young gentlemen. Secular, wealthy, and well-connected Etonians began to swell the college. There were no entrance exams; students had "the right to claim a degree without sitting for an examination"; and the degree, once conferred, entitled its holder to a life fellowship, so putatively all graduates, and all masters at Eton, had lifelong refuge in King's.

By the 1880s, the medieval structure of the university had begun to give way to the social necessity of educating a crop of men to fill the needs of a rapidly growing professional class. The imperial civil service in particular had a hungry mouth. In Asia and Mesopotamia, India and Ceylon, Egypt and southern Africa, and in London, too, now a world city, professional men were needed, bright men, organized men, men with a head on their shoulders for business, hearty, clubbable, oar-pulling men. Some Kingsmen still lived by the public school ethos, with its reverence of "team work . . . and cricket"; some still believed that "firmness, self-complacency and fatuity . . . between them compose the whole armour of man."

But within the university King's began to earn a distinctive place, threading the needle between the demands of rigor and the call to modernity. In 1869 King's began to require that all undergraduates sit the Tripos, the university examinations toward an honors degree, which had real intellectual bite; and King's students disproportionately took first-class honors in classics, which Morgan had chosen for his subject. The result was a crop of graduates inclined to public service and intellectual pursuits. Kingsmen became schoolmasters and parsons, professors and lawyers, doctors or diplomats, but rarely stockbrokers or businessmen. Fewer Etonians were admitted. The college began to make room for "oddities and the crudities— people who had not enjoyed their public schools or had been to the wrong school or even to none."

His father, Eddie, had been a Trinity man, but on the advice of family friends Morgan chose the less-rugged ethos of King's, just next door. So King's made room for Morgan, a suburban day boy from a middling school. Like his character Rickie Elliot in *The Longest Journey*, Morgan "crept cold and friendless and ignorant" from public school to university. At Michaelmas term 1897 Morgan and forty-seven other boys entered King's for a three-year course of study. The college was small and civilized, with fewer than two hundred undergraduates and eighteen Fellows in residence. Morgan was eighteen, tall, gangly, impossibly shy, unformed, terribly underprepared, but more clever than he knew.

The atmosphere at King's was conducive to Morgan's growing agnosticism. King's abolished the compulsory religious tests that other colleges retained. Mandatory attendance at chapel was relaxed; students who missed services were nevertheless obliged to sign a roster by eight in the morning, and Morgan, along with many other young men, shuffled out in slippers and dressing gowns to the Porter's Lodge to autograph the book. In freshman year his lodgings were near the present-day Guild Hall, and daily Morgan "could be seen rushing up St. Edward's Passage to mingle with the larger flood which surged from the College itself."

More significantly, the college had abolished the requirement that Fellows must subscribe to the articles of faith in the Anglican Church (which had been a condition of employment at Cambridge for centuries), along with the rule of celibacy that accompanied it. The newer dons had progressive views, and under their influence the classical curriculum of Greek and Latin history, literature, and philosophy—in place since medieval times—was widened to include more modern subjects: first modern history and politics and the natural sciences, then the modern languages. But King's continued to emphasize the teaching don, the bachelor don, the man who recognized that college life should rightly belong to the undergraduates. The teachers who made the greatest impression spiritually and intellectually on the young Morgan published very little, but they *listened* to young men.

To be listened to, one must first have something to say; but Morgan was too callow, too "stupefied" by Cambridge life to contribute to the conversation. He had earned a small Exhibition scholarship on the strength of his entrance exams. Socially and academically he found his first year "bewildering." He seemed to view himself from the outside. In November 1897, after he had been in Cambridge a month, Lily requested a photograph of him in cap and gown, but he was "unsure of my clothes," and anxious about his hair—"as I have my cap on, I don't think my hair will matter." Two months later he tried a new and unconvincing persona: golfing for the first time in his life, with some Tonbridge School acquaintances. In nine holes, he shot 133. The following week, he worsened his score.

For many young people, going off to university is the time when grownups become characters—it is possible to step away from them sufficiently to walk around them, so to speak, and ascertain or at least speculate on their motives. By practice and pretense, a young person can become a self, thinking through what he really believes and knows. So slowly Morgan became a character too, who found himself best when he was alone. Years later, he observed that "it is difficult for an inexperienced boy to . . . realise that freedom can sometimes be gained by walking out through an open door."

In Morgan's case, this feeling of freedom was achieved by cycling through a college gateway. Fluid movement on a bicycle gave this suburban boy his earliest sense that he had discovered the taproot of real traditions, the *real* England. The geography of Cambridge became a kind of psychic landscape, alternately claustrophobic and liberating. Walking or cycling in the city, Morgan squeezed through the pinched wet alleys between the stone walls of college buildings, down the narrow streets that wound to the river Cam or ended abruptly in a cul-de-sac of a college gatehouse. From these confined spaces he found himself plunged without warning into astonishing vistas—the green expanse of Parker's Piece, Jesus Green, the Midsummer Common, or the marshland at the backs of the colleges, where the sky hung broadly like a Dutch painting, the weather scrolling across it like a film projected at high speed. Even within sight of the bridge at the back of King's, docile cows lifted their heads from grazing to watch cyclists and students bustling by. The colleges huddled together tightly. Many turned their faces to the street, the market, and the town, but their backs were exposed to wide watermeadows that reached as far as the eye could see, with only the tiny spire of the church at Grantchester visible in the distance.

In the spring of his first year, Forster rode his bicycle out into the open countryside west of the city, alone. Near the village of Madingley he came upon a strange feature in the landscape, an abandoned open chalk pit that had sprouted a copse of pine trees. In the "shelter of the dell" he felt as if he had entered a separate magical world. At the time Morgan recorded the discovery prosaically: "Walked into old chalk pit full of young trees." But within a decade, the sensation blossomed into a narrative: "The green bank at the entrance hid the road and the world," and from within the circle he "could see nothing but snow-white ramparts and the evergreen foliage of the firs."

In *The Longest Journey*, Morgan would step back and use what Cambridge had taught him to shape his younger self into the anxious, priggish character of Rickie Elliot, who retreats to the safety of this place to "tell most things about my birth and parentage and education." And, most important, in the novel Rickie would not be alone. Morgan would populate the dell with sympathetic friends. The first third of his novel was a valentine to Cambridge.

During the long vacation that summer. Morgan went house hunting with Lily, who had no further ties to Tonbridge after he had left school there. She settled into a semidetached house in Tunbridge Wells—to Morgan a town even more stultifying than Tonbridge had been. On his return, he was delighted to move into the bosom of the college. His set of rooms on the top floor of Bodley's Building had glorious views—from his bedroom into the symmetry of the Queen's College gardens and from his sitting room, a long, lazy northern look at the pastures, the King's and Clare College bridges, the meandering river, and presumably at a philosophical cow herself, who would reappear, immortal, in the first scene of *The Longest Journey*, as the young men lying on the carpet in front of the coal fire debate whether she is *actually* there or only *perceived* by their senses. Bodley's was faux-Gothic, having been built in 1893; its stone matched the golden flank of the chapel, but it lacked the chapel's damp chill. It was a hospitable place. In these rooms, for the first time in his life, Morgan discovered that he had a gift for friendship.

At the head of stairway W7 lived a handsome, genial young man with pale skin, a flop of dark hair, and angular eyebrows that telegraphed his exquisite skepticism about things as they are. Hugh Owen Meredith, known by his initials as HOM, was one of the new breed of genuinely brilliant Cambridge undergraduates. His father was an Irish shorthand clerk who sacrificed a great deal to educate his eldest son. To Morgan, HOM's brains, beauty, and grace were intoxicating. Meredith was a college Scholar, he had racked up prizes in classics and every kind of sport, and he had a shattering confidence about his own beliefs that belied a parallel habit of self-scrutiny amounting to self-hatred. The model for both George Emerson in *A Room with a View* and Clive Durham in *Maurice*, HOM loved to "épater the narrow-minded."

Within weeks of meeting Morgan. Hugh boldly announced he was an atheist, and proceeded to separate Morgan from the last remnants of his faith. To HOM it was clear that not only was church practice hypocrisy, but the very concept of Christ was humbug. Along with John Maynard Keynes. who would become perhaps the greatest economist of the century, HOM led a public attack under the banner of secularism on the college's sponsorship of a Christian mission in the slums of East London. Like many undergraduate political protests. the atheists' "sincere and bellicose" display verged on comedy. They sent a representative to present a petition of grievances timed to interrupt prayers at High Table. Just as the provost intoned. "In the Name of Jesus Christ our Lord." there was a scuffle; the rude emissary was escorted out of the hall, and a don piped up loudly: "Would you mind pass-ing the potatoes?" The renegades won the day; it was decided that college work with the London poor could be done through a secular organization.

Under Hugh Meredith's influence, Morgan lost his faith "quietly and quickly."

> The idea of a god becoming a man to help man is overwhelming to anyone possessed of a heart. Even at that age I was aware that this world needs help. But I had never much sense of sin, and when I real-ised that the main aim of the Incarnation was not to stop war or pain or poverty, I became less interested and ended by scrapping it.

Examining the Gospels carefully to discern the personality of Christ ended the matter permanently: "So much moving away from worldliness towards preaching and threats, so much emphasis on followers, on an elite, so little intellectual power . . . such an absence of humour and fun that my blood chilled."

The Meredith family had been scandalized by the news of HOM's athe-ism, but Lily responded more phlegmatically to Morgan's "pompous" pro-nouncement that he had lost his faith. His mimicry of rebellion, though sincere, proved a bit of an anticlimax. "It so happened . . . that my father had lost his faith about 30 years previously and had recovered it after a short interval. My family assumed that I should follow the paternal pattern."

Losing his faith cleared the way for Morgan to divine a new philosophy. It is hard to imagine that a young man so kind, so bright, so sensitive could live to the age of twenty with no real experience of friendship, but it was so. With "no formula for unknown experience," Morgan used the tools at hand. He discovered the beautiful ideas of ancient Athens just at the moment he found the brilliant and beautiful Hugh, and in the alchemy of mind and heart he began to inch toward an ethics of human "warmth."

Hellenism was an intermediate step toward his personal philosophy. For many a late-Victorian man, the classics served as an excellent looking glass. If you were inclined toward empire, the study of ancient Greece reinforced your belief in the inevitability of Britain's wealth, the rectitude of its ideals, and the justice of its global sway. Young men like Morgan, wrestling with how to *be*, and how to be *good*, found that "Athens in particular had expressed our problems with a lucidity beyond our power." And for homosexual men,

Hellenism served as both an ideal and a disguise. From J. A. Symonds to Oscar Wilde himself, they justified the legitimacy of their desire by invoking the halcyon days of ancient Greece. Just two years before Morgan entered King's, speaking from the dock, Wilde had summoned the redoubtable troika of the Bible, Hellenic practice, and Shakespeare himself to defend his love affair with the young Alfred Lord Douglas:

> The love that dare not speak its name in this century is such a great affection of an elder for a younger man as there was between David and Jonathan, such as Plato made the very basis of his philosophy, and such as you find in the sonnets of Michelangelo and Shakespeare. It is a deep spiritual affection that is as pure as it is perfect . . . It is beautiful, it is fine, it is the noblest form of affection. There is nothing unnatural about it.

Wilde's greatest error had been to believe that the homophilia of his cloistered Magdalen College life could be practiced in the public world. The men of King's would not make the same mistake. Anxiety and fascination with homosexuality reverberated just under the surface, but the subject itself was carefully contained. Describing tutorials at Cambridge in *Maurice*, Morgan would demonstrate the knowing evasions of the dons: "They attended the Dean's translation class, and when one of the men was forging quietly ahead Mr. Cornwallis observed in a flat toneless voice: 'Omit: a reference to the unspeakable vice of the Greeks.'"

Such behavior deflected attention from the homophilia at the heart of the King's notion of friendship between the faculty and students. The college's most famous don, Oscar Browning, "saw in King's the material of a new Athens." Practically speaking, this meant that he loved both Greek literature and beautiful boys. Browning's reverence for young men was eccentric and pronounced. He had retreated to King's in 1876 in a spectacular scandal, claiming his life fellowship in the wake of being fired as a master at Eton. At that time he was forty, but he had already earned the jocular nickname "The O.B.," and he had swelled to the vast walrus bulk that made him the recognizable subject of caricature in undergraduate magazines.

Browning's ostentatious romance with a pupil, Lord Curzon's son George—who, at fifteen, was decades away from his lofty position as the viceroy of

India—had proved to be too much for his colleagues at Eton. Not that the relationship was overtly sexual. Browning never laid a hand on an English boy. That he reserved for the safer, grubbier Greek and Italian boys he encountered on holiday. But his chaste pedophilia might best be described as "soul-fingering." This practice he continued with the slightly older students at King's. Morgan understood and appreciated Browning's fractious power: he found him to be "a deposit of radium, a mass of equivocal fire." Browning generated a torrent of adjectives—one colleague's list included "Falstaffian, shameless, affectionate, egoistic, generous, snobbish, democratic, witty, lazy, dull, worldly, academic," to which Morgan later in life added "a bully and a liar." Despite these shortcomings, Morgan believed, "Whatever his make up, he did manage to educate young men."

Browning was "the hero of a lost play by Shakespeare." The memoirs of his colleagues and students are studded with extraordinary vignettes. "His corpulent person was consistently to be found in a state of primitive nudity," either sporting with undergraduates in the Cam or holding impromptu office hours in his rooms *en déshabille*. He habitually chose handsome young men with indeterminate skills to be his secretaries. His student (and later Morgan's great friend) Goldsworthy Lowes Dickinson recalled finding him undressed "in his inner room, where he slept behind a screen, in the act of getting up. On one side of him was a secretary writing letters to dictation, and on the other another [boy] playing the violin." Browning may have been unregenerate, but his younger colleague Nathaniel Wedd, always alert to hypocrisy, defended him. Wedd observed trenchantly, "Eton sacked OB for introducing the very things on which it now prides itself."

Inside the insular all-male world of King's, Browning ruled. The college was virtually cloistered; the gates were locked at nine in the evening. Within this world freedom was defined in part by extravagant misogyny. There is nothing so sure to make a young man feel invincible and important as the cocoon of excluding others. The college porter is always ready to spot you the money for a cab if you should arrive late and penniless in the fog; outsiders—even, famously, Virginia Woolf—are scooted off the lawns in front of your eyes. Fewer than a tenth of the university's students were women, who were denied degrees and were contained in two women's colleges at the margin of the city; Browning, who marked their exams for extra money, announced that the best woman's essay was markedly inferior to the worst of the men's. He prided himself on his ignorance of women. When asked if he found the Venus of Botticelli to be lifelike, Browning replied that he could not answer the question, since he had never seen a woman naked.

In the city, too, women were curtailed in unconscionable ways. University rules superseded British common law and applied to all inhabitants. Under rules established in the Elizabethan era, university proctors were empowered to arrest women "suspected of evil" (that is, presumed to be prostitutes), hold them without notice to civil authorities or their families, and incarcerate them in a private prison known as the Spinning House. In the 1890s Cambridge was transfixed by lawsuits brought in Crown Court by two innocent young women who sued the university for false imprisonment. Jane Elsden and Daisy Hopkins lost their cases, but the publicity incited political pressure to limit the university's power to control civil life. By the time Morgan left King's, the Spinning House courts had been abolished by Act of Parliament.

For Morgan it was a relief to live in a world so different from the one dominated by Lily and the Aunts. True, he was steeped in the reflexive misogyny of Edwardian culture. When discord in any relationship occurred he would believe that "as usual the women have precipitated the trouble." But he was attuned to bigotry and aware of his own ignorance of women. In a few years he would begin to explore why the price of justifying oneself as a homosexual should be exacted in the hatred of women. In *The Longest Journey* he would show Rickie Elliot to be obtuse and discourteous when Agnes Pembroke came to visit King's. The Schlegel sisters, two of the most complex and sympathetic female characters in any novel, would anchor *Howards End*. One New Year's resolution in December 1904 would be to "get a less superficial idea of women."

The diary entries from Morgan's second year at King's read like the letters of the young Keats: absorbed in ideas, reading rapaciously, unaware that the whole world is not composed of art and literature. The Boer War had just begun, but Morgan was oblivious to political events. All his attention went to his widening circle of friends. There was Sydney Waterlow, who seemed preternaturally middle-aged—he had grown a huge mustache while at Eton, was a great talker, and would take any side of an argument, even both sides. (Later in life, he was embroiled in two simultaneous lawsuits: the first to annul his marriage on the grounds of impotence, the second a breach-of-promise case brought by his pregnant mistress.) And there was Waterlow's friend Edward Dent, who shared both an unrequited crush on HOM and a deep love of music with Morgan. A brilliant musicologist who followed all the latest European composers, Dent played piano with Morgan, and invited him to the university's weekly chamber recitals. And Malcolm Darling, generous of spirit, who would soon serve in the Indian civil administration (and invite Morgan to come visit). Darling was sweet-natured, unworldly, and resolutely heterosexual. When two of his friends were expelled from Eton and left the college in the same car, Darling "could not make out why their friends should have pelted them with rice." ·

There was always company, always music, always laughter in Morgan's rooms in Bodley's Building. Every day consisted of long walks through the city, a disquisition or a dispute on art with a friend. Morgan sublimated his love for HOM, watching him dominate passionate discussions. Daily life was a sort of modern symposium.

5 Nov. (Sunday) [1899] Spencer, Mounsey & Gardner to breakfast. Lunched with Meredith . . . Wilderness in the afternoon . . . 20th Nov. . . . Ainsworth came in & ate bacon; then he and Meredith argued about beauty. Enter MacMunn with whom I walked up Huntington Road . . . Tea with Miss Stephen [Virginia Woolf's aunt]: talked of Tenn. & Browning. Coffee with Lubbock: beautiful rooms and books; admirer of R[obert] L[ouis] S[tevenson] . . . 27th Nov. . . . Debate going on: "Trinity is too big." Worked. Meredith came in and discussed beauty again.

Morgan was fortunate to be assigned Nathaniel Wedd as his supervisor. Wedd balanced the bad news—that Morgan's education at Tonbridge had not taught him how to *think*, and thus that he was likely to do poorly on the looming Tripos—with a wholehearted recognition that his student had a delicate, unusual, promising mind. "To him more than to anyone," Morgan later wrote, "I owe such awakening as has befallen me."

Wedd was a perfect mentor. Morgan's first impression was of a young Mephistopheles. Wedd smoked excessively. He grew a huge walrus mustache and wore bright red ties. Only thirty-five, he was not far past his radical Fabian days. As a King's undergraduate in 1882, Wedd had goaded the college elders by inviting G. B. Shaw to lecture at King's, prompting the provost to object unless Shaw wrote to reassure him that he did not plan to "dynamite" the college. Wedd was asked to query the incendiary speaker on his "moral basis" for coming to King's. Shaw duly responded by mail that his moral basis was the same as Wedd's, an equivocal response if a gentlemanly one.

As a don, Wedd remained steadfastly "cynical, aggressive," and anticlerical. He would ostentatiously spit on the ground when he saw the procession lining up for chapel. He swore and blasphemed liberally, and even taught his colleague the mild-mannered Goldsworthy Lowes Dickinson to swear too—which Morgan found "a desirable accomplishment for a high-minded young don."

Wedd "gave all his time and energies to undergraduates, was at home to them at all hours of the night, stimulated, comforted, amused" them. He encouraged Morgan to write not only academic essays but small pieces for the *Basileon* and other Cambridge undergraduate magazines. Morgan adopted the pseudonym of Peer Gynt, the Ibsen character whose dark search for identity ends in despair, burying his head in his mother's lap. But despite the serious pen name, his incidental essays were light ephemera: "On Bicycling"; "On Grinds," a whimsical skit based on *Agamemnon*. In letters home to Lily he was already beginning to display a distinctive sensitivity to literature; he was reading Shaw's plays, he told her, and they were "wonderfully clever & amusing, but they make me feel bad inside." Alongside his syllabi for lectures and essays, Morgan was greedily reading for pleasure. He plowed through Milton and Shakespeare; Sophocles and Pindar; Robert Browning and Rosetti; Housman's new book of poems, *A Shropshire Lad*; Tennyson, Maeterlinck, Pinero, and Ibsen; and all the great eighteenth-century English novels.

He developed a knack for pulling together a compelling essay, provided he could choose the subject. At the end of his second year, Morgan won a college prize for a stylish paper on the history of the novel. But he faced the unrelenting Tripos in his third year, and Wedd was not sanguine about his chances of doing well. His poor performance on the interim exams in May 1899 rendered him ineligible for the plum home civil service jobs, like the one his friend Leonard Woolf would take on in Ceylon. Morgan wrote Lily that Wedd "advises me to think of journalistic work as one of the things I might do . . . I don't think I shall be good enough." Though he could live frugally on the legacy from Aunt Monie, it began to be clear that he must choose some sort of profession. When the marks for the Tripos were announced, Morgan was relieved to have earned a solid upper-second-class Honours. But still, what to do? He had little confidence and no vocation.

The better part of valor is discretion, Falstaff mutters as he tentatively pokes Hotspur's corpse with his sword. In the absence of any solid idea about the future, Morgan decided to stay on at King's for another year. He changed his subject to history. Though he hoped to work with Wedd, Oscar Browning buttonholed him instead, insisting he must supervise his reading. Browning was viewed by most students as entertaining but harmless, but as a tutor he was nugatory: "While his pupil read out his essay he would put a red spotted handkerchief over his face and go to sleep. Awakened by the cessation of the droning, he would exclaim 'My boy, you're a genius!'"

Morgan later wrote charitably, "I came towards the end of O. B.'s glory, nor was I ever part of its train." Which is to say that by the time they encountered each other—when Browning was in his sixties and Morgan just twenty-one—Morgan was neither seductive enough for the old man nor callow enough to be seduced by Browning's dodgy ideas of romantic boy-worship. In any case, Browning's instruction was beside the point. For his birthday, Aunt Laura Forster had bought him a sensitive and fortuitous gift—a life membership in the London Library. In Morgan's last year at King's, Wedd and HOM opened new doors for him.

It was not so much *what* Wedd taught him as *how* Wedd encouraged his intellectual hunger that Morgan remembered in later years. He "had helped me" by casually observing "in a lecture that we all know more than we think. A cry of relief and endorsement arose from my mind, tortured so long by being told that it knew less than it pretended." Gently, understatedly, Wedd encouraged Morgan:

> He tells me that I might write, could write, might be a writer. I was amazed yet not overawed. Like other great teachers of the young, Wedd always pointed to something already existing. He brought not only help but happiness. Of course I could write—not that anyone would read me, but that didn't signify . . . I had a special and unusual apparatus, to which Wedd called my attention . . .

This precise description, read aloud to friends thirty years later, records a moment of revelation. There is a special poignancy in the fact that even at the origin of his life as a writer, Morgan imagined, understood intuitively, that his creative force might have to be cut off from sympathetic readers. There would come a time when what he wanted to write would be unpublishable. Morgan came to understand that homophobia had its source in a special kind of anxiety on the part of heterosexuals: "What the public really loathes in homosexuality," he would write decades later, "is not the thing itself but having to think about it." So Maurice would confess to his family doctor, using a circumlocution he hoped Dr. Barry would comprehend: "I'm an unspeakable of the Oscar Wilde sort." But the doctor, who has known the young man all his life, doesn't want to hear about it. He recoils from Maurice: "Rubbish, rubbish! . . . Who put that lie into your head? You whom I see and know to be a decent fellow! We'll never mention it again. No—I'll not discuss. I'll not discuss. The worst thing I could do for you is discuss it."

Morgan's "unspeakable" subject dominated the last fifty years of his writing life. Much of this writing would languish unpublished in archives. But the fact that no one would read it would "not signify." He would continue to write anyway.

On February 9, 1901, Morgan was elected to the secret intellectual coterie known as the Apostles. Established in 1820, the Cambridge Converzatione Society—its proper name—was designed to bring older undergraduates and younger dons into informal social and intellectual comradeship. Only a dozen new members were elected from the entire university each year— hence the nickname—but those elected in previous years could attend the gatherings. Hugh Meredith, elected the year before, had urged his brethren to consider Morgan since the autumn, and formally sponsored him for election. It was a signal achievement.

Tennyson and his great friend Arthur Hallam, to whom *In Memoriam* was dedicated, had forged their friendship in the society. And the young men who welcomed Morgan to their circle would go on to great things too— Maynard Keynes, who devised the new economics that would lift Europe and America out of a great depression; Leonard Woolf, husband of Virginia, publisher and political writer; Roger Fry, the art critic, don, and painter who introduced Cézanne and Matisse to British eyes; and the philosophers Bertrand Russell and G. E. Moore, still both in their late twenties. But the point of the Apostles was to unravel the concept of achievement itself. They eschewed all external measurements of the good and the true, the whole Victorian bourgeois drooling over money and medals and fame, all utilitarian and worldly values, anything "associated with action or achievement or with consequences."

And a good thing, too. Morgan certainly would not have merited membership in any other kind of fraternity. He had first met Lytton Strachey by tripping over an ottoman in the historian G. M. Trevelyan's rooms at Trinity and landing on him sideways. Lytton, brilliant, sardonic, pale as a vampire, unfolded himself from under the heap. He was impressed.

Like all young people vibrating with passionate intensity, the Apostles could behave insufferably to those outside the group. Leonard Woolf's friends at Trinity could not stand them, accusing Strachey, particularly, of being *ungentlemanly* toward the pious. Just so. Keynes, looking back, explained, "We were at an age when our beliefs influenced our behaviors, a characteristic of the young which it is easy for the middle-aged to forget." The young men gathering in front of the coal fire took their shoes off and ate anchovies on toast. They applied a strict Socratic method, debating all aspects of Truth, however arcane: "Are crocodiles the best of animals?" "Is self-abuse bad as an end?" "Should things be real?" "Is anything as good as a person?" "Is the cow *there*?"

They persuaded themselves that the method by which they reached their conclusions was entirely rational, secular, and determined only by individual "plain common sense"—a phrase they adopted from G. E. Moore's analytic approach to ethics. For Woolf and Keynes, in particular, Moore's 1902 book *Principia Ethica*

suddenly lifted an obscure accumulation of scales, cobwebs and curtains, revealing for the first time, so it seemed, the nature of truth and reality, of good and evil and character and conduct, substituting for the religious and philosophical nightmares, delusions, hallucinations, in which Jehovah, Christ and St. Paul, Plato, Kant, and Hegel had entangled us.

The young men's faith in themselves, in truth, and in beauty was in effect a kind of neo-Platonic religion. But Keynes later acknowledged, "We should have been very angry at the time with such a suggestion. We regarded all this as entirely rational and scientific."

If Morgan seemed the wrong sort of young person to embrace this method, he was at home in the circle because his friends recognized that he understood the secrets of humanity by some means other than purely rational discourse. The Apostles' belief that only an individual can determine ethical behavior emphasized scrupulous honesty and a willingness to listen to others' views. In a room full of talkers, Morgan's steadfast silence demarked him as a peculiar kind of genius. Lytton

> nicknamed him the Taupe, partly because of his faint physical resemblance to a mole, but principally because he seemed intellectually and emotionally to travel unseen underground and every now and again pop up unexpectedly with some subtle observation or delicate quip which somehow or other he had found in the depths of the earth or of his own soul.

Maynard Keynes called Morgan "the elusive colt of a dark horse." Leonard Woolf, too, was intrigued: "He was strange, elusive, evasive. You could be talking to him easily and intimately one moment, and suddenly he would seem to withdraw into himself; though he still was physically there, you had faded out of his mental vision, and so with a pang you found that he had faded out of yours."

Woolf delighted in the elliptical way Morgan arrived at insights by employing "a streak of queer humour." Just when the tone of high seriousness would reach its apogee, he would drop the trump card: an explosive bark of laughter like a sneeze, which veered off into uncontrollable high-pitched giggles.

One might conclude that all this talk of brotherly love in the company of so many young homosexual men might ignite an orgy of passion. Not so. The Apostles were not yet the Bloomsbury Group. They were doubtless more tolerant of the notion of homosexual love than their fathers and grandfathers had been, but they remained thoroughly Edwardian, progressive in a delicate, high-minded, academic way. Heterosexual Apostles such as George Trevelyan held an "idealistic attitude towards homosexual love." But Strachey had not yet begun his systematic seduction of his friends. Keynes captured the odd tone of their discussions, bold but austere: "Strachey issued [an] edict that certain Latin technical terms of sex were the correct words to use, that to avoid them was a grave error, and, even in mixed company, a weakness, and the use of other synonyms a vulgarity. In 1903 those words were not even esoteric terms of common discourse."

The furthest Lytton and Maynard went was to apply a pragmatic, if chaste, approach to the selection of new members, "jockeying to procure [the] election" of "beautiful young men" to the society.

Goldsworthy Lowes Dickinson was neither beautiful nor young. He was almost forty, and though he had been a don at King's for the whole of Morgan's residency, they had known each other slenderly before Morgan's election to the society. "Goldie," as his friends knew him, had a striking, sensitive face and the gentlest mien. As a King's undergraduate, he had found his heart and mind utterly transformed by reading Shelley, and he remained a bit of a political romantic all his life. He had trained in classics, absorbing politics through Plato and Aristotle. More than anyone at the university, Goldie had created the new discipline of political science. For a short time after the Treaty of Versailles in 1919, Goldie became an essential public man, helping to shape and define the League of Nations. But his more profound influence was to be private and vicarious: his lectures "Modern France," "The Transition to Democracy in Modern England," "The Machinery of Administration under Democracy," and "The Theory of Law and Government" educated generations of young men who would take his lessons into the public world.

In Dickinson, Morgan found the adult most like himself in temperament. Goldie's life was "not dramatic." He "tended to inhabit the university spiritually." All his adult life he was anchored in a set of rooms in the Gibbs Building of the central court at King's. Like Wedd, who was also an Apostle, Dickinson's energies were expended more on teaching than on publishing. His teaching method was to "rope . . . people in to get ideas on some problem which puzzled him"; he would "talk more about the problem itself than [his student's] treatment of it"—an egalitarian process that "disconcerted his weaker pupils, who wanted to be shown where they went wrong." Mildly but firmly he would tell them, "It hasn't come yet," and leave them to revise yet again.

His profound influence was best preserved in the memory of those students who became his close friends. Morgan, who would write Goldie's biography in 1934, found in his mentor's ineffable character the key to what is most real and most valuable in human experience. Morgan would dedicate the biography to "Fratrum Societate," to both the brotherly society where he first came to know Goldie well, and the idea of brotherliness itself. The book would be a case study in the falseness of external measurements of worth in understanding a human life. That it described the life of a gay man, a man consumed with unrequited and inexpressible love, marked it for Morgan as quintessentially *mortal.*

For Goldie's writing itself did little to preserve the quick warm essence of the man. The self-consciousness that uncoiled in him in the act of setting things down distorted and darkened his natural good humor: "a thin veil of melancholy . . . interposed between him and the paper as soon as he sat down to type." His handwriting was so illegible that it subjected him to terrible, comic misunderstandings. One man whose sister attended Goldie's extension lectures in the Midlands felt her honor had been attacked, and wrote him a minatory letter beginning: "My sister has a bone to pick with you, Mr. Dickinson!" Both the student and her sibling had misread Goldie's scrawl of "good!" in the margin. They thought he had written "Fool!" Mechanical means of communication proved to be no more reliable. Goldie was notorious for being "the only man who could make a Corona type upside-down."

Goldie had, to use Morgan's word, a "maieutic" gift. That is, he served as a midwife, bridging people and ideas, between people and the vision of themselves at their best, the midwife between the intellect and the heart. He traveled widely, loved Chinese and Japanese culture, and was especially adept at explaining alien cultures to the British mind. His *Greek View of Life*, published in 1909, popularized Athenian ideas for the general reader. In *Letters from John Chinaman* (1901), he so thoroughly appropriated the voice of a Chinese official to describe Chinese attitudes to the West that most reviewers believed it could not have been written by a European. Morgan admired, and later would emulate, Goldie's uncanny ability to befriend younger men, to accept them as true equals. Dickinson was a great man and a great professor because "teaching . . . could not be distinguished . . . from being taught."

Four months after he joined the Apostles, Morgan calmly let go of Cambridge. He knew these friends would stay with him all his life. His 2:1 on the history Tripos cemented the conclusion that he would not become a don like HOM, or his friend George Barger, who took up a position teaching chemistry at Edinburgh. There was no immediate prospect of work, no design for life that magically appeared.

So Morgan spent the summer of 1901 contemplating his next step. He began an untitled novel—which he would later abandon as a fragment— about an inhibited young man from the suburbs. Packing up his pages, his books, his rumpled tweed suits, his academic gown and mortarboard, he took off on a brief round of family visits with Lily—to Aunt Laura at West Hackhurst, and Uncle Willie, his father's youngest brother, in Northumberland. He bought a pocket guide to learning Italian. His most immediate plan was to tour Italy with his mother. Baedeker in hand, he began to plan their journey. They would be away from England for over a year.

3

"A Minority, Not a Solitary"

Morgan and Lily embarked on something considerably more middle-class and Edwardian than a Grand Tour. Their assault on Italy was ambitious in its thoroughness if not its delicacy of sentiment. Every church, every monument, every fresco, every museum, every sight was planned, viewed, ticked off the list. Morgan confessed to the more urbane and adventurous Wedd that his traveling was all by the book: "Baedeker-bestarred Italy . . . is all that I have yet seen." To Goldie, his most intimate correspondent, he wrote discontentedly, "Our life is where we sleep and eat, and the glimpses of Italy that I get are only *accidents*."

He might have done differently if he had not been traveling with Lily. There was an odor of duty about their approach that unsettled Morgan even at the outset; he wrote Dent, whose travels were more off *piste*, that "the hotels are comfortable and costly I hate it." Pensione life offered all the conventions of suburban England, slightly askew: wallpapered rooms where the carpet and antimacassars smelled a bit sour, services at the local Anglican church listening to a droning sermon by an undistinguished Oxonian vicar, stewed prunes for breakfast, boiled beef for supper. The Pensione Simi on the banks of the Arno may have offered a room with a view, but it was run, improbably, by a Cockney landlady.

Even viewed through this keyhole, Italian culture was undeniably stirring. Little observations wormed their way into Morgan's imagination: the look of a handsome Italian waiter as he stepped through French doors onto the pergola, the way a sharp burst of wind sheared through the trees on a hillside, the shimmer of oppressive heat, the sudden sting of grit in his eye from a passing railway train. He absorbed the plebian poetry in the cadence of the

Baedeker. His first published novel, *Where Angels Fear to Tread*, ironically captured its encyclopedic tone: "Philip could never read 'The view from the Rocca (small gratuity) is finest at sunset' without a catching at the heart."

Their constant movement—a month or even two in Florence, Rome, and Milan, a week in Siena, Pisa, Naples, a retreat to the Alto Adige in the heat of summer—only partially disguised the profound regression in Morgan's relations with his mother. Months before, he had been in the company of his friends, debating the meaning of beauty. Now he was setting out for the day with guidebook, smelling salts, and a parasol. Lily sensed that something was odd: "M is much quieter than he was before he went to Cambridge," she wrote to her mother. Edward Dent, visiting with the Forsters as they overlapped in Italy, noted how sharply Lily reprimanded her son. He disapproved of Morgan's timidity. Dent, too, had an imposing Victorian mother, but he drew a line: he "took her to buy butter dishes, but he would never, ever have gone to Italy with her."

For her part Lily "never saw anybody so incapable" as her son, who missed trains, misread directions, lost his gloves, mislaid guidebooks, left maps behind at every stop. Each day their progress unraveled as they sought to retrieve items misplaced hours before. Long after her death, when Morgan was in his seventies, he reflected on how hapless he must have seemed to her:

> Now I am older I understand her depression better . . . I often think of my mistakes with mother, or rather the wrongness of an attitude that may have been inevitable. I considered her much too much in a niggling way, and did not become the authoritative male who might have quietened her and cheered her up. When I look at the beauty of her face, even when old, I see that something different should have been done. We were a classic case.

But the young Morgan could discern only that something was missing in his sensory apparatus. To prepare so carefully had made each experience an anticlimax: "I missed nothing—neither the campaniles, nor the crooked bridges over dry torrent beds, nor the uniformity of the blue sky, nor the purple shadows of the mountains over the lake. But I knew that I must wait for many days before they meant any thing to me or gave me any pleasure." Even at the beginning of his travels, he dimly understood what would become the central premise of his two Italian novels: that the best lessons of

Italy for the Englishman were corporeal. The art he encountered was ecstatic, irrational. The Madonna of Mantegna in Milan was "surrounded by a circle of cherubims, who are warbling—not singing, but with their tongues out and their mouths open, like birds." The Italians had retained the classical ideal: "[C]herish the body and you will cherish the soul. This was the belief of the Greeks. The belief in wearing away the body by penance in order that the quivering soul might be exposed had not yet entered the world." Even the tourist venues were admirably unprudish and practical. High above, on the roof of the cathedral, the local authority had installed a lavatory.

In the winter of 1901, "very discontented" with the novel fragment *Nottingham Lace*, he abandoned the story of young Edgar and his meddling, status-conscious mother. The attempt had given him a grip on his aesthetic goals, however unrealized. He explained to Goldie,

> I've tried to invent realism, if you see what I mean: instead of copying incidents & characters that I have come across, I have tried to imagine others equally commonplace, being under the impression that this was art, and by mixing two methods have produced nothing. I think I shall have a try at imagination pure & simple . . .

Instead he began to sketch essays of his impressions of Italy. He channeled his damnable self-consciousness into a virtue. Now each destination became food for future writing. Some places, alas, were already spoken for. "Perugia would be nicer, I think, if Symonds had not written an Essay on it." In March 1902 he complained to Goldie, "Traveling does not conduce to work. I have a few sentimental articles on Italy, and have got a plan for a new novel." After a long labor, this would become *A Room with a View*.

When the corporeal lessons of Italy intruded, they came suddenly, precipitously, unasked for. He sprained his ankle in late January, and languished indoors for days at the little hotel near the Trevi fountain. Here he was marooned among "all females, and not very amusing." A week later he tripped on the steps of St. Peter's and broke his arm, which necessitated canceling a side trip to Greece in the welcome company of his Cambridge friends. The second injury rendered him utterly helpless. Lily had to bathe him, and each morning he woke up riddled with fleabites. Everything conspired to make him feel inept.

As he recovered through the spring, the warmth of Naples unsettled him in a different way: he became consumed by erotic dreams about men. They were inchoate but urgent. For the moment, not wishing to understand them, he simply savored the intensity of feeling—"It is not what happens in dreams but the strength of our feelings that is so wonderful." But a few years later in *Maurice*, he would write:

> Where all is obscure and unrealised the best similitude is a dream. Maurice had two dreams . . . they will interpret him. [In the first dream he] was playing football against a nondescript whose existence he resented . . . The nondescript turned into . . . [a] garden boy. But he had to be careful or it would reappear. [The boy] headed down the field towards him, naked and jumping over the woodstacks . . .
>
> The second dream is more difficult to convey. Nothing happened. He scarcely saw a face, scarcely heard a voice say, "That is your friend," and then it was over, having filled him with beauty and taught him tenderness.

Even in his dreams Morgan felt he had to be careful not to penetrate the boundary between body and soul. The naked boy and the tender male voice came to him on separate nights. But the homoerotic muse would not desist, and in mid-May it apprehended him with full, unexpected force. One sunny morning Morgan walked alone in the country outside Ravello, nothing in view but little trees occasionally ruffled by a little wind, and the town in the distance framed against a dark blue sea. In an instant a story emerged: "I would bring some middle-class Britishers to picnic in this remote spot, I would expose their vulgarity, I would cause them to be terribly frightened they knew not why, and I would make it clear by subsequent events that they had encountered and offended the Great God Pan." For the next two days Morgan cloistered himself in the hotel writing out the first drafts of "The Story of a Panic." Never before had he sat "down on the theme as if it were an anthill."

The form of the story he inherited from Ovid. It was a pure fantasy of metamorphosis. But the pinched perspective of the narrator—male, married, middle-class, middle-aged—was Morgan's creation. Never has a more pedestrian mind encountered bacchanalian forces.

The plot of the story is both simple and mysterious. Some inexplicable terror strikes the group of tourists—so suddenly that they neglect to protect the youngest among them. The peevish schoolboy Eustace has been left behind. The narrator and the rest return to find the young man transformed by the sensual spirit of Pan: he wears a "disquieting smile," comes "whooping down . . . as a wild Indian," barks like a dog, and sings scattered tuneless songs in the small hotel—"five-finger exercises, scales, hymn tunes, scraps of Wagner." Most disconcertingly, Eustace becomes physically demonstrative, searching out the Italian waiter and embracing him. The story ends with the waiter's sudden unaccountable death, and Eustace's escape into the Italian night. The narrator remains utterly puzzled by what has happened.

"The Story of a Panic" captured many themes that would permeate all of Morgan's subsequent fiction. The contrast between the tumultuous warmth of Italy or India and the chilly English heart. The genius loci as a source of both inspiration and fear. The strange, often estranging, significance of a plotless discovery about one's inner self. All at once Morgan seemed to have grasped how to use his complex empathy, the thing Wedd had called his "apparatus," both to be *inside* bourgeois British culture and to demonstrate how absurd such a position was.

It was a masterful beginning for a writer of twenty-three. But it was also an unwitting gloss on Morgan's own sexual panic. The immediate reaction of his Cambridge friends to "The Story of a Panic" "horrified" and disgusted the young Morgan. They treated it like a salacious tidbit. Someone gave the manuscript to Maynard Keynes, who shared it with Charles Sayle, a university librarian who cultivated a baroque effeminacy. "Oh dear oh dear, is this Young King's?" Sayle asked in knowing mock horror. "Then he showed Maynard what the Story was about. B[uggered] by a waiter at the hotel, Eustace commits bestiality with a goat in the valley where I had sat. In the subsequent chapters, he tells the waiter how nice it has been and they try to b[ugger] each other." Thus opened the abyss between men like Sayle and Lytton Strachey, who took satisfaction and pride in calling homosexuals "buggers," and Morgan, who even years later would not spell out the whole word.

It was not until two decades later—in the mid-1920s—that Morgan had the detachment to observe how much the story of writing "The Story of a Panic" was the story of his own sexual anxiety. Morgan read this little fable of authors and critics to a sympathetic group of friends, many of them the Apostles whom he had known at Cambridge. He never published it. By the time he was forty he could laugh at his priggish younger self. That he, at twenty-three, had been "horrified" by Sayle's lascivious reading later confirmed to the mature Morgan how close to the truth this unwelcome interpretation lay. When he had conceived the story "no thought of sex was in my mind"; but, looking back, later he acknowledged, "I had been excited as I wrote and the passages where Sayle had thought something was up had excited me most." Nevertheless, he could not forgive the librarian for his hamhanded literal reading of the story. A reader like Sayle, he concluded, cannot be countenanced "because he thinks he knows and slips out after twilight in his strongest spectacles . . . for a peep of a nightshirt." To the end of his life Morgan recognized the sexual force as a wellspring of his creative work. But as an artist he resisted looking too closely at anything so "sacred and mysterious" as the mechanics of creation.

The long tour of Italy seemed merely to postpone the reckoning of what to do with his life. Anticipating his return to London in the autumn, he confided to Dent, "I watch my own inaction with grave disapproval but I am still as far as ever from settling what to do." Fortuitously, George Trevelyan offered an intriguing stopgap: "Would you care to do some teaching at the W[orking] M[en's] College, next October?" The prospect was welcome, not least because it would offer proximity to Hugh Meredith, who was studying economic history at the London School of Economics and had rooms just around the corner from the college on Guilford Street.

In September 1902 Morgan and Lily returned to London. With no permanent home, they took up residence at the Kingsley Temperance Hotel just opposite the British Museum. Temperance indeed. The Kingsley was crammed with the sorts of people who frequented the pensiones they had stayed in over the last year: dowagers and earnest students, and young ladies traveling with an aunt as a chaperone. This was a very different Bloomsbury than the bohemian playground that Lytton Strachey, Vanessa Stephen, and her sister, Virginia Woolf, would establish just a few years later in a shabby townhouse blocks away on Gordon Square. There was very little privacy for Morgan at the hotel, but the city beckoned. The museum held wonders: beautiful naked Attic sculptures, a giant pair of winged Assyrian bulls carved out of stone, designed to be seen from two perspectives—they had four legs from the front, five legs from the side. In *Maurice*, just here, between the two "monsters," the gamekeeper Alec Scudder would corner the stockbroker Maurice Hall and unsuccessfully try to blackmail him.

By month's end Morgan was teaching Latin once a week at the Working Men's College on Great Ormond Street. In this he joined George Trevelyan, HOM, and other idealistic young Cambridge men. He also applied for a position as a lecturer for a university extension service in regional towns near London. He proposed a syllabus on the history of the Italian city-states. It was a great relief to him to have something to do, and especially to be in the company of robust, attractive male students. Morgan wrote to Dent that he thought he wasn't a very effective teacher. "I am afraid I enjoy it more than they do."

The Working Men's College was the fruit of Christian socialist idealism. It had been founded forty years before by a man called F. D. Maurice to provide a university-style education for men of the working classes. There were already mechanics' institutes devoted to vocational training, but F. D. Maurice's liberal imagination was not satisfied. Did workingmen not yearn for knowledge for its own sake? Did they not deserve the human fellowship of university life? So the course of the Working Men's College was set to self-consciously mirror the most advanced curricula of the day: systematic study of controversial political subjects, great literature, and art. The founders' ideals emphasized "rational enjoyment and hard work mingled with education" and encouraged "the formation of friendships" between faculty and students. The opportunities for friendship centered on manly pursuits—boxing and other sports. For the less hearty there was a library.

Though the intended clientele were laborers, most of the students who attended the college in fact came from a rung up the social ladder. These were clerks and lower-level professionals—men like Leonard Bast in *Howards End*, or indeed like Hugh Meredith's father, men who stood on their feet for twelve hours a day, filing cards in the new modern systems of cross-ledgers and indexing, or scratching out copies of business documents with inky fingers. Manual laborers, the reformers discovered, "demanded more practical subjects." No reading of Ruskin's "Stones of Venice" for them. They wanted to *get on* in the world.

There is very little record of Morgan's time teaching at the college. It was essentially a private pleasure. But he did succeed at making one lifelong close friend. One of his students was a brilliant young man who worked as a clerk in a Crosse and Blackwell pickle factory. E. K. Bennett, known as Francis, was quiet, gentle, and homosexual. Despite his tendency to denigrate himself, Bennett's career was a remarkable success story: he rapidly progressed from student to teacher at the Working Men's College, and after George Trevelyan supplied money for a scholarship, he went on to a brilliant career at Cambridge, as a Fellow of Caius College in modern German literature. Bennett was one of a very few pioneering working-class dons.

So in the dank November of 1902, Morgan traveled back and forth across Russell Square, between the bustle of the male world of the Working Men's College and the Kingsley Hotel, where, like Jane Austen at her writing table, he had almost no time to write and almost no privacy. He was picking his way along on a new Italian novel. A heroine named Lucy, a wide-eyed tourist, was his surrogate. He planned to dedicate the novel to HOM.

Meredith was living in Bloomsbury to retool—to begin an academic career as an economic historian, which would lead him first to Manchester and finally to Queen's College, Belfast. He remained a romantic, penning "weekday poems" from the point of view of working-class Londoners. Hugh was indecisive, intensely self-critical, and prone to appreciate things just after they had gone out of reach. Perhaps inadvertently, perhaps because of his mixture of darkness and adamantine wit, he continued to exert a magnetic, quasi-sexual attraction on a whole circle of friends long after he left King's. A kind of soap opera of alienated affection swirled around him in these years. Dent was crushed to discover that Hugh had plans to marry. But perhaps because he had been the golden boy in his own family, Hugh had "a horror of people who depend on me."

Just before Christmas 1902, HOM initiated an ardent turn in his friendship with Morgan. It began with the theoretical framework of fraternal affection, but it evolved into a peculiar and very unsatisfying love affair. About its details both men were scrupulously silent. The closest thing to a record of this is the portrait of Clive Durham in *Maurice*, a portrait that Morgan could paint only after he had outgrown both Hugh's platonic affections and the sting of recognizing their limitations. Between the young men there was some very tentative and inept lovemaking—long, earnest, fully clothed embraces, chaste kisses, and florid talk of the Hellenic ideal of friendship. But the intensity of the encounters awakened Morgan's heart. In his diary two years later he looked back on the two great discoveries of his youth—that he could no longer remain a Christian, and that he desired only men. Both he owed to the influence of HOM. These insights were still so raw, and so dangerous, that he wrote about them at the close of 1904, elliptically: "I've made my two discoveries—the religious about 4 years ago, the other in the winter of 1902—and the reconstruction is practically over . . ."

For his part HOM retreated from real intimacy, but the residue in him was a sense of diminishment and loss. In 1903 he broke off an engagement to marry. Later that year he had some sort of nervous breakdown. Morgan traveled up to Manchester to visit him, walking beside him for hours in silence, keeping him company, asking for nothing. Even in the midst of his depression, Hugh recognized that Morgan was a remarkable friend. He confided glumly to Maynard Keynes, "I think I am dead really now. Or perhaps I should say that I realise now what was plain to others two years ago. I come to life temporarily when I meet Forster."

In the spring of 1903, Morgan traveled to Greece with Wedd and a group of Kingsmen, picking up the plans that had been postponed when he broke his arm the year before. This time he took Lily only as far as Italy, leaving her there while he peeled off to join the tour. If Italy had been disappointing because he had been overprepared for it, Greece was anticlimactic because it confirmed what he had already come to know about himself. A second great short story was born there, a variation on "The Story of a Panic." "The Road from Colonus" ended poignantly, with the elderly Mr. Lucas unable to acknowledge the touch of Hellenic inspiration offered to him. On the road to Colonus he comes upon a natural "shrine," a tree with water gushing out of its bark, and for a brief moment he knows that "something unimagined, indefinable, had passed over things, and made them intelligible and good." But he resists the muse. He ends up back in suburban England, untouched by the momentary epiphany, "irritably" complaining about "intolerable" neighbors and barking dogs. But the mysterious sound of running water in his ears haunts him still. Morgan felt a bit like Mr. Lucas. The reprise of Italy was a disconcerting sense of déjà vu: it was a "depressing thing to look down the table" at the pensione "and honestly believe that you are the cleverest person seated at it, which is what I do day after day."

At the end of the summer, mother and son returned to London and faced facts. Hotel living had lost its charm; they found a flat, their first ever, in South Kensington, in one of the "mansions"—the modern euphemism for the clean, anonymous buildings of flats then proliferating in West London.

Morgan had a very light footprint there. He spread out an early draft of *A Room with a View* in his bedroom, but did not settle in. His lectures at Harpenden and Lowestoft on the Italian city-state took him out of town weekly, and at Cambridge he was always welcome in Goldie's rooms at King's, or Dent's (who had just been made a Fellow). He joined Apostles meetings and went to concerts frequently.

Goldie, Roger Fry, and George Trevelyan had just established a little magazine they named *The Independent Review*, and the first of Morgan's travel essays were published here. It was an amenable place to come into print. The journal's aim was mainly political, "to advocate sanity in Foreign affairs and a constructive policy" against Chamberlain's jingoist and imperialist domestic platform. This editorial position was carefully placed so as not to align with party politics: "not so much a Liberal review as an appeal to liberalism from the Left to be its better self." So from *Basileon* and the *Cambridge Review* to *The Independent Review*, Morgan found a home for his writing supported by his friends from King's.

In December 1903 Morgan, unsatisfied with the structure of the "Lucy novel" he had been writing fitfully for more than a year, began a wholesale revision. He cracked open a notebook and labeled it "New Lucy." Unlike the "Old Lucy" drafts, this revision brought Lucy Honeychurch and her pathetic cousin and chaperone Charlotte Bartlett back home from their Italian travels to England. For Lucy Honeychurch to have real moral agency, she would need real choices, and would need to face real antagonists to her narrow and protected view of the world. So Morgan spiced up the sedate crowd of characters in the "Old Lucy" drafts, introducing the iconoclastic, plain-speaking Emersons, father and son, and the sexually ambiguous, insightful clergyman Mr. Beebe. And Cecil Vyse, the aesthete with whom Lucy breaks off an engagement, was given startling and sympathetic depth. The basic premise of the plot remained just as Jane Austen might have conceived it: Whom should Lucy wed? But the new draft placed the heroine in a modern, unstable world—because, as he explained in a lecture to the Working Men's College, "the woman of today is quite another person" than an "early Victorian woman."

Lucy thinks she is safe when she returns in the second half of the novel to "Windy Corner," the sprawling Victorian house in Surrey where she had led a cosseted childhood—Pimm's cups and tennis on the lawn, and tidy, complacent ideas about the proper place of People Like Her. But the threat of something modern and unorthodox stalks her even in the parish of Summer Street, emanating from suburban villas with twee little names such as Cissie and Albert. The Emersons have moved into the neighborhood. "The fatal improvement" of the train lines from London and the advent of the bicycle have made it impossible to keep even this quiet part of the Home Counties from becoming a "perfect paradise" for the wrong sorts of people—bank clerks, men who work for the railways and in trade, ambitious freethinkers such as George Emerson. When they heard the siren song of love from these unorthodox quarters, neither Lucy nor (it turned out) even Charlotte would make the mistake of Mr. Lucas in "The Road from Colonus." But Morgan would have to bring them home to test the full effect of the touch of Italy upon their dutiful English hearts. Even with this conceptual advance, something still stalled the novel's progress toward completion—a quaver, a spasm of self-consciousness, a sense that he was "not a real artist."

A month later Morgan turned twenty-five. It was difficult to tell what he *was* but rather easy to determine what he *wasn't*, and wasn't likely to become. Morgan wasn't the same son who had left Lily for King's. He couldn't pretend to be an undergraduate any longer. He wasn't a gentleman. He wasn't a published writer, or a proper academic, or a career man of any sort. He wasn't to be like his friends Sydney Waterlow and George Barger and Malcolm Darling and George Trevelyan's brother Robert, who, one by one, settled into marriages. Even HOM, who had broken off his engagement the summer before, and entered into a second (later aborted) plan to marry, seemed inevitably destined to be a husband. In a few years, Morgan would categorically reject his friends' path. He would define his identity in opposition to them, writing in his journal, "I do not resemble other people." But at twenty-five he was still unwilling to be decisive.

From this quiet interior space in a world of fixed social rules—a world where passing the jam the wrong way at the tea table could invite a sharp glance—Morgan summoned a miraculous burst of creativity. Few artists have ever had a year like Morgan's in 1904. In the span of twelve months, he set aside the manuscript of *A Room with a View*, conceived and wrote the whole of his first published novel, *Where Angels Fear to Tread*, mapped out his second published novel, *The Longest Journey*, revised, wrote, and published "The Story of a Siren," "The Eternal Moment," "The Road from Colonus," "The Story of a Panic," and most of the other short stories that he would collectively publish in *The Celestial Omnibus*. He also began to write short stories with explicitly homoerotic themes, stories that would be published only posthumously. In her rich diary, Morgan's friend Virginia Woolf would record each wisp of idea, every iteration of her creative thoughts, all her strategies for revision. But Morgan was taciturn on his extraordinary creative flowering. He jotted down only a comment or two on his writing process in his diary. He did not even mention when he completed *Where Angels Fear to Tread,* or note the day it was published.

The years since he had left Cambridge looked like indolence or indecision, but they had been fruitful and reflective. For though his early fiction was not autobiographical in the strict sense, it worked through the three questions that had gnawed at him since his adolescence. What he was, what he would do, and how he was made up sexually were wholly intertwined. In his annus mirabilis the answer to these questions hatched all at once.

Like Cézanne relentlessly painting and repainting the silhouette of Mont Sainte-Victoire, or Jane Austen sketching her moral vision on the "little bit of ivory" of provincial domestic life, Morgan discovered the richness and complexity of his entire oeuvre, his whole aesthetic enterprise in a single subject: the search of each person for an honest connection with another human being. Especially someone unlike himself. He would return to it again and again. He was well aware that this subject was a spiritual inheritance from the women writers who came before him, and he adopted their foundational forms as the template for his moral world. He would anchor his plots in the domestic sphere that had been so richly explored by Austen and George Eliot. He would concern himself with their themes: the right choice for a marriage, the tug-of-war between propriety and personal freedom, the moral complexities of an interior life, the pressures of a small community upon an individual's moral actions. He would not need wide vistas. But he would redefine the old conventions. Out of the remarkable isolation of his upbringing and despite his characteristic timidity, Morgan found a way to displace the center of these time-honored plots. He would discomfit his readers by looking all around a question, asking them to identify with unlikely characters—an Indian doctor, a working-class clerk struggling for an education, a headstrong young widow who falls impetuously in love with the wrong man. He would make complicated use of the "question I am always discussing with myself"—"whether I am conventional or not." The answer was yes and no.

Always he was alert to the tension between the constraints he faced in his daily life and the possibilities presented by his imagination. The vision of a beautiful world, a world in which he might love and be loved by another man, beckoned to him like a mirage. He glimpsed it in 1904 when he contemplated the *kouroi* in the British Museum: "Each time I see those Greek things in the B.M. they are more beautiful and more hopeless . . . That wonderful boy with the broken arm—who I suppose is to be called sugary because he's new-Attic—stands all the afternoon warm in thick sunshine. He simply radiates light . . ." Despite his belief that Christianity had fatally separated the soul from bodily pleasure, despite his conviction that passion was the key to redeeming the English soul, with the ironclad certainty of youth, Morgan concluded,

> I'd better eat my soul for I certainly shan't have it. I'm going to be a minority, if not a solitary, and I'd best make copy out of my position. There is nothing contemptible or cynical in this. I too have sweet waters though I shall never drink them. So I can understand the drought of others, though they will not understand my abstinence.

His frustrated desires gushed up like a wellspring, fueling his urge to write. If he could not make love, at least he could "make copy."

This passage from his most private journal is significant for several reasons. The term Morgan chose at that time to describe his "position" as a homosexual in Edwardian England was "a minority." By selecting it, he repudiated the mainstream culture, which abhorred homosexuals, criminalized homosexual acts, and made even the thought of such desire "unspeakable." But the choice of the term also signaled a rejection of the few models for homosexual expression that were known to Morgan. Whether embodied by provocative aesthetes such as Oscar Wilde and Charles Sayle, or by bohemians living in Bloomsbury such as Lytton Strachey and the painter Duncan Grant, the public personae of homosexuals felt inauthentic to him, and not because he was an innocent or a prude. Both Wilde's public posture and Strachey's iconoclasm were too precious, too clever, too arch, too intellectual, and too self-referential to appeal to Morgan's sensibility. The oscillation between *conventional* and *not* was in his marrow. He did not have a form for it yet, but what he wanted for himself—and for other men like him—was something he had never seen in the world. He wanted intimacy, love, and domesticity akin to marriage.

Morgan contemplated his "position" because he earnestly considered the moral implications of his sexual identity. To be sure, his "abstinence" was born of caution and fear of offending his mother. But he sought to express himself in his own language. By choosing the word *minority*, he eschewed some of the technical terms that were coming into vogue in progressive circles, terms such as *invert* and *intersexual* and *Uranian* and *homogenic* and *homosexual*—seductive theoretical explanations as to why this queer attraction happened between men, terms that scientists and doctors devised and intellectuals in the know embraced with relief, even with zeal. Morgan rejected the pigeonhole of medical labels. He was not interested in being a "case study," as J. A. Symonds had been for Havelock Ellis in his groundbreaking *Sexual Inversion* (1897). Morgan was deeply suspicious of explanations for the *cause* of homosexuality, whether the explanations came from Germany—where K. H. Ulrichs and R. von Krafft-Ebing were promoting theories of congenital "morbid predispositions"—or from England. (He would later distance himself from Freud as well.)

In his journal, Morgan imagined himself suspended between two kinds of hostile misapprehension—those who could not imagine the idea of homosexuality, and those, like Lytton, who would find his "abstinence" cowardly or risible. But Morgan never imagined that he would be utterly alone. Even in this plaintive defense of his "position," Morgan held on to a vision of a communal sexual identity—"a minority" to be sure, but not a "solitary." He grafted the Apostles' belief in personal relations onto an erotic ideal of a lover and friend *different* from himself. His fantasies concerned the garden boy and the laborer, the clerk and (eventually) dark-skinned men. Since he had begun teaching at the Working Men's College, the romantic idea that love could be both an expression of lust and of tolerance was incarnated in a particular form. That this was both a conventional trope—Wilde himself had sex with working-class boys, after all—and an unconventional one was emblematic of Morgan's character and his personal philosophy.

A few months after he wrote this entry, "an idea for an entire novel—that of a man who discovers that he has an illegitimate brother—took shape" over a weekend in July 1904. It hung in his mind as he and Lily searched for a more permanent and amenable place to live than the dreary flat in South

Kensington. Taking a break from house-hunting, mother and son traveled to Wiltshire to visit Maimie Aylward, a cousin by marriage on Eddie's side of the family, and a dear friend of Lily since before Morgan's birth. Maimie lived near Salisbury, "the heart of our island: the Chilterns, the North Downs, the South Downs radiate hence." The great stone circle of Stonehenge stood just outside the city, not far from the cathedral's magnificent spire. "The fibres of England unite in Wiltshire," Morgan believed. It was a place to escape into, and a place to come home.

In mid-July, leaving the ladies to talk, Morgan set out alone into the Wiltshire landscape. Long country walks were a popular pastime. Since Wordsworth's poetry had been published a century before, finding oneself and finding the Real England through its unspoiled countryside had been a rite of passage for literary men of romantic outlook. Since his days at King's, Morgan had been impressed by A. E. Housman's collection of poems *A Shropshire Lad* and Matthew Arnold's *The Scholar Gypsy*. As only a displaced suburban man can be, he was especially ambivalent about the erosion of ties to the land and to the past. Three miles east of Salisbury Morgan came upon an ancient hill fort from the Iron Age, a series of undulating concentric embankments about twelve feet high, overgrown with long "gray and wiry" grasses. As antiquities go, they suited Morgan perfectly: they were "unobtrusive," "curious rather than impressive." As he walked toward the single tree at the center of the Rings, Morgan saw "the whole system of the country" before him. And there, in the shade of the small tree, he came upon a shepherd boy with a club foot. Suddenly, as it had been for him in Ravello, "the whole landscape" became "charged with emotion."

From the air, the Figsbury Rings look like a fried egg with an enormous yolk, albeit an egg with an area of fifteen acres or so. Each of the two concentric circles has a breach for entry at the east and the west. The force of human will upon the landscape is best revealed from above—the Rings are part of a great constellation of circular shapes pressed into or carved from the chalk hills on Salisbury Plain: tumuli and stone piles and Stonehenge itself, with its grand avenue to the river Avon, and the city-fort of Old Sarum, the first site of Salisbury. The view from above exposes the scars of forgotten conquests. The Romans appropriated Old Sarum and built roads threading from fort to fort, as befits an occupying army. Some of these roads, lean and straight and strong, form the spine of the A roads, a later conquest still. Others, long abandoned, thrust headlong through farmer's fields. The farther the distance, the more palpable the pattern of scars. The best images of the Figsbury Rings come from satellites.

If you stand at its highest point on the plateau of the fort, the evidence of human toil is subtler. The prospect presents a paradoxical feeling of being both atop the world and sheltered by it. Morgan called this feeling a "system" of understanding the relations between people and the natural world. The whole of Wiltshire is laid out like a private revelation from here, a God's-eye view of nature and man's attempts to work on it—forest and field in patchwork, the river meandering, and on a good day, the cathedral's emphatic spire. Embraced in the long arms of the embankment, you are hidden from all who might approach.

For Morgan, lying at the spot in the Rings brought back a reiteration of the cosmic feeling he found inside the chalk circle at Madingley. The haphazard encounter in this magical place magnified the mystery. Forster's conversation with the shepherd boy took less than a quarter of an hour. It was not a galvanizing *plot*. Resting in the shade of the single ancient tree that abutted the top ring, they passed the time talking about "nothing—still one of my favourite subjects." The boy was genial and not the least bit obsequious: he didn't call Morgan "sir." Despite his deformity, he seemed happy and at ease. In a flourish of generosity that Morgan found quite touching, he offered a "pull at a pipe." Since he did not smoke, Morgan declined. As he got up to leave, he offered the boy a tip of sixpence, which was rebuffed without hostility.

No spark of human warmth has found more willing kindling. Morgan "caught fire up on the Rings." "In that junction of mind and heart where the creative impulse sparks," the boy had touched him. It was a subtler touch than the spirit of Pan that had transformed Eustace in "The Story of a Panic"; Morgan was imbued with a spirit of *home*. The boy's spontaneous kindness convinced him "that the English *can* be the greatest men in the world: he was miles greater than an Italian; one can't dare to call his simplicity naïf." And the idea of home engendered a surrogate family, the brother he had always hoped for and missed, the sense of belonging that his rootless condition had denied him. He would be father to his fiction—a more positive and impassioned position than "making copy" instead of making love. "I created, I received, I restored," Morgan wrote decades later about this seminal moment. All at once the shepherd boy "gave birth" to the character of Stephen Wonham in *The Longest Journey*.

Morgan had already begun to imagine a character like himself, a bright and shy young man who is transformed by "the fearless influential Cambridge that sought for reality and cared for truth," the Cambridge . . . "which I knew at the beginning of the century." But now he realized that Cambridge would be only part of a larger story. The orphaned Rickie Elliot, Morgan's surrogate in the novel, would discover by chance that he has a bastard half-brother in Stephen. Stephen is everything Rickie is not—a hard drinker, a shepherd and farmhand, an autodidact, cantankerous, as comfortable in himself as he is uncaring about the opinion of the world. He is at once the spirit of Brotherhood, distilled from the Apostles' love of Greece and of one another, and a quintessential common Englishman. So the weaving of life into art began: "Figsbury Rings became [the fictional] Cadbury Rings. The valley of the Winterbourne below them turned into the Cam . . . *The Longest Journey* was born." Tellingly, Morgan transferred the club foot from the figure who had inspired Stephen to the character of Rickie. It was a mark of his difference, and his inadequacy. Citified and sissified, Rickie, the head to Stephen's heart, would carry the defect that set him off from others, make him unable to play sports at school, and after his unfortunate marriage render him genetically unsuitable to father healthy children.

Just a day after the incident in the Rings, Morgan's self-consciousness began to erode his confidence. He minutely parsed his own behavior toward the boy. How stiff and stupid he had been! How denigrating to offer him money! This, his first record of the encounter in his private journal, was already haunted by the feeling of being belated—"I walked out *again* to Figsbury Rings"—he began his account. As he denigrated himself, he elevated the boy's motives until the shepherd became an emblem, not merely of chance friendliness, but of peasant "wisdom," national character, the spirit of Englishness itself. He decided that, "whether he knows it or not," the boy was "one of the most remarkable people I've ever met."

Characteristically, Morgan mulled over the scene as it might have appeared from the boy's point of view. The boy's refusal to accept his money manifested "great wisdom" and a simple courage. "I was simply bound to think myself unsympathetic," Morgan concluded in his diary that September, "whether I offered that sixpence or not, and I get a comfort in the rebuff." Looking at the scene in retrospect, overcome with lust, guilt, and anxiety, Morgan turned to Italian to encode his powerful feelings: *"Vorrei cercario ancora—ma come si può vivere quando si domanda sempre 'cosa fa?', 'dove va?"* (I would still like to search for him, but how can one live when people are always asking "what are you doing?" "where are you going?")

Twice more, on Monday and Tuesday, Morgan walked back to the same spot to see if he could find the young shepherd again. (One imagines him fretfully planning to do so over the weekend, thinking up a pretext to disentangle himself from Maimie's and Lily's "Where are you going?"s.) But it was not possible to recapture the radiance of effortless synchronicity. The boy and his flock had gone on to Wilton, six miles away. Morgan learned this fact on his third visit in pursuit of the boy, from the boy's father, also a shepherd "neatly dressed" and friendly, but "altogether less wonderful" than his son. Morgan took comfort that neither father nor son would call him "sir."

In later years Morgan was at pains to emphasize that there was nothing sexually illicit about his behavior toward the boy. Charles Sayle, the Cambridge librarian, may have been canny about the motives for "The Story of a Panic," Morgan admitted, but he must misconstrue the story of the shepherd boy: "Charles Sayle wipes his glasses but our interview was of no interest to any type of observer." So much was true: Morgan was exceptionally careful to act with propriety. But his mind buzzed with emotions, and his behavior at the time suggests that the encounter had a mesmerizing erotic power—an alloy of lust and gauzy romance. Nowhere in his writing does he acknowledge that the chance meeting between himself and the shepherd was an iteration, in inversion, of the moment from his school days when he encountered the pedophile on the Downs. But the incident had the same silhouette: a man and a boy; the offer of payment rejected; the tumult of excitement; the palpable urge to detail and explain his innocence.

With reluctance, years later, Morgan discovered that though the event "fructified" his novel, "test[ing] the magic" was inevitably disappointing: "The Rings survived . . . the Tree remained." But his companion on that visit, Lytton Strachey, proved to be immune to the scene's charms. He was "not one to countenance fanciful transferences." And during this visit to Wiltshire in the early 1920s, Morgan had cause to measure even for himself how much of the scene's significance derived purely from his yearning imagination. On a long walk he encountered the shepherd again, recognizing him "because he would have been, and was, a mangy farm labourer, with a club foot. I felt no pleasure, no sadness, nothing at all except a passing fancy that everyone and everything I encountered was equally unreal." Morgan said nothing to the man, nor, he remarked drily, did he "hand over his share in the royalties of *The Longest Journey.*"

4

"The Spark, the Darkness on the Walk"

The inchoate idea for a new novel lingered when he and Lily returned to London later that month. After months of searching, "we have got a house, too small and with no garden." They signed a lease for fifty-five pounds per year on a semidetached house in the little village of Weybridge, which was being built up into a commuter town at the far western edge of London. A railway line meant that Waterloo Station was little more than half an hour away, and the walk from the station to the foot of the village a brisk twenty minutes through woods and country lanes. The house was "small and somewhat suburban," he told Dent, but fortunately "not genteel." It stood at the margin of the village's high street, opposite an old coach inn. The little village was compact, and it absorbed the burst of Victorian development rather gracefully: the faux-Gothic church of St. James was only decades old, but nestled in an ancient churchyard. There were undeveloped woods and fields leading down to the Wey, a tributary of the Thames, where he could row Lily about on a fine day. Less than a mile away was the beautiful wetland the Chertsey Mead, alive with birdlife.

The face of the three-story brick house had an attic gable, and broad windows that looked out onto the postage-stamp-sized Monument Green. A tall marble column dedicated to the memory of a local Hanoverian patroness anchored the green. It had been transported from the notorious London neighborhood of Seven Dials to this suburban safe haven and bore "an inscription to the effect that it really pays to do good: the last line is 'are registered in courts above.'" To Robert Trevelyan, Morgan offered a parodic sketch. To the rear, a view of "a field full of dropsical chickens." From the parlor, the phallic monument. "The villa . . . has a beautiful brass bound door step which we are taking on from the last tenant. None of our neighbours have one."

Like Adam in the garden, Morgan's first act upon moving into the house was to name it. Built only three years before, it came with the grandiose designation Glendore, which was "too trying." Instead he called it Harnham, after the watermeadows within sight of Salisbury Cathedral, and the hill to the southeast of the city—the Wilton side—from which there was a remarkable view. Thus the Forsters grafted old England onto their new suburban home. Lily might find that the name reminded her of Maimie. For Morgan, it was a secret link to the place where he had met the shepherd boy.

Harnham was not Rooksnest, but it was "quite pretty in some ways," far roomier than their Kensington flat, and it radiated Edwardian comfort. On the ground floor were a drawing room with a piano, a dining room, and a kitchen; two large bedrooms for Morgan and Lily and a bathroom occupied the next floor; and tucked up in the attic were three small rooms—one each for Ruth Goldsmith, who had been Lily's cook at Tunbridge Wells, and Agnes Dowland, the parlormaid, and a workroom for the nascent writer. Downstairs functioned as a purely Victorian middle-class household; upstairs, something more modern was brewing. The tiny study was Morgan's aerie: twin windows looked out over the green and the road. He rose late in the morning, and divided each day into practicing piano and writing in the little room where he would finish the Lucy novel—which he would eventually call *A Room with a View*—and write five more. He would live here with Lily for the next twenty-one years.

In December 1904, a year after his first major revision of the Lucy drafts, he set aside that novel yet again, breaking off at the moment when the engagement with Cecil Vyse is put to Lucy Honeychurch in earnest. Very quickly Morgan began to sketch out a wholly new novel based on a scrap of conversation, a "sorry bit of twaddle" he had heard and remarked on during his first Italian travels in 1902, a tidbit about a disastrous marriage between a young English widow and a younger Italian man.

Where Angels Fear to Tread is a novel Henry James might have written if he'd had a sense of humor. Like the Lucy drafts, the novel was conceived as a clash of cultures between middle-class English people and ordinary Italians. Forster's working title was "The Rescue": Philip Herriton, lover of Italy, and his hidebound sister, Harriet, are dispatched by their formidable mother to rescue his brother's widow, Lilia, from Signor Gino Carella, the son of a dentist in Monteriano. But Lilia's hapless chaperone, Caroline Abbott, has utterly failed, and by the time Philip arrives Lilia has already married.

The plot unravels in unexpected ways. Mrs. Herriton's poisonous sense of duty at first obscures the reader's sympathy, but she turns out to be right; the marriage *does* make Lilia miserable. Real sorrow is the consequence. Lilia dies in childbirth. The rescue of her infant son—in fact, a kidnapping by his English relatives—ends in the baby's accidental death. Philip breaks his arm when the carriage with the stolen baby overturns. When Gino discovers his baby has been killed, he tortures Philip by twisting his broken arm. (This was the scene that Morgan later admitted had "stirred" him erotically: "I knew not nor wondered why, and even if I had heard of Masochism I should have denied the connection.") The British interlopers limp away from Monteriano, where they have done so much harm with such righteous intentions. At the conclusion of the novel, Philip feels transformed by his experience, and decides that he must declare his love to Caroline. But Caroline, too, has learned a lesson from the ordeal. She confides to Philip that she loves Gino, and Philip withholds his true feelings from her, in a Jamesian renunciation. In the end, it is not clear who is being rescued, or from what.

Forster composed the novel "almost with physical force"—ten short chapters in just over a month. His first readers didn't quite know what to make of it. Aunt Laura' s elderly friend, the Victorian critic Snow Wedgwood complained that her "fundamental objection to the story was that [Morgan] did not make up his mind at the start whether it was to be a tragedy or comedy. It seemed quite a new idea to him . . . that one ought to have any conception of one's intentions in this respect. I feel that in a tragedy everything ought to convey some intimation of seriousness." But should one laugh or cry at Philip's ridiculous narrow life—or at his sacrifice? In his first completed novel, as in all of Austen's, even prigs and petty tyrants have moral agency: Morgan recalled "[d]iscovering that Lady Bertram [in Austen's *Mansfield Park*] had a moral outlook shocked me at first." He "had not realised the solidity of an art," he confided in his Commonplace Book, "which kept such an aspect in reserve, and placed her always on the sofa with pug."

In *Where Angels Fear to Tread* Morgan tried to convey what he labeled "intermittent knowledge"—the "ability to expand or contract perception without being detected . . . [O]ne of the advantages of the novel form . . . [it] has a parallel in our perception of life: we are stupider at some times than at others." He defended the novel against Robert Trevelyan's rather "severe" criticism that the turns in the plot should be more clearly telegraphed, the characters more sympathetic, the English setting more "amusing." The ethical question, Morgan replied, was how much people can *change*.

> The object of the book is the improvement of Philip, and I did really want the improvement to be a surprise . . . [I] dislike finger posts, and couldn't bear . . . the thought of inserting "Philip has other things in him besides these: watch him" . . . [I] should have felt that the suggestion that a book must have one atmosphere to be pedantic. Life hasn't any, and the hot and cold of its changes are fascinating to me.

On his birthday, New Year's Day in 1905, Morgan reported to Leonard Woolf that he had completed the manuscript and sent it off to Blackwood's in hope of serial publication. He had accomplished something important, but felt weighted down by his personal insignificance. In his diary he set down a sober accounting of his life's progress. From the little room at the top of the stairs, his life looked bleak:

> My life is now straightening into something rather sad & dull to be sure, & I want to set it & me down, as I see us now. Nothing more great will come out of me. I've made my two discoveries—the religious about 4 years ago. the other [his homosexuality] in the winter of 1902—and the reconstruction is practically over . . . I may sit year after year in my pretty sitting room, watching things grow more unreal, because I'm afraid of being remarked . . . I still want, in all moods, the greatest happiness but perhaps it is well it should be denied me.

Having always thought that "twenty-five is the boundary of the romantic desirable age," he was nearly certain that no one would ever love him.

Fifty years later, Morgan reflected on his premature despair. He concluded that it was a symptom of how humans often feel "not altogether at home in the world of time . . . Growing old is an emotion which comes over us at almost any age. I had it myself violently between the ages of twenty-five and thirty, and still possess a diary recording my despair . . . This unpleasant sensation . . . is probably only another form of the sensation of being too young, which irritates adolescents." But the young Morgan could not muster the long view.

He steeled himself for the future, writing New Year's resolutions to discipline his wayward sloth and lust. He vowed to get out of bed by nine in the morning. To "keep the brutes" of physical desire "quiet," he would adopt a regimen of exercise. He would attempt to overcome his paralyzing shyness. And, in the event he might encounter another young man like the shepherd, he decided to teach himself to "smoke in public: it gives a reason for you & you can observe unchallenged." More practically, without a manuscript to anchor him, he began to plan his next escape from Lily and his dead-end life.

Again, a friend from King's came to the rescue. Sydney Waterlow had an eccentric aunt who needed an English tutor for her three eldest children. Elizabeth, the Countess von Arnim, was ostensibly from the minor German nobility, but she came to such a position by a wildly circuitous route. She was a cousin of the novelist Katherine Mansfield. Born in New Zealand to a British father who had made a fortune there, at twenty-two Elizabeth had married a German aristocrat twenty-five years her senior, and coming to dislike both him and his milieu, fashioned a separate existence for herself and her five young children in a rambling seventeenth-century stuccoed *Schloss*, one of his many ancestral properties. Life in Berlin tired her. She set about building an idyll in Nassenheide in the Pomeranian countryside. The estate comprised more than eight thousand acres of farm and piney woods; here she set up a little matriarchy with her adoring children, a private system of schooling them, a study with a typewriter for herself, and a beautiful English garden as a sort of rebuke to the German way of doing things. Her three eldest daughters she rather coyly nicknamed April, May, and June, after the months of their birth. Her (mainly absent) husband she christened "The Man of Wrath." These circumstances she depicted in a roman à clef, *Elizabeth and Her German Garden*, published in 1898. The domestic myth of Elizabeth floating about her garden with happy children in tow became a late-Victorian bestseller. Elizabeth would go on to write twenty more novels. Two in particular lived on after her death: *Enchanted April*, a romance of female friendship in Italy; and *Vera*, the stark tale of her abusive second marriage.

His sojourn in Nassenheide afforded Morgan the chance to write letters home to Lily, the sort of comic travelogues that periodically renewed their affection and reinforced their shared sense of the ridiculous. In them, he would become her "Poppy," or "Popsnake"—his childhood nickname of endearment. He detailed to her an arrival at Nassenheide as a gothic comedy of errors "beyond my wildest dreams." Traveling by rail through the unknown dark, he was let off the train in a driving rain—"pitch dark, no station, no porter, no one of any kind." Morgan persuaded a local farmhand to lead him to the *Schloss*—"Slosh! We trod in puddles . . . we waded in manure"—and, after trudging alone up a rough drive full of potholes, he arrived at Elizabeth's darkened mansion. When he rang the bell, "a hound bayed inside." A "dishevelled boy" led him through "a long low white washed barrel vaulted hall, hung with trophies of the chase," while he followed after, his "boots oozing manure." The countess had expected him to arrive the following day. The next morning after breakfast he encountered his employer. She was not quite what he had expected: "indifferent false teeth & a society drawl." "How d'ye do, Mr. Forster!" she announced firmly. "We confused you with one of the housemaids. Can you teach the children, do you think? They are *very* difficult."

He stayed with Elizabeth and her entourage from April to August 1905. Germany did not much impress him—"the country is unthinkably large and contented and patriotic," he wrote in his diary—but his daily teaching duties were not onerous, and the three girls, ages thirteen to eight, took instruction well. He liked the other tutors, and had plenty of time to himself in a large and comfortable suite of rooms. Within a few days of his arrival he got word that Blackwood wanted to publish his novel, though on parsimonious terms. He showed Elizabeth, an established author, and she offered her opinion of the novel as she read it in stages—the first few chapters "very clever, but most unattractive, and she felt as if she wanted a bath." Reading further, she decided that the novel was "beautiful," only to "retract . . . and [go] back to her original opinion." Morgan and Blackwood had a brief tussle over the title. Blackwood rejected Morgan's first choice, "Monteriano," but accepted his second, taken from the famous adage from Alexander Pope—"Fools rush in where angels fear to tread." Quite quickly author and publisher "settled into contentment" with each other. All July he read proofs.

While in Nassenheide, Morgan turned to his diary to ruminate on the wider question of how he fit into the world. He felt out of touch with modern writers. In its infancy, the novel had been *novel*—of all the literary forms, it made the unique promise of showing life truthfully—but the conventions of the nineteenth-century novels Morgan revered had begun to feel a little like a cage. It seemed to him wrongheaded, even trivial these days simply to end a novel with "the old, old answer, *marriage*": "Artists now realise that marriage, the old full stop, is not an end at all . . ." Resolving a plot with a marriage was part of the imperative of comedy, but the blind optimism of lesser writers seemed dishonest to him: "The writer who depicts [life as a bed of roses] may possibly be praised for his healthy simplicity. But his own conscience will never approve him, for he knows that healthiness and simplicity are not, in all cases, identical with truth."

The modern writers whom he most admired, from Dostoyevsky to Ibsen to Hardy, were convinced that truth lay in a tragic vision. But his temperament, his need to see both "hot" and "cold" in the world, could not find sympathy with these brooding minds. This set of aesthetic problems reflected the most pressing questions in his inner life. As one by one his closest friends disappeared behind the "astonishing glass shade . . . that interposes between married couples and the world"—HOM, George Barger, Malcolm Darling—he was beginning to feel certain "I do not resemble other people." Must intimacy always take the form of marriage?

He mulled over a correlative. What social force made people so herdlike, so inclined to divide between *us* and *them*? The strange insular world of the von Arnim household, from one angle, seemed merely an iteration of the strange insular world of Weybridge, or any other enclave of privilege. Most people he knew had very little sense of the lives of people unlike themselves. It was all very well to read Dickens or Mrs. Gaskell's *North and South*: "To be enthusiastic & sentimental over the picturesque poor is no difficulty." The comfortable world he knew best concerned itself only with finer gradations of status. Lily, his aunts, their friends, spent endless hours determining who was too "vulgar," who "genteel" enough to visit or invite to tea. The approach to people unlike oneself, he believed, was a moral obligation, but an obligation with risks.

To know and help [the poor] are we to lose our souls—or how much of them . . . [C]onditions are appalling: poverty, matrimony, much of family life all work against love and clear vision: and to those are added the rules of the game—death and decay yet people contrive to get in touch—I believe because they are radically good.

For the time being, these ideas remained a mere wisp in his diary. Within the year he would work them into a lecture called "Pessimism in Literature" to be delivered across the class divide to students at the Working Men's College. How to "contrive to get in touch" with people would remain the great ethical question that illuminated his life and art. He would face its difficulties squarely, unflinchingly, in his last and greatest novels, *Howards End* and *A Passage to India*. In the meantime he would try to live his life according to the ideals of his art.

Morgan returned to London in the autumn of 1905 to enthusiastic reviews of *Where Angels Fear to Tread*. Friends, especially Dent and Dickinson, offered effusive praise. But the experience of being published sharpened his keen sense of his limitations as an artist. He told Robert Trevelyan,

> I know I am not a real artist, and at the same time am fearfully serious over my work and willing to sweat at atmosphere if it helps me to what I want. What I want, I think, is the sentimental, but the sentimental reached by no easy beaten track—I cannot explain myself properly erly . . . [M]y equipment is frightfully limited, but so good in parts that I want to do with it what I can.

What he *could* do was to try out a life in fiction that he felt unable to live in the world. In the first six months of 1906, he took up the fragment of plot that the shepherd boy had sparked in him. He borrowed the title *The Longest Journey* from Shelley's *Epipsychidion*—which loosely translates to "the story of a soul." Rickie Elliot's search for love would take him from Cambridge to the Sawston school, to the Wiltshire countryside. The novel, like Shelley's poem, asked how best—in family or friend, man or woman—one might find intimacy.

> *I never was attached to that great sect*
> *Whose doctrine is that each one should select*
> *Out of the world a mistress or a friend*
> *And all the rest, though fair and wise, commend*
> *To cold Oblivion—though it is the code*
> *Of modern morals, and the beaten road*
> *Which those poor slaves with weary footsteps tread*
> *Who travel to their home among the dead*

By the broad highway of the world—and so
With one sad friend, perhaps a jealous foe,
The dreariest and the longest journey go . . .

This exhortation to take the road less traveled, to stick by a band of brothers, had been the Apostles' creed at Cambridge. In a tribute to both his intellectual brothers and the ideal of brotherhood embodied in his years at King's, Morgan dedicated the novel simply, "Fratribus." But by the time he wrote *The Longest Journey*, Morgan felt the strength of those bonds eroding. The "code of modern morals" seemed ineluctably to lead toward "the beaten road" of marriage.

No summary of the plot can convey how peculiar and uneven a novel *The Longest Journey* is. It was an autobiographical fantasy. Of all Morgan's creations, Rickie is the one who most closely resembled himself. For the first third of the novel, through a lonely childhood and an awakening into friendship at Cambridge, Morgan anchored Rickie in the circumstances of his own life. But then he set his surrogate loose into a speculative future. After university, Rickie wants to become a writer, but out of cowardice chooses the more "slavish" life, teaching at Sawston, a mediocre public school that Morgan later remarked drily "owes something to my public school."

Agnes Pembroke's brother teaches at Sawston, and she is engaged to marry Gerald Dawes, a rather dim but virile specimen of an English public school man, who bullied Rickie when they were at school. (Gerald's attractions are all physical—the narrator tells us that "just where he began to be beautiful the clothes started.") After Gerald dies suddenly in a football match, Rickie decides to marry Agnes though his motives are obscure, even to him. Rickie's greatest friend, Ansell, counsels against it. He "foresee[s] the most appalling catastrophe": "You are not a person who ought to marry at all. You are unfitted in body: that we once discussed. You are also unfitted in soul: you want and you need to like many people and a man of that sort ought not to marry . . . and if you try to enter [a marriage] you will find destruction."

This syncopation of the plot was deliberate—Morgan placed Rickie's marriage to Agnes in the *middle* of the story, for in a modern novel "marriage is most certainly not an *end*, either for [a woman] or for her husband. Their courtship [is] but a prelude . . . the drama of their problems, their developments, their mutual interaction, is all to come."

As if the drama of his own life could be played out like a game of chess in the novel, Morgan plotted out the consequences of marriage and the alluring prospect of having a brother very unlike himself. As he began writing, he worried that his structure was too calculated to bear the novel's emotional weight. "Doubt whether the novel's any good: all ingenious symbols, little flesh and blood."

From his very first drafts, the plot had centered around the triangle of Rickie, Agnes, and a male character who became Rickie's illegitimate brother, Stephen Wonham. Agnes, all middle-class values, abhors Stephen. Agnes is the sort of woman whose devout Christianity leads her to believe in "the soul and the body," a dialectic that Morgan had known to be irredeemably flawed, since Italy had taught him to "cherish the body." He summarizes her character with devastating wit. "'The soul's what matters,' said Agnes, and tapped for the waiter again."

Stephen's drunkenness, his illegitimacy, his country ways all threaten Agnes's domestic stability, and she counsels Rickie to cut him off. But he cannot, and his love for his brother, complexly transferred from Morgan's erotic vision of the shepherd boy, eventually costs Rickie his life. He dies after being hit by a railway train while pulling the drunken Stephen off the tracks. In the end, Rickie's stories are published posthumously, to modest acclaim, under the title *Pan Pipes*.

The reviewers of *The Longest Journey* labeled the novel "clever" so often that one suspects they believed its author to be insincere. They could not know how much of this story of a soul was taken directly from Morgan's deepest yearnings and fears. Morgan told Dent that he had written a scene of pure panic—a chapter in which Rickie runs naked when touched by the spirit of nature—but struck it from the novel because it threw the ending off balance. (He joked to Dent that "only students of the Master's Juvenilia will now twig what he's driving at.") Looking back on *The Longest Journey*, Morgan acknowledged that while it might be the strangest and the "least popular of my . . . novels" it was "the one I am most glad to have written." It was cathartic for him to work through in fiction what a terrible idea it would have been for him to marry. But the structure was prescient in ways he could not know. In years to come he would learn how painful a triangular relationship between two men and a woman could be.

In the summer of 1906, with the novel well under way, Morgan made two sentimental journeys, as if to test the roots of his identity and the promise of sustaining them. The first was to Manchester to visit Hugh Meredith, who had finally settled on the idea of marriage. His fiancée, Christabel Iles, was a bright university woman with progressive ideas about education, child rearing, and suffrage. The trip was not a success. Morgan returned to London disconsolate, sickened by how much he felt "cut off from HOM." It was not only the prospect of HOM's marriage that disturbed him. Something essential about their friendship had dwindled, and this disquieting realization fueled a sense that their previous years of friendship had been a chimera, and not the truly intimate connection he had believed them to be. On the trip home, he commented bitterly on the forbidden sights he saw from the train window: in the June heat "the bodies of men drying off after bathing in the Thames."

In August he returned to Stevenage for the first time since Lily and he had left Rooksnest when he went off to school. He found Frank Franklyn, the garden boy he had played with as a child. In letters to Lily he described the house in detail, noting changes—"you can hardly see the house for creepers: huge ivies are growing towards the larder window." But he did not brave a visit inside. The town, too, had changed: "There is a whole new street, parallel between the High Street and the railway . . . towards us it's all exactly the same." Thirteen years after their departure, Rooksnest was still *us*.

Down the road about a mile at Highfield he wandered shyly into the garden of Lily's old friends the Postons, catching them unawares in a memorable domestic tableau. Years later the Postons' daughter recalled her mother going into the rose garden on that day, "wearing a sweeping blue gown. It was hay time and . . . she paused to pick a handful of newmown grass for my rabbits." At the margin of the garden "a tall gangling young man in ill-fitting tweeds" appeared and introduced himself as Morgan Forster. "My mother welcomed him with her ravishing smile. 'Of course, you're an old friend,' she said. 'Come along in and have lunch.'" So the glorious image of Mrs. Wilcox in the first chapters of *Howards End* was imprinted on Morgan's imagination.

In October, Morgan and Lily toured the chateaux of the Loire Valley. He joked to Dent that there was "no escape from Table d'hôte." Back in Weybridge there were tea parties, talks at the local literary society, Thursdays with friends in London, walks to the margin of the village where gardens gave way to lush meadows, sonatas to practice on the piano in the drawing room, and protracted discussions with Lily and Ruth about which cheese to order from the market. Each afternoon he retreated to the attic to press on with *The Longest Journey*. But just when it seemed to Morgan that his narrow suburban life would stretch out interminably, unchangingly into the future, Weybridge yielded a spectacular surprise. A wonderful dark-skinned boy bounded up the Harnham attic stairs.

Syed Ross Masood was seventeen—a decade younger than Morgan—but from the first moments he dominated their friendship. Well over six feet tall, he looked at the top of Morgan's head, and he was barrel-chested and virile, willing to pick a fight if he felt his honor was impugned. He was profoundly handsome, in a matinée-idol exotic sort of way, with large, wide-set, almost black eyes, and a fierce black mustache. He had come from Delhi to live with Lily's Weybridge neighbors Sir Theodore and Lady Morison. Sir Theodore had recently retired from two decades at the Anglo-Oriental College in Aligarh, first as professor of English and finally as principal of the college. The ostensible purpose of Masood's arrival in their English household was to prepare him for entrance exams to Oxford—hence the need for Morgan to tutor him in Latin—but the real story was a dark family drama back home in India.

What a family it was! Masood was descended from the Muslim intelligentsia, with a lineage of great power and significance. He was the only grandson of Syed Ahmad Khan. Sir Syed, as he liked to be known after being honored by the Crown, had begun as a clerk in the East India Company, and risen by hard work, intelligence, and loyalty to become a high-ranking official for the Raj. He was a bold and decisive man. During the 1857 revolt, he had risked his life and reputation to evacuate the British from Bijnor, and took charge of the district for a time to protect European residents from violence; subsequently he published a treatise blaming the origins of the mutiny not on rebellious soldiers, but on the "pride and arrogance" of Indian civil service officers who "consider the Natives of India as undeserving of the name of human beings." He looked back to the Mogul empire as the halcyon moment of Indian culture and stability. In 1875, Sir Syed founded the Anglo-Oriental College with the twin aims of creating a rigorous western-style scientific university and promoting Muslim unity. (He promoted Urdu as the proper language for the future of India, believing Hindi to be vulgar.) He was forward-thinking in a very particular mode. He revered British education, sent his own son to study law at Christ College, Cambridge, and designed the Anglo-Oriental College to be a sort of Muslim Cambridge. His vision of the school included both Sunni and Shia boys—who would be forbidden to provoke disputes along doctrinal lines. To win back the glory of ancient Muslim days, he published a weekly journal, *Tahzib-al-Akhlaq*—"The Training of Morals"—which disseminated Muslim culture, the revival of Urdu, and a pan-Islamic proto-national identity for India. In his day these ideas earned him enemies: Muslim clergymen derided his ecumenicism within the faith, and Hindu leaders were equally hostile to his triumphalist view of Muslim culture and what they viewed as his hand-in-glove attitude toward the Raj. Syed Ross Masood was only eight when his grandfather died, an old and venerated man in his community.

Masood's father, Syed Mahmud, had trained as a barrister and ascended to the "highest position a 'Native' could hold in the British Government of India"—he was appointed a High Court judge at the age of thirty-seven. But he stood uneasily under the long shadow of his famous father. He gave his only son the name Ross after his English friend the barrister George Ross, but he rankled over discrimination and ill-treatment by the British authorities. An alcoholic, he resigned from the bench when a British judge blamed his tardiness in issuing opinions and absence from work on drunkenness. Syed Mahmud returned to Aligarh, but he alienated Sir Syed by drinking in front of him. He had hoped to be appointed as his father's successor to the college, and his life unraveled further when this did not happen.

Masood suffered at the hands of his unstable, unhappy father. His mother intervened with British authorities and friends, including Sir Theodore Morison, to protect her young son. One night Syed Mahmud—drunk and in a rage—dragged the ten-year-old Masood outdoors in freezing weather, forcing him back and forth across the college lawn to teach the boy how to break up the sod with a wooden plow. He had in his addled mind some sort of lesson about India's place in the world, and the political history of agriculture. Terrified, the boy's mother called upon Sir Theodore, who interceded, "wrapped up the shivering . . . boy in his greatcoat" and took him home. And there he stayed. Masood's father "was driven out of Aligarh," reciting a snatch of Urdu poetry, "All that splendor is left behind / When the gypsy packs up and goes." For the three years before the family moved back to England, the Morisons were effectively foster parents to Masood, whom they loved dearly. Sir Theodore had a son about Masood's age, and he always referred to them both as his sons.

Despite completing preparatory school in Delhi, it was not at all clear that Masood was ready for a British university. He was a mercurial character. There was a bit of his father's hot temper in him, and a bit of his grandfather's grandeur. He habitually made big plans—to memorize all the verse of the Urdu poet Ghalib, to take up tennis, to learn to play the banjo—but only fitfully followed through. Masood was generous, especially when he didn't have money, princely in his manner toward both his own countrymen and Englishmen, whom he regarded as "poor fellows." All his life he was the center of a coterie of admirers, who listened to him tell tall tales in his "sonorous and beautiful voice; one could not fail to notice his voice, for he never stopped talking." He had "the vast self-confidence that comes from being able to trace one's ancestry back through the Prophet Mohammed at the thirty-seventh generation to Adam at the one hundred and twentieth." To Morgan, who had been parched for so long, this fountain of effusiveness was irresistibly charming. Not all of Morgan's family shared his enthusiasm. When his cousin Maimie Aylward heard he was tutoring a black man, she exclaimed, "Oh dear, I do hope he won't steal the spoons."

Morgan romanticized his new friend; in Masood he thought he had found the perfect embodiment of his belief in the primacy of human warmth. On Christmas Eve 1906 he wrote in his diary, "Masood gives up duties for friends—which is civilisation. Though he remarks—'Hence the confusion in Oriental states. To them personal relations come first.'" The personal relations between Morgan and Masood remained chaste, if unorthodox. Not much Latin got learned during their tutoring sessions. When Masood got bored—which was often—he would pick Morgan up, turn him upside down, and tickle him. When Masood went up to Oxford, Morgan visited him, and returned to Weybridge with a hookah, but without his cap, which Masood had "borrowed" without consultation.

Their friendship seemed to achieve an unprecedented intimacy almost immediately. In correspondence Morgan called Masood "My dear boy" while Masood returned magisterially "My dearest Forster." His proportions were extravagant; after a short interruption in correspondence, he began a letter—"Centuries may pass, years may turn into 2000 centuries, and you never hear from me, and you are not to think that the great affection that I feel for you has in any way diminished." Masood scolded Morgan for his English temperament, his way of carefully "measur[ing] out [his] emotions as if they were potatoes."

The emotional whirlwind was salutary, in the end. Looking back, Forster believed that Masood "woke me up out of my suburban and academic life, showed me new horizons and a new civilization and helped me towards the understanding of a continent . . . There never was anyone like him and there never will be anyone like him." Over the course of several years, the young man eclipsed HOM in Morgan's imagination. For the time being, all Morgan's emotions were below the surface. He wrote cryptically in his diary about his deepening love for Masood: "We like the like and love the unlike." But his life remained so bifurcated that even in his private diary he divided his end-of-year insights into "inward events" and "outward events."

The Longest Journey was set to be published in mid-April 1907. Disgruntled by his dealings with Blackwood, Morgan had found a new publisher and better terms. (He remained with Edward Arnold for the rest of his life.) The week before the novel came out, Morgan set off on a walking tour of the Lake District, the fifth wheel to two couples—HOM and his wife, Christabel, and George and Florence Barger. Florence was George's cousin and wife, a university graduate whose spirited support for socialism, suffrage, and women's education made clear she planned to be her own person.

Morgan enjoyed the long treks across magnificent scenery and "pigging it" at meals. But he peeled off alone on a personal pilgrimage, following the route of rural place-names in A. E. Housman's elegiac *A Shropshire Lad*. HOM had introduced him to these poems during their second year at King's, and his valedictory sense of the receding friendship with HOM magnified Morgan's romantic appreciation of both the text and the terrain. "The home-sickness and bed-sickness" in Housman's poems, "the yearning for masculine death— all mingled with my late adolescence and turned inward upon me." Shrewsbury he found "unspoilt and alive: a city of vigor still adjusted to its beautiful frame. Poetry—or luck—in every inch of it." Suddenly, he read Housman's poems as a kind of code that "concealed a personal experience" of its author: "I realized the poet must have fallen in love with a man." Just outside of Ludlow, Morgan was seized by a desire to communicate his understanding of this hidden connection with Housman. At a rickety oak table in front of a peat fire in the Angel public house, Morgan composed a fervent letter of admiration. It was his first experiment with homosexual author worship. From Housman, silence. Much later, Morgan realized that he had not affixed a return address.

Back in Weybridge he encountered a pile of positive reviews in the newspapers. Most read *The Longest Journey* as an extension of the satirical attitude of *Where Angels Fear to Tread*. The *Times Literary Supplement* wrote, "Mr. Forster fastens himself again, like some sharp wholesome insect upon the life of the suburbs . . ." An unsigned review in the *Morning Post* faulted his spasmodic plotting: "the sudden death rate among the significant characters, exclusive of the two children . . . is 44%." But the Cambridge friends who found themselves portrayed in the novel were not as sanguine. Lytton Strachey resented Morgan's commercial and critical success. He described to Leonard Woolf how he had heard something "burrowing in a corner" of the London Library.

> It was the Taupe . . . He's a little changed—very bronzed and healthy-looking, and with very nearly the air of a settled establishment. His book [*Where Angels Fear to Tread*] has gone into a second edition, and he sits in Weybridge writing another, and will go on doing so all his life. He admits he's "successful," and recognises, in that awful taupish way of his, the degradations that that implies. But he's of course perfectly contented. The thought of him sickens me.

He added, "The morals, the sentimentality and the melodrama [of *The Longest Journey*] are incredible, but there are even further depths of fatuity and filth." Robert Trevelyan characteristically took it on himself to tell Morgan that his Cambridge friends had found "things in [your novel] which are very bad. They are not the only things in it that are bad, oh no, not by any means, but these . . . things are so bad that it is only common friendliness to let you know." But criticism didn't dent his spirits. Morgan was always hardest on himself. Once he had committed to print, he could let it go without much fretting.

With the promise of a contract for a new novel, he returned to the unfinished Lucy manuscript with a growing sense of dread at how pallid and artificial its inner life seemed to him now. "I have been looking at the 'Lucy' novel. I don't know. It's bright and sunny and I like the story. Yet I wouldn't and I couldn't finish it in the same style. I'm rather depressed. The question is akin to morality."

Five years had passed since he sketched out a list of characters in an Italian notebook—

Lucy Beringer. Miss Bartlett, her cousin.
 H.O.M.
Miss Lavish . . .

—but only one of them had been named after an actual person, and this was HOM. That character had disappeared in revision, and the person himself, ensconced in a middle-class life, his wife pregnant with twins, seemed to Morgan more dead than the notebook sketch he had inspired. The whole premise of a romantic novel seemed false.

The new style, if one could call it that, twinkled still, but underneath it was a hard diamond edge of disgust at the work and his pandering. It took more than a year to hammer out revisions. Morgan adopted a tone of semi-comic desperation as he described his efforts. In a parody of the last line of Wordsworth's "Strange Fits of Passion," he wrote Robert Trevelyan, "Oh mercy to myself I cried if Lucy don't get wed." Writing began to feel like a kind of ventriloquism. He even appropriated Miss Bartlett's voice to accept an invitation to visit the Trevelyans:

Sir,
    I hesitate to address you but you have again confused me with my young cousin Miss Honeychurch . . . I am of very little consequence, I do not matter, living in a very quiet way as I do at Tunbridge Wells . . . I beg you therefore for her sake to remember that I am
                                    CHARLOTTE Bartlett

In revision he retained the arc of the plot—Lucy Honeychurch's choice between the intellectual aesthete Cecil Vyse and the impetuous romantic figure of George Emerson—but began to insert private jokes to keep himself amused. The Reverend Mr. Beebe takes down Emerson's copy of *A Shropshire Lad* from a bookshelf and announces, "Never heard of it." He had always planned to dedicate the novel to HOM, and he did so. But his friend need not know that this was a valedictory.

Writing the Lucy novel had become a mechanical exercise. But jolted by reading Walt Whitman's Calamus poems, Morgan began to take Whitman's declaration to heart: "I will escape from the sham that was proposed to me."

He began a systematic reading of the gay canon. If he listened with a newly attuned ear, the panpipes of erotic music he had detected in Housman could be heard everywhere. He jotted down a cryptic list of names in his diary without commentary, as if someone reading over his shoulder might discern the hidden pattern. There were the authors of "Etonian meditation[s]," stories of "delicate sensitive little schoolboys" who fall hopelessly in love with older boys, but whose "devotion only ends with death." These Edwardian novels and their writers are long forgotten: A.E.W. Clarke's *Jaspar Tristram*, H. N. Dickinson's *Keddy*, Howard Overing Sturgis's *Tim*, and the schoolboy fantasies of Desmond Coke, who published under the delicious pseudonym "Belinda Blinders." There were defenses of homosexuality by J. A. Symonds and the Victorian sage Edward Carpenter. And there were the overtly sexual poems of Whitman, Michelangelo, and Shakespeare. Slowly and tentatively, Morgan began "contriving to get in touch" with an unacknowledged body of gay literature.

In mid-January 1908 Morgan was offered a decisive opportunity to meet a homosexual author whom he might imagine as a master and mentor. Sydney Waterlow lived in Sussex near Rye, and through his wife's family he had befriended Henry James, insofar as it was possible to move toward intimacy with that august presence. Waterlow attached himself to the Master in toadying admiration, and the old man, now approaching seventy, seemed content to bask in it.

The myth of James, contrived by his own careful hand, was well under way. Ensconced in the cool and dark of Lamb House, James had fashioned himself into not merely an elder statesman of literature and guardian of the future of the novel, but a member of the English gentry. Through his friendship with Waterlow, Morgan was invited to take Sunday tea with James, keenly aware that James was purportedly "a really first class person." Half jocular, half eagerly sincere, he wrote to Lily and Dent about the impending occasion: "I felt all that the ordinary healthy man feels in the presence of a lord." The austere brick house had formal gardens and pristine lawns; inside, Morgan and Waterlow stole a glimpse as they walked past the darkened study where James composed at a massive table.

The Master was sixty-six, rotund, and "effectively bald"; Morgan, tall, stammering, and shy, only twenty-seven. In *The Albany* magazine he had just published "The Celestial Omnibus"—a story of a boy who takes an ordinary bus to heaven on a fantastic journey—and feared that James would "know better" than to like it. But he was unprepared for the confusion that their actual meeting unleashed. Morgan was introduced as a published author. But James, who was a bit deaf and unlikely to be budged from his initial impressions, somehow decided that he was meeting the young philosopher-Apostle from King's. "Your name's Moore," he announced firmly, grasping Morgan's shoulder in a proprietary grip. Nonplussed, Morgan did not clearly correct the mistake, and a cascade of other small misunderstandings ensued: Was Forster from Wakefield or Weybridge? Had James or had he not known Forster's great-aunt?

In retrospect it was clear that James had wanted his guests to be comfortable, if only comfortable in their willingness to hear him hold forth on his opinions of the day. He had recently read Queen Victoria's letters, and pronounced that she was "More of a man than I expected." But the whole atmosphere of the place, and the compulsory reverence for James himself, repelled Morgan. The American transplant seemed to him to take on the worst attributes of "the English character." There was no spontaneity, none of the kind of haphazard but reliable warmth that he had so loved in Masood, and even in HOM in his earlier days. James's house and his person were like his novels, "disembodied" and fastidious in their emotional control.

Twenty years later, while preparing the lectures that would be collected in *Aspects of the Novel*, Morgan would single out James for particularly savage criticism, in part because an artist of such great talent seemed to him to have a moral imperative to *be human*. James's novels were beautifully designed, he acknowledged there, but their "pattern [is] woven—at what sacrifice? Most of human life has to disappear—all fun, all rapid motion, carnality, etc., and 9/10ths of heroism. Maimed creatures can alone breathe in his pages." Characters in James's novels are "gutted of the common stuff" in "the interest of the pattern" their godlike author seeks to impose, and "this castrating is not in the interests of the Kingdom of Heaven" since "there is no philosophy . . . no religion (except an occasional touch of superstition), no prophecy, no benefit for the superhuman at all. It is for the sake of a particular aesthetic effect which is certainly gained, but at this heavy price." Though he did not say it aloud, Morgan concluded privately that the source of James's cramp was repressed homosexuality—James was "merely declining to think about homosex, and the knowledge that he is declining throws him into the necessary fluster."

The disappointment he felt in meeting James may have been inevitable, and it was certainly partly Morgan's own fault. In letters to his friends and in his own diary, he had built up the encounter into something auspicious, and the consciousness of these expectations dampened any chance of finding something magical in even the lackluster humor of his own inept performance. He wrote to Lily a brief comic sketch of himself as a hapless visitor, which played a familiar score but deflected the deeper lesson. The arid atmosphere of high art in Lamb House, the fawning and the hush, repelled Morgan. This kind of authority "was not my own road."

As he stepped out, literally, onto the gravel road outside Lamb House that blue-gray evening after tea, from down the lane framed by tall privets a bright flicker of flame flared and guttered. In the distance a workman walking home had paused to light a cigarette. It was not a deliberate call sign—the man never saw Morgan at all—but the glow set Morgan ablaze in a synaptic burst. It was a private revelation. Suddenly, Morgan felt impelled to travel a different road, to walk away from the house of Art toward the rougher, more real life he knew he desired.

In his private diary, he wrote a sharp little sketch of the evening's impressions to capture the feeling of the meeting with James. And then, without any context to frame it, a poem spilled out onto the page:

> *I saw you or I thought of you*
> *I know not which, but in the dark*
> *Piercing the known and the untrue*
> *It gleamed—a cigarette's faint spark.*
> *It gleamed—and when I left the room*
> *Where culture unto culture knelt*
> *Something just darker than the gloom*
> *Waited—it might be you I felt.*
>
> *It was not you; you pace no night*
> *No youthful flesh weighs down your youth.*
> *You are eternal, infinite,*
> *You are the unknown, and the truth.*

Yet each must seek reality:
For those within the room, high talk,
Subtle experience—for me
The spark, the darkness on the walk.

For the time being, he would not approach such men. He would spin his heart's insights into art, captured in a rarefied, disembodied ideal of "eternal, infinite" manly beauty. But the impulse set his compass toward the human. He would go with the spark.

5

"Ordinary Affectionate Men"

Working over the typescript of *A Room with a View* in early May 1908, Morgan dismissed the novel as "bilge." His own words sounded inauthentic to him, but he had found a voice worth listening to: "I opened Walt Whitman for a quotation, and he started speaking to me . . . he is not a book but an acquaintance, and if I believe him, he's more." In *Leaves of Grass* Whitman had vowed to "dissipate this entire show of appearance," to celebrate the poet's love not merely of mankind, but of *men*. Morgan saw that Whitman, too, had been "stifled and choked" but he had shaken off his chains. Celebratory, effusive, manly, democratic, Whitman's poems promised that there need be "no more fighting between the soul and the body." So much of Whitman echoed Morgan's hopes and desires. How wonderful it would be to "believe him," to share his courage and his optimism. Whitman's erotic poems were electrifying in their own right, but they gained greater power because they were part of a larger human yearning to *connect*.

> *Passage to India!*
> *Lo, soul! seest thou not God's purpose from the first?*
> *The earth to be spann'd, connected by net-work,*
> *The people to become brothers and sisters,*
> *The races, neighbors, to marry and be given in marriage,*
> *The oceans to be cross'd, the distant brought near,*
> *The lands to be welded together.*

Just days after Whitman spoke to him, Morgan felt the "[i]dea for another novel shaping" in his quickening imagination. In a single short paragraph, he sketched out virtually the whole conception of *Howards End*. This story would be an answer to the thin, brittle quality he had come to detest in the long revisions of *A Room with a View*. *Howards End* would take a wider view. He would ground his characters in the modern world—the London wincing at the din of new construction, motor cars, and the pounding of steam pile drivers, and the timeless English countryside rapidly eroding into endless suburbia.

Morgan balanced two families with very different values, each equally convinced of the supremacy of their way of seeing life: Margaret and Helen, the Schlegel sisters, who cherish personal relations and the liberal values of "temperance, tolerance and sexual equality"; and the Wilcoxes, who believe in money, business, and power, and who know to their marrow that the sisters' outlook is "sheltered [and] academic"—"that Equality was nonsense, Votes for Women nonsense, Socialism nonsense, Art and Literature, except when conducive to strengthening the character, nonsense." Morgan understood that "the spiritual cleavage between the families" must be tested by Margaret's marriage to Henry Wilcox, and that she must marry him even after she discovers that though "impeccable publicly," Henry has been hiding a sexual secret—a past liaison with "a prostitute." *Howards End* explores the tension between respectability and personal morality, and the tremendous gulf between the standards for men's and women's sexual behavior.

He also wanted to give the principles of liberalism a long hard look. It was all very well to dismiss the world of the Wilcoxes, the world of external things, of money and business—but Morgan knew that the world where young men could sit toasting crumpets on a long fork in front of the fire talking about ideas and art depended on things and money, depended, too, at its foundation on the unseen clerks and office boys who toiled in it. Where Henry and his children believe that they have earned their wealth, the Schlegel sisters feel a twinge of guilt about their privilege. The Schlegels' politics are vaguely well-meaning: "they desired that public life should mirror what is good in the life within." Their intervention on behalf of Leonard Bast—a young clerk whom they meet at a concert—begins the chain of events that leads to his death, and Helen Schlegel's pregnancy and disgrace.

Howards End is a house, the ancestral house of Ruth Wilcox, the first Mrs. Wilcox. It is a replica of Morgan's child's-eye view of Rooksnest, right down to the chimneys and the wych-elm with the boars' teeth pressed into it. And Ruth Wilcox is a sort of spiritually attuned matriarch. She can read people's hearts. Oblivious to the modern world, in touch with nature, content with her role as mother and wife, she is everything that the Schlegel sisters detest about women of their mother's generation. And yet they both come to discover that Mrs. Wilcox is extraordinary, for reasons they cannot explain. Mrs. Wilcox is the female equivalent of Stephen Wonham.

Morgan based his complex characters on models from his life. He told Dickinson, "Your home at All Souls Place somehow suggested the Schlegels' house to me . . . and your three sisters seen as it were with a sideway glance and then refocussed." In their unorthodox habits the Schlegels also resemble the orphaned daughters of Sir Leslie Stephen, who would soon marry to become Virginia Woolf and Vanessa Bell. Leonard Bast, wary, believes that "to trust people is a luxury only the wealthy can indulge." His character originated from Morgan's observations of one of his proud and striving students at the Working Men's College. Alexander Hepburn was a printer who fiercely wanted to become *cultured.* As Morgan watched the changes in "throbbing stinking London," he worried that "Money is power, and nothing else is, as far as I can see." He would test this principle as he worked on drafts of the novel throughout 1909.

Just as Morgan began to imagine in an abstract way that Henry Wilcox's sexual misconduct might set the story of the two families' conflict in motion, a story of real sexual danger interjected into his life with horrifying force.

Malcolm Darling's impending wedding was the event of the summer in Morgan's circle of Kingsmen. Darling had come home on leave from the Indian civil service, eager that Morgan should meet his best friend and groomsman, Ernest Merz. Merz was twenty-seven, a lawyer with the heart of a poet, good company, bright and funny, "a continual bubble of suppressed laughter"—Morgan liked him immediately. On Thursday, July 8, the three young men shared a congenial, leisurely bachelor supper at a Soho restaurant. After dinner Darling peeled off, leaving Morgan to stroll with Merz toward his club. They talked amiably, and said their goodbyes. Shortly after, Merz went to his rooms in the Albany, the fashionable bachelor apartments next to the Royal Academy, walked upstairs, poured himself a whisky, and hanged himself.

The suicide shook Morgan deeply. He detailed the events in his diary five days after Merz's death:

[H]e left me, normal, at about 9.40. Next morning he was found dead . . . The inquest today reports that there was no evidence as to the state of mind. As yet no clue. I may meet sadder things, but never a more mysterious. However horrible the explanation, there surely must be one. He had even taken a holiday for D[arling]'s wedding on the 21st. He was charming . . . I can't think it has happened.

Normal. It was truly awful to have been the last person to see Ernest Merz alive, more awful still to be Malcolm's confidant as he tried to make sense of the unfathomable facts just days before his wedding.

However horrible the explanation. On Monday morning, the day before the inquest, Malcolm confided to Morgan obtusely that he feared his friend Merz might have been a homosexual. Perhaps this dread secret—or the threat of exposure—might have caused his death? Letters shot back and forth, and Morgan suggested they could have "a few minutes talk alone." Morgan, who had surmised the same explanation long before Malcolm, warily replied, "The more I think of it the more distressed I get. My own theory—one must have one—is that he was either insulted disgustingly or saw something disgusting. You mustn't be annoyed at me for writing so freely. The man whom I saw has never made a mess of things, I know that." Even as he sought to reassure his stricken friend, Morgan plumbed the full weight of the scandal. Did the verdict of suicide "prevent ecclesiastical rites?" he asked Malcolm. He was thinking of the "distress" to Merz's family.

The more distressed I get. No wonder, since comforting Darling meant retreating further into deception. He could not tell Malcolm he was homosexual now. Merz's death brought home to Morgan how *something disgusting* could happen suddenly—there was always the chance of an inadvertent slip and exposure. But even more palpable than the fear this instilled was the terrifying truth that Merz had seemed happy, *normal,* to him when they parted just minutes before his death. What a tragedy that Morgan had been unable to sense another human being was in so much pain and fear.

The incident of Merz's death made Morgan feel ever more cautious and frozen, ever more despairing about the prospect of a brave Whitmanesque life. His diary went quiet for weeks. Then news of the death of an acquaintance compounded his emotional paralysis: "I feel that I cannot feel." Weeks after Merz's suicide, Morgan set aside the notebook that had been his diary since 1904, though there was still room in it to write. He bought a new book covered in sturdy leather, with a lock with a hasp. The "Locked Diary" would be the repository for his inward thoughts for the next sixty years.

His entries in the Locked Diary over the next few months focused disproportionately on stories of sexual anxiety and danger. He jotted down a report he had heard about a young Frenchman who was told by a pettish lover that she had syphilis. "Going home, he wrote a letter explaining what had happened, & then shot himself. He was examined. No traces of poison were found on him. It was all a joke." He began and abandoned a fragment of a new novel—called *Arctic Summer*—breaking off with the suicide of a young man after the discovery of a sexual misdeed. Though Lance March's sexual crime is unnamed—all that is said is that he "disgraced the college and himself"—he is sent down from Cambridge, and shoots himself after his brother confronts him, asking, "Have you thought of mother at all?"

Everything conspired to make him feel edgy and disgusted with the world. He had just read Frank Harris's psychobiography of Shakespeare—a bestseller—which suppressed all discussion of the homoerotic sonnets.

> Was going to reflect sadly on life, but what's the use of my abuse? A wrong view of S[hakespeare]'s sonnets in a book . . . lent me, and an attempted blackmail in this morning's paper are the main cause. How barbaric the world! If a tiny fraction of the energy would go to the understanding of man, we would have the millennium. This bullying stupidity.

Just before Christmas "the biggest thing" of the year occurred when Masood invited him to spend a week together sightseeing in Paris. They shared a glorious time—walking up the steps at Montmartre, attending the Comédie Française—and when they parted at the train station Masood, "plunged in despair," was full of histrionic goodbyes. "Do buck up," Morgan told him, embarrassed at the scene. He was satisfied that Masood loved him, but what did this love mean? His year-end reflections focused on "the enigma" of Masood's feelings: "Will [his love] ever be complete? Is the enigma him or his nationality? That he forgets me in between I could bear, but what is he thinking of at the time?" Back in London, Morgan continued to spend "joyful but inconclusive" evenings with Masood. Unable to gauge Masood's sincerity, Morgan decided to take a jocular, self-deprecating tone in his letters. He signed off one letter, "From Forster, member of the Ruling Race to Masood, a nigger."

But privately he was as unsatisfied with himself as he was with Masood. He parsed his own character, admitting to himself that "my bourgeois cuteness and desire to know where I am" was "perhaps no less fickle" than Masood's wild effusions. Masood had shown him an Urdu poem: "'o love, each time thou goes out of my sight, I die a new death.' How can I keep it quiet when I read such things? My brain watches me, but it's literary. Let me keep clear from criticism and scheming. Let me be him. You've stopped me. I can only think of you, and not write. I love you, Syed Ross Masood: love."

These were Morgan's final words for the year. The rest of the diary's page is blank.

His yearning for Masood was all "literary," but in daily life, Morgan was overwhelmed by powerful waves of lust. The beauty of men on the street "tormented" him. He was haunted by the image of "a khaki great coat," of "eyes so indifferent to mine & of manhood's hidden column." He had a frightening brush with blackmail: "After lunch in the Savile . . . I said something about a 'charming boy' and one of the members lowered his paper looked at me and raised it in a lightning flash. Then I went to have my [hair]cut, and the man hinted that he would like to borrow 10 pounds—! I had never seen him before . . ."

He tried hard to suppress these feelings. It was best to be safe, he concluded rather priggishly: "However gross my desires, I find I shall never satisfy them, for the fear of annoying others. I am glad to come across this much good in me. It serves instead of purity."

But by the end of 1910, Morgan could no longer settle for the "joyful but inconclusive evening[s]" he had spent with Masood, with their tantalizing embraces. The crisis came after an evening at the opera. On December 28 he took Masood to Covent Garden, to see Richard Strauss's adaptation of Oscar Wilde's *Salome*. By the end of the evening, Morgan was at a fever pitch, and he blurted out his confession of love to Masood in a cascade of emotions. Masood listened quietly and calmly. He waited a moment, and then very softly said, "I know."

Alone, on the train home to Weybridge Morgan was in a tumult. He sent off a letter to Masood—which does not survive—reiterating his love and demanding some sort of commitment for the future. It was maddening, but at this moment family obligations intervened: Morgan and Lily paid a New Year's call on Aunt Laura at her house at West Hackhurst. Days went by without a response from Masood—Morgan chafed and squirmed "in an awful stew all Saturday and Sunday" as the silence persisted. All he had was his diary: "*Non respondit*, and though I do believe it's all right, my breast burns suddenly & I have felt ill. He has sent me such a horrid ugly birthday present! tray with candlestick match box and sealing wax rest, colourless message inside: probably posted before my letter reached [Love, Love.]"

On January 2 a letter arrived from Masood. Unaccountably, wonderfully, he let things stand where they had always stood. He seemed to treat this revelation from Morgan as one more of the strange things Englishmen did. Morgan chastised his friend—"you devil! Why didn't you write at once?"— but he was deeply relieved. "There is nothing to be said, because everything is understood. I agree," he told Masood. As he wrote these words, Morgan had just turned thirty-two. He was back where he had begun, grateful only for not having shattered the friendship that meant the most to him in the world.

The chasm between Morgan's public and private personae began to widen in this year, 1910, for the publication of *Howards End* made him a literary celebrity. As he completed the manuscript in July, he assessed his oeuvre. He liked the new novel well enough, but *The Longest Journey* was the "book to my own heart. I should have thought it impossible for a writer to look back and find his works so warm and beautiful . . . To have written such a book is something. My next heroism will be to stop writing."

(Forty years later, in 1958, Morgan would revisit this question. In retrospect he decided humbly, "*Howards End* [is] my best novel and approaching a good novel.")

The novel came out on October 18. Its rapturous reviews, oddly, reawakened the *tristesse* Morgan had felt while writing the revisions of *A Room with a View*. *The Daily Telegraph* announced, "There is no doubt about it whatever. Mr. E. M. Forster is one of the great novelists. His stories are not about life. They are life." The *Athenaeum* pronounced him "one of the handful of writers who count." To Goldie, Morgan confessed that the adulation made him uneasy. "I go about saying that I like the money, because one is simply bound to be pleased about something on such an occasion." In his diary he reflected, "I am not vain of my overpraised book, but I wish I was obscure again." He was disquieted that Lily "is evidently deeply shocked" by Helen's pregnancy in *Howards End.* Maimie and Aunt Laura—all the Victorian ladies—concurred. "Yet I have never written anything less erotic."

The truth was that more than ever he felt the "sterility" of his creative life. It would be another six months before he could diagnose its source with accuracy:

> main causes of my sterility 1. Inattention to health—curable. 2. Weariness of the only subject that I can and may treat—the love of men for women and vice versa . . . 3. Depressing & enervating surroundings. My life's work, if I have any, is to live with a person who thinks nothing worth while.

After the crisis with Masood at New Year's 1911, something began to disintegrate in the relations between Morgan and his mother. It became impossible for both of them not to resent the sclerotic state of their shared lives. Louisa Whichelo, Lily's mother, suddenly became ill and died in mid-January at the age of eighty-four; her death plunged Lily, who was fifty-six, into a depression that seemed permanently to diminish her. Lily began to make little cutting remarks. She told Morgan that if Masood ever came back to live in Britain again, his friendship with Morgan could never be on the same footing. Morgan believed that "sorrow has altered her, and I had to alter too, or leave." He tried to squelch his anger at her, which made him feel "trivial and effeminate."

To his disgust, he found himself acting like a little boy. When Aunt Laura asked him how he liked a cheese she had served them at West Hackhurst, Morgan pretended he had not tasted it though it had gone rotten; Lily was left to bear the bad news, and later excoriated him, saying that he was "just like his father, unable to put his foot down at the right moment." It was the first time that Lily had spoken about Eddie in a denigrating way, and Morgan felt afterward that he could not respect her any longer. When he cracked a vase he "feared to tell mother," but was disgusted by his "cowardice." On the anniversary of his father's death, he had a private "Satanic fit of rage against mother for grumbling and fault finding" and imagined that he would sweep all the china figurines off the mantelpiece and cut his throat. But Hamlet-like, he could not act. He knew that "mother does not think highly of me. Whatever I do she is thinking 'Oh that's weak.'"

The final ignominy came when Roger Fry painted his portrait—a rather modern rendition of him as "a bright healthy young man, without one hand, it is true, and very queer legs, perhaps the result of an aeroplane accident, as he seems to have fallen from an immense height on to a sofa." Despite the comical description to Florence Barger, he was rather proud of the painting, and bought it. But he gave it to Florence after a local vicar came to visit Lily in Weybridge, and seeing it in the drawing room, exclaimed, "I say! Your son isn't queer, is he?"

In the summer of 1911, anticipating Masood's permanent return to India, he and Morgan arranged a monthlong walking tour of the Italian lakes. In retrospect, he found the trip to have the flavor of "a honeymoon slightly off colour" though it "was clear he liked me better than any man in the world." Eventually he tore up his letters home because they were so "wet" and colorless. All that remains of the visit "is a photograph of us there . . . I starry eyed with a huge moustache, looking very odd indeed." It was to be the first of a series of formal domestic portraits with friends and lovers he would preserve throughout his life.

Impressive sales of *Howards End* brought Morgan enough money to undertake a six-month journey to see Masood and Malcolm Darling in India. Lily remained fragile after her mother's death, but Morgan persuaded her that a holiday in Italy with her friend Mrs. Mawe might warm and solace her. He agreed to travel with the ladies as far as Rome to tuck them into their hotel. For the onward journey he would meet up with a group of Cambridge friends. Morgan joined Robert Trevelyan in Naples; Dickinson joined the party at Port Said.

In anticipation, Morgan began furious planning for the trip. He read up on Buddhism and tackled the Bhagavad Gita. There was much correspondence with Robert and Goldie over provisions for the trip—which deck chair to buy at the Army and Navy Stores, the best sort of celluloid underwear. He practiced some Urdu phrases—while riding a bicycle one was supposed to shout, "'Out of the way brother' or 'Mother, do not take up all road.'" Leonard Woolf, back from Ceylon, did what little he could to teach Morgan to ride horseback. On Putney Common the two men made quite a scene. Morgan discovered there was the problem of steering the animal, and then there was the problem of *stopping* it. Atop even the gentlest mount, he always felt as if the horse had six legs.

The prospect of leaving home catalyzed a deepening friendship with Florence Barger. She was exactly his age, compassionate, fiercely intelligent, and quite lonely: her husband, George, was consumed with work while she was marooned at home with two sons, aged two and five. On a visit to the Bargers just before he left, Morgan steeled himself and told her that he was homosexual. She surprised him. Quite instinctively, she took up discussion of his "inner life" as analogous to her own, and with frankness that happily outstripped his expectations she talked about sex—telling him of a miscarriage, her unhappiness about George's infidelity, how women were slower to sexual excitement than men. It was a "[v]ery great happiness" to have a woman as a friend. "She loves me and I her."

At Port Said, Morgan finally began to feel as though he were entering another world. Goldie climbed aboard ship from a tiny boat, looking unconvincing in a pith helmet. The greasy little boys on dockside called out to tourists, "Here smut postcard." Flying fish danced at the ship's bow, glinting in the sun. On deck the Cambridge clique sat apart from the body of staid English civil servants on their way to Bombay, who dubbed them "the Professors" in a tone with "a little nip of frost." Their cloud of disapproval brought out a schoolboy irreverence in the group. They perched on bollards on deck instead of playing games, and "argued about the shape of the earth at the breakfast table." Although he was fifty, Goldie was "evanescent . . . shooting out little glints of nonsense."

Morgan struck up a conversation with a handsome young army officer who lay on a deck chair reading a book of poems in the hot sun. Kenneth Searight was returning to his unit at the Khyber Pass. Searight melded a Byronic sensibility to the soul of a colonial accountant. "It's not a star that's beautiful, it's its effect on one," he told Morgan. Searight was "very intimate with the natives," Morgan confided to Florence. Indeed. Searight unveiled a leather diary containing his own encyclopedia of colonial pedophilia, row upon row of young native boys: name, age, race, sex acts, and number of his orgasms all totted up. He had also written a long poem in the Romantic style about being "perpetually in love with some boy or other" and a "minorite story." Morgan spent hours with him in "amazing conversation."

When the cabins became unbearably hot, Morgan moved his cot to sleep on deck. After two weeks of sailing, the party arrived in Bombay, and hired personal servants to travel with them for the duration of the trip. Morgan made a beeline to Masood at Aligarh, nine hundred miles away by first-class railway. The Anglo-Oriental College, "spread . . . out over the plain like red mushrooms," was beginning to fray at the seams: there were fractious disputes between the English faculty and the remnants of Sir Syed's Muslim friends. Masood was cordial, but Morgan was clearly his showpiece, and it was impossible to gauge the state of their friendship through the scrim of his elaborate and public hospitality. Each day Morgan met dozens of Masood's friends; a large supper was organized in Morgan's honor where they ate bad English food. There was much manly camaraderie, and much expense. One of Masood's friends put on a nautch, a stag party with dancing girls who sang at deafening pitch; after hours of this, Morgan realized that the event would continue until he left. Pressed into kissing the women goodbye, he settled for shaking their hands instead.

From Aligarh, Morgan (joined by Robert and Goldie) headed north to the Afghan border to visit Searight, "superb in his uniform." They drove along moonlit roads to attend a formal dinner in the officers' barracks. In a scene he would refigure in *A Passage to India*, Morgan lost his collar stud; with dinner ever more delayed, he gave up looking for it and went off with his collar askew. Afterward the officers danced together under the stars, Searight commandeering Morgan into a foxtrot. It was the last Morgan ever saw of him.

Morgan was more or less "adrift in India," with no fixed itinerary or clear purpose in mind. Besides visiting Masood, his one object was to spend some weeks with Malcolm and Josie Darling in Lahore. The couple "fitted indifferently into official circles at Lahore . . . indeed sometimes . . . did not fit in at all." Malcolm had startled some of the local English officials when he inspected a local prison wearing robin's-egg blue pajamas. Morgan found Josie in particular to be "unconventional, ardent, fearless." He told Lily,

The Darlings are ideal hosts and friends. Not many Anglo-Indians would encourage a guest to do queer unusual things, still less to join in them themselves. Everyone is in such a terror of being out of the ordinary. Classical music, literature, intellectual tastes generally—as a rule all is dropped in a couple of years and husbands and wives . . . meet other husbands and wives in a dense mass at the Club.

Morgan was as well equipped as any Englishman to comprehend the thicket of Indian politics, in large measure because his interests were so "peculiar and personal." "I didn't go there to govern . . . or to make money or to improve people," he said later. "I went there to see a friend." From October 1912 to March 1913 Morgan constructed a spider web from friend to friend across India, from the club at Lahore to a wedding feast in Dewas, from the Anglo-Oriental College to the Barabar Caves, on bicycle and atop elephants, on foot and "in a sort of starved omnibus."

He arrived at a moment of relative calm for the Raj. In 1905 the viceroy, Lord Curzon (the same Lord Curzon who had been the object of Oscar Browning's affections), partitioned Bengal, ostensibly to make the administration of such a large area less difficult. Like so much of British mapmaking, the effect was destabilizing: Muslims became the majority in Eastern Bengal, and both Hindu and Muslim nationalists magnified tensions as their populations jockeyed for power. The partition was rescinded in time for King George V's triumphal imperial tour the year before Morgan arrived. The Indian Councils Act reforms of 1909 solidified the Raj, leaving two nominal consultative power bases to Indians, an impotent National Congress, and a loose confederacy of provincial councils, elected indirectly, which kept homogeneous ethnic groups geographically localized and set in uneasy equipoise. As Morgan traveled from Muslim to Hindu states he kept his ears open, hearing a chorus of contradictory ideas about which was the *real India*, and what should become of the country.

Of one thing he became certain: even the most well-intentioned British people were coarsened and spiritually corrupted by the experience of imperial power. One Englishwoman told Morgan, "I came out with no feeling against Indians, and now I can't bear them." After the rebellion of 1857 the British, afraid of contagion both bacterial and cultural, had retreated into their little rectilinear compounds, eating boiled beef and bottled peas and putting on musicales at the club in a hideous parody of suburban life. Even "a cultivated man with a good sense of unimaginative humour" could only muster the half-joking admission that "I despise the native at the bottom of my heart." Morgan wrote Florence Barger that he had met a schoolmaster at Benares, "so kind, but whatever I wanted to do, he told me it wasn't done and whatever I said he replied archly 'Oh, but that's seditious.'" When the military chaplain at Chhatarpur suggested to the maharajah that he should eat beef to gain strength, Morgan "winced with horror," but his private secretary

noted serenely, "The padre sahib is a very nice man indeed, he has no interest whatever in religion and that is suitable for a clergyman."

After such familiarity with Masood and his Muslim friends, Hindu India
was more impenetrable to both Goldie and Morgan. At the "paradise" of
Chhatarpur, Morgan met the maharajah, who had been tutored for a time by
Sir Theodore Morison; at Dewas Senior, "the oddest corner of the world outside of Alice in Wonderland," he met the man he would familiarly call "Bapu,"
the Maharajah of Dewas. Malcolm Darling had served as a kind of regent
to the young rajah before he assumed power, and Morgan and he were invited to attend a grand wedding in honor of a local British dignitary. Morgan
was dressed for the occasion, in jodhpurs of white muslin and "a waistcoat
the colours of a Neapolitan ice—red, white and green, and this was almost
concealed by my chief garment—a magnificent coat of claret coloured silk,
trimmed with gold . . . [which] came to below my knees . . . Cocked rakishly
over one ear was a Maratha Turban of scarlet and gold . . ."

After the wedding came a feast. Morgan detailed the items on the *thali*:
"brown tennis-ball, not bad . . . three dreadful little dishes that tasted of
nothing till they were well in your mouth, when your whole tongue suddenly
burst into flame. I got to hate this side of the tray . . . Long thin cake, like a
brandy snap but salt." And a mound of seed "As for canaries . . ."

At Chhatarpur, Goldie noted, the maharajah "turned out" to be homosexual, though he had melded his sexual inclination to a kind of perverse
religiosity, in which the boys who were the object of his yearning became
figured as the god Krishna, the god who like the Messiah was always promising to come but never came—Krishna as a kind of "ideal friend." For
Dickinson, who himself practiced a kind of chaste version of Hellenic boy
worship, this was a familiar and melancholy theme.

Masood's young friends who had studied law at Cambridge chafed at the
indignities of their daily lives under the Raj, and were unabashed at explaining this to Morgan. In Allahabad, he recorded the conversations between the junior magistrate Abu Saeed Mirza and his friends at a Mogul
dinner they served. They had to be ever so careful with European women,
they complained—"not even a little flirt." Whipped into honest anger, Mirza
told him, "It may be fifty or one hundred years but we shall throw you out."
Morgan transposed this comment to the mouth of Dr. Aziz, though even when
he finished *A Passage to India* in 1924 he could have no idea how prescient
it would prove to be.

The weeks spent with Masood did not resolve the question of their friendship. Almost from the beginning of the visit Morgan was lamenting "he who might be slipping away," and in mid-January, spending two weeks with Masood at his work in Bankipore, Morgan learned that Masood planned to marry the following year. The two men had some sort of long conversation and reckoning, which survives only in the poignant entry in Morgan's journal for January 13: "Long and sad day . . . Aie-aie-aie-growing after tears. Mosquito net, fizzling lamp, high step between rooms. Then return and comfort a little." The next day Morgan rose early to visit the Barabar Caves. Masood did not see him off on the journey.

Perhaps because of this farewell, India always conveyed a sweet sense of *wanting* in Morgan—both a sense of desire and a sense of loss. He recognized that the narrative of perpetual longing was embroidered into a larger tapestry of Orientalism, that India would always reflect British desires for the exotic, would always tantalize and disappoint. The essays he wrote in the immediate aftermath of his voyage are full of little deconstructions of his own attitudes, making the man who yearns too much into a figure both poignant and comical. Whenever Morgan looked for magic in India his expectations were deflated, but often in the places he was not looking for it, it found him. Morgan came away from his first visit to India certain that there was no certainty. But he was brimming with images and scenes: the nationalist Muslim wedding where the gramophone played "I'd Rather Be Busy with My Little Lizzie," competing aurally with the orthodox call to prayer; a long conversation on the road with a completely un-self-conscious naked boy; the inadvertently comic carved inscription "God si love" on a marble wall; in the courts at Aurangabad a punkah wallah pulling the blades of a huge leaf fan back and forth "with the impassivity of Atropos"; hundreds of naked men waiting to bathe in the Ganges; the blank sheen of the walls in the Barabar Caves. Each of these visions would burn its way into his great novel of India, but not for a long time to come. As Morgan traveled the subcontinent, he felt sterile, and convinced that these impressions would be of no use to him. He told his new friend, the Belfast writer Forrest Reid, "I am dried up. Not in my emotions but in their expression . . . To have done good work is something."

As he left Bombay for Marseille on April 1, Morgan already conceived that his incomplete understanding of India was a crystalline example of the human muddles that obscure and distort love. He wrote a final letter to Masood from aboard ship. "It's an awful pity when people who love each other and might live together don't. I'm coming to live with you in our old age, but till then you must make some other arrangement."

Morgan came home from India bearing gifts—yards and yards of brightly colored silk that he arranged atmospherically: the dining room table "with silks strewn and incense burning," so beautiful that Lily gave a "gasp of joy." She called Ruth and Agnes in to witness the unpacking. It was a "radiant moment."

Lily was fifty-eight, stout, and plagued by gout and rheumatism; in September 1912 she decided on a month's water cure at Harrogate, in the north of England, to soak her bones in the glorious Orientalist fantasy of the recently renovated Turkish baths. Morgan spent some of the time in Belfast, visiting HOM and Forrest Reid, for whom he had written a letter of praise for his novel *The Bracknells* earlier in the year. Reid was a few years older than Morgan, buttoned-up and terribly middle-class. He had paid his own way through Cambridge after inheriting some money, and lived a very quiet bachelor life, penning delicate novels celebrating schoolboy virtues. Morgan appreciated being Reid's mentor, and their epistolary friendship had meant much to him during his time in India. In mid-September, Morgan joined Lily in Harrogate, and with her safely placed at the spa, he made a secret pilgrimage about an hour's travel south, to visit Edward Carpenter.

By the time he died in 1929, Carpenter was considered a Victorian relic, but as Dent defended him then, this was true only because "modern life had absorbed so much of his message that one can hardly understand that it was ever necessary for him to utter it." Carpenter was approaching seventy when Morgan made a visit, the most recent in a long line of admirers and supplicants who made their way to the cottage and garden and writing shed that comprised the old man's "Thoreau ideal" in the tiny hamlet of Millthorpe, south of Sheffield. A romantic and a socialist, a Victorian guru of radical causes, Carpenter had cast aside a life of comfort and privilege (and the Anglican priesthood) to live among working-class people in the slums of Sheffield and agitate for class equality, women's rights, and social acceptance of homosexuality. Tall and skinny, with a great shock of white hair and a beard like an Old Testament prophet, he lived with his much younger working-class lover, George Merrill, in a cottage on seven acres of land. Carpenter had rescued Merrill from destitute poverty in Sheffield. Now Merrill cooked and cleaned and gardened—at first growing produce to sell in local markets, and eventually for subsistence only. He worked wearing sandals—sometimes *only* sandals—among the vegetables. Carpenter had traveled to America to meet Whitman, who inspired him and slept with him. The two men shared a belief in the principles they labeled *democracy*.

What Carpenter believed and how he lived were indistinguishable. Because he despised economic inequality, he gave up his privilege; because he abhorred how modern life atomized people, separated them from one another and their physical nature, he lived simply and off the grid. He did not distinguish between the forces that oppressed women's lives and the ignominy heaped on homosexuals. He composed extravagant Whitmanesque poetry promoting "homogenic love," free sex, and women's liberation, and lived openly as Merrill's comrade for almost forty years. The simple example of his life proved inspiring for generations. Goldie and Roger Fry, when they were undergraduate lovers, had stayed at the cottage with Carpenter a generation before; G. B. Shaw and William Morris revered him the generation before that.

Carpenter himself was grateful to have found his calling and lived his ideals; Merrill felt that he had been rescued by his life with Carpenter. The younger man defended their isolated idyll—he once chased away a pair of roving missionaries, shouting, "We're *all* in heaven *here*." For his part, Carpenter described in his autobiography how he had given his dress clothes away, and eschewing respectability, found that he could change the world and earn real happiness by settling down with his lover as "two bachelors." Morgan described how Carpenter, by "escap[ing] from culture by the skin of his teeth," became "not only charming and lovable, but great." Carpenter's "candor about sex, particularly about homosexuality" was what drew Morgan to visit him, and the occasion would utterly change Morgan's life.

In the kitchen of the little farmhouse Carpenter sent off a spark of ideas. But it was the dark, handsome Merrill, then in his forties, who (unbeknown to the old man) made a play for Morgan, touching "a creative spring," which was located—it turned out—"just above the buttocks." Morgan had never been touched there like that before, and could still recall its thrill almost fifty years later: "It was as much psychological as physical. It seemed to go straight through the small of my back into my ideas, without involving my thoughts."

What Forster "conceived" in that furtive touch was his fifth, and only truly honest, novel—*Maurice*. He imagined a happy gay love story between two "ordinary affectionate men"—Maurice Hall, a suburban stockbroker, and his lover Alec Scudder, a restive working-class man who takes on the job of gamekeeper to a threadbare gentryman's estate. Together, Maurice and Alec end up much as Carpenter and Merrill did, in isolation but defying society in two significant ways: by being unregenerately and openly homosexual, and by loving as equal partners despite their class differences. (The gamekeeper-as-salt-of-the-earth lover may have become a stereotype since the publication of *Lady Chatterley's Lover*, but it is well to remember that Morgan's story was written almost twenty years before D. H. Lawrence's.) Returning to Harrogate after a few short days, Morgan began to write as if he were on fire.

"A happy ending was imperative" to the plot of the new novel. Morgan had seen miseries enough in life—Merz's suicide, Goldie's unrequited loves, rumors and stories of blackmail, doctor's "cures" and prison with hard labor, self-abnegation and miserable "loneliness." A story in the newspaper might end "unhappily, with a lad dangling from a noose," or with the poor man facing the "penalty society exacts." What was art for, if not to show a new way forward? "I was determined that in fiction anyway two men should fall in love and remain in it for the ever and ever that fiction allows." Only in the isolated example of George Merrill and Edward Carpenter had Morgan seen even an inkling of the domestic life for gay men that he had glimpsed in Whitman's poems, that he believed in and desired.

In shaping the plot, he tried to remain faithful to the spirit of his deepest wishes, but in the character of Maurice himself "I tried to create a character who was completely unlike myself or what I supposed myself to be, someone handsome, healthy, bodily attractive, mentally torpid, not a bad business man and rather a snob." He wanted to make clear that the novel was wish fulfillment rather than autobiography—to make the point not only about his inner life, but also that the actual world, the place where a man like Henry Wilcox might feel most at home, was a little different than custom would have us believe.

The third figure in the tense triangle of *Maurice* is Clive Durham, who meets Maurice in his rooms at Cambridge. Clive is ahead of Maurice, and introduces him to the "hellenic temperament," drawing into an embrace Maurice's at-first-unwilling arms. As Clive "deteriorates" into hypocrisy, denial, and marriage, he comes more and more to resemble the HOM of recent days, who had become a "ghastly old boy" in Belfast, lecturing on economics, obtuse, morose, and self-involved when Morgan came to visit. Years later Morgan felt he might have been "unfair on Clive" in this portrayal, but the revisions to his character betray Morgan's unmistakable disappointment— not only for the death of the friendship that had meant the most to him when he was young, but of the painful discovery that HOM had lost his sensitivity and compassion.

He showed the manuscript to no one for several months. Then, gingerly, he began to share the work-in-progress with his most intimate friends, almost as a currency of trust, aware that they could hurt or expose him. He discovered much about the state of his novel from these first forays into sharing his secret—and much about the state of his friendships as well. He had made the mistake of showing Meredith a very early draft, and was dismayed to discover that "it bored him dumb—I shan't show him the rest." He concluded, "Hugh can't again be in my life as he has been . . . I was very badly hit by his indifference to *Maurice* and the pain has opened my eyes little by little to his general indifference."

This fact Morgan could confide only to Florence Barger, who was untainted by association from King's College days. At first he approached her tentatively:

> I have talked to you so much, that I have decided to add another piece of news—i.e. That I <u>have</u> almost completed a long novel, but it is unpublishable until my death and England's. As it is improbable I shall ever show it you, I had not meant to say: but I know that you will be cheered by this proof of fertility, and I hope when it is off my mind I may be free for more practical themes. I have been pretty busy over it for the last 9 months. I think I would rather you didn't tell George this.

To a heterosexual woman like Florence, he feared that *Maurice* might be "a new and painful world, into which you will hardly have occasion to glance again! A tiny world that is generally unknown to all who are not born in it. My only fear is that it may make me seem remote to you—not for one instant repellent, but remote." But Florence praised the book. "I am so happy that you think the thing's literature," he wrote her. "It was meant to be, but that naughty Hugh disconcerted me; so much that I nearly chucked it."

Carpenter predictably "took to" the figure of the gamekeeper, but Morgan was surprised to find that he was "blind to" the sexual troubles of the women in the novel—here, at least, he was ahead of the prophet. Roger Fry told Morgan that the novel was "beautiful . . . the best work I have ever done," which pleased him immensely; and Sydney Waterlow gave a heterosexual stamp of approval to the love affair, though he felt the novel was most effective as "a sociological tract."

Morgan entrusted his most heartfelt discussion of *Maurice* to three friends with expertise in its "tiny world"—Goldsworthy Lowes Dickinson, Lytton Strachey, and Forrest Reid; but in different ways all three men disappointed him. His defense of the novel allowed him to articulate the clearest vision of what being homosexual meant to him.

He made the mistake of showing Goldie some short stories on homosexual themes. His mentor's shocked reaction momentarily shattered Morgan's confidence. He burned the stories, and the sting of Goldie's disapproval spilled over to dampen the writing of *Maurice*. "My smooth spurt is over," he wrote in his diary, "ended by Dickinson's disgust." Just as when *A Room with a View* had stalled, Morgan was left with "3 unfinished novels on my hands"— the first few chapters of an Indian novel, the fragment of *Arctic Summer*, and the very beginning of *Maurice*. By the end of the year, he bucked up, determined to look "Forward rather than back." He set his sights on a different muse: "Edward Carpenter! Edward Carpenter! Edward Carpenter!"

Morgan shared a later draft with Goldie, after rewriting a section of the novel. Goldie had objected to "the Scudder part"—presumably a portrayal of rather inexact lovemaking between Maurice and Alec—though he admitted he had little "personal contact" with such people and so might be a poor judge of its veracity. He told Morgan that the novel "breaks my heart almost . . . When Maurice goes back after [Clive's] marriage—it's unbearably right." Goldie had quite a lot of experience with this sort of heartbreak; for the better part of a year he had been telling Morgan about the peregrinations of his lover, Oscar Eckhardt, who had left Goldie for a woman. For his part, Morgan was happy to have used the book for a concrete purpose. He and Goldie, he wrote in his diary, "are on a basis of comrade's life at last. *Maurice* has done it."

Forrest Reid's response was even more pointed than Goldie's had been. Reid was in love with young boys, but self-hating and consumed with a sense of sin. He professed to be surprised that Morgan was homosexual, surprised as well to be discerned as one himself. He had distilled his homosexuality in both life and art into a "sublimated . . . sublime," a kind of Peter Pan worship of schoolboys' innocence, schoolboys' perfections, schoolboys' disembodied and unerring perfection. All his life he lived with one young boy or other, delighting in making up elaborate stories for them until they left him and grew up. The *idea* of lovemaking between men was sinful, he believed, and *Maurice*, even with its gauzy description of Maurice and Alec "sharing" their bodies, seemed repellent and perverted to him. He asked Morgan to burn the letter that told him this. Morgan's letter in return began quite delicately:

Dear Reid.

. . . My perspicacity is equally at fault, for I quite thought you realised my interest in these subjects—something you said my last visit to you quite convinced me. I also thought, and still think, that if expressed in detail much of this interest must give you pain, but of late I am crediting others with the strength to bear the pain, and that is why I sent you the book. Earlier I couldn't have—should have feared to lose your friendship. I don't fear now.

But he had come too far in his own inner life to accept the premises that underpinned Reid's critique. Whitman had inspired him. He was prepared to argue not only for the legitimacy of homosexual love but also for its necessary bodily expression. He rejected the stink of Christianity in Reid's response.

I do want to raise the subject out of the mists of theology: Male and female created He not them. Ruling out undeveloped people like Clive (who "grow out of homosexual feelings")—one is left with "perverts" (an absurd word, because it assumes they were given a choice, but let's use it). Are these "perverts" good or bad like normal men, their disproportionate tendency to badness (which I admit) being due to the criminal blindness of society? Or are they inherently bad? You

answer, as I do, that they are the former, but you answer with reluctance. I want you to answer <u>vehemently</u>! The man in my book is,
roughly speaking, good, but society nearly destroys him. He nearly
slinks through his life furtive and afraid, and burdened with a sense
of sin. You say "If he had not met another man like him, what then?"
What then indeed? But blame Society, not Maurice, and be thankful
even in a novel when a man is left to lead the best life he is capable
of leading!

Morgan argued that it is "right . . . that such a relation should include the
physical . . . if both people want it and both are old enough to know what
they want." Morgan told Reid that he measured the "success" of his writing on the subject by whether a "normal" reader might see the *human* in
the expression of gay desire—to forget "the form of the passion and only
remember . . . it was passion." (He was bucked up by Waterlow having seen
the novel in this way.) It was natural for each person to be prejudiced about
"the particular local forms that desire takes"—after all, "we all find it difficult to tolerate a form that isn't our own."

It was the "social fabric" and not nature itself that made homosexuals
what they were, Morgan argued to Reid. "My defence at any last Judgement
would be 'I was trying to connect up and use all the fragments I was born
with.'"

To give these people a chance—to see whether Paradises are really
nearer any Hell than penal Servitude, whether their convictions of
Sin are really more than the burrs in the social fabric that the heart
and brain, working together, can pluck out—that's why I wrote *Maurice* and let him meet Alec—not saints or aesthetes either of them but
just ordinary affectionate men.

It was a powerful statement of belief, especially since it was wholly a product
of Morgan's idealistic imagination. He had created two lovers who escaped
into a utopian world without ever having had the courage to touch any man
himself.

This was precisely the point, from Lytton Strachey's perspective. He acidly told Morgan that his tender vision of gay domesticity was impossible. At
the end of the version Strachey had read, Maurice and Alec went off together

to the north of England to pursue a life apart as woodsmen and comrades. Don't be so romantic, Strachey argued. Men like this don't find each other. Even if they do, they do not *stay* together: "I should have prophesied a rupture after 6 months—chiefly as a result of . . . class differences— . . . [E]ven such a simple-minded fellow as Maurice would have felt this—and so your Sherwood Forest ending appears to me slightly mythical."

Strachey's second criticism was that he didn't "understand why the copulation question should be given such importance." Not understanding how close to home these comments might be to Morgan, Strachey sharpened his argument: "I really think the whole conception of male copulation in the book rather diseased—in fact morbid and unnatural." He discerned a double standard in the book, contrasting the two years of "chastity between Maurice and Clive . . . which you consider (a) as a very good thing and (b) as nothing very remarkable" with Clive's decision to marry "and promptly, quite as a matter of course, to have his wife." With these provisos, Strachey informed Morgan that he enjoyed the novel very much.

In his reply, Morgan conceded Strachey's expertise in sexual matters, without quite acknowledging how deep his own ignorance of the practicalities was. He told Lytton that he agreed with the criticisms more than he "would have liked." At its heart, *Maurice* was designed to be a visionary statement, and Strachey's critique that it was too fantastic and utopian was beside the point. More than a year earlier, he had written Lytton, "No one ever breaks" conventions "in the right place." The exchange stripped away some of the shiny veneer of Strachey's condescension toward Morgan's commercial success, and made the men much closer friends.

It also pressed Morgan to articulate his aesthetic objectives in writing *Maurice*. Thanking Dent for his words of praise, "You can scarcely imagine the loneliness of such an effort as this—a year's work!" he outlined his accomplishment: "I do feel that I have created something absolutely new, even to the Greeks. Whitman anticipated me, but he didn't really know what he was after, or only half-knew—shirked, even to himself, the statement."

But his hope that writing an unpublishable novel might end his creative sterility was not borne out. By June 1914 the manuscript of *Maurice* was complete. But there was nothing to show Lily, who could not help noticing the long days and nights that Morgan was squirreled away in his attic writing. He shaped an explanation for her somewhere between a true confession and an outright lie—telling her, "My work is all wrong."

The "diminution" of his intimacy with Masood, which had been growing since he returned from India, "was to be expected" now that his friend had married, and Morgan did not worry over it much. About the rupture with HOM, he decided, "[I] do not think I am to blame." His old friendships took a backseat to two new relationships that burst into his life but foundered quickly on the thorough misapprehension of his character. First, a small embarrassment: Florence Barger's sister Elsie Thomas fell in love with him. But writing *Maurice* had fortified his resolve, and he let her down quickly and gently, without revealing anything but his respect for her. In late January 1915, Morgan met D. H. Lawrence and his new wife, Frieda, at a dinner party held by the Bloomsbury patroness Lady Ottoline Morrell. The son of a miner, Lawrence had crawled out of poverty and a miserably unhappy family life to become a school inspector. But the educational system was stultifying, and he broke free—by stealing the affection of his favorite professor's wife. Lawrence was almost thirty and had completed his autobiographical novel *Sons and Lovers*. He and Frieda lived by the kindness of friends who lent them a cottage in Sussex. The couple were about to begin their restless hegira to find a place in the world—Australia, France, a ranch in New Mexico— where they could feel at home and free.

Lawrence was categorical about *everything*. In *Howards End*'s unease with the class system, and the stories of Pan in *The Celestial Omnibus*, Lawrence thought he had found a kindred spirit in Morgan, but he accused him of not going far enough. Lawrence was "a sandy haired passionate Nibelung," Morgan told Forrest Reid, and "really extraordinarily nice." Frieda had warmed to *Howards End*, telling Morgan it "is a beautiful book, but you must go further." The couple invited Morgan to come to their cottage for what turned out to be an alarming weekend: Lawrence held forth, linking Morgan's temperament to a whole cosmology of what was wrong with modern man, keeping him up till all hours to accuse him—"you belied and betrayed yourself"—and urging him to fulfill "the natural animal in you." Forster returned to Weybridge, and Lawrence immediately sent a hectoring letter: "In [your] books . . . you are intentional and perverse & not vitally interesting. One must live through the source, through all the racings & heats of Pan, and on to my beloved angels & devils witn their aureoles & their feet upon the flowers of lights." And then he demanded that Morgan come again the next weekend, breezily signing off, "Auf Wiedersehn."

It emerged that Lawrence's diagnosis of Morgan's problem was that he must "satisfy" his "implicit manhood" but "He tries to dodge himself—the sight is painful." "Why can't he take a woman and fight clear to his own basic, primal being?" Lawrence lectured Bertrand Russell. Because, he confidently concluded without pausing for an answer, Morgan "sucks his dummy—you know, those child's comforters—long after his age." If Morgan would only act, he could become "pregnant with his own soul." Lawrence told a friend that he found Morgan "very nice." But he wondered "if the grip has gone out of him." For his own part, Morgan suspected a different problem in Lawrence's psyche: suppressed homosexual tendencies. The "Poem of Friendship" in Lawrence's *The White Peacock*, "which is beautiful," was also "the queerest product of subconsciousness that I have yet struck," Morgan told Dent knowingly. Lawrence "has not a glimmering from first to last of what he's up to."

The final straw came when Lawrence spoke derisively about Edward Carpenter in Morgan's presence. Here again Lawrence was quick to judge but off the mark. To Lawrence, the old man was a sexual pioneer in a fusty Victorian vein whereas he alone was clear-thinking and modern. It was another case of Lawrence blindly misreading stylistic clues. Carpenter wore a beard, true, and he had campaigned for sexual freedom since before Lawrence was born, but he had only recently founded the British Society for Sex Psychology. The society was cautious about its members getting ensnared in the recently enacted Defense of the Realm laws against sedition: one had to be sponsored by two members, and to pay dues. But its agenda was genuinely radical—promoting open discussion of sexual matters, women's right to sexual pleasure, access to birth control, and homosexual rights. At Carpenter's urging, Morgan had quietly joined the society. Months later, so did Lawrence. In his diary, Morgan realized that he couldn't forgive Lawrence's insulting Carpenter. "With regret" he let go of the irascible friendship.

Even when Morgan had been at Nassenheide, British anxiety about the Hun was palpable. In August 1914 war was declared against Germany. The shadow of war had lingered for so long that "up till the last moment it was impossible to believe that the thing was really going to happen." The fact of war frayed Morgan's friendships. Even Malcolm's wife, Josie Darling, who was dear to his heart, became irritable. Stop dreaming, she told him, enlist in the army, and "face facts." He gave her a sharp answer. "Don't say 'face facts' to me, Josie. Everybody keeps saying it just now, but the fact is, it's impossible to face facts. They're like the walls of a room . . . If you face one wall, you must have your back to the other three."

He decided he would not enlist, and instead took on a civilian "war assignment," cataloguing paintings at the National Gallery. *Maurice* was unpublishable, and there were no more novels in him, he felt sure. He confessed to Goldie, "What's to occupy me for the rest of my life, I can't conceive." It was impossible not to comprehend his predicament, and impossible to do anything about it. He told Florence, "I am leading the life of a little girl so long as I am tied to home."

6

"Parting with Respectability"

On the ship from Marseille to Alexandria, the men discussed conscription. It was mid-November 1915, and after fifteen months of total war the British Army was hopelessly depleted. A draft seemed inevitable. The small company of Red Cross volunteers bound for British-occupied northern Africa considered this looming fact. As noncombatants on the margins of the war, they found a bright side: the draft would pull Britain together as a nation, give men a renewed sense of purpose and pride. Both the working-class ambulance driver and the Tory doctor agreed. What a good idea it would be to have all "Englishmen" together in the fight!

In his diary Forster recorded the conversation as if his companions were minor characters in an unwritten expatriate novel. He sat quietly apart from the passengers sunning themselves on deck. Morgan was almost thirty-seven, but gave the impression of someone much younger—"a very pale, delicately-built young man, slightly towzled and very shy, with a habit of standing on one leg and winding the other round it." He had perfected the art of eavesdropping.

Setting out for Alexandria, it was hard to tell if he was running from or running toward something. In England, Morgan was suspended between two camps, alienated by both the ardent pacifism of Strachey, Dickinson, and his Bloomsbury friends, and the rabid—*female*, he felt—call to arms. War fever grew poisonously. And it was poisonously linked to sexual politics. Zealous self-described "brigades" of young women invented a novel kind of street theater, pressing white feathers into the lapels of men in civilian dress to shame them into enlisting. He had rebuffed an unsolicited letter from the mother of an old school friend, impugning his patriotism, and by extension, his masculinity. Her attitude was ubiquitous. The *Daily Mail* had just published Jessie Pope's poem "The Call," with its insistent goading against effeminacy:

> *Who's for the khaki suit—*
> *Are you, my laddie?*
> *Who longs to charge and shoot—*
> *Do you, my laddie?*
> *Who's keen on getting fit*
> *Who means to show his grit*
> *And who'd rather wait a bit—*
> *Would you, my laddie?*

Aboard ship, among strangers, Morgan mulled over the transformative power of an ill-fitting khaki suit. The Red Cross uniform was comically unimpressive: "khaki of sorts with some sort of rank sewn on to it, which later on came out in the wash." Despite this, despite the least military posture of any male creature alive, despite his distracted academic mien, Forster discovered that clothes made the man. He felt uneasy, in disguise. In his diary he noted wryly, "My uniform is well received. Some think me a soldier, some a chaplain."

He called the uniform his "costume." It suited him for an ambiguous role. His official title was Searcher in the Wounded and Missing Department of the Red Cross. He held no rank, but the position afforded the modest privileges of an officer: half-price travel on Alexandria's new electric trams, a rudimentary salute in greeting. Nevertheless, he was a civilian, and was expected to find his own lodging and pay his own way. As he traveled by rail across the Nile Delta, from Port Said to Zagazig to Tanta, he knew only the barest outline of his duties. He was to interview the wounded in military hospitals to determine the status of soldiers gone missing in the disastrous months of fighting in the Dardanelles. By early December, Forster began his work. He planned to stay three months. He stayed more than three years.

In donning the khaki, he had evaded Miss Pope's call, but nevertheless found himself subject to the dictates of women. In London, he had been vetted for the role of searcher by the formidable Near Eastern specialist Gertrude

Bell, who handed him on to Miss Victoria Grant Duff, the head of Alexandria's Red Cross Wounded Department. The daughter of a notable Victorian polymath—a Liberal MP and former governor of Madras State—Miss Grant Duff had an exacting education in the ways of empire and the slightly officious air of a young woman who, given her first proper posting, was determined to do it by the book. Morgan, prone to prickliness when it came to professional women, found her "shrewish." He did not know that her closest brother had been killed in France the year before.

And there was a third woman in the picture, as usual. The choice of Alexandria was a compromise between his aspirations for romantic escape and Lily's fears about losing him to the war. The first plan was to set out for his beloved Italy as an ambulance orderly. But "mother was too much against it" and Morgan abandoned the idea, mulling the balance of cowardice and filial devotion in the decision to succumb to her wishes. The ambulance proposal had a hint of grandeur. Reading about Walt Whitman's nursing work in the American civil war fired his imagination, and offered a masculine identity he could reckon with—at once tender and adventurous. To Masood, he confided his vision of himself in the ambulance unit in Italy. "All one can do in this world of maniacs is to pick up the poor tortured broken people and try to mend them." But in Alexandria, there would be no picking up of tortured broken people, in fact no touching them at all. He would be a pastoral bureaucrat.

The *idea* of Alexandria retained some literary romance. To the boy who read classics at Cambridge, Alexandria had resonance as a mythological first point in an ancient, noble gay past. In the fourth century B.C., had not Alexander the Great left his friend and lover Hephaestion's side to explore the improbable spine of rock between the Mediterranean Sea and Lake Mariut and give the place his own glorious name? His Ptolemaic successors had built the great lighthouse Pharos as a beacon at the entrance of the harbor. This was the city of Hellenic enlightenment and Hellenic sensuality. The city of Alexander, of Antony and Cleopatra, adrift from Roman law, the city where the greatest library in the world had been built. There was something tragic, something hopeless and beautiful about the possibility of Alexandria.

Alexander had died just eight years after the founding of his city. His body was brought back there to be buried. The great library founded to be a beacon of learning burned to the ground, all its treasures lost. To Dickinson, Forster confided the stirrings of "a vague scheme for a book or a play about

Alexander." But the reasons he could not follow through were familiar and banal. The weary roundelay of self-censorship: "Here we are again. Unpublishable."

The real Alexandria, as the "real India" would be for Adela Quested in *A Passage to India*, was a profound disappointment. Not a trace of the ancient grandeur remained. All the "things to see" were just miles to the east, in Cairo or the Nile Delta. The city's treasures seemed to have been recently sold to the highest foreign bidder by some occupying force or other; the great twin obelisks called Cleopatra's Needles, commissioned by Cleopatra in honor of Mark Antony, now stood three thousand miles apart, domesticated trophies in New York's Central Park and on the Thames Embankment, to be wondered at by people eating ice cream. Everywhere he looked, Morgan was almost comically deflated by the erasure of former glories. The archaeological museum paled in comparison with the British Museum. Describing its treasures in a guidebook of Alexandria he composed in his later years there, he evokes a deadpan, weary tone: "This room contains nothing of beauty . . . These monuments . . . may have been imported . . . at some unknown date . . . Then come to some painted tombstones protected by glass; they are inferior to some in the rooms farther on . . . Dull colossal statue of Marcus Aurelius . . ." Even Forster's eye for phallic monuments was dimmed. The glamorously named Pompey's pillar wasn't very tall, and turned out to be someone else's pillar anyway. He commented drily that the "specimen is not even well proportioned."

His first impressions of the city were so quotidian they couldn't even evoke strong feelings. No doubt to reassure Lily, Morgan wrote, "One can't dislike Alex . . . because it is impossible to dislike either sea or stones. But it consists of nothing else as far as I can gather; just a clean cosmopolitan town beside some blue water." From his "comfortable" room in the modern Majestic Hotel, tidy French gardens to the north gave way to symmetrical palms planted along a waterfront promenade. The great lighthouse was now no more than a stub of stone on a fitful spit of breakwater.

The real Alexandria was an *administered* city. Its strategic position on the bottom lip of the Mediterranean Sea—just west of the Suez Canal—had made it irresistible territory for the larger struggles of European power since Napoleonic times. A French colony in the late eighteenth century, for the better part of a century it had been ruled first by the Turks, who appointed a

Khedive, and then, when they were foreclosed in bankruptcy, by a British vice-consul. In the modern city the harbor was shaped like two parentheses back-to-back. The western harbor, its mouth open to the sea, was busy and industrial. The eastern, once Alexander's ancient site, had settled into a decorative beachfront called the New Quay. Morgan politely called Alexandria "cosmopolitan." In fact it was commercial. Refugees from the wreckage of the Ottoman Empire, and sharp-eyed merchants of many nations, found its geography and its laissez-faire attitude congenial. Alexandria harbored more expatriates than Cairo, a city of ten times its size. Italians, leftover French, stateless Armenians, Jews, Maltese, Palestinian traders from the Levant, and especially Greeks had been deposited as if by sequential tides. It was possible to find or buy almost anything English: the Baedeker enumerated English clubs, English beer, confectionaries, preserved meats, Anglican churches, English theaters, ready-made clothing, baths, banks, doctors, pharmacists, booksellers, woolen goods, cigars . . .

The latest iteration of flotsam was a garrison of twenty-five thousand British troops, stationed in the mercantile hubbub. The city proved to be an ideal location for managing supplies and censoring mail. Just a year before Forster arrived martial law was imposed on the population of almost half a million people. In 1915 and 1916, the great fight over the Dardanelles was coordinated from Alexandria. The wounded of the ill-fated Turkish campaign were shipped here, to the margin of safety, to heal or to die.

Forster was unaware that he entered an especially uneasy sexual climate. One constant anxiety for both British military and civil administrators was the difficulty of containing Alexandria's inclination toward commercial vice. Sexual hygiene was the key to social hygiene in their view. The "civilizing process" linked morale to morals. But the administration of decent rules of order was complicated by the dual legal structure left over from the French occupation. One could *manage* the soldiers and the British population according to British custom. But "bachelor" army troops were naturally susceptible to all sorts of risks. The army and the Sanitary Commission began the laborious work of counting, sifting, and regulating: studying venereal disease, registering brothels, compelling medical examinations, regulating interracial marriage, "rescuing girls from vice," actively deporting "undesirable Europeans" and known homosexuals. The distasteful but practical belief prevailed that female prostitution was a necessary evil. Without it,

British soldiers would inevitably succumb to the worse, and ever prevalent, "depraved methods of sexual gratification"—the vice of "traffic in boys."

Policing purity was endless, maddening work. The vast majority of the occupants of Alexandria were beyond their reach, subject by default to the Egyptian Native Penal Code. Under these laws, inherited from the Napoleonic Code, neither consensual homosexual acts nor male prostitution was illegal. To one administrator charged with developing new "offenses against morality" for a draft penal code, the native population's blind eye to homosexual practices was particularly galling. It was "unthinkable," he wrote, that young people, "the most precious asset of a State," should be "exposed to the moral and physical corruption in the toleration of unnatural offenses." Martial law allowed the British authorities to begin making the crooked straight and the rough places plain.

The first friend Forster looked up when he arrived in Alexandria, his fellow Kingsman Robert Furness (called Robin), was part of this administrative apparatus. Furness had been a minor magistrate before the war. His own account, in a letter to Maynard Keynes, betrayed a more bemused than exasperated tone: "I have long been a policeman . . . in this disorderly town: daily I feed my disgusted eyes on drunken Welsh governesses and stabbed Circassian whores; I peer into the anus of catamites; I hold inquests upon beggars who die and are eaten by worms." For Furness, the city indefatigably—even cheerfully—resisted the rule of law, and he went about adjudicating petty infractions of the most sordid sort. He was well aware of the registered brothels and the census of boy prostitutes.

Like many British gentlemen, Furness had little trouble maintaining wholly disparate public and private roles. He had a taste for smut and a ribald joke. He detected a hint of seductive play in ordinary sights, such as a young Egyptian man touching one button after another on a soldier's tunic as a gesture of farewell. Most of all, he adored the Hellenistic Alexandrian poet Callimachus, whom both he and Morgan had studied briefly at Cambridge. He began his own translations of this underappreciated poet, whose work had been dismissed as decadent by the dons. Furness was drawn to Callimachus' poetic form, the elegiac epigram, with its "frugal, pungent" style. The little vignettes gave the taste of immediacy. Though dating from the second century B.C., they had a freshness of form; the delicate, almost off-hand observations, their "intimate and whimsical realism," made them feel very modern. And they were often frankly sexy, unapologetic about their homosexual lust. They demanded a translator sensitive to nuance. When war came, Furness joined the civil service. By day he applied his editorial skills in a new vein. He managed the Press Censorship department.

Back in London, Miss Bell suggested firmly to Morgan that the best way to hold to the straight and narrow was to keep to the bright expanse of the central town. When he asked her "what the inhabitants of Alexandria would be like . . . [s]he replied I would have no opportunity to find out. I should only see them in the streets as I went to and fro on my work." The dangerous parts of the town were the Byzantine ones—in both senses of the word. Just look straight and avoid the meandering and crooked byways, she advised. Rectilinearity begets rectitude. Thus "disguised" in khaki, Forster wrote years later in bemusement. "I went to the Red Cross office and the hospitals and back to the hotel and for a time looked neither to the right hand nor to the left in the streets, as Miss Bell had enjoined."

The British world was oriented toward Place Mohammed Ali, named after the "ambitious and westernising Ottoman adventurer from northern Greece who made himself master of the country after Nelson forced Napoleon's withdrawal." His large equestrian statue cast in Paris by Jacquemart dominated the public space that the English resolutely called "The Square." From the square the streets reached out, broad and open, wide vistas framed by palms. It was perfectly possible to join a British club and spend all one's time smoking cigars and gambling and following "a good deal of horse racing."

Indeed, the view from his room was of a clean, modern city. His newly built lodgings in the Hotel Majestic were steps from the square to the east and formal gardens to the north. That much of this celebrated modernity arose from wholesale rebuilding after British gunships leveled the square to quell Egyptian attempts to resist enforced occupation in 1882 was lost on the writers of Baedeker's 1914 guidebook. Just next to the Anglican church at the northeast corner of the square lay the eponymous St. Mark's Buildings ("belonging to the British Community"), which housed the Red Cross offices where Forster worked each day. These the Baedeker described unreflexively as "the only buildings" on the square "which escaped the fury of the natives in 1882."

During his first winter in Alexandria, Forster's daily life was contained almost entirely within the orbit of the Baedeker's recommendations for a day-and-a-half stay. From the hotel to the Red Cross office was less than ten

minutes' walk on the perimeter of the square; from the office to the Mohammed Ali Club ("handsomely fitted up; patronized by Europeans of all nations; introduction by a member necessary") was an equal distance to the
east. From the club Forster took the recently electrified city tram several
miles to the east to the Red Cross hospital to interview the men. The name
of the branch line was Ramleh, Arabic for "sand."

The irony of trading a suburban existence in Weybridge for a bureaucratic existence on the Mediterranean was keen. To Masood he described his
daily routine: "I . . . start out about 10.0, returning for lunch and finishing
about 7.0." Foursquare. Twice daily, he commuted between grandiose modern monuments to colonial dreams of the Orient. At the western end was the
four-story white stone Majestic, all mod cons, with twin cupolas in an eastern style. At the eastern margin past suburbs along the undulating coast lay
the Khedival Palace—a vast Orientalist confection, built at the turn of the
century by the Turkish Khedive for his Austrian mistress: light stone, Moor-
ish arches, pergolas, tile roof. The palace site was beautiful, surrounded by
fragrant gardens atop a rocky cliff, with steps cut in the rock down to the
"intense and unbelievable blue" sea. By the time Forster arrived the palace
had been commandeered. The gardens were fenced off, the palace domesticated into rooms for convalescent soldiers.

For friendship, at first he relied on the familiar network of university
men, which never quite "coalesced into a set." He began closest to home,
with Kingsmen and Furness's colleagues at the censorship office. Besides
Robin Furness, a tall, "cerebral and ruffled heron" of a man, there were a
"Syrian" and a "Greek," George Antonius and Pericles Anastassiades. Antonius, only twenty-five, was cosmopolitan and sympathetic. Born in Alexandria to Palestinian parents, he had made his way from an English-speaking
public school in Ramleh to King's. Now he returned the favor, taking a sympathetic Englishman into his world. In his company, Morgan began fitfully to
explore the city, "discarding my uniform . . . [to] plunge . . . into the Bazaar."
Antonius exemplified what Forster came to describe as the "typical Alexandrian" identity, which "symbolizes for me a mixture, a bastardy, an idea
which I find congenial and opposed to that sterile idea of 100% in something
or other which has impressed the modern world and forms the backbone of
its blustering nationalisms." Here was a young man whose very being connected East and West.

Anastassiades, a cotton broker, also reached out to Morgan. Ambitious and striving, and eager to appear polished, he paid Morgan four pounds a month for English lessons. Through Furness, Forster met an extraordinary woman, Aida Borchgrevink.

Aida was a force of nature. She was born in America, the daughter of a Midwestern corn king. Trained as an opera singer before her marriage, she had been literally translated by Verdi—hearing the opera on her honeymoon, she added a fateful *i* to her pedestrian given name, Ada. She had married a Norwegian judge presiding at the Mixed Courts, the special courts for civil cases between Egyptians and foreigners. Now in her mid-fifties, after a decade of widowhood, she lived an extravagantly romantic and eccentric life with her daughter in a fashionable suburb of the city. She burst into arias from Wagner's Ring whenever she was behind the wheel of a car. Partly under her benign but spirited influence, Furness and his friends sponsored a membership for Morgan in the men-only club, the Mohammed Ali. Here he uneasily donned the white linen uniform of an expatriate gentleman. By spring, he had decamped to live with Furness in a villa east of the city center, with wide views of the sea. By all appearances, he was getting settled nicely—saving a bit of money, making a bit of money, finding congenial acquaintances.

But to Masood, he opened his weary heart. "All that I cared for in civilisation has gone forever, and I am trying to live without either hopes or fears." It was not only that the war had shattered a sense of progress and possibility; it was also the concomitant sense that his sojourn in Alexandria seemed so unreal. In the spring, he wrote Virginia Woolf,

> I imagine it is here that civilisation will expire. It is already dead in Cairo, which has war correspondents and 119 Generals and clubs of perturbed and earnest men. But in Alexandria it still seems possible to read books and bathe. It's true I talk about the war all day, but to people who can say "we fought every inch as dirty as the Turks," and whose deepest wish is peace at once.

The cruel parody of this new suburban life began to disgust Morgan. Alexandria roused a disturbing herd instinct in him. Watching the Arabs on the street each day infuriated him. He wrote Malcolm Darling in India:

I came inclined to be pleased and quite free from racial prejudice, but in 10 months I've acquired an instinctive dislike to the Arab voice, the Arab figure, the Arab way of looking or walking or pumpshitting or eating or laughing or anythinging—exactly the emotion that I censured in the Anglo-Indian towards the native . . . It's damnable and disgraceful, and it's in me.

It was *in him*, all right. Far from instinctive, Morgan's reaction came from careful, painful observation of these Arab men. There it is: that odd self-made term *pumpshitting*, which signaled his most intimate erotic thoughts. Watching Arab men look at him, watching them piss on the street, watching them laugh and be separate from him inflamed his desire, and his self-loathing. The damnable disgrace was his timidity, which coiled back on itself into a kind of displaced hatred. He hated what he did not have the courage to touch.

But he was good at his work, which was listening. Day after day, notebook in hand, Morgan sat down gently on the beds of wounded men and asked them to tell him their most horrific memories. He was struck by their vulnerability. The men were underfed, short, fragile, and terribly young. And the stories they told, in little fragments of trauma, made their bodies seem ever more tender and absurd. Miss Grant Duff praised the clarity of his reports, which were forwarded to the men's families and to the great Red Cross apparatus in London. But privately, for himself, Morgan began to build a counternarrative to capture and to understand the voices of these men.

It was a recapitulation of his months at the Working Men's College, but this time Morgan was the pupil. He found the young working-class men "so pleasant and grateful, and some of them quite charming." Appreciative of his kindness and care, they told him flatly of the most appalling scenes. In wartime every human effort seemed to backfire in ludicrous ways. A small group of men picked away to build a trench only to be summarily drowned in it by a flash flood days later. The bones of fallen comrades reappeared ghoulishly in the mud. One young private "in the Herefords spoke of a dead Australian who was in the way when they were making a parapet, so they cut him at the neck and knees and fired through him."

Morgan was patient with the men. His stillness allowed them to open to the horror slowly. His notebook captures even the cadence of their words. The frozen stammer: "After giving careful evidence for 20 minutes, without reproof, [a private from Manchester confided] "I never like anyone to ask me about it—it leaves a bad taste in the mouth. I think of the days again, of the days again . . ."

The disorienting panic: "He says 'I'm vomiting tell the Captain I'm vomiting' There was no guts in the 6.6.—Then I see the Captain with 2 bullets in his Privates. Froth comes out of his mouth."

The poignant resignation: "'Goodbye Sergeant. I'll turn over and die quietly' Dead in 1/4 hour."

In the face of these surreal stories, Morgan found solace in practical ministrations for the men. Sometimes he did small errands, lending them books, writing dictated letters, taking their watches to be mended. He played chess in silence. Sometimes he simply kept them company. One young man, Frank Vicary, sat up in bed and to Morgan's amazement, said, "'I'm awfully interested in ideas—I'm more interested in ideas than anything'—and blimey so he was." Morgan gave Vicary books by Goldie Dickinson, and their friendship warmed platonically until Vicary was sent back to England with a bad heart and jangled nerves.

In his own routine tenderness, Morgan detected a parallel feeling to the love of the men for one another in the muddy trenches. Like them, he found his intimacy disguised by the shape of his duties. Gradually, without sentimentalism, he came to feel that the greatest story of the war was to be found in compassion. And he heard beneath their words a truer story of gay love and friendship. The small notebook collated fragments, but to him the fragments glowed with meaning. Here was the deeper record of the meaning of the war: individual and human, not political. From the verbatim snippets of men in their most extreme trials he gleaned a hidden story that could not be erased. He named this section of the notebook "Friendship." Under this title, he collected little tessellated fragments to recover its power.

The story of friendship was often told as a story of loss. Chasing down the stories was dispiriting work: "If one does get news about the missing it is generally bad news." But it had unexpected compensations for him. In searching for the *missing man* he found the suppressed story of gay love. One boy told him shyly, "All the boys what I mated with is dead." Morgan was touched by the working-class locution, "mates," with its ambiguous elision of comradeship and sexual intimacy. So much had been erased and eradicated, and yet the love of one man for another endured. In another case, the only proof of existence of a missing soldier named Dodds emerged elliptically, even unconsciously, as a tale of lost love. An infantryman told Morgan of a pal who had died near him in the trenches: "I got to know the name [Dodds] through hearing a man call it out so much in his sleep. I slept near him. It used to be Dodds this and Dodds that. They must have been bosom chaps something special."

The (still unpublished) "Incidents of War" notebook unconsciously transformed Morgan's workaday task of writing reports into a new kind of historical record. Everywhere, he could discern the code that seemed to be illegible on the surface of things. He identified with the human instincts he saw, the timid, the antiheroic, the ordinary kindness in these slight men. In the single, wounded voices, he heard the chord of friendship. His notebook was the beginning of a new enterprise as a writer, to gather an anthology of men's experience. It was a compensatory narrative, honest and fragmented, the narrative of men who fought as dirty as their enemies and craved only peace. Ideas about patriotism were supplanted by epigrammatic observations, "little nameless unremembered acts of kindness and of love." The alchemy of patience and silence distilled his skill at eavesdropping into a new, nonfictional form. By honoring how hard it was for the men to relive these horrors, by recognizing the intimacy of both telling and witnessing, Forster became a gay historian.

Morgan's sense that he was witnessing the last moments of an old order turned out to be prescient. The conscription that the Red Cross volunteers had predicted in the autumn became a reality by the spring of 1916. Casualties, especially in Flanders, necessitated a precipitous loosening of physical standards for the young volunteers: from a minimum height requirement of five feet eight inches in the first months of the war, to five feet five inches in October 1915, to five feet three just a month later. Now the net of compulsory conscription reached wider than even the Red Cross workers had imagined. All unmarried men between the ages of eighteen and forty-one were required to present themselves for service. Forster was furious, and terrified. Though almost forty, he was clearly included in the order; the new conscription laws rescinded an earlier agreement whereby Red Cross personnel were excused from direct military service.

The means by which the conscription scheme worked were particularly loathsome to him. For a few months, until the end of June 1916, the army offered a fig leaf: rather than submitting directly to the draft, men could "attest," or certify to military tribunals their willingness to serve, subject to medical approval. Entering the military machine in this way offered a slender hope of evading active service, but it required at least lip service to the legitimacy of the government's claim. Forster found the whole exercise to be in bad faith—cruel, coercive, and servile. He felt the Red Cross was complicit too; by releasing its able-bodied volunteers for military service, the organization finessed its earlier agreements with them and capitulated to the war machine. As a matter of principle, he would not simplify his position. He refused to argue, as Strachey and Duncan Grant had done, that he was a conscientious objector. The crisis of conscience briefly shattered him psychologically: he found himself staggering and bumping into furniture, mysteriously falling to the floor. Only his friends kept him from feeling "crushed" by the experience.

A brief but pointed exchange with the Red Cross commissioner yielded no results, and he began to summon every means to excuse himself from the military maw. He wrote Lily: "I am quite shameless over the wirepulling. If I can't keep out of the army by fair means then hey for foul! . . . I haven't the least desire to pacify the parrots who cry 'All must go.' One will lose a certain amount of friends of course, mainly female . . ." One of the parrots surprised him a bit. Miss Grant Duff supported Morgan's position vociferously, arguing for his continued service as a Red Cross volunteer on the grounds of his exceptional efficiency. To Morgan, this "obscured the issue" by substituting "the question of utility" for the question of conscience, but her advocacy sharpened his sense of alienation from organized structures of power. He told Florence Barger that in her defense of him Miss Grant Duff "is a splendid creature, but she holds the Gospel of work which I don't and oughtn't to. I am an artist—after a week of stress like this one has the right to utter that discredited word—and the artist must (yes! I am actually going to say this too!) live his life, and it was my life not to attest." The "wretched business" was ironically put to an end by the medical board's conclusion that Morgan's body was unfit to fight. In the end, a weak body conquered a strong mind. It was a monumental relief.

The episode galvanized in him an increasingly pointed political view. He began to conflate the "march of civilisation" with the great machine of social oppression. Slowly he inverted the term which had once been his lodestar into a form of alienation. *Civilisation*, like *respectability*, became anathema. In his little notebook he concluded that the real political lesson of the war was that "[w]e must have a numerous and well fed lower class to fill our army."

Social hypocrisy, the theme that had generated so much comedy in his novels, now took on a more serious cast. Since his defense of *Maurice* to Forrest Reid three years earlier, he had understood homophobia to be a social rather than a spiritual ill. But now homoeroticism itself seemed to be a political stance. One evening by the sea, at the base of the palace at Montazah, Morgan witnessed a scene that he shaped into a parable:

> I was bathing myself on the deserted beach and a man galloped up on a donkey, stripped, and tried to pull it into the water with him. The lines of a straining nude have always seemed academic to me up to now but hereafter I shall remember red light on them, and ripples like grey ostrich-feathers breaking on the sand. He didn't—to grow less serious—get the donkey to follow him, but I don't know that I want to grow less serious. I come away from that place each time thinking "Why not more of this? Why not? What would it injure? Why not a world like this—its beauty of course impaired by death and old age and poverty and disease, but a world that should not torture itself by organised and artificial horrors?"

He told this story to Dickinson in the spirit of homosexual solidarity. Like him, Goldie had despaired of finding sexual intimacy. And he had despaired for the future of the world. Morgan saw a connection between these two forces. The arbitrary horrors of war making were inextricably linked to the horrors of persecuting gay men. He could only hope, as he had done in the dedication of *Maurice*, for a more tolerant, if distant, future: "It's evidently not to be in our day, nor while nationality lives, but I can't believe it Utopian, for each human being has in him the germs of such a world." In these private writings, he began to shape a politics of quiet resistance, to celebrate the power of the individual and to preserve his own kind of human meaning, not within, but against society. These ideas would achieve full flower years later, in the celebrated essays on personal freedom published in *Two Cheers for Democracy*.

Morgan seized upon what he understood to be a precious final moment to open himself to the unknown city. Walking without a guide became a quasi-political act. He set out on foot, this time deliberately looking to the left and the right, trying to engage the people whom Miss Bell has assured him didn't exist. The key to his method was the antithesis of Miss Grant Duff's gospel of *utility*—deliberate aimlessness. The city opened up like a flower. He followed the margins set by water, not by pavement: the canal near the Nouzah Gardens, the unchartered seafront, the shores of Lake Mariut. He taught himself to swim. There were unexpected surprises in this rambling. On the southern shore he found a tiny fishing village cut off from the main city by slums.

He found that his nondescript khaki served not merely as a "costume," but as a disguise. Even a uniform with indeterminate and ephemeral rank was a passport to travel freely. Just as he became mercenary in protecting himself from the draft, he traded on male privilege and his status as a British officer to wander with impunity. No one need know the inside of his heart.

This restless rambling was the half-sublimation of intensifying unfulfilled lust. Everywhere there were invitations that couldn't be accepted. The very air seemed to call out to him poetically, in the voices of the tram conductors as they announced the approaching stations—"Come here Mustafa Pasha, come here Sidi Bashr . . . yes yes come here Bulkeley and Glymeno-poulo." In *A Passage to India* these plaintive calls would be transmuted into Godbole's hopeless and mysterious song, "come come" to the reticent gods who never do. It seemed to him he would die without ever having a sexual encounter with another human being.

The sexual climate of Alexandria was enticing but dangerous. Though Aida and Furness were understanding, he had few real confidants. So he wrote to friends in England, braving the military censor's eye. His chief respite was his old mentor Edward Carpenter's sympathetic ear:

I don't want to grouse, as so much is all right with me, but this physical loneliness has gone on for too many months, and with it springs and grows a wretched fastidiousness, so that even if the opportunity for which I yearn was offered I fear I might refuse it. In such a refusal there is nothing spiritual.—It is rather a sign that the spirit is being broken. I am sure that some of the decent people I see daily would be willing to save me if they knew, but they don't know, can't know—I sit leaning over them for a bit and there it ends—except for images which burn in my sleep. I know that though you have heard this and sadder cases 1000 times before, you will yet be sympathetic, and that is why you are such a comfort to me. It's awful to live with an unsatisfied craving, now and then smothering it but never killing it or even wanting to. If I could get one solid night it would be something.

Clearly the young wounded soldier Frank Vicary, for all his warmth and sympathy, was one of the men whose images burned in Morgan's dreams. With Frank he could "do the . . . brotherly" thing—but he could not bring himself to risk touching him.

Everywhere he found absence, and in the absences he discerned codes of repression. A sign painted at a blocked-off entrance to the hospital read "No admission this way even if the fence has fallen down." To quell his feverish desires, he began to write, publishing small essays in the *Egyptian Mail*, the Saturday edition of a Cairo English-language newspaper. The narrative of these small travelogues was in itself subversive. He set up parallels between Alexandrian and British attitudes, leveling their ethical field. An essay on the strangeness of the Egyptians' bastard "Gippo English" was balanced with an essay on the risibility of "Army English." These short sketches, some still unpublished, some later collected in *Pharos and Pharillon*, were disguised as amusing travelogues. But they were more pointedly a self-conscious antidote to Baedeker's smug and secure Eurocentrism. Close reading of them reveals a complex narrative sympathy—an attempt to bring across his insights in a different key, one that Morgan would come to describe as an invitation to view life at an angle.

He explored the meandering streets of Alexandria, the places where a man without a map would get lost. And he actively researched the secret city of vice. Using his connections within the Censorship Office, Morgan befriended an Egyptian official in the police. He asked him to find a hashish den outside the purview of the British authorities. Hash was thought to be a more lurid drug than opium. In the public account—"The Den," in *Pharos and Pharillon*—he shaped the expedition as an amusing sketch of local color with a twist. The den disappoints. No drugs are found, and the trip becomes an occasion to mock the English yearning for a titillating exotic experience. But in his raw private letter to Edward Carpenter, he confessed a very different story with a very different moral.

Here Morgan made clear that the episode sexually stirred him. Drug vice and sexual vice had the same root, and he was deeply implicated in the search for both.

> We went up pitch black stairs in a slum and scratched at a door at the top . . . We push in and find a small and well mannered company smoking the drug, quiet and languorous. There was an Arab girl, barefoot, very young and tired, and some boy attendants, playing cards together—not to speak of odd noises in unopened rooms. One of the boys made a sign to me. I did not respond, but he came and sat down . . . on the bench. He was a young man, really, of extra-ordinary beauty and charm, very big and well built and manly, despite delicacy of lip and softness of eye. He wore garabia and tar-boosh and wouldn't talk Italian and I no Arabic. The other boys—in European dress and less charming—also made signs. Everyone—except ourselves—smoked. I would have smoked if I had been alone.

This seductive episode was interrupted, as it was so often for Forster, by the arrival of Europeans. "Three . . . dapper young men in straw hats, probably Italian shop assistants," came in and spoiled the mood. Not only did they make Morgan fatally self-conscious, they also enacted the familiar kabuki dance of homophobia. The Italian men, he wrote to Carpenter "were horrified at our sight. Boys tried to sit on their knees but they were not having any of it at all . . ." Even in recounting the episode to Carpenter, self-consciousness made him step back mentally. "Well, now with due regard for the censor, I have indicated what was to me an interesting and even attractive evening. I felt curiously at home in that den of vice."

Morgan's letter makes clear that he felt tarnished not by the boys' sexual invitation, but by his own fatal timidity. As with his protestations about the repulsiveness of Arab men, he turned the ethics of the episode back on itself. In the immediate aftermath of the visit, Morgan discovered that the Egyptian policeman had revealed the existence of the hash den to the British authorities. To Malcolm Darling he derided this as "an act of pure mud."

> A few days after I heard from Furness that the owner had been hauled up, and on mentioning this to my Egyptian friend was sickened to the vitals that *he* had gone straight to the police and peached. "Oh yes"— smiling modestly. "It was my duty. I am a private gentleman in the evening but a member of the administration (he's in the Police himself) by day. I keep the two apart."

No doubt a promise to keep the den a secret had been broken. But Forster's terror and disgust—"sickened to the vitals"—must have come from the realization that he, too, had been vulnerable to exposure. He told Carpenter that the commandant at the hospital was a "purity fanatic" who put men with venereal disease in "prison conditions in a wire enclosure." No doubt he could imagine a similar fate if he were "peached on." The episode only fed his sexual anxiety.

At the time the draft scare was brewing a propitious event opened the secret city still further. At dinner in the Mohammed Ali Club in early March, Pericles Anastassiades introduced him to an old friend, a lifelong Alexandrian and expatriate Greek, whose family (like Anastassiades's) had made a fortune in exporting cotton. But the man, Constantine Cavafy, had been down on his luck for decades; the ninth and last child, Cavafy had been educated in England, but lost his father at a young age, and lived like Balzac's Père Goriot in meaner and meaner circumstances.

Now he presented almost a cartoonish sketch of his more prosperous former self. He was impossibly vain and self-important. Though fifty-four, he styled himself "middle-aged." He was fastidious and formal. And he somewhat absurdly embalmed his physique. He circulated airbrushed and quite dated photos of himself to his admirers. He wore spectacular black circular spectacles, and brilliantined his hair with some special coal-black concoction. A friend described him as having the air of a boy who had inexplicably aged. He was palpably artificial, and palpably homosexual. And he was utterly intoxicating to Forster.

It took some weeks before the full magic of Cavafy revealed itself. By August Morgan wrote his mother that he had been invited into the inner circle—to "a literary evening." Cavafy was something special and "delightful," a "Greek gentleman in a straw hat, standing absolutely motionless at a slight angle to the universe." He was a poet utterly divorced from the commerce of art. Part of Cavafy's attraction for Morgan was his "tilt," the complete bifurcation of his public and his inner, essential life. This entailed separating day from night.

The daylight world consisted of an almost comic resistance to the British work ethic as espoused by Miss Grant Duff. Despite his great erudition, Cavafy was a clerk for the government office improbably named the Third Circle of Irrigation. For him it was more like the third circle of hell. He cultivated an exquisite sloth. His colleagues there described his elaborate strategies—covering his desk with papers "to give the impression he was overwhelmed with work," answering the telephone with the plaintive lament "I am very busy," arriving late but eschewing the elevator to take the stairs, walking slowly as if deep in thought. Most of the day, he composed poetry at his desk. His coworkers observed him: "We saw him lift up his hands like an actor, and put on a strange expression as if in ecstasy [as] he would bend down to write."

In the dark world of his salon Cavafy seductively embraced the seedy as the best part of life. He had devolved to a small apartment in the Greek quarter northeast of the square, off limits to the casual visitor because of its impenetrable winding and narrow streets. The flat was on Rue Lepsius, known to the wags as "Rue Clapsius" because of the preponderance of whorehouses in the neighborhood. Indeed, the apartment was on the second floor, directly over a male brothel. Cavafy found the location to be efficient and ideal: "Where could I live better? Below, the brothel caters for the flesh. And there is the church which forgives sin. And there is the hospital where we die."

Every evening between five and seven he was at home. Though he had lived there for years, Cavafy dithered about whether to electrify the apartment at his own expense. He never did. As a consequence, the flat was veiled in a kind of mysterious and romantic gloom. Cavafy lit the rooms by lantern and candlelight with studied effect.

continuously adjusting the light; he himself invariably sat in shadow, timidly avoiding the eyes of others while yet examining them closely. He would get up and open or shut or half-shut the shutters in different parts of the room, or half-draw the curtains . . . He would light or snuff a candle or two, sometimes adding another if a beautiful face appeared in the room.

The décor was a Fauvist's dream. There was a dark green hallway, a faded mauve dining room decorated by his late brother Paul, and a tiny red salon with a balcony onto the noisy street below. Here he received special visitors, surrounded by "his better furniture . . . old carved wood, lustres of pierced copper, little tables inlaid with mother-of-pearl . . . silk cushions embroidered with birds and flowers . . ."

In this exotic locale Forster had a significant scene of gay self-recognition. Almost thirty years later, the moment was still vivid enough for Morgan to capture its every detail in the present tense:

> I am back from my work, costumed in khaki . . . We have been introduced by an English friend, our meetings are rather dim, and Cavafy is now saying with his usual gentleness, "You could never understand my poetry, my dear Forster, never." A poem is produced—"The God Abandons Antony"—and I detect some coincidences between its Greek and public school Greek. Cavafy is amazed. "Oh, but this is good, my dear Forster, this is very good indeed," and he raises his hand, and takes over, and leads me through.

Cavafy led Morgan through to a new world and a new lexicon for homosexual experience. Even picking his way haltingly along the lines of this one poem, Forster knew he had encountered a major poet, more formidable for being so unconcerned with a wide audience. The subject, tone, and diction of Cavafy's work was of a piece, and completely original. His poems were graceful, unrhymed, offhand. They captured a sense of intertwined insight and loss. Alexandria, "the Alexandria you are losing," the fateful Alexandria whose "invisible procession of exquisite music," was his locus and his muse.

Whether set in Antony's moment, or Callimachus', or even in the recent past, Cavafy's Alexandria was a sensual city. It was a city for unabashed gay men. He celebrated the knowledge that beneath layers of erasure lay a meaning, perhaps known only to one person, which retained an afterglow. That such insights were hidden made them all the more precious. The poems were ravishing and plain. They captured the transcendent power of lust.

> *sensation that I love come back and take hold of me—*
> *when the body's memory awakens*
> *and an old longing again moves into the blood,*
> *when lips and skin remember*
> *and hands feel as though they touch again.*

> *Come back often, take hold of me in the night*
> *when lips and skin remember . . .*

And Cavafy's poems were intoxicatingly honest. They focused on physical passion rather than intimacy. Often the sexual encounters were fleeting, the speaker resigned to the fact that "it wouldn't have lasted long anyway—" But what pungent memories remained! "How strong the scents were, / what a magnificent bed we lay in, what pleasure we gave our bodies." Even more exciting was Cavafy's belief that this all-male erotic world was superior to the heterosexual world. He was unapologetic, and without timidity or guilt. Cavafy serenely believed in the normality, even the superiority, of homo-erotic love. To him the Greek way of love, attached as it was to centuries-old Alexandrian society, was far greater than the debased contemporary world. His oeuvre legitimized both the powerful immediacy and enduring history of gay desire.

For his nighttime self, Cavafy constructed an artful persona, superior, detached. He chose to be an outsider, forging a linguistic method in which outworn ways of expression were reborn in a new key. In speaking, Cavafy was equally at home in English, French, and Greek. He proudly held himself apart as a Hellene. Though he had lived all his life in Alexandria, he knew only enough Arabic to direct the kitchen staff. But in his poetic form he literally invented a new language for his subject.

At the time Cavafy composed these poems, there was a vast abyss between written and spoken Greek. Through long decades of political subservience the written language had ossified into a stilted official "classical" jargon, called *katharevousa*. Demotic Greek, a bastardized spoken language, was crammed with low neologisms and considered unfit for poetry. Cavafy boldly chose bastardy. His poems shocked the ear with "expressions . . . that one might actually hear in a shop." He seized the colloquial and spoken language and dragged it into "the world within." To Forster, Cavafy's innovation was as arresting as the quotidian and original language of the first chapters of Joyce's *A Portrait of the Artist as a Young Man*, which he eagerly read while in Alexandria. But this new means of expression was galvanizing, and far more moving. Here was a way to freshly uncover the gay past.

And the salon provided another benefit. Cavafy's salon connected men, literally through literature. He carefully selected a coterie of beautiful young men to show his poems. Cavafy wrote them out by hand, and left them, unbound, in little piles on the bookshelves in his simple back room. He would bring the manuscripts out, in different configurations, to flatter or please the individual reader. Reluctant to part with them, he claimed he was still polishing them, often for years. From time to time, he walked to the Grammata bookshop to give the owner a small handful of poems—erotic enough to "burn . . . his fingers"—to print in its eponymous journal. But more often he insisted that they could be viewed only as pages passed from hand to hand.

Up until now, Morgan had not imagined any way to be a writer but to partake in a public world of letters. Inability to find an audience had always led him to what he called "sterility." But Cavafy proved there was a different path: by exercising authorial control he forged a homosexual culture. Sublimely detached from the dictates of the public, he refused to encounter the world on any other than his own terms. Cavafy's strange, secret world cemented trust and interdependency. Morgan had grown up in an English world where even *to be seen looking* exposed gay men to danger. Now he found a place where a writer shaped intimacy with steely determination. Elated, Forster described his newly discovered gay network to Dickinson: "The best Alexandrian I know—Cavaffy [*sic*]—reminds me of Callimachus or some such poet—sensitive, scholarly and acute—not at all devoid of creative power but devoting it to the rearranging and resuscitating of the past. And another poet—Sinadino—lately typed me for a present a series of extracts from Pierre Loüys [*sic*]."

Agostino John Sinadino is a poet now almost completely unknown. A devotee of Mallarmé, after the war he became a close friend and correspondent of André Gide. Sinadino was three years older than Forster, but temperamentally a world apart. He was swish, campy, and liked his own outrageous jokes; his laugh was a "treble cackle" that was uniquely discernable and contagious. "A small middle-aged man with a long prehensile nose," Sinadino had a way of sniffing out the latest delectable literature from every avant-garde and decadent local scene. He was a peripatetic fellow, popping up in Paris, Alexandria, New York, and Milan in a single decade, cross-pollinating every literary circle he entered. The extracts he copied out from the pseudonymous Pierre Louÿs were explicitly pornographic, and hard to come by.

Morgan couldn't resist this colorful figure. Not just in the dusty past, the laments of Callimachus or the celebrations of Whitman, but *here, now*, the magic of gay life revealed itself. Even eight years later, back in the drought of Weybridge, Forster remembered these encounters. He took up a pen to write a rare poem in Cavafy's casual colloquial style:

> *To see a Sinadino again–*
> *The thought fell into my heart like rain*
> *And then began like a seed to sprout*
> *To see Allesandro coming out*
> *Or Agostino going in . . .*
>
> *Or even to know that wherever I went—*
> *A policeman's beat or a General's tent,*
> *A brothel, a café, the Cavers at Home,*
> *Ramleh's remote and echoing dome,*
> *The sea when tepid, the streets, when cool,*
> *The stairs, when dark, or a Greek girls' school*
> *Always to know that wherever I go*
> *I never know*
> *When next I shall meet a Sinadino.*
>
> *The thought has blossomed in exquisite flower*
> *And Alexandria returns for an hour. Weybridge 29-1-24*

This unpublished poem argued for a special power in gay men's lives, unavailable to those who could rely on sanctioned conventions to discover their lovers and mates. The possibility of a chance discovery of a lover, found as if by instinct through a surreptitious encounter, seemed magical to Morgan. After Cavafy, Morgan saw the promise of this world everywhere, hidden in the ordinary world. But its features could be discerned only by relaxing and relying on instinct.

Cavafy offered Morgan not corporeal but emotional and conceptual fulfillment. Morgan was not physically beautiful enough to tempt Cavafy, who in any case was past his sexual conquests, wary and controlling. He had a Warhol-like detachment, and loved to create a scene just to watch it happen around him. But his impenetrability made Forster ever more eager to have a place in preserving and translating this precious thing. "It was not my knowledge that touched him but my desire to know and to receive. He had no idea then that he could be widely desired, even in the stumbling North. To be understood in Alexandria and tolerated in Athens was the extent of his ambition."

This "desire" for knowledge, figured in such explicitly sexualized terms, sought a way to give Cavafy a future to match his bold appropriation of the past. In his poem "Hidden Things" (1908), Cavafy had acknowledged that his sexual identity was a practical "obstacle in [his] way," and—like Morgan in *Maurice*—he imagined a utopian future:

> *All the times I wanted to speak out.*
> *My most unnoticed actions,*
> *Discreet writings those most disguised—*
> *From these alone they'll understand me . . .*
> *A long time from now—in a more perfect world—*
> *Some other made like me will appear*
> *And, to be sure, he will act freely.*

Morgan took it upon himself to wrest Cavafy's work for an audience that would appreciate and preserve it. His need to do this was far greater than Cavafy's need for recognition. Until he walked across the street to die in the Greek Hospital in 1933, Cavafy maintained a scrupulous formality with Forster. The letters from Forster to Cavafy were always more intimate, and more yearning, than the formal and polite letters that came back from the other direction. The imbalance of affection settled into a compensatory filial relation for Forster. He would be a kind of good gay son.

While in Alexandria, Morgan buttonholed George Valassopoulos, a fellow

Kingsman and frequenter of Rue Lepsius, and cajoled and nagged him for the next decade to provide a delicate translation of Cavafy's poems to be published by the Woolfs' Hogarth Press. Forster came to believe that meeting Cavafy was one of the great strokes of fortune in his life. The corollary is also true. The English translations awakened the world to this fresh voice, which by mid-century was recognized as the greatest of the modern Greek poets. Forster made Cavafy's reputation in the world.

Paradoxically, as Cavafy's world liberated Forster's mind, it exacerbated the problem of his body. It was embarrassing to be so sexually belated, at thirty-seven not to have any more sexual experience than these terrible cravings of lust and an occasional wank under the stars. Trust was hard to come by in this militarized world. Morgan turned with increasing fervor and frankness to friends abroad. To Florence Barger, exactly his age, married and sexually experienced, whose unjudgmental response made her the perfect interlocutor. To Carpenter, to Dickinson, and in a jocular but veiled guise to Masood. These heartfelt and detailed letters preserved the record of his sexual awakening in striking detail.

He began a campaign to have sex of some kind with someone. For several months, in the summer of 1916, this plunged him into a physical paradise just short of sexual activity. Characteristically, he told Dickinson,

> I wished you were here with me at Montazah this morning. It is the country Palace of the ex-Khedive and has been turned into a Convalescent Hospital. Among its tamarisk groves and avenues of flowering oleander, on its reefs and fantastic promontories of rocks and sand, hundreds of young men are at play. fishing, riding donkeys, lying in hammocks, boating, dosing, swimming, listening to bands. They go about bare chested and bare legged, the blue of their linen shorts and the pale mauve of their shirts accenting the brown splendour of their bodies; and down by the sea many of them spend half their days naked and unrebuked . . . It is so beautiful that I cannot believe it has not been planned.

Glimpsing Cavafy's world had convinced him that, far from some sort of heroic sacrifice, celibacy was the embodiment of moral cowardice. Respectability, the internalization of fear itself, became his enemy. Finally, in mid-October—almost a year after he arrived in Alexandria—Morgan mustered the courage to be spontaneous. When he made this decision, he approached it with almost bureaucratic resolve. On the beach at Montazah, in the shadow of the hospital, suspended between terror and courage, he found a recuperating soldier as hungry as himself. The sex was brief and anonymous. To Florence Barger, he didn't specify the act, which was most likely a hurried sucking off. Instead he described it by what it meant for his soul: "parting with Respectability."

The sexual encounter was a calculated attempt to bring his body in line with his ravenous imagination. The next day, October 16, 1916, he examined more dispassionately what he called his "lopsided" life. He wrote to Florence unsentimentally: "Yesterday, for the first time in my life I parted with <R>. I have felt the step would be taken for many months. I have tried to take it before. It has left me curiously sad." The shorthand—"<R>"—was a practicality to evade relaying an obvious conclusion to a military censor. This wasn't misplaced paranoia. Unbeknown to Morgan, earlier that summer some letters to Masood had been intercepted. Their tone of affection aroused the suspicion of the postal censor in Bombay, who sent it on to his superiors, voicing the conclusion that the writer was "a decadent coward and apparently a sexual pervert." Only the fortuitous presence of one of Goldie's friends saved him from disaster. Lieutenant-Colonel C. E. Luard, in the Bombay Political Office, assured the censor that while Morgan might be "a poor creature" and no real man, "there is no foundation for the suggestion that he is a sexual pervert." Thus did the tightly knit network of Kingsmen protect their own.

Even as he reported his escape from sexual isolation to Florence, Forster understood that the kind of casual anonymous sex of Cavafy's most erotic poems was unsatisfactory for him. He characteristically blamed himself, sensing that in his debilitated state he didn't have the capacity for real intimacy. The episode stopped short of guilt. But he relentlessly aspired to greater spiritual growth. He summed up the lesson:

I realise in the first place that I am tethered to the life of the spirit—tethered by habit, not by free will or aspiration. (Why do people assume that only the flesh binds?) To put it in other words . . . the step would *not* have left me with these feelings had I taken it at the usual age—though it might have left me with remorse instead.

This was not a tragic vision. Nor was it wholly pathetic. He recognized and condemned a thread of narcissism in his belated sexual experience.

The moment became an invitation to digest something beyond the insights Cavafy had opened for him. He wanted to tie together the human and the political. He wanted to place the sorrow that sex could bring into the context of the meaning of his life. Morgan believed that Florence, who had not only had children, but had lost them to miscarriage, could best understand this complicated feeling.

> Well, my dear, this is odd news for a Matron to receive, but you've got to receive it because you're the only person in the world I want to tell it to . . .* I am too old to change to other food . . . My life has *not* been unhappy, but it has been too dam lop sided for words and physically dam lonely.
>
> * I don't even know if it's important news.

It *was* important news. The fierceness of his diction—*damn* lopsided and *damn* lonely—said so. For even in this half-realized moment, he sensed a utopian possibility that set him apart from Strachey, Cavafy, and the cynical set of gay men who found enough in pure sensuality. Sex promised not only the possibility of intimacy, but a sense of what it is humanly *for.* Morgan had diagnosed what was wrong with Britain and with warmongering nationalisms as a real disease of the soul. He felt the nation becoming "tighter and tinier and shinier than ever—a very precious little party, I don't doubt, but most insistently an island." He wouldn't settle for sex as an isolating phenomenon. But there was no doubt it was a relief to be in the physical world.

In his war notebook, he pulled together the personal, the sexual, and the political, examining his own part in the lockstep toward self-censorship and jingoism. He began to speculate on the bond that brought men to this place, in words that could well reflect his own desire to see into the life of these men: "To merge myself. To test myself. To do my bit. To suffer what soldiers suffer that I may understand them. These—apart from compulsion—are the motives that send men to fight." Here was the spectacular insight of a Red Cross searcher who discovers what he didn't expect, something in his own character. As if looking in a mirror, he diagnosed the spiritual ills: "Human nature under war conditions. The obverse of love is not hatred but fear. Fear is only one of the forms being taken, cowardice being another and efficiency a third."

The sexual awakening was not possible to describe publicly. So he slyly translated it for straight ears in coded form: in 1922, in *Alexandria: A History and a Guide*, Morgan described the place where he first had sex.

> Montazah Sta.—Close to the station is the *Summer Resort* of the ex-Khedive . . . The road leads by roses, oleanders and pepper trees . . . Beautiful walks in every direction, and perfect bathing . . . During the recent war (1914–1919) Montazah became a Red Cross Hospital; thousands of convalescent soldiers passed through it and will never forget the beauty and the comfort that they found there.

He never did forget this moment. For sex was not everything. But sex was a start.

7

"A Great Unrecorded History"

Almost immediately he plunged into "unappetizing gloom . . . depressing his friends, mangling his work, boring the prostrate soldiery." It was not a metaphysical condition, he discovered, but a prelude to a case of jaundice that began with a spectacular, humiliating bout of vomiting at a dinner party. A week later, comfortably ensconced in the General Hospital's officers' quarters, he had sufficient humor to pen a third-person comic grotesque: "gleams of primrose passed over his face, and his eyes glowed with celandines, and his ankles wobbled like two cuckoo flowers." Three weeks in the hospital restored him enough to wanly celebrate his thirty-eighth birthday on New Year's Day. But in early February he sprained one weakened ankle, and was back in a hospital bed for two more weeks. What a contrast to those beautiful young bodies on the beach! He felt himself "an inoffensive blossom."

It was not an auspicious response to his sexual awakening. Submitting to the care of his new landlady, Irene, he settled into an attitude of poetic resignation. On his birthday he copied out a passage describing the unquenchable longing of Marcus Aurelius for an Ideal City. To achieve the Beloved Republic, Plato demanded virtue, wisdom, and beauty. But Marcus Aurelius yearned also for tenderness and pity. From Irene, Morgan received both.

Irene had been Aida's housemaid. Another Alexandrian "bastard," she was Greek by ancestry but raised on Corfu, where Morgan's beloved Italian was the lingua franca. She retired early from domestic service to buy two small boarding houses and "shifted about the sandy wastes that lay east of the city with the intention of making money." Unwilling to impose upon Furness's largesse any longer, Morgan rented a cheap room from her, and got more than he bargained for: vigorous nursing to a stream of Italian chatter, a

cat and kittens, and frequent unannounced decampments to her other property. "Wherever she went she took me," he wrote, "remarking '*Lo porto con
me*' as if I was a doll."

Cautiously he resumed his hospital duties, the commute on the tram line
halved by his move to the suburbs. One cold night in late January, Morgan
rode back from Montazah alone in the dark. In the tram three young Egyptian
conductors casually chatted, riding on the footboard. The youngest approached
Forster. Would he mind standing up, so he could retrieve his coat from under
Morgan's seat? The man spoke good English, "charming and polite, I said
yes, cold, and we smiled." Like a melody that becomes palpable only after
being heard again and again on a distant radio, Forster's sense of this man
as an individual swelled into focus slowly. For several weeks the Egyptian
half saluted him as he stood at the terminus when the tram came in. Morgan
half responded. "Each knew the other wasn't someone else. No More."

Soon Forster began to realize that he had been looking *through* this face
for more than a year. He reconnected scattered impressions. Looking up as
the young man rode past, thinking, "'nice' and the morning was fresh and
sunny." Smiling when the conductor laughed broadly with a soldier. Remarking on his playful caress of each button on the soldier's tunic as he said
goodbye. This was the handsome boy with "some African-Negro blood" he
and Furness had admired the previous spring! He began to discern the beautiful dark face, with its full lips and wide-set black eyes, from the thousands
of anonymous faces that streamed by each day.

Discovering this genuine. bright young Egyptian—who introduced himself as Mohammed el Adl—seemed a prophetic answer to a pressing question. "Often as I let myself in at night, so safe and dull, I wondered 'Will this
go on forever?' Seeing you"—he wrote to Mohammed in a private memoir—
"I felt it would not, and determined not to be afraid until I was obliged."
Since 1909 when he wrote *Howards End* Morgan had believed, without much
evidence in his own life, "that to be trusted and to be trusted across the barriers of income race and class, is the greatest reward a man can receive . . ."
The prospect of real friendship galvanized his theory into practical courage.
He recognized the dangers, but felt curiously unmoved by them, confiding to
Florence:

> I have plunged into an anxious but very beautiful affair. It seemed to
> me—and I proved right—that something precious was being offered

me and that I was offering something that might be thought precious . . .
I should have been right to take the plunge, because if you pass life
by it's jolly well going to pass *you* by in the future. If you're frightened
it's all right—that's no harm; fear is an emotion. But by some trick of
the nerves I happen not to be frightened.

Sangfroid and determination were all very well, but finding the right tone
for such a friendship proved rather difficult. For one thing, he had to find el
Adl without giving the impression that he was stalking him. The night after
the encounter with the coat, Morgan tucked a copy of *Punch* intended as a
gift for Mohammed under his arm. With studied casualness he waited unsuccessfully for hours. Not knowing the young man's schedule, for several
weeks he loitered at the terminus of the Bacos line, hoping for a glimpse of
Mohammed's attractive head stooped over the accounting book as the tram
"c[a]me up into the swirl," all the while pretending each encounter was accidental. "God knows how many hours I stood waiting . . . that April and
May," Morgan ruefully wrote Florence. Once Mohammed realized he was
sought, he laconically said "second car," where they met on the sly while
Mohammed explained his work schedule. He, too, was attracted by this
strange blossoming friendship.

El Adl's insouciant air, unusual among the "servile" Egyptians, was refreshing. He was young (perhaps only seventeen) and bantam (five feet six
and about 130 pounds), but carried himself with the quiet authority of an
ambitious self-made man. At just the same time Forster arrived in Alexandria, he had come to the city alone to seek his fortune, leaving his parents
and brother in a sleepy village in the Nile Delta. And he was resplendent in
his khaki uniform, with a dark red tarboosh and blue silk tassel. With his
eager idiomatic English and his charm, Mohammed seemed potentially a
stock character—the colonial gigolo—but he proved surprisingly generous
and human: prickly but honest, willing to risk a great deal for friendship.

Linguistically and culturally Mohammed had the upper hand. Riding
side by side, talking softly, they always spoke English. (Forster expressed a
wish to learn Arabic, to read *The Thousand and One Nights*.) Mohammed
understood only too well what the British were saying sotto voce. Riding with
Morgan out to the hospital, he abruptly asked "a question about Mohammedans which please answer truly, sir." Why did the English hate Muslims
so, he wondered? Forster protested, but Mohammed pressed back; he had

overheard a soldier say to another, "There's a Mosque for fucking (I beg your pardon) Mohammedans." There was no answer for this but the most personal. Forster confided his great love for his Muslim friend Masood, telling Mohammed he had gone all the way to India to see him, and would again. That must have cost a lot of money, Mohammed commented drily. But the gesture impressed him.

Sensing Forster's earnest vulnerability, Mohammed reciprocated by taking a bold risk of his own. In late March, grandly and impulsively, he refused to allow Morgan to pay the fare. Unused to being treated as a human being by the British (he had been upbraided and even struck by imperious riders), he warmed to Morgan's impeccable courtesy. This episode would work itself poignantly into a scene in *A Passage to India* when Dr. Aziz, having paid for every ticket on the train, informs his obtuse English guests that seats on the Marabar line are always free. But Morgan understood that "the reprehensible habit of joyrides" was a shared transgression. Slowly, they were building their own separate world.

Yet even their mutual efforts to connect could not forestall a cascade of small misunderstandings. Excessive generosity seemed to exacerbate them. Once Forster offered a cigarette only to be rebuffed: "I seldom smoke—my ministry of Finance does not permit it." Mohammed's reply puzzled Morgan— was he asking for baksheesh, or repelled by the notion? The small change from the fare became a currency of intercultural squabbles—the older man insisting on punctilious payment and asking Mohammed to keep the change, the younger refusing. This drama reached its point of bathos when Mohammed emphatically closed his fist and the coins fell to the floorboards, sending Forster to his hands and knees to recover them. Forever overshooting or undershooting the mark of proportion, Forster persisted gamely, telling Florence that in retrospect "I can only say I have been less stupid than most people."

It was soon evident that the Egyptian had as much to fear as Morgan himself. When a tram inspector discovered that Forster had not paid his fare, Mohammed quickly replied with a pretext in Arabic: "It had blown away or that I had a Pass—anyhow something that wasn't true." But the ruse was discovered. This precipitated a crisis, enacted in the familiar dance of colonial racism. "No suspicion or blame attached to" Forster, who "was far too important a personage," but after a terrific scene Mohammed's job was imperiled. "With a sort of regal detachment," Mohammed shrugged off the threat, saying simply, "I have performed a good action." Desperate moments followed. The tram idled while the inspector spoke darkly with headquarters by telephone. Mohammed stood quietly beside Morgan, making small talk to defuse the tension. Then, just as Forster was to be left on the verge, Mohammed urgently turned to him: "'Please answer me a question. When you went to India, how many miles was it?' 'I don't know or care' I cried. 'Whenever shall I see you again?' He replied 'I might try to meet you one evening in my civil clothes perhaps.' Then I got off."

Stunned, Forster turned to the machine of privilege he so abhorred. He pulled strings. Luckily, the station manager knew Furness, and owed him a favor; by noon the next day—just as with the Bombay censor the year before—the King's College network came through. All was well. But Furness was willing to go only so far. In a welter of protectiveness, he warned Forster not to see Mohammed again, playing both sides of the game: "most sympathetic and helpful" but "harp[ing] on about general conditions, onlookers, etc." Years later, Forster was able to see that he had been "an awful nuisance" by approaching Furness in this way. But at the moment his defence of Mohammed was "the thing I am proudest of in all my life," in part because it represented the triumph of friendship over fear. Morgan found the young man, told him his job was secure, and asked if they could meet again. "He replied vehemently 'any time any place any hour,'" and their great friendship commenced in earnest.

Throughout the summer, the two men inched toward physical intimacy. Forster's carnal feelings grew as he took greater and greater risks. He wrote in a memoir that "sensuality . . . came violently when you first agreed to meet me. I got off your tram at Sidi Gaber and stumbled home in the dark." The location is telling, for Sidi Gaber was well short of Irene's lodgings. Danger and excitement had taken hold: Morgan had to walk off the feeling of triumph and cool down.

Only in public spaces could they have privacy. Chastened by Furness's response and keen to Mohammed's concerns, they sought a neutral ground for their first assignation. Mohammed set the terms. He christened the location "Chatby Gardens," using the name of the closest tram stop as an orientation point. But he gravely counseled Forster to get off at "Mazarita not Ramleh, up the road by the column." This way each man would debark at an anonymous, "dark and unfrequented" station. Morgan inscribed Mohammed's directions on the back of the ticket stub, and kept it for the rest of his life.

The Ptolemaic column at the mouth of the Municipal Gardens was a tall shaft of pink granite visible and beckoning all along the road. Celebrating an earlier conquest, it had been reerected in honor of Lord Kitchener's capture of Khartoum in 1898. The gardens themselves were edged by an old city wall and the Farkha Canal. Though their margins were picturesque and ancient, like much else in Morgan's Alexandria, they were a modern invention styled to "look mediaeval by moonlight." By day the highlight was an artificial pond—"an abode of ducks"—surrounded by benches. This was where the men arranged to meet.

The encounter began like an O. Henry story. Forster brought another hapless gift, the kind of expensive sticky cakes he had heard were a particular delicacy for Egyptians. He did not know that el Adl's mother had warned him against taking sweets from strangers. Though we know Forster to be an unimposing and sincere personage, el Adl later told Forster he feared they might be drugged. For his part, el Adl stood beside Forster for some time, unrecognized. Morgan didn't see him because he came in an unexpected disguise: in complete tennis whites, right down to the gutta-percha-soled shoes. For ten full minutes, the sensitive Red Cross searcher had been looking past him, unconsciously seeking the familiar uniform. But Mohammed came disguised as a British gentleman.

The conversation was not propitious. Acutely aware of his low social status, Mohammed came off as familiar and contemptuous: "I do not care for cakes. What did you pay for them? . . . How many centuries ago did you buy them?" Then he shifted tactics. To this "gentleman" he confessed to being "only a boy," and the son of a butcher at that. When Morgan called him "gentle boy," he relented, and smiled. Suddenly, unaccountably, the two men broke through mutual suspicion into something more volatile and vital. Mohammed invited Forster back to his room. "Would you like to see my home of misery? It will be *dreadful*." With comic grandeur he disposed of the cakes on the tram, passing them out to the startled riders on the long ride home.

Mohammed lived in Bacos, a working-class district east of the central town. His house was not dreadful, but quite ordinary. It comprised a single stark room, more spare than shabby: the only furnishings were a platform bed and a small wooden trunk, which he impulsively flung open and emptied to Morgan's astonishment. He "showered everything in the room down to 'This is lip salve' and . . . flung all that he had in his trunk to the bottom saying 'Very little, all clean . . . Now I have shown you all there is to show.'" Perhaps because he sensed that the British believed Arabs were unclean, Mohammed overcompensated. But his "immaculate" clothes and his guileless self-exposure spoke expressively. Morgan told Florence, "I remember thinking at the time that the man who did that would also hide no secrets in his heart if he decided to open it." The caveat was a telling bit of projection, for Morgan had not yet told Mohammed his name.

At that moment, it turned out, Mohammed made the decision to trust this odd Englishman. He showed Morgan a photograph of his fiancée, a young woman waiting back in the countryside. He told him about the missionary school where he received his rudimentary education. Significantly, he confided to Morgan that though he was very close to his mother, he had always felt like a stranger in his own family: "I have always ate apart and lived apart, and thought apart. Perhaps I am not my father's son." It was clearly exciting, and a great honor, to be treated as an equal by a British man. As Forster left later that evening, Mohammed told him quietly, "This is the very happiest evening of my life."

Their next meetings were not quite as promising. A few days later, the men arranged to meet for a walk at Glymenopoulo (another unfamiliar station), but the weather was miserable. Another evening Forster returned to Mohammed's room to be introduced stiffly as a trophy to an assortment of the young man's friends. Finally Forster invited Mohammed to his room at Irene's, where they sat on the bed and played chess. But on this occasion Morgan, who had finally introduced himself, "clouded" the advancing intimacy by evading questions about his life in London.

On their fourth meeting, in Mohammed's room, Forster and el Adl got into a literal scrape over sex. "Fascinated by [Mohammed's] character and talk," Morgan sprawled nearer to the young man on the bed, and they kissed for the first time. Even years later, the sensation of Mohammed's arm under his head remained "vivid." He noticed that as they lay together Mohammed kept his hands in his pockets to hide his groin. Sensing that el Adl's erection was an invitation, Morgan asked, "How fond are you of me?" and moved to unbutton the boy's flies. The two men tussled—Mohammed "defending himself"— and the scene ended with Forster staunching the blood from a scratch on his face and el Adl nursing a black eye. Morgan was mortified, Mohammed frightened and distressed. Briefly, anxiety pressed them into hardened postures. Morgan "found it hard to believe [Mohammed] was neither traitor nor cad" and became convinced that he had been deliberately insulted. Mohammed retorted by drawing a firm line: they could remain friendly on the trams, but never again meet privately. Morgan flew off in a huff.

But by the next morning on the tram tempers cooled and the misunderstanding became ridiculous to them both. Forster apologized. Comparing wounds, they laughed out loud. It was a moment of refreshing vulnerability. The two men found themselves in uncharted terrain. In retrospect, Forster observed how unnatural behavior could be fueled by panic. The incident reminded him of the preposterous aborted "engagement" between him and Florence's sister Elsie Thomas just before he left for Alexandria. "I have often thought of your sister. And wondered . . . whether she, like me, suddenly found it impossible to behave otherwise but in the most extraordinary way . . ." Now he felt a new serenity in the tumult of emotion.

> It isn't *happiness* it's—rather offensive phrase—that I first feel a *grown-up man* . . . The practical difficulties—there is a big racial and social gulf—are great, but when you are offered affection, honesty, and intelligence with all that you can possibly want in externals thrown in (*including a delightful sense of humour*), you surely have to take it or die spiritually.

Their shared sense of the absurdity in this rigid world pulled them through.

They came to this understanding from vastly different places. Forster was awed at how frank and relaxed the young man's sexual education had been. "One morning I woke up and said O mother what is this? My mother told me, so then I knew." His attitude toward sex and love had "so much cheerfulness in it—none of the solemnity which Christianity has thought essential to Romance." Though Mohammed had been brought up a Christian in a Muslim world, he calmly rejected his faith, saying, "I did not like Christianity." Morgan marveled that he seemed impervious to its pernicious influence. Comparing the "inroads on free thought made by Christianity and Islam," Morgan concluded Mohammed must have been saved by his culture, for "Islam makes less mess."

They talked a lot about sex. It was a relief to have a serious interlocutor on the subject. But the talk was also partly sublimation, for as much as Morgan campaigned for a full sexual partnership with Mohammed, he made little progress on this front. (He returned to the beach in early June to have anonymous sex for a second time.) In mid-July Mohammed's mother died suddenly, and he traveled home to Mansourah for her funeral. Forster's acute sympathy pulled them closer together. When Mohammed returned they had an honest conversation about their sexual expectations.

Mohammed had kissed him and embraced him, stroked his "short hair but crisp," telling Morgan it was "beautiful." But he recoiled from genital sex. Forster sketched out the chasm humbly in a letter to Florence. He recognized that his yearnings distorted things. Not at all sheepishly, he admitted he had exaggerated his sexual intimacy with Mohammed in an earlier letter to her.

> We hadn't entirely [parted with Respectability] and I wish to—it indeed seems right to me that we should, and I thought his objections trivial and beat back against them. He has made me see that I must not do this . . . but he has made me see it with so much tenderness and affection that I feel our friendship is only now beginning . . . As soon as he can give more he will give it.

This economy of sex, this emphasis on giving and getting, made el Adl uneasy. He was terribly sensitive about his relative poverty, and Morgan's tenacious insistence compounded his anxieties about being unworthy. It also awakened the old fear of exploitation.

> Completely to part with Respectability he refuses—"Never! Never!"— then with an indescribable mixture of detachment and tenderness turned his head away and said "I want to ask you a question. Do you never consider that your wish has led you to know a T.C.? And do you not think that a pity for you, and a disgrace? While answering my questions you are not to look at me."

T.C. was el Adl's shorthand for Tram Conductor. The question was a goad, and a test of Morgan's sincerity: Would he betray a taint of class-consciousness? Could Morgan's hungry eyes be trusted? They must look away. Mohammed wanted to be not a sexual toy but a true intimate.

By early October he felt capable of honestly articulating his own desire:

If we are to be friends forever you must promise me something. (Do you wish to be friends forever?) If you wish (I do) You must promise at once to tell me if I wrong you so that we make its place clear. 1.2.3.4. wrongs may not matter but if we have more then all may become evil . . . But I must be independent—if I do not want to meet you I must say "I do not", if I am not sure I must be able to say perhaps. You must respect me as I respect you.

The sexual impasse was now clearer to Morgan, who realized that Mohammed "feared he was only externals for me." But even with the muddle sorted out, it was clear that sex meant different things to each of them. The scuffle over el Adl's erection—his sudden ambivalence in the midst of so much physical affection—puzzled Forster enough to ask about its meaning later in their friendship. El Adl insisted that it didn't indicate any particular desire. He explained, "My damn prick stands up whoever it is, it means nothing." For Forster, who had concluded by this time that being homosexual was the core of his identity, el Adl's casual polymorphous attitude was fascinating. He told Morgan he had slept pleasurably with both men and female prostitutes, and he blithely expected to marry and have children. Like most Egyptian men, he viewed all kinds of penetrative sexual behavior as a natural expression of male prerogative. Centuries-old Islamic practice took a pragmatic approach to official morality: sex with men made "a sinner, but did not imperil the status and honor due him as a man." The Napoleonic Code coincided easily with local custom; it viewed gay sex as distasteful, but a private matter. In this context, el Adl's statement "My damn prick stands up whoever it is" may well be the equivalent of Forster's "I feel a grown-up man."

Mohammed told Morgan, charitably, that his desire was "Foolish." Morgan replied, "All have their foolishness and this is mine." But to Mohammed, sexual subordination was a peculiar, even preposterous, choice for an adult man. Morgan's lobbying for more frequent and intimate sexual expression in their relationship, his barely unexpressed desire to be penetrated, must have been read by the younger man as an inexplicable concession of social power.

Living after Freud and Foucault, we parse the misunderstanding differently than the men did at the time. In a sense they lived on either side of a great (although still permeable) conceptual divide, between sex being sex and sex being identity. Forster anticipated modern ideas about sexuality, but only vaguely. He grasped only that what was happening between him and el Adl was more in the nature of "an understanding rather than an agreement." He was willing to wait. And if he had to choose, he concluded he would opt for intimacy over mere sex.

It befell that he didn't have to choose. Just days after the passionate request for respect and honesty, Mohammed gave Morgan a "sudden hard kiss" and after "a gruff demur" leaned back, untied his linen trousers, and let Morgan masturbate him. This was a milestone. The struggle was over:

> Dearest Florence,
>
> R. Has been parted with, and in the simplest most inevitable way . . . I am so happy—not for the actual pleasure but because the last barrier has fallen . . . I wish I was writing the latter half of *Maurice* now I know so much more. It is awful to know of the thousands who go through youth without ever knowing. I have known in a way before, but never like this. My luck has been amazing.

The affair with Mohammed intensified his romantic conviction that gay men could be connected to each other deeply, even permanently. And while the relationship seemed to him resolutely modern and unclassifiable, perhaps because of Cavafy's influence he extrapolated from his individual experience to a collective, hidden past. One starry late-summer night the landscape once again related a parable. It was similar in tone and power to the glorious revelation of the naked man pulling the donkey on the beach of which he had written Goldie a year before. This time he shared it with Florence. As he sat on the veranda of the Sultan Hussein Club near the Bourse,

> The half moon, with beautiful blue markings on its primrose, stands looking at the sunset . . . It is very sweet of you to think of us both—I feel so touched and happy: yet, considering the relation from outside,

I imagine it is indeed worthy to be thought about; it is such a triumph over nonsense and artificial difficulties: it is a sample of the . . .
other triumphs that I am sure come off but of which we hear nothing
through the brassy rattle of civilisation so called . . . When I am with
him smoking or talking quietly ahead . . . I see beyond my own happiness and intimacy, occasional glimpses of the happiness of 1000s
of others whose names I shall never hear, and I know that there is a
great unrecorded history.

Unlike "the thousands" of wretched repressed Englishmen he imagined
in his other letter to Florence, here Forster conjured a more benign multi-
tude. Beneath the brittle veneer of civilization, beneath history as the official
record of the powerful, was a transcendent alternative history that only a
softened heart could glean.

But even this worthy vision was subject to the noisy wartime world. After
Mohammed's mother died, much about living in the city became less pleasant to him. Privacy was becoming scarcer. His half-brother inexplicably
came to stay at the Home of Misery for almost a month, literally and figuratively squatting in the corner of the room that Morgan noted sourly
"would otherwise be ours." Once while conversing innocently the two men
were discovered in Morgan's room by Irene, who let out a muffled scream.
Forster fumed to Florence, "It's absurd he can't stop here. Only when one
feels seriously does one realise how false is the constitution of society." Conditions, never ideal, became more pinched at just the moment the relationship deepened.

And Mohammed's job, already precarious, had become even more unten-
able. Although he knew it to be against his more selfish interests, Forster
lobbied Furness to find a better-paying position for his lover. In October
1917 Mohammed left for Kantara, in the Canal Zone, where he served as a
clerk in the British military apparatus at more than twice his wage on the
tram. The work was mundane, but deliciously subversive. Mohammed told
Morgan slyly that he was going "to be a spy."

By doing low-level intelligence work for the British in the Canal Zone, it
could be argued that Mohammed was being co-opted. But Forster's letters
indicate that this joke was a shared conspiracy. He asked Florence: "Do you
not think it is very bad to have made him a spy? *We* do not think it is so bad."

El Adl told Forster his philosophy in all things was "some lies is necessary to life." Now Forster and his lover were lying together, as it were, in the service of friendship over allegiance to empire.

The sexual breakthrough coincided with Mohammed leaving Alexandria. It may have been a parting concession on his part, but it was also a promise for the future. In preparation for their time apart, Forster helped Mohammed pack his things, and gave him some money he could ill afford. (Weeks earlier, with Lily's rent in Weybridge going up usuriously, he told her to sell his typewriter to pay for expenses.) With so much of their world in flux, each man was anxious to fix the moment in his own way. Morgan persuaded Mohammed to sit for a studio photograph, dressed in a tarboosh, Western suit, bow tie, and shiny spats. The boy was handsome, young, and very earnest. Like Morgan, he took off his spectacles for the occasion. A fly whisk of white horsehair—which belonged to Morgan—in his right hand draped over a small table. For his part, Mohammed offered a desperate goodbye. As his train left the station "it felt like the fall of a curtain after an act." He called after Morgan, begging, "Don't forget me, don't—" The plangent voice lingered despite Forster's assertion that "by now our relationship is too deep and firm to fear separation." Years later, he recalled a similar scene of separation: "You called out my name at Bebbit el Hagar station after we had seen that ruined temple . . . that no one else seems to have seen. It was dark and I hear an Egyptian shouting who had lost his friend: Margan, Margan—you calling me and I felt we belonged to each other, you had made me an Egyptian."

Though Mohammed wrote "affectionately" from the Canal Zone every few days, and they counted the days toward his planned leave of absence in March, the loss of the secret world the two men shared inevitably isolated Forster. "Everything seems breaking here" in Alexandria, he told Florence: Furness was departing for war work in Cairo, and he was "losing" Mohammed. His pool of friends seemed so shallow. Aida, who had been sympathetic during the draft scare, now seemed bored by him. And after the importuning over the hash den, over Mohammed's joyrides, over finding Mohammed a job, Furness had begun to express real irritation at being drawn into Morgan's entanglements. By late fall Miss Grant Duff, never a friend of the bosom, had become "Miss Goose Duff" in letters to Lily.

Routines offered no solace. Though he had been promoted to "'Head

Searcher for Egypt' whatever that means," his Red Cross work now seemed terribly mundane. The promotion disrupted the balance of power between Miss Grant Duff and himself, inviting poisonous and unfamiliar office politics. She justifiably felt underappreciated and trumped by a male conspiracy. To compensate, she took up a tone of aggrieved sarcasm. All winter petty encounters between them magnified his misery. News from the hospital almost disappeared from his correspondence. In March 1918 she resigned, leaving him relieved but without even this little drama to distract him.

He felt the "stupidity and deadness" of life without Mohammed. And he chafed at having news so "worthy to be thought about" with no one to tell it to. Defying the military censor, he turned to Florence, Goldie, Strachey, and Carpenter to pour out the exquisite details of his love affair with Mohammed. This turned out to be a very good thing for gay posterity.

Each correspondent received news from a particular angle. Morgan was touched by Florence's genuine interest in Mohammed. She wrote him separate letters (none survive) and treated them as a legitimate couple. "It is very sweet of you to think of us *both*—I was so touched and happy," he told her. His letters to her focused on untangling the emotional muddles at the heart of such a complicated love affair. With Dickinson—whose affairs were always unrequited—Morgan adopted a heartier tone, telling him, "I have actually at my age had *adventures*." But he was initially unable to break free of cliché in his description of Mohammed. It "is more like an affair of Searight's than anything else I can indicate! This will convey to you age, race, rank, though not precisely relationship." Perhaps because he sensed that Dickinson was romantically underdeveloped, he quickly ceased describing the inner workings of his emotional life with Mohammed to him. Listing Mohammed's good qualities—"reliability cleanliness, intellectual detachment, charm . . . test after test comes along, always with the same result"—his letters to Goldie had an arid air. To Edward Carpenter, who followed every move forward with vicarious delight, he hinted flatteringly that Mohammed was like George Merrill. He shared the precious photograph of Mohammed to seal the comparison. Carpenter responded warmly:

> Your good friend. Mrs. Barger, sent me the photograph, for which I was grateful to her (& you). I was sorely tempted to keep it. But what a pleasure to see a real face after the milk & water mongrelly things

one sees here! It was a literal refreshment to me. Those eyes—I <u>know</u> <u>so well</u> what they mean. and I think you do too. <u>now</u>! And that very charming mouth! I wish you would send me one for myself, to keep.

Morgan drew his circle of English friends and acquaintances closer by invoking their mutual interest in his growing love for Mohammed. By Forster's command, they circulated the little trophies: his narrative, enclosing Mohammed's letters and photograph. Morgan even gave Florence homework on what it was like to be homosexual. recommending that she read Carpenter's autobiography, *My Days and Dreams*, and complimenting her on liking and understanding it. Eventually, he even told Masood about Mohammed. But to Lily, Morgan said nothing about his Egyptian friend.

In the bleak midwinter, after Mohammed had been in Kantara for a full two months, Morgan turned afresh to writing. He worked in earnest on the research for a planned guide to Alexandria, exploring the past since the present was a vast military zone. And he began another much less veiled history, a complete account of the affair with Mohammed. Maimie had just died, and though he decided not to make the long journey back to England for the funeral, the event and his New Year's thirty-ninth birthday set a firm cast of memento mori in his mind. He told Florence soberly, "I want to put a few things on record . . . My personal interest in it apart, I feel it oughtn't to be lost. It's a little the starved artist writing in fact. I don't mean this to be an ordinary letter. except it contains my love to you. Let me know if you get it. And keep it, for one forgets."

These letters were galvanized by the confidence that his love for Mohammed was both an experience in itself and "proof of something larger and wider." He approached the history as a novelist. adopting the sweeping temporal perspective he had invented for the unnamed narrator of *Howards End*: keen insight into immediate events nestled into the serene detachment of a very long view.

That novel had begun with the famously offhand sentence "One may as well begin with Helen's letter to her sister." The narrator's odd interjections from the distant future gave the story an impulsive, if slightly imbalanced, momentum. Of course, this present tale was clearly still incomplete: six months earlier he had admitted to Goldie that he couldn't envision how his friendship with Mohammed might end. He felt it was capable of developing into something, since "romantic curiosity seems on both sides to be passing into something more permanent." But then he shrugged and let go, asking rhetorically, "How does anything end? One should act as if things last."

Now being separated from Mohammed made him grasp the reality of his love affair very tightly. He pointedly returned to the previous spring, dissecting the smallest incidents and trying to recall Mohammed's words verbatim. The method had the twin advantages of contemporaneous impression and retrospection. But it also pointed toward permanence, if only for the eyes of gay men at some distant time. He was becoming convinced that "nothing in my life will ever be as great." And this view, like many of his instincts, proved prescient: almost forty years later, from the perspective of old age, Forster confirmed that his friendship with el Adl was one of the two "greatest things" in his life.

But he did not yet have a name for this sensation. It only seemed certain to him that the pseudo-empirical categories developed by sexologists such as Krafft-Ebing and Hirschfeld—which he called "German physiological pigeon holes"—were threadbare ways of expressing the complex conditions of human experience. He told Goldie, "I never did find one to fit me . . ." What he had with Mohammed, he was sure, was as revelatory as a whole new way of seeing and being. As much as he could, Forster took pains to preserve the evidence of their affair as a dialogue, carefully copying out almost fifty letters from Mohammed (while burning all of Florence's) and keeping a cache of ephemera from ticket stubs to photographs. The best way to respect Mohammed was to give him his own voice.

He relished how being with Mohammed had sharpened his capacity for surprise. He told Florence he envied her three "children's sense of looking at life, with each person a new species." Especially entertaining was the shared practice of inverting social expectations in canny ways. Both men relied on fixed racial attitudes and their shared male privilege in public spaces, sometimes to walk together side by side, hiding in plain sight. Of course he and Mohammed had honed rules to make them safe, but these often involved the creative use of others' prejudice and obtuseness. Adopting a sardonic voice, he told Florence, "He is unfortunately black—not as black as a child's face or ink, but blacker than . . . Masood—so that our juxtaposition is noticeable . . ." So they made the most of el Adl's color when they must.

What else could he be thought to be but Morgan's servant? Disgusted by co-lonial power, Forster nonetheless employed it to extend metaphorical cover to his friend.

Their clothing often belied their station. Mohammed took great pleasure in teasing Morgan about his shabby clothing and great pride in the care of his own dress. "Taking me by the sleeve last night he said gently, 'You know Forster, though I am poorer than you I would never been seen in such a coat. I am not blaming you— no, I praise—but I would never *be* seen, and your hat has a hole and your boots have a hole and your socks have a hole.'"

"Good clothes are an infectious disease," Mohammed admitted. "I had much better *not* care and look like *you*, and so perhaps I will, but only in Alexandria." He wouldn't be seen like that at home. The young man who first appeared in blinding tennis whites knew how to distinguish himself and how to become inconspicuous. Sometimes paradoxically: in April 1918, Morgan arranged for a second photograph of Mohammed, as a keepsake while he was away in the Canal Zone. The young man surprised him by arriving for the session dressed in Forster's shabby military uniform. What a delicious appropriation! What a parody of the way uniforms both mark the distinctive position of their wearers and make them indistinguishable from other men! El Adl knew the portrait would be circulated to Edward Carpenter and to Forster's other English friends. This photograph boldly proclaimed their intimacy. In another queer cultural cross-dressing, that summer the men commissioned a single dress suit, too big for Mohammed, slightly too small for Morgan, for them to share.

There is a third, even more revealing and mysterious self-fashioning, a tiny snapshot dating from the period before Mohammed left for Kantara. It was taken out of doors in heavy sun. Wearing a soft collarless cotton shirt unbuttoned at the neck, Morgan sat alone on a volcanic rock like those on the shoreline at Mex, in three-quarter profile, looking down at a book in his hands. There's no notation of who stood behind the camera. Could it have been Mohammed? Of the thousands of photographs in the King's College archives, it is one of only a few where he is smiling. It's tempting to think of this and the photograph of Mohammed in Forster's uniform as a diptych, in ghostly dialogue, as close to a gay domestic portrait as they could manage at the time. Years later, Forster would pioneer this genre, but not now, not yet.

This new worldliness and sense of play made plain how insufficient his attempt at gay fiction had been, how imponderable and solemn. "The whole

ending of *Maurice* and its handling of the social question now seems sad timorous half hearted stuff." Some of the novel's idealism still seemed right—"I
have known in a way before, but never like this," he told Florence. But he
had written it too soon, before he realized that "some lies is necessary to
life." "Oh Florence," he wrote, "what a mean, truncated life if this had never
happened." For once, his corporeal life had outstripped his imagination.

As best they could, that spring they arranged to see each other during
Mohammed's rare military leaves from his work. The long-anticipated visit
in March dissolved into a muddle. Mohammed did not write as he had
promised, and briefly Morgan suspected he had been insulted or forgotten.
But Mohammed was very ill—"he went to hospital with some slight ailment
and caught some filthy fever there." Moreover, he had been mistreated by
the British authorities, having to pay a bribe just to get a hospital bed. Disbelief turned to disgust and a welter of displaced anger when Morgan discovered the truth. He bitterly complained to Florence that the army "shovels
[Egyptians] around like dirt." The episode convinced Morgan that he must
"make an effort over A or we shall lose one another for ever. I can't think how
to get him away from this military zone which will neither let him come out
nor me in."

An Alexandrian reunion in mid-May, however, went off as planned. But
with Mohammed now homeless and Irene suspicious, they had to stay in
Bacos with an Egyptian friend. These complex arrangements awkwardly coincided with the arrival of E. K. "Francis" Bennett, Morgan's former student
at the Working Men's College. Before they met, Francis had been a factory
worker. (He would eventually climb into an impressive academic career as
a German professor at Cambridge, on the foundations of Morgan's support
and his own brains.) Like Morgan, Bennett was homosexual, but he was
still clinging to Forrest Reid's repressed belief in Respectability. Morgan
was "obliged to tell him the bare fact" of Mohammed's existence and Bennett received the news "with more sympathy and interest than I had expected . . ."

A different plan to integrate Morgan's Egyptian and his English lives was
frustrated at the last moment, when a rendezvous with the poet Siegfried
Sassoon was aborted because Sassoon did not get permission to leave ship.

Sassoon's correspondence was so sympathetic that this was a real disappointment. (They would meet in England in the coming year.)

Morgan took Mohammed to the remote rocky beach at Mex, where they swam, sunbathed, and sat "as Maurice and Clive sat at Cambridge" on their delicious day playing hooky. Mohammed told him "two days have passed like two minutes." The idyll was like "some lovely cloud" that interposed between him and the war. "He has hidden my home life too," he told Florence. But did the cloud obscure or did it clarify? By the end of May the vision jarred him into thoughts about their future together. Florence had recommended that Morgan decamp from Irene's to avoid her hostility, and set up an alternative domestic arrangement supporting the young man. "Your new arrangement isn't possible," he replied. Mohammed's "bloody independence for one thing wouldn't consent . . . [He] expects marriage and life among his own people, so far as he looks forward at all, and I scarcely look forward to anything different." But these facts belied Mohammed's attitude. "He strikes me as more fully attached to me than hitherto: says he had awful dreams about me when he nearly died." The idea of living together was improbable, but it wormed into his brain, even "[m]onth after month with my life in a box . . ." Their restlessness over the future jarred Mohammed into action. At the end of May, without other prospects, he "chucked that infernal job" and left for Mansourah. But life—or rather, death—intruded suddenly in June.

Mohammed's father died two days after he returned home, and two days later in a cruel double blow he "received a wire from Tanta [in the Nile Delta] stating that my brother—the tailor—drowned in the Nile." "Griefs never come one by one," Mohammed told him, "they always come in battalions . . . What am I going to do? I have always asked myself the question but I did not find the answer yet." Mohammed had never felt close to his father, but his brother Ahmed was beloved, and the death bewildered and shattered him. "He was a good swimmer and the Canal [where he drowned] is not so deep. I did not realise it yet." Morgan immediately traveled to Mansourah to console him. The visit "was even better than either of us had hoped. Does one experience a renewal or a deepening of emotion each time?" he asked Florence.

Mohammed now found himself in a middle-class predicament: jobless, but a homeowner. For once, the men had some privacy—"perfect conditions"—

though they were a reiteration of the Home of Misery. The house was more like three tiny houses connected together in a slum near the railway station, and Mohammed had rented out all but one small room to keep to himself. This was considerably less clean than the room in Bacos, but no matter: the men "seldom touched [the muddy floor] bottom." They headed straight for the bed. Food was brought in to them by a "semi-slave" who "squatted in the passage while we ate." To wash they stripped in a passage under the stair, "pour[ing] little tins of water over each other." Though Mohammed was "awfully grave at first," he rebounded the next day, wrestling and ragging with Morgan in the bed, playfully threatening, "'Morgan I will hurt you—Edward I will kill you' and we went on fooling until we fell asleep."

Here there was no need to be coy. Mohammed gave him quite a tour of Mansourah by boat and carriage, introducing him to "Mr. Ganda and all [his] other friends." The two men cheerfully planned Mohammed's next step: marrying his brother's widow and adopting their two-year-old child, of whom he was fond. Morgan told Florence: "I am rather in favour of it. He likes her and has often seen her, and she likes him and approves the scheme . . . She requires no dowry, and—being a widow—there will be no expense over the wedding." Morgan prided himself on his pragmatism and knowledge of local customs, pointing out that he returned by third-class ticket, traveling like a proper Egyptian to spite British hauteur.

Mohammed's wedding plans did not diminish their intimacy. While lying in bed they had another frank conversation about sex. "I theorised to him . . . rather deeply against R[espectability]—how afterwards I found it even more important than at the time. He said very gently 'I quite understand'"—neatly accommodating both Forster's sexual needs and his conviction that loving Mohammed meant hating the British. Now Forster had "the happiness of knowing that things are sound even on an intellectual basis." In a parallel confidence, Mohammed told Morgan that he had blackmailed men over sexual advances when he was younger but abandoned this "low down" behavior over sympathy for his victims. He concluded, "All is exceptions in men as in English grammar." Now they were both firmly on the same side.

"Sick of" Mansourah, Mohammed returned to Alexandria late in July to visit Morgan. He teased him about finding a pair of Morgan's socks—distinguishable by the hole in their toe—which he had left by the latrine in the dark. On the fourth anniversary of the start of the war, while everyone else was watching military exercises, they slipped off to the remote beach at Mex, beyond Ramleh, "bathing and sprawling among the rocks on the breakwater." Mohammed had decided to marry a different woman, his widowed sister-in-law's unmarried sister, Gamila. This was a "more romantic" choice, with "more probability of nice children in consequence—at least isn't that so? . . . I hope he may yet live 'as a happy man in my own paternal home.'"

But by the fall, with marriage plans advancing, Morgan became deeply worried about Mohammed's health. Perhaps it was tuberculosis—Mohammed was coughing and had alarmingly lost weight—"his back looks hollow." Perhaps he was only ground down by the sorrows of the summer. Morgan's concerns were magnified by a new sense of urgency, for big political events augured an end to the war, and to their idyll. The British had already taken Jerusalem, and in October Damascus fell. Everywhere the Turks were being pushed back. Soon he must leave Egypt. As the wedding approached at the beginning of October, Morgan became seized with dread. He wrote Florence:

> I think A's [Adl's] must be the saddest letter a man ever wrote on his wedding eve. The marriage disconcerts me more and more. It seems just a hygienic measure. He says he has read about love in books, but he just doesn't know what it means. Now I wonder whether I should have dissociated with him. I was so anxious for him to have whatever might enlarge his life . . . I trust it is not this disease. I feel morbid as well as sad so I won't go on . . . In my calmer moments I tell myself he merely hasn't eaten enough, and that this desolating breakdown of spirits is natural in one who has suffered as he has. If he should die I shall cable to you as it will relieve me.

A week after the wedding, Morgan developed an exaggerated fear that telling Mohammed he would leave might actually kill him.

> I have just been writing a ghastly letter to him . . . telling him it is unlikely I shall be in Egypt much longer. They are bound to move us. The breakup of Turkey leaves Alexandria nothing to do . . . I understand A's psychology but not his physiology and I tremble lest it have at such a time a bad effect—the mixup of his marriage and illness and then me coming on the top.

To Morgan's relief, marriage made Mohammed feel serene, happy, and manly, as if he "was scarcely in the world before." And a doctor, paid for by Morgan, told him, "[h]e has not actually got consumption—is on the verge." Even better, "Our relationship just doesn't change. He wants me to stop with him. I shall once again before I go."

In mid-November, just after the Armistice, Morgan traveled again to Mohammed's home in Mansourah to meet his new wife. The arrangements were entirely unorthodox and to Morgan "the first twelve hours of my visit were as perfect as I have known." The only disquieting fact was that Mohammed, though "fatter," still felt ill. Morgan massaged him to sleep, but he awoke with terrible itching, and Gamila took over.

Morgan crashed the honeymoon by invitation, but the visit was a severe breach of local custom. The companionship of a European with a married man was unthinkable, and Morgan realized that Mohammed had made "more sacrifices for me than I ever had for him." Gamila herself stayed out of the way except for "glimpses." Morgan liked her a great deal, though the Egyptian form of marriage seemed as strange to him as (no doubt) Forster's presence must have seemed to her. "She is like some tame and pretty country animal, and he will be kind to her as all, but the idea of companionship seems never to have entered his head. It is queer even to me, who know the East a little . . . At present he regards her alternately as a [play—scratched out] comfort and a financial anxiety."

Mohammed had moved to the larger part of the house, much nicer, and with a capital loan of seventy pounds from Morgan, set up as a cotton broker, "buying cotton from the country people & selling it to the dealers." A second visit in late January 1919 confirmed Morgan's sense that Mohammed was happily settled in his marriage. This time he brought the gift of an inlaid wooden box to the stunned Gamila, and he and Mohammed took turns teasing her by exaggerating its cost. "God help the man—he must be mad," she exclaimed, hearing one estimate. But neither man admitted to the lie: it was a shared secret. Choosing presents for Florence's children—a hat, some small tin whistles—Mohammed offered a startling suggestion. "Why not take them costlier gifts? Why not take them a pair of Egyptians?" Morgan wished he could. Was it possible to transplant what they had grown together? It seemed unthinkable, an even greater fantasy than Maurice and Alec in the greenwood.

The wedding offered one advantage: now he could tell Lily about the marriage of a new Egyptian friend. Fit and happy, Mohammed followed Morgan back to Alexandria to see him off to the ship, promising to stay in touch. Three eventful years! As he sailed off, Morgan was officially separated from his Red Cross service. And though neither she nor her husband knew it yet, Gamila was already pregnant with a son they would name Morgan.

PART TWO

Happiness Can Come in One's Natural Growth

8

"Do Not Forget Your Ever Friend"

Three years later Morgan took up his pen to dedicate a little notebook:

To Mohammed el Adl,
> who died at Mansourah shortly
> after the 8th of May, 1922,
> aged about twenty three: of consumption;
> his mother, father, brother, and son
> died before him: his daughter has
> died since, his widow is said to
> have married again:

and to my love for him.

August 5th 1922.

He gathered up ephemera: several small studio photographs of his lover, a ticket stub from their first tram ride together, and a pathetic little packet comprising all of Mohammed's letters to him. Each day he walked alone at Chertsey Mead, the watermeadows a mile from Harnham, pausing at the entrance stile to slip on the ring Mohammed's widow had sent him—a circle of gold set with a cheap red stone. Each night he slept with the ring under his pillow. "I am sure that I could have lived with him had he been in occupation and good health," Morgan wrote to Florence. But now that dream was dead. Save for this little trove Mohammed was completely erased from the world.

• • •

Three years before, as he climbed off the ship at Gravesend in January 1919, Morgan was sure he could never be the same man he was when he left for Alexandria. He tried to be philosophical—"with my present freedom what a life I would have led. But the war gave and the war took away." In gratitude for his safe return, Lily gravely insisted on saying prayers at the dinner table for the first time since his childhood. But it was alienating to feel so completely changed internally, and to have the world of Harnham revert so quickly to its old rhythms. "I see my middle age as clearly as middle age can be seen. Always working and never creating. Pleasant to all trusting no one. A mixture of cowardice and sympathy." In a half-conscious way he tried to imagine a different path than being a writer—"I don't see what it is clearly yet, but I know what keeps me from it."

As soon as possible, Morgan made a beeline to visit friends he had not seen in the long years of the war: to the Bargers, now in Edinburgh, where George was professor of chemistry; to the Merediths and Forrest Reid in Belfast; to Edward Carpenter and George Merrill, who had moved south to Guildford when the rural winters hobbled the infirm old man. Morgan took a leisurely holiday with Goldie in Lyme Regis. And there was a new friend as well. After so many missed opportunities, he finally met Siegfried Sassoon. Sassoon was just over thirty, tall, rangy, and angular of aspect; he was famous as a war hero, and notorious for his public opposition to the war. Right off the bat he told Morgan that he was homosexual, and quickly became a confidant. They shared a common distaste for "the outward nonsense of England"—the grotesque "unbroken front of dress-shirts and golf" that remained "absolutely untouched by the war."

From this archipelago of tolerant households he always returned home. It was important to keep alert around Lily, to whom he dared make only "[a] couple of sly references to Mohammed my Egyptian friend." One morning, reading a letter from Mohammed, Morgan "broke down" at the breakfast table, and vowed thereafter to be on his guard—"very unwise as it puts me in mother's power. She is very sweet but it is unsafe to be seen in pieces."

The news from Mohammed was troubling. So was the news from Egypt generally. The British government had promised to dissolve the protectorate when the war ended in favor of some kind of self-rule for Egypt, but immediately reneged. With widespread unemployment and hunger, ordinary Egyptians began to agitate; in March 1919 hundreds of people were killed in riots in Cairo. Unrest spread into the countryside. The British answer was a crackdown. Saad Zaghloul, a prominent nationalist politician who had been selected to represent Egypt at the Versailles talks, was arrested and exiled to Malta. Rural agricultural workers were forced to work as "volunteers" on behalf of the British occupiers. Morgan wrote an impassioned letter to the *Manchester Guardian*. "The Trouble in Egypt," he argued, was a consequence of "disgraceful" and "brutal" British policies.

As Morgan feared, Mohammed had been swept up in the chaos. Still out of work, he had sold some black market goods. He was picked up by the British on a spurious charge of possessing a firearm and sentenced to six months in prison and a steep fine. One of his friends managed to get a letter through to Morgan in French—a kind of code to the monolingual censors— telling him the gist of the story. Morgan sent money to pay the fine, but the silence from Mohammed frightened him.

When Mohammed was released in the autumn, his letters were tinged with a new bitterness. The baby Morgan, always sickly, had died. And Mohammed's attitude had hardened. "I wish you was American," Mohammed wrote. "I noticed a bad habit to English during the Court Martial. The English are revengable." And corrupt. Conditions in prison were abysmal, and Mohammed found he could ameliorate them only by bribing the guards or granting coerced sexual favors. "I found in my dictionary that english [*sic*] means cruel."

To Morgan, Mohammed's treatment reflected a "cynical" and "secret" British government, which had passed draconian laws limiting civil liberties under the euphemism of the Defence of the Realm Act—known as DORA. (Lytton Strachey's friend Dora Carrington had dropped her first name in protest—thereafter signing her letters and paintings simply "Carrington.") But the populace as a whole seemed to be asleep: the newspapers were consumed with stories of film stars, and a failed transatlantic flight.

In Egypt the native population is being arrested wholesale. Similarly in India. In Russia our troops are being employed on some unknown adventure. At home prices are rising . . . our homes are full of the wreckage of four years' war . . . Do we clamour for facts, for the removal of the censorship, for the repeal of DORA? No. In Paris a handful of generals and diplomats are deciding the future of the world. Are we interested? . . . Not in the least. This planet is passing through the supreme crisis of its history. It is being decided whether we shall be

governed openly, like a free people, or secretly . . . [H]ow the cynics who
govern us secretly must have gloated . . . "There goes the mob!" they
must have thought, "just the same as ever after four years of suffering—
indifferent to truth, incapable of thought, and keen only on trifles."

Leonard Woolf urged Morgan to channel his outrage by contributing to a
white paper proposing reforms on behalf of a progressive think tank. *The
Government of Egypt*, with Morgan's pointed critiques, was published in 1921.
But protesting felt like shouting into the wind.

Just then Malcolm Darling's old friend the maharajah of Dewas renewed
his invitation for Morgan to come serve as secretary to the court of Dewas
Senior, a central Indian principality. His Highness's current secretary had
requested a leave of six months from March to October 1921. The opportunity to see the other side of India appeared with striking symmetry to Morgan: the Hindu court to balance Masood's Islamic India; the tiny maharajah,
pious and provincial, to contrast with Masood and his worldly, Anglicized
manner; the summer timetable to round out the winter months of his previous visit. It would be Morgan's first proper job, subordinate to someone else.
But the duties were rather unclear. He wrote Forrest Reid that he was "going
as Prime minister or something." Ten days before he sailed Morgan had
lunch in Berkeley Square with his old friend the Alexandrian George Antonius, now working as an aid to Faisal ibn Hussein, the newly installed king
of Iraq. The whole map of the Middle East was being redrawn after the war,
and London was abuzz with men jockeying for power. At the margin of the
gathering stood a slight blond young man with a long face and burning blue
eyes named Lawrence. Morgan was intrigued by the young man's enthusiasm
for the future of the Arab world; he dropped him a note afterward, but Lawrence did not reply.

Mohammed surprised him in the short stopover at Port Said, bribing his
way aboard; he was still unemployed, but fit and cheerful, and the two spent a
few "dream like" hours together, drinking Turkish coffee, walking along the
deserted beach to have sex at the toe of the grandiose statue of de Lesseps.
It was cold and foggy: Mohammed wore "a great coat and blue knitted gloves
with which he repeatedly clasped my hands, saying how are you, friend, how
are you." Both men felt as if they had never parted. Morgan arranged to
spend at least a month with Mohammed in Egypt on his return journey.

His Highness Tukoji Rao III—whom Morgan called Bapu Sahib—ruled a tiny state that had been forged out of a splintered Hindu empire in the eighteenth century. He was exactly nine years younger than Morgan: they auspiciously shared a birthday on January 1. He was very small, with a huge mustache, dark eyes, and an impish body, bright but mercurial in temperament, and even by the time Morgan arrived—years before he fled his palace in advance of a mob—unreliable, "deceitful and impractical" as a ruler. Morgan wrote to Florence, "I wish he used his intelligence more. It is mostly employed in the detection of intrigues. The truth is that the fundamental in him is religious, not intellectual, and that I must understand his religion better before I can understand him." But Morgan liked him. "He was a charming creature, gay, witty, affectionate, generous, and with a strong religious element in him . . . [H]e made a tragic mess of his life in the end . . . I went out to be his secretary . . . I had never been a secretary before and he did not know how to employ one. So it was a strange affair."

Morgan thought the visit might revivify his Indian novel, dormant since before the war. He had told Lily that another visit to India might help "finish it—it is stuck now because all the details of India are vague in my mind not for any other reason." But India, like Egypt, had shifted under his feet. The same British government that had seen fit to elevate Bapu Sahib from rajah to maharajah in 1919 as a way to placate the Hindu states had in the same year ordered the slaughter of unarmed religious pilgrims in a garden near Amritsar. Hundreds, perhaps thousands, were killed. Malcolm Darling had written to Morgan days afterward:

> [P]anic and cruelty—the two go together. I understand now why Germans did those terrible things in Belgium, they . . . fell blindly upon the people whom they feared. So with us . . . We did not rape and hack to pieces, but one day in Amritsar they shot down hundreds, mostly zemindars, there by religious hazard . . . I have seen the place—a death trap. 5 or 6,000 there, the kernel of them thoroughly seditious, but the majority lookers on . . . Enter infuriated general—"I took 30 seconds to make up my mind," said he to Watkin—and then—1500 rounds. God it makes me sick to think of it. Yet I was told by my chief 10 days later—"people at the Club (Lahore) say you ought to be court martialled for criticizing."

The pace of political change in India was more rapid than either Forster or Darling could have imagined a decade before. Anxieties about sedition engendered repressive new laws in India, as they had in Britain, too. The Rowlatt Act authorized the government to arrest anyone suspected of terrorism and to hold prisoners indefinitely without trial. In response an obscure lawyer named Mohandas Gandhi, who had just returned from South Africa, began to organize peaceful protests against the government. In the context of calls for self-rule the sclerotic condition of Dewas Senior pointed up the compromised and antique British ideas of Indian government. Morgan explained to Florence,

> In his social life (e.g. the abolition of Purdah) [His Highness] is most revolutionary. But in his politics, and particularly in his attitude to British India . . . he is conservativissimus, and I rejoice that the political problem is not urgent yet in Dewas . . . The attitude to the English officials . . . is much more friendly than when I was here before and at the same time more independent: the explanation being that the ruling classes, whether English or Indian, find a common menace in Gandhi.

Morgan understood that H.H. was a complicated figure, a pawn to both sides of the chess board, and pressed by political forces well beyond his control.

Nevertheless, arriving in Dewas Senior in the spring of 1921, Morgan found the court in chaos. Parts of the palace that had been under construction when he visited a decade before were already crumbling into ruin. He wrote to Lily, "You would weep at the destruction, expense and hideousness, and I almost do." The scene below his bedroom window was a case in point: in the courtyard workers ineffectually scrabbled in the dirt, five thin brown men passing a single bucket hand to hand to deposit the pile on a molehill a few yards away. "For acres around the soil is pitted with similar efforts, slabs of marble lie about, roads lead nowhere, costly fruit trees die for want of water, and I have discovered incidentally that £1000 worth (figure accurate) of electric batteries lie in a room and will spoil unless fixed promptly . . ." As he wrote this letter, Morgan watched a squirrel boldly walk up a long flight of steps, disappearing into the innards of one of the several unused grand pianos in the palace hall.

Morgan knew that His Highness disapproved of homosexuality and had dismissed a previous secretary when he was discovered to be gay, and he told himself, "The least I can do is to cause no trouble." An ill omen as he approached the palace brought on an uncanny sense of dread. "It was a dull evening at the end of March, the road was straight and rough and edged with small dreary trees and we passed a dead cow round which vultures were standing. I . . . had the definite thought 'That's how it will end.'"

Now that his body had been touched by Mohammed, Morgan's lust was unquenchable. It swelled in the "grilling heat" of midday, and masturbation— even "thrice in one afternoon"—offered no relief. Self-control was no use. As he rode in a carriage one afternoon, the mere thought that his wrist might brush the arm of the young Indian beside him made Morgan ejaculate into his trousers. The panopticon of courtyards and hallways at the palace robbed him of privacy—or so he imagined. Despite a miasma of paranoia, he began to flirt with a Hindu coolie, a slim boy of about eighteen who seemed to reciprocate his advances—the lingering touch of a finger echoed by a sensuous salaam. But surreptitious efforts to consummate his desire devolved into farce—every time the two got close, they were interrupted or discovered, and broke away from each other. Morgan began to believe that the court gossip, always feverish, was centered on his indiscretion. Sick at heart, he confessed to Bapu Sahib. "I think you know I am in great trouble," he announced miserably. But H.H. told Morgan he had heard nothing. "His voice was kind, but I wished I was dead."

Morgan recorded the conversation verbatim in a little diary. Despite his prejudice against homosexuals, the maharajah was both curious and pragmatic.

He continued gravely but without reproach. "Why a man and not a woman? Is not a woman more natural?"

"Not in my case. I have no feeling for women."

"Oh but then that alters everything. You are not to blame."

"I don't know what 'natural' is."

"You are quite right Morgan—I ought never to have used the word. Now don't worry."

His Highness reassured him, and promptly arranged to find a sexual partner from among the palace servants. For this kindness, among others, Morgan came to think of the maharajah as a "kind of saint."

Kanaya was a barber at the palace, a slender, pretty, devious boy. Shaving Morgan became the sanctioned pretext for their sexual encounters. His Highness instructed Morgan to cheerfully agree with any scurrilous rumors that he and Kanaya were having sex as the best way to dispel gossip. The boy was already "budgeted for," he reassured Morgan. The only caveat was that Morgan must do nothing that could be interpreted as sexual passivity. And so for some weeks Morgan sodomized the boy, who punctually arrived to satiate his lust. Soon Kanaya tried to parlay his secret into a bigger salary, and bragged to his friends at the court that he slept with Morgan. H.H. boxed the boy's ears.

The arrangement corrupted Morgan's soul. He discovered with some disgust that complete power over the boy made him sadistic.

> I resumed sexual intercourse with him, but it was now mixed with the desire to inflict pain. It didn't hurt him to speak of, but it was bad for me, and new in me . . . I've never had that desire with anyone else, before or after, and I wasn't trying to punish him—I knew his silly little soul was incurable. I just felt he was a slave, without rights, and I a despot whom no one could call to account.

With a clinical eye Morgan watched his own complicity in the privileges of race and caste. He came to see how his brief stint of perverse cruelty was part of the grander temptations of colonial power. He decided that he could no longer think of Searight and his colonial adventures with benign curiosity.

These reflections led Morgan to deeper questions. Was his desire for some "emotional response" from Kanaya merely a projection of Western erotic conventions? "It is difficult to find the emotion of a man whose aim it is to give pleasure to others." Was it ludicrous to ask for sincerity from a whore? How much of his own desire was just a veneer of romanticism over a cold-blooded expression of power?

On the other hand, it seemed grotesque to Morgan to deny consciousness or agency to Kanaya (or to Mohammed for that matter) just because they weren't white. In the murky world of English-colonial relations wasn't skepticism that a brown man could feel affection for him simply a different sort of bigotry? He asked Goldie, "Do 'fondness' and 'love' lead to intimacies that are different in quality? . . . When I was with M[ohammed] those 3 hours in Port Said I was overwhelmed with a feeling of safety: overwhelmed on ac-

Morgan, age three, under the protective gaze of his recently widowed mother, September 1882.
(By permission of the Provost and Scholars of King's College, Cambridge)

"I often think of my mistakes with mother. [I] did not become the authoritative male who might have quietened her and cheered her up . . . We were a classic case."

Clockwise from top left: Lily, care-worn and in mourning clothes, at age thirty-one, with Morgan, age seven (Courtesy P. N. Furbank); Morgan, about ten years old, with Lily (By permission of the Provost and Scholars of King's College, Cambridge); Lily in old age, with Morgan, still deferential, in his mid-fifties (By permission of the Provost and Scholars of King's College, Cambridge)

Rooksnest in 1885: Morgan on the pony, with his mother holding the bridle. (By permission of the Provost and Scholars of King's College, Cambridge)

West Hackhurst, the house Eddie Forster designed for his sister Laura. Morgan and Lily moved here in 1924. (By permission of the Provost and Scholars of King's College, Cambridge)

Kingsman. Morgan in his lodgings at Cambridge, c. 1900. (By permission of the Provost and Scholars of King's College. Cambridge)

Goldsworthy Lowes Dickinson as a young Fellow at King's, 1889. (By permission of the Provost and Scholars of King's College. Cambridge)

Hugh Meredith—"HOM"—at King's, May 1900. (By permission of the Provost and Scholars of King's College. Cambridge)

Nathaniel Wedd, Morgan's astute tutor. (By permission of the Provost and Scholars of King's College, Cambridge)

Edward Dent in Italy, 1903. (By permission of the Provost and Scholars of King's College, Cambridge)

Virginia and Leonard Woolf during their engagement, 1912. (Mortimer Rare Book Room, Smith College)

Malcolm Darling (left) and Morgan (right), before Darling's posting to India. (Courtesy of P. N. Furbank)

"A honeymoon slightly off colour"—Morgan and Masood in Switzerland, August 1911. (By permission of the Provost and Scholars of King's College, Cambridge)

Clockwise from top left: Florence Barger, 1917 (By permission of the Provost and Scholars of King's College, Cambridge); C. P. Cavafy in Alexandria, c. 1930 (By permission of Cavafy Archive); Edward Carpenter and George Merrill, Sheffield, 1905 (By permission of Sheffield Archives & Local Studies Library)

Mohammed el Adl wearing Forster's khaki uniform. (By permission of the Provost and Scholars of King's College. Cambridge)

The tram ticket from their first meeting, pasted on the back of a photo of Mohammed (By permission of the Provost and Scholars of King's College, Cambridge)

Morgan's snapshot of soldiers swimming at Montazah. 1917. "Down by the sea many of them spend half their days naked and unrebuked . . . It is so beautiful that I cannot believe it has not been planned." (By permission of the Provost and Scholars of King's College. Cambridge)

Secretary to the maharajah of Dewas in full official robes, 1921. (By permission of the Provost and Scholars of King's College, Cambridge)

Bapu's family, 1910. The maharajah of Dewas is at right. (By permission of the Provost and Scholars of King's College, Cambridge)

Josie Darling peering from a window of the Dewas Palace guesthouse, Christmas 1912. (By permission of the Provost and Scholars of King's College, Cambridge)

The maharajah of Chhatarpur, 1912. (By permission of the Provost and Scholars of King's College, Cambridge)

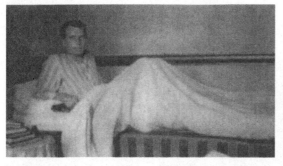

J. R. "Joe" Ackerley in bed in Hammersmith. Taken by
Harry Daley in the 1920s. (Courtesy of P. N. Furbank)

Harry Daley in uniform with a friend from the Hammersmith Public Baths. (Courtesy of P. N. Furbank)

Right, top to bottom: Morgan's photo of the Weybridge bus
driver Reg Palmer (By permission of the Provost and Scholars of
King's College, Cambridge); W.J.H. "Sebastian" Sprott, 1920s
(Courtesy Patrick Belshaw); Charles Lovett, 1930s (Courtesy of
Patrick Belshaw)

Boat-race day near Joe Ackerley's Hammersmith flat. Front row, from second from left: Masood's son Anwar, Tom Wichelo, Mrs. Ackerley with dog, General L.E.O. Charlton, Akbar Masood, Joe Ackerley, and Morgan.

R. J. "Bob" Buckingham, Morgan (in a cloth cap), and Joe Ackerley on the promenade in Dover, 1930s. (By permission of the Provost and Scholars of King's College, Cambridge)

Right, top to bottom: Bob Buckingham, 1935 (By permission of the Provost and Scholars of King's College, Cambridge); May Buckingham in her nurse's uniform, 1929 (Courtesy of the Buckingham family); William Plomer (Private Collection)

HOM and Morgan, photographed the week after Mohammed's death in 1922. (Courtesy of P. N. Furbank)

T. E. Lawrence, 1928. (By permission of the National Portrait Gallery, London)

Christopher Isherwood. Morgan. and two German friends in Brussels, 1937. (Huntington Library)

Morgan and Bob Buckingham, c. 1934. Their first domestic portrait, taken by the Spender-Edmiston studio. (By permission of the Provost and Scholars of King's College, Cambridge)

Paul Cadmus—painting a nude Forster in *What I Believe*—with Jerry French and George Tooker in the background, at St. Luke's Place, 1948. (Archives of American Art, Washington D.C.; copyright the Estate of George Platt Lynes)

May Buckingham, Morgan, Joe Ackerley, and Robin Buckingham (facing away from the camera) in London, 1949. (By permission of the Provost and Scholars of King's College, Cambridge)

Morgan and Mattei Radev, c. 1965. (Copyright the Estate of Frances Partridge. By permission of the Provost and Scholars of King's College, Cambridge.)

Aldeburgh, October 1949: Morgan and Benjamin Britten composing *Billy Budd*. (Collection Hutton Archive, Kurt Hutton/Getty Images)

Morgan in his rooms at King's, Christmas 1949. He amended Edith Oliver's card to read "Love." (Courtesy of the Estate of Edith Oliver, née Goldsmith. By permission of the Provost and Scholars of King's College, Cambridge.)

Opposite: The George Platt Lynes session, New York, June 1949. (Photo top left courtesy of Beinecke Rare Book and Manuscript Library, Yale University; photo top right by permission of the Provost and Scholars of King's College, Cambridge; photo below courtesy of P. N. Furbank)

Top to bottom: Morgan, age ninety, in Keynes's rooms at King's. In the forecourt of King's, March 1970. The last photograph of E. M. Forster: Morgan makes his way across the King's lawn. Taken from Goldie's rooms in the Gibbs Building. (Photos courtesy of Mark Lancaster)

count of the route, but the *feeling* was identical with what I experience when I am with Florence or you . . ." But in India he couldn't gauge intimacy. It was a hall of mirrors.

Morgan concluded that he was ill-equipped to interpret the sexual lexicon of this strange world. Sexual attitudes at court seemed prudish, but the religious festivals were chock-full of erotic play. During the holiday of Holi, "the Hindu Dionysia," Morgan watched a troupe of male dancers enact some sort of sexual farce featuring a married couple. He wrote to Goldie,

> I was struck with the remoteness of their sexual gestures: in most cases I didn't know what was up. One "girl" lay on her face and extending her hands before her clasped and unclasped them alternately. This indicated the act of copulation. "If it had really been a girl" said H.H. "it wouldn't have done, it would have been too much. But they have a boy which makes it all right." I wonder! All very odd. I shall never feel the surety in these matters here that I felt in Egypt. The sphere of "naughtiness" seems wider, and perhaps this it is that makes it faintly distasteful to me.

A visit to Chhatarpur a few weeks later compounded his bafflement. The maharajah of Chhatarpur, a grotesque little man whose face folded in on itself like a Pekinese dog, had long indulged his passion for beautiful boys by keeping a retinue of actors and singers who, wearing only loincloths, put on skits of the life of Krishna for his daily pleasure. Ten years before, he had hired dozens of them to embody Krishna in all his lovely forms—but the religious cast to his sexual sublimation had consumed much of the court's budget, and as a consequence of British-imposed thriftiness he was down to a single Krishna boy as an attendant. In a flourish of generosity, he offered the boy as a suitor, arranging a serenade in a romantic tableau. Young Krishna was "intelligent and forthcoming, but the face is sensual and melancholy and probably cruel. I hear his acting and singing were not good, but he must have looked striking, and when we got back he played quite sweetly to me on a flute."

That night Krishna came to Morgan on a white horse, riding bareback in the blue moonlight, his long black hair streaming down his back. He was strikingly glamorous, wearing enormous diamond stud earrings, and singing a strange tuneless song. It was a remarkable sight. But the next morning the romance was dispelled. The boy, it seemed, had overplayed the part. He was not authorized to wear the earrings, Morgan was told. He was not supposed to ride the horse.

> Today . . . began exquisitely with K in diamond earrings and upon a horse that he could not ride. We taught each other English and Hindustani for a couple of hours. He was friendly and simple, and only 4 servants were watching us, which is solitude in India . . . [He] is to be punished for calling on me with a horse and earrings. He was told to walk quietly up, avoiding ostentation, because as soon as there is talk he may have to go and with him will depart my last channel for visions of the Deity.

The next day, crammed into the backseat of a motorcar with the maharajah of Chhatarpur and the Krishna boy, Morgan sought to explain himself. They were traveling to see the erotic sculptures on the temples of Khajuraho. As they bumped along the rutted road, Morgan leaned "across the slender sphinx who sat wedged between us" to confide in his benefactor. "I want him to keep house for me like George Merrill," he told the maharajah with heartfelt sincerity. His Highness was puzzled. He asked Morgan, "What is to keep house?"

Out of these muddles—Comic? Tragic? Pathetic?—Morgan would embroider the rich tapestry of his final novel. Morgan's careful observation of his own erotic conundrum pointed out how impossible it was for him to understand India through the lens of his cultural assumptions, however well-meaning. In *A Passage to India* yearning for connection became indistinguishable from desire as Morgan sketched out the friendship between Dr. Aziz and his English friend Cyril Fielding. Riding side by side at the end of the novel, furious, "half-kissing," Fielding asks Aziz, "Why can't we be friends now? . . . It's what I want. It's what you want."

> But the horses didn't want it—they swerved apart; the earth didn't want it, sending up rocks through which riders must pass single-file; the temples, the tank, the jail, the palace, the birds, the carrion, the Guest House, that came into view as they issued from the gap and saw the Mau beneath: they didn't want it, they said in their hundred voices: "No, not yet," and the sky said: "No, not there."

It was bootless to ask what was "natural" in this tragic, muddled world.

. . .

Well before his term was up, Morgan began to suspect that the Dewas court finances were impossibly in arrears. In August he asked to forgo his salary. He had tried to be effective at representing Bapu Sahib, lending some order to the management of accounts, but it was like pouring water through a sieve. Ruefully, he left the court early. He spent his final ten weeks in India sightseeing near Hyderabad with Masood. Morgan was happy to see him married, and they seamlessly renewed their friendship. They spent a glorious New Year's birthday together, garlanded with flowers and eating sweetmeats. On January 23, 1922, the ship arrived at Port Said, but instead of Mohammed's sweet face, there was a shock. Morgan learned from a messenger that "Mohammed collapsed under consumption about a fortnight before I landed," and was lying mortally ill in his house at Mansourah.

Morgan rushed to be at his lover's side. He took Mohammed to Cairo to be examined by the leading medical specialist, who confirmed that the young man had at best weeks to live. It was "an unhappy time for me in the local daily sense," Morgan told Florence, because Mohammed was irritable and in pain. But the "central truth" of this fatal moment distilled into a calm, pure sensation on both sides—a mixture of awe, gratitude, and love. Morgan was "thankful to be on the spot," and to have the money to make Mohammed and his family comfortable.

Morgan and Mohammed's extended family—Gamila, their baby daughter, hangers-on—repaired to the Nile resort of Helouan. Mohammed rallied enough to take some short expeditions on camelback to see the ruins at Wadi Hof. Morgan nursed him through "all the traditional symptoms, haemorrhage, night-sweats, exhaustion" lovingly, but without hope. Lying awake on a cot beside Mohammed's bed, Morgan drank in the image of Mohammed's thin face. By day he read proofs of his guide to Alexandria, gently shooing flies off Mohammed as he dozed. The dying man was in strangely "radiant spirits . . . charming and talkative . . . a jolly companion." Encircling his lover with good wishes from around the globe, Morgan urged both Masood and Florence to write to Mohammed, which they did.

Mohammed was well enough to come to Cairo to see Morgan off on the day. I trust that the end will come without suffering poor dear little fellow. His face is unchanged. In the house he wears a yellow velvet cap, shaped rather like Goldie's, and folds his body up as only an Oriental can, so that the intelligent beautiful head seems to be resting on a pyramid of clothes. Ah me—but everything is bearable, it is the betrayal from within that wears away one's soul and I have been spared that.

Morgan climbed aboard ship for London knowing he would never see Mohammed alive again.

A month later, in March 1922, Virginia Woolf was shocked at the sight of Morgan when she encountered him on the street in London. He seemed to her

depressed to the verge of inanition. To come back to Weybridge, to come back to an ugly house a mile from the station, an old, fussy exacting mother, to come back having lost your Rajah, without a novel, & with no power to write one—this is dismal, I expect, at the age of 43. The middle age of buggers is not to be contemplated without horror.

She was wrong about the object of Morgan's affection, but correct in assessing his state of mind. Leonard, ever practical, invited him to dinner, and urged a resumption of work on the Indian novel; work had always been their solace when Virginia was ill. Goldie, too, urged him forward.

Days later, impulsively, Morgan burned all his homosexual stories. It was not so much that he was ashamed of them, but he felt they were the equivalent of masturbation, written "to excite myself." Keeping them around "clogged me artistically." When he had begun writing them fifteen years before he was convinced that he was "doing something positively dangerous to my career as a novelist." Now they seemed tame, inconsequential, "[t]he wrong channel for my pen."

Mohammed's last letters came to Harnham, where Morgan read them secretly at his little desk under the eaves.

dear Morgan
    I am sending you the photograph
    I am very bad
    I got nothing more to say

the family are good. My compliments to mother.

My love to you

My love to you

My love to you

Do not forget your ever friend

Moh el Adl

By the time Morgan received this letter in early May 1922, Mohammed was already gone.

In the little notebook Morgan began to write back to his dead lover, "although I know that a putrid scrap in the Mansourah burial ground is all that was you." If he was not to forget his "ever friend" it seemed an urgent necessity to examine their love affair clearly and dispassionately, to record all that could be known about Mohammed. So much was at stake. "One slip of my mind would make a spook of you." But fighting sentimentality opened Morgan to dark thoughts. He was tortured by the possibility that "determined my life should contain one success I have concealed from myself and others M's frequent coldness towards me   And his occasional warmth may be due to politeness, gratitude, or pity." One thing he knew to be true. In *Howards End*, Morgan had summarized his philosophy: "Death destroys a man; the idea of Death saves him." The sweet paradox—death erases everything; but without death nothing has meaning—had been written in innocence, before the sting of death had really touched him. Mohammed was rotting, of this Morgan was certain. There would be no reunion with his lover in heaven. But Morgan must simply trust the words—"My love to you / My love to you / My love to you."

But the utter erasure of Mohammed and his line—the surviving child was a *girl*, and didn't count—made the whole question too poignant and final. It was as if in dying Mohammed had dragged Morgan into the shroud with him.

The *mater* is a misfortune for me as well as a grief for at my age I need someone of another generation to speed me up and direct me from the pottering-kindness which is naturally required of my life. I cannot think what he and I together might not have developed into. The end is so final. If his boy had lived there would have been that possibility, but I have no inclination to grapple with a female Oriental infant.

When Morgan took up the Indian manuscript again in the autumn of 1922, the whole process of revision was suffused with this sense of loss. The epigraph of *Howards End*—"only connect!"—now seemed hopelessly naïve to him. He told Masood, "When I began the book I thought of it as a little bridge of sympathy between East and West, but this conception has had to go, my sense of truth forbids anything so comfortable. I think that most Indians, like most English people, are shits, and I am not interested whether they sympathize with one another or not." But somehow he managed to rescue his new writing from simple despair and misanthropy. His "sense of truth" forbade it.

The final draft of *A Passage to India* was darker and more complex than the first few chapters he had written and set aside in 1913. The novel would remain a meditation on the limitations of human connection, but in a bold and honest decision, he chose to succumb to India's incomprehensibility. He abandoned omniscience, and emptied out the plot until key elements of the original story became deliberately unknowable. The early drafts of the novel were shaped as a straightforward courtroom melodrama. Adela Quested was sexually accosted in the caves, and Dr. Aziz was the culprit. But in revision the plotline became deliberately murky. At the moment of the attack, Morgan shifted the narrative perspective to follow Aziz into a nearby cave as he smokes a cigarette. What happens cannot be known, but the reader effectively affirms Aziz's alibi. At the rape trial Adela bravely admits that she does not know who assaulted her, or even if she was assaulted at all.

Adela's moral courage permits a just verdict for Aziz, but Morgan refused to tip the scales of his novel toward benevolence. The same terrifying unknowability that faced Adela in the Marabar Caves affects the serene Mrs. Moore during her visit there: she enters as a tourist, but leaves as a broken woman. The experience of hearing the echo in the cave unravels her psychologically. Her Christian faith disappears because in the darkness all words—from "Let there be Light" to "It is finished"—carry no meaning. She concludes nihilistically, "Pathos, piety, courage—they exist but are identical, and so is filth. Everything exists, nothing has value."

All through 1923 Morgan worked on his last novel. He planned to dedicate it to Masood, "the only person to whom I can open my heart and feel occasionally that I am understood." The only *living* person. By day, he walked alone and thought of Mohammed; by night, he continued his long letter to his dead friend.

. . .

In May 1924, after a final illness that unhinged her mentally, Morgan's aunt Laura Forster died at the age of eighty-five. She had lived at West Hackhurst since her younger brother first designed the rambling brick house, and she willed the remainder of her tenancy lease to Lily and Morgan. Though he was always to feel like a nephew at the Abinger house, though "he never possessed it," in a very real sense this invitation was a kind of homecoming for Morgan. With its six bedrooms and its two great chimneys, its north and south verandas, its gables and stables and large rose garden, the house limned Eddie's aesthetic, and it was the only commission he completed in his short life. It was also a bit of a fossil in 1924. "There was . . . no gas, no electric light, no central heating, no hot water supply or baths. The drinking water is pumped from a well and carried to the kitchen in buckets," heated on coal stoves by Agnes, and, if one wanted to bathe, carried upstairs in copper kettles. Morgan had known the house intimately since he was born; he visited Aunt Laura faithfully twice every year. But it would never be Rooksnest; it was not quite *home*.

Faced with a move she had long wished for, Lily dithered. Should she move to Abinger, or keep the house in Weybridge? West Hackhurst was well in the country—a long walk up rutted lanes from the little station at Gomshall near Dorking. Unable to make up her mind, Lily extended the lease on Harnham for a time, keeping two houses. In fact, three. After going back and forth in her mind, Lily began the arduous process of moving her belongings to Abinger. Morgan decided it was the moment to take rooms in London—after all, West Hackhurst was considerably farther afield than Weybridge—and he carved out a little freedom in a pied-à-terre in Brunswick Square, close to his Bloomsbury friends. It was a strange feeling, becoming a country squire in middle age. Leaving London for Abinger one day, Morgan told Carrington wryly, "I have to visit my estates."

Alongside the work on *A Passage to India*, Morgan began to compile his Egyptian essays into a collection. Virginia and Leonard Woolf promised to publish it. *Pharos and Pharillon* was conceived as a tribute to Mohammed, but when the time came to dedicate the volume, Morgan could not summon the courage to put down his lover's name. He wrote to Florence, one of Mohammed's cherished circle of friends, to ask her help:

The Hogarth Press are bringing out some of my Alexandrian things
this winter. It should be a nice little book. I have dedicated it
"To————" because I wished my next book to be Mohammed's whatever his relation to me, but now I do not like the dedication. All his
life I hushed him up and I feel I ought to put his name in full. Yet I
don't want questions from outsiders as to who Mohammed is. Have you
any advice, or rather sentiment, on the matter? I could allude to him by
some literary paraphrase, but I hate such. Though it occurs to me—
two words in Greek—that fit both book and him extraordinarily well.

In the end he inscribed it in Greek "to Hermes, leader of souls," a cryptic
allusion to the friend who had led him from sexual ignorance into the new
world. He told Florence that Mohammed had inspired something else—a
new and serious homosexual short story.

I have just written a short story which is his in another sense, though
I did not realise that when I started. It is violent and wholly unpublishable, and I do not know whether it is good . . . The characters are
a missionary and a young chief of the vague South Seas, who he con-
verts and does inasfar as this world is concerned; in the next world
the situation is reversed.

The story, published posthumously, he called "The Life to Come." As he was
with the *Maurice* manuscript, Morgan was chary with this new homosexual
fiction. "I may show it to Goldie, but there is more sensuality in my composition than in his, and it might distress him." For the time being, only Florence
and Sassoon were trusted to see it.

Sassoon traded him, contraband for contraband. He lent Morgan his copy
of a new book, very hush-hush and privately printed, by a young man detail-
ing his extraordinary adventures among the Bedouin during the war. Morgan
realized he had met the author, the "fair-haired boy" from the luncheon with
Antonius! *The Seven Pillars of Wisdom* was a revelation—"exactly what I
want," he told Sassoon. His excitement over reading it lit a creative fire—
under the spell of the beautiful Arab memoir, Morgan hurriedly finished
writing the final chapters of *A Passage to India*.

When Morgan met him for the second time in the winter of 1923, T. E.
Lawrence had not yet been transformed into the legendary "Lawrence of

Arabia." (The publication of *The Seven Pillars of Wisdom* would see to that.) Though he was only thirty-five, Lawrence had already compiled a huge, restless résumé—as an archaeologist, linguist, scholar, diplomat, and soldier-adventurer. He was tiny—a few inches over five feet tall—and reed-thin; from across a room he looked like a luminous boy. Lawrence had been studiously trying to shake off any notion of grandeur, resigning from the colonial office and attempting to enlist in the Royal Air Force under an assumed name. But he had been found out and discharged.

Morgan wrote Lawrence an effusive letter, with sharply detailed suggestions for revising the manuscript of *The Seven Pillars*. Lawrence replied quickly this time, honored to be approached by a writer "among the elect. I feel giddy at the idea of you taking the trouble." He was just discharged from the service, and had bought a tiny cottage in Dorset, no more than a shell really, which he romantically christened Clouds Hill. It was near the army base, so he could frequent the local pub with his buddies; Clouds Hill was so cramped that Morgan put up at the Black Bear. The visit seemed promising: Lawrence was attracted to Morgan by something like hero worship, Morgan to Lawrence by something like lust. On his return to London, Morgan performed the next step in his familiar dance toward intimacy, offering up "The Life to Come" while warning Lawrence of its "unpublishable" content. The young man was excited to be invited into Morgan's confidence. "I'd very much like to see the unpublishable stuff, any of it you feel able to show me. It shall be safely kept, and quickly returned," Lawrence promised him, adding reassuringly, "'Unpublishable' is a relative, even passing, qualification. *The Seven Pillars* earned it two or three years ago: and have lost it in that little time."

Then, a month's silence. Then Lawrence wrote disconcertingly to tell Morgan that it was "one of the funniest things I'd ever come across." He "laughed and laughed" at the story of lust and murder. Morgan replied, clearly taken aback, but game. He told Lawrence that his reaction made him laugh in response. "I am glad you wrote," he wrote Lawrence, "as I had assumed you were disgusted and was sorry though I knew in such a contretemps neither the disgusted nor the disgusting party would be the least to blame." So the friendship rested delicately, for the moment. As a billet-doux the story was a flop. Lawrence was immensely attractive, but he was also very *strange*.

● ● ●

Leonard Woolf had become a stalwart supporter, urging Morgan to forge on with the Indian novel. So, in late January 1924 Leonard and Virginia were the first to hear that "I've put the last words to my novel." Morgan was pleased and moved, but he knew in some obscure way that it was the end of an era for him. He had a revealing conversation with Virginia about their shared craft, which she recorded in her diary: "Talking of Proust & [D. H.] Lawrence he said he would prefer to be Lawrence; but much rather would be himself. We discussed his novels. I don't think I am a novelist, he said. Suddenly I said 'No, I don't think you are.' Ah! He exclaimed eagerly, interested, and not dashed." Virginia was onto something, but she was not in a position to understand fully why Morgan seemed so serene in response to her perception. She thought that Morgan meant to fall back on a career as a journalist and reviewer. But Morgan had not shared his homosexual fiction with her—she was not privy to the *Maurice* manuscript, did not know how rapidly and avidly he was writing new short stories: "Dr. Woolacott," a psychological tale of a soldier haunted by his lover, killed in the war, or "The Obelisk," a ribald fantasy of seduction.

Morgan's choice of literary models was telling in ways she could not wholly understand. Proust, the master of memory and despair, had indeed been an inspiration as Morgan finished *A Passage to India* and as he mourned Mohammed. Virginia was making a similar assumption to the one D. H. Lawrence had made about Morgan. It was true that her mousy friend, at least on the surface, seemed a writer more in the mold of the moody Proust than the irascible D. H. Lawrence. But a notation in Morgan's diary a decade later illuminates the exchange with Woolf. He had been talking with her about *sex*—

> In the best love making I have known there has been a sort of laughter and the most violent embrace gets softened by it. That's to say my problem as a writer hasn't been as awful as some's. It is these lower class youths, rather than any special antic with them, that has bothered me. [N.B. I have never tried to turn a man into a girl, as Proust did with Albertine, for this seemed derogatory to me as a writer.]

In his conversation with Virginia, Morgan exclaimed "Ah!" because she had helped him to make a discovery about the literary identity he would pursue for the rest of his life, the problem he had understood, in an inchoate way, when he had written, in 1919, "I don't see what [my path] is clearly yet, but I know what keeps me from it." His path would be not so much one of renunciation as one of literary bifurcation. He would continue to write, as D. H. Lawrence had done, honestly and fiercely, but he would accept that much of this writing would forever—or at least until the "happier year" he had imagined in *Maurice*—remain "unpublishable." He told Virginia that day, "I am not at all downcast about my literary career," because he had radically reimagined its terms.

Only Morgan knew that *A Passage to India* would be his valedictory. He dedicated it to "Syed Ross Masood and to the seventeen years of our friendship." Reviewers welcomed his novel as a "great book," but they saw it as a return to the stage after a long silence rather than a swan song. In India and in England the novel was recognized as something greater and deeper than a work in the universally admired vein of Forster-the-sensitive-novelist. It was a masterpiece. In a bemused, slightly uneasy mood Morgan watched his "good luck" pile up as the novel took hold in the public consciousness, winning the James Tait Black Award for fiction, and becoming a bestseller. The gush of royalties and his inheritance from Aunt Laura suddenly made him a rich man.

The day after he turned forty-six, Morgan soberly took inventory:

Famous wealthy, miserable, physically ugly—red nose enormous, round patch in middle of scalp which I forget less than I did and which is brown when I don't wash my head and pink when I do. Face in the distance—mirrors of Reform Club—is toad-like and pallid, with a tiny rim of hair at the top of the triangle. My stoop must be appalling. [I] am surprised I don't repel more generally: I can still get to know anyone I want and have that illusion that I am charming and beautiful . . . Stomach increases, but not yet visible under waistcoat. The anus is clotted with hairs, and there is a great loss of sexual power—it was very violent 1921–22. Eyes and probably hearing weaker.

9

"Toms and Dicks"

As Mohammed was dying, Morgan happened upon an elegy in a magazine called the *London Mercury*. The poem's premise was commonplace enough four years after the war—a man in mourning, poring over a bundle of letters from a dead friend. But its diction startled him because it echoed word-for-word phrases from his secret letter to Mohammed, and his lover's final letters:

> *Seeking my dead*
>
> *Hearing him yet*
> *Saying "Good-bye!"*
> *Hearing his sigh,*
> *Murmured so low,*
> *"Ah, but I know . . .*
> *You will forget."*

Reading "Ghosts" evoked an uncanny sensation of déjà vu, "the horror, beauty, depth, emotional and mental insecurity" of being in thrall to longing and loss. Impulsively, Morgan wrote a letter of praise to the young poet. J. R. Ackerley was only twenty-five. The poem was his first published writing, and he was flattered to hear from a celebrated author. Ackerley preserved the letter as a treasure—as he did every one of the nearly eleven hundred more Morgan would write him over the next fifty years. Thus a spontaneous gesture of encouragement began a deep friendship between two men a generation apart.

Like many survivors of the First War. Ackerley in his mid-twenties was both older and younger than his age. He had left Cambridge to become an officer in the trenches of France, where his only brother had been "decapitated" by a "whiz-bang" in the final months of the war. Twice wounded, captured by the Germans, Ackerley was transported from camp to camp as a prisoner of war, and eventually interned with other British prisoners at Hotel des Alpes in Switzerland, "guilty and frustrated" at being held in such luxurious conditions. There he fell in love with a young officer dying of tuberculosis. After the war he returned to London with a cold heart and no patience at all for the fustiness and cant of the generation that had sent him to war. Pleasing himself, which had always been his inclination during his indulged childhood, now became a badge of honor and a personal rebellion. Joe Ackerley was unapologetically homosexual, and determinedly promiscuous. He was tall and rangy, and strikingly handsome—with chiseled cheekbones, a sharp strong nose, brown hair. and icy blue eyes. He honed his seductive charm. Sure only of his fierce intelligence. wit, and love of literature, he wandered about from country to country and bed to bed. spending his father's ample allowance and *finding himself*.

Morgan's first impression of the young man was that he had an undeveloped heart. "I don't quite like A. though he has intelligence and charm. I suspect him of cruelty, but perhaps it's merely because I suspect all young men. I have no friend under thirty now." But being with Joe made Morgan feel less antediluvian. They never slept together, but they became fast friends. Morgan fell into an avuncular role with Joe, making suggestions on what he should read. and chastising him for his romantic scrapes. In turn, the young man, though hapless in his own love life, served as an unjudging and experienced confidant on sexual matters. Morgan sculpted his young protégé into Pygmalion. brokering a position for him as secretary to the maharajah of Chhatarpur. Joe wrote *Hindoo Holiday*—a hilarious account of his five months there—but he was far less appreciative of Indian mysticism and Indian muddles than his mentor had been, and soon he was back in London, driving around in a green MG with the top down, seducing guardsmen and yearning for the Ideal Friend. His list of qualities for this imagined person—which he later catalogued in his autobiography, *My Father and Myself*, as if he were ordering up a dish at a restaurant—was exacting enough to preclude most ordinary mortals: the man had to be loyal, physically attractive, circumcised, younger than Ackerley, healthy, no bad breath. And rather more improbably, he had to be *heterosexual*.

Just when *A Passage to India* came out in the summer of 1924, a second, quite corporeal, ghost appeared unexpectedly. Of all places, it chose to haunt Weybridge. Walking back from the railway station to Harnham one day as he shuttled between West Hackhurst and Weybridge, Morgan was shocked to see Mohammed driving a taxicab. Or rather a man with the same wide face, the same delicious color of skin, the same bemused expression, the same casual attitude as his forearms rested on the steering wheel. The young man disappeared for some weeks, and Morgan almost believed that he had been a ghost. Then he reappeared, this time driving the station bus. "It was like a return from the dead, and upset me," Morgan wrote in his diary.

The event unsettled the sense of resignation he had so carefully cultivated since Mohammed's death. He had resolved, "No personal relationships— you bring too little and are too old." Days before the ghost appeared, Morgan had caught a glimpse of "a man of my own age & class watching rough across the river at Shepperton" and thought with disgust, "I am like that." But did his disgust stem from "envy or shame?" he wondered. Now, very cautiously, he allowed his hopes to reawaken. Morgan began a flirtation with the driver, who lived with his wife and child in a flat carved out of a large, derelict house in the fields just behind Harnham.

With the tutelage and encouragement of Joe Ackerley, Morgan plotted how to test the boundaries of the driver's affection. Affable but cagey, the man went through several pseudonyms before Morgan found out his real name, Reg Palmer. Reg was of mixed race—"some black blood," Morgan noted in his diary; he had a mashed boxer's nose and stood stocky and strong. The men exchanged cigarettes each time they met—thank heavens Morgan had learned how to smoke since he met the shepherd boy!—and soon Reg "asked me rather shyly whether I'd care to come round to his place one evening and 'have a crack.'" This auspicious phrase turned out to mean having a meal with Reg's wife and toddler. Morgan adopted an amused tone in explaining the situation to Florence.

> She was a very nice woman—better educated than he—and we all had
> biscuits and coffee, and I nursed the cat. The man is not intelligent

and rather rough, and I don't think anything important will come from it. But he is perfectly straight—a simple response to friendship—so I mean to go on. I told mother about it (in passing), for now I must ask him here, and I had to get her leave. She thinks he hasn't placed me socially, and will collapse when he sees the splendours of Harnham. I'm not sure. I must arrange that Agnes doesn't open the door to him, however!

Reg shared Morgan's pleasure in conspiring against the women—both Lily and Reg's wife, Bess. The pretext for visiting Harnham would be to obtain "French lessons"—"he learned some strange sounds in France which it pleases him to repeat." Reg showed up for his first lesson bearing the gift of a photograph. Lily, who "didn't trust his face," commented acidly, "How like the lower classes to have given you his photograph as a first call. They always think one in love with them after the slightest civility."

Reg came by Harnham several times to move carpets and heavier furniture as the Forsters prepared to debark permanently to Aunt Laura's house. Morgan decided to be practical: "I had better have such adventures while I can, for there will be no place for them in the pseudo-feudalism of West Hackhurst." The two men creatively found ways to be alone together. In January 1925 they made love in the half-empty parlor of Harnham while Lily was at West Hackhurst unpacking the china—"a queer ending to my almost 20 years sojourn in this suburb."

Reg told Morgan that he had never had sex with a man before, but he was quite keen and confident as a lover: "The visit was sticky, but friendly and physically superb." Considering the evidence, Morgan concluded that his new friend was a habitual but harmless dissembler, whose lies were "mere social behaving." In July, Morgan felt "nearly off my head for happiness" from an extended sexual romp, made more delightful since it played out like a Feydeau farce—the window cleaners arriving at the front door at just the moment when the two men tiptoed out the back. Morgan composed a picaresque for Joe all in French—"Madame n'est pas sans soupçons"—before breaking off, "Oh Joe—it is like before—I want to die, but then it was only 10 minutes happiness, and today it was 9 hours." It would have been longer, but Bess was about to go into labor with her second child.

Decades later, Morgan's friend Eudora Welty admiringly reviewed his posthumously published gay fiction. But she added one telling caveat: "when the women went out of his stories, they took the comedy with them." The same could be said for the tone of the personal relationships Morgan developed in his late forties, after he met Joe Ackerley. Under Joe's tutelage, Morgan explored gay London—places beyond the "tatty pubs in Soho . . . dull clubs frequented by elderly queers" and "dark and smelly urinals"—and by entering this completely male secretive world, he developed a taste for categorical misogyny that would have been unthinkable to him in previous years.

Like many young homosexuals of his generation, Joe Ackerley defined his homosexuality by opposition to everything feminine. Contempt for women was a badge of honor. This attitude amplified Morgan's latent profound misgivings about female power. He broadened his personal resentment of Lily and Bess into a worldview, writing in his "Commonplace Book,"

> *Women have got out of hand* . . . Twenty years ago I thought "It's unpleasing to me but it won't go further" and spoke with false enthusiasm of women's rights. She shall have all she wants, I can still get away from her, I thought. I grudged her nothing except my company. But it has gone further . . . This, I begin to see, is sex-war, and D. H. L. has seen it . . . and is far more on the facts than Bernard Shaw and his Life Force.

The temptation to play up the drama of his encounters with Reg to a virulently misogynist audience of friends may have encouraged Morgan to exaggerate their antic tone at the expense of the women at the margins of his tales. But it is disquieting to hear Morgan record with such heartlessness Bess's complaint to her husband as he leaves once more for a day to roll in the hay with his new friend:

> I have just discovered the trouble over [Reg]. Bess won't let him come . . . Then today—I left Cambridge early for the purpose—I asked if I might come and see him; when I got round, Bess was in the dark and a temper . . . He said "she's a bit nervous—she don't like to be left"—no doubt true: and she said crossly "I see nothing of you all the day." So I retired, defeated I suppose.

Morgan had been in Cambridge for an Apostles meeting. He discovered after a long drought that his old Cambridge connections could also provide a wellspring of young friends. Chief among them was Sebastian Sprott. The name, like the young man himself, was a creation: he had been born Walter John Herbert Sprott in a resolutely middle-class family from a suburb of Birmingham, but decided early on that his affections were with the proletariat, and once at Cambridge, chose to go by the simple name Jack. But Jack Sprott was ridiculous, his King's friends insisted, too near "Jack Spratt" for comfort. A loud and sustained debate took place while Walter-John Herbert Jack listened, when Dent (then a Fellow of King's) appeared in Sprott's rooms, carrying a large sheaf of music by J. S. Bach. *Sebastian!* his friends suddenly proclaimed. Sebastian would be a mellifluous name! And he agreeably adopted it for a decade or so, gradually reverting simply to Jack.

Sprott was bright and emotionally acute—at university he studied social psychology—but he applied these virtues elliptically: he demanded to be adopted by someone and then molded to a frame. Maynard Keynes had sponsored him for the Apostles, and taken him to bed. Sebastian fell deeply in love; he accompanied Keynes on a journey to South Africa and was paid to index his book, but Carrington thought his real job title should be "attendant slave." He tutored Vanessa Bell's children for a time. Hovering around the alluring margin of the Bloomsbury circle, hungry for culture and just plain hungry, Sprott spent what little money he had on books and clothes. He was a bit of a dandy, with a special eye for odd colors, notable scarves, and a crisp hat. He came across as an exquisite—with fluttering hands, his "voice shooting up and down the scale or suddenly pouncing on some selected word." But he would lend his last penny, and often did, to anyone more hard up than himself. He was forever adopting strays from a raffish collection of young toughs and crooks in and out of prison whom he befriended easily and without judgment. When Sprott answered the phone, he could be overheard saying with infinite compassion, "I *knew* you were to be released this afternoon."

Sprott took up a position as a lecturer in psychology at the University of Nottingham—"a dreary nowhere at the apex of a pyramid whose basis is Blackpool and Wigan"—moving into a huge, damp, rickety row house in the deepest slums of the city. In his first months there he picked up an affable working-class man in a public toilet. Charles Lovett followed Sebastian home and never left. Lovett was a doughy, sweet, tractable, moon-faced young man, abject in his adoration for Sprott. He lived with Sprott for decades, happily cooking and cleaning for him, a patient witness to countless comings and goings, always waiting for Sebastian's latest affair to burn out.

After moving out of his parents' baronial mansion in Richmond, Joe Ackerley had discovered the ideal neighborhood in London to meet Lovett's sort of jaunty young men, unemployed and spending most of their time in petty larceny and booking small bets, the kind of honest crooks who knew how to keep their heads just above water, knew when to push off, and knew how to have a good time. Unlike the handsome Guardsmen for whom casual prostitution was a lucrative sideline, these men were happy to go to bed in exchange for a meal and comradeship. Some of them had girlfriends or wives to whom they went home.

Joe rented a set of rooms at the top of a once-elegant Georgian townhouse at 6 Hammersmith Terrace, which backed straight onto the muddy bank of the Thames. The actor John Gielgud recalled the décor as an admixture of Spartan and camp: "a statue of a Greek youth, a large bunch of bananas on the dining table, and a rather anonymous young disciple ironing shirts in the kitchen." The house had a spectacular view of Chiswick Eyot at the bend in the river, and served as an ideal vantage point to observe the annual Oxford-Cambridge boat races. Joe was given access to the large terrace on the riverbank by his landlords, an eccentric trio of ancient siblings who had inherited the house. The eldest, an old queen, wearing a dressing gown barely tied, peered up the staircase eagerly when Joe and his friends arrived and departed. "[I]n this négligé . . . he was always overcome by a genteel, simpering embarrassment: 'Fancy you catching me like this!'"

After the war, Joe had written a play about his experience as a prisoner of war. Doing so was an expiation of the painful love affair he had suffered through with the young and cruel officer who was interned with him. *Prisoners of War* charted the psychological deterioration of Ackerley's double, the virile, manly Captain Conrad, who falls in love unrequitedly with the nineteen-year-old tubercular Lieutenant Grayle. The shattered state of returning soldiers was a raw subject in the immediate aftermath of the war, and Joe found it difficult to mount a production—"I do not think that any theatre would undertake a play of so harrowing and distressing a character," he was told. The problem play was an allegory of broader social problems, but these were perceived very differently by straight and gay audiences, to Ackerley's advantage. To avoid the scrutiny of the Lord Chamberlain, the official government censor of plays, it was produced in its first showcase by a club theater devoted to producing controversial, uncommercial plays. The sponsor, Mrs. Whitworth, was a progressive woman, the wife of a theater critic and arts editor at Chatto and Windus. She promoted the play convinced that it depicted a universal and deplorable phenomenon, the sad state of psychologically damaged young veterans, each in his own way mangled by the experience of war. It did not occur to her that scenes in which Grayle lays his head on Conrad's lap while the older man strokes his hair, or the hurried warning "Look out! Someone might come in!" had any homosexual content, and thus she was disconcerted when the theater was inundated with requests for tickets to "the new homosexual play." Word was out. She demanded a meeting with the playwright.

Ackerley did not demur or back down. He argued that if Mrs. Whitworth had missed the subtext, other theatergoers would as well; the production went forward, with Ackerley's friend Frank Birch directing, never mentioning to his actors the groundbreaking theme of the play. The realistic portrayal of the characters—none of whom comported himself according to the effeminate stereotype of a nancy boy—offered plausible cover for the unaware. But Mrs. Whitworth had forever lost her innocence—watching Ackerley embrace his sister at a rehearsal, she hissed, "You see! Incest as well." In September 1925, when *Prisoners of War* transferred to the West End for a short commercial run, it became the first play with an explicitly homosexual plot to pass the obtuse scrutiny of the Lord Chamberlain.

Morgan took the opportunity of the production to introduce Joe to Goldsworthy Lowes Dickinson. He encouraged Joe to send on a draft of the script to Goldie, who offered a long list of enthusiastic suggestions for revision. Morgan's attempt to bridge his old and new friends backfired when Goldie fell promptly and miserably in love with Joe. It was an ill match: Goldie was famously repressed, and never acted on his physical desires, painfully sublimating them into a shoe fetish. For his part, Joe was notoriously uninterested in older or gay men and had decided that "unable, it seemed, to reach sex through love" he should instead "start . . . upon a long quest in pursuit of love through sex." Ackerley made matters worse by not only telling Goldie after an overnight visit of passionate talk that he had not had this much fun as an undergraduate at Cambridge, but kissing the old man passionately on the lips when he left in the morning. Poor Morgan was left to interpret the mysterious chemistry between the bewildered protagonists, in long letters seriatim.

Morgan was too wise to advocate for Goldie, but he diagnosed an emotional problem at the root of Joe's perennially unsatisfactory love affairs. Morgan told him so directly: "I think you are scared or bored by response . . . I think love is beautiful and important—somehow I have found it so in spite of all the pain—and it will sadden me if you fail in that particular way." Days later, while agreeing with Joe that the best love should not be "disembodied," Morgan sharpened his critique. "Proust seems to think that a certainty of success in love stops one from proceeding; that rebuffs or jealousy are the only stimuli that keep one interested in a person. This isn't my experience, and I don't want it to be yours." He counseled Joe not to waste his time on his current lover, a scamp who, however charming, had fenced stolen goods and habitually run into trouble with the law.

His own friendship with Reg was gaining footing at the moment Joe's affair was disintegrating. "It is curious," Morgan told Joe, "how my affairs generally move upwards, yours downwards. Moralists prefer me. See chart opposite." At the bottom of this letter Morgan helpfully drew a little graph of two lines pointing in opposite directions, with the facetious attribution of "The Royal Metrogenital Society."

One Sunday morning Ackerley went out into the river mist of Hammersmith Terrace at dawn to get the milk bottle off his stoop, and came back inside with the milk and a brilliant young policeman who had been walking the beat. Harry Daley was only twenty-four. He had grown up in Lowestoft like one of the "unthinkable" poor of *Howards End*: his orphaned father was a fisherman, and his mother a charlady. When Harry was a boy his father drowned at sea; Mrs. Daley moved her four young children to live near Dorking. Harry worked as a delivery boy in Abinger, where (by coincidence) he had brought groceries to Aunt Laura Forster at West Hackhurst. He intended to join the navy, but instead was recruited into the Metropolitan Police.

Harry was voraciously hungry for the pleasures of the glittering city. He had chosen the police force for its human drama and its proximity to the West End. He enjoyed being posted to T Division, with a beat from Chiswick to Hammersmith, since "Hammersmith Broadway was the pleasure centre of this end of London in the same way that Piccadilly Circus was supposed to be for London as a whole." An aficionado, Harry had unusual discernment in matters of culture: he impressed Joe Ackerley when they first met by asking if he was the same man who had written *Prisoners of War*. He drank in Beethoven, Brahms, and Franck, listening to concerts on the wireless or playing scratchy records on the gramophone with an outsize horn he set up in his cubicle at the police barracks where he lived. Harry never forgot the afternoon at West Hackhurst when he listened, rapturous, as Morgan played a Mozart sonata with a "heavenly touch" on a tiny new piano he had installed in his study. Morgan's delight in the music "made him wonderfully loveable." It was a golden moment made especially memorable because, music lover that he was, Harry had never before heard a piano played live.

Almost immediately after Joe introduced them in the summer of 1926, Harry and Morgan became lovers. Through Morgan and Joe, Harry was unexpectedly drawn into a glamorous, "gay and all embracing" world, a secret world unlike any he had known, where men from all walks of life shared sex, talk, and friendship. They were a colorful and eclectic bunch. His circle of new friends included aristocrats and heirs to great fortunes— Eddie Sackville-West, the music critic (and cousin to Vita Sackville-West), who had inherited Knole, a vast Elizabethan country house in Kent; and Christopher Wood, willowy, effete, sporting a monocle, whose money came from a family business in canned jams. And there were Bloomsbury artists— Duncan Grant, who painted a portrait of Harry in his uniform, and Raymond Mortimer, later the critic for *The Times*, whose flat was crammed with Picassos and Braques.

There was General L. E. O. Charlton, known as Leo. This stern, almost priggish chief of Air Staff in Iraq was a principled man who had quit the RAF to protest its policy of bombing civilian targets. He lived quietly with his partner, a shy working-class RAF man named Tom Wichelo. Through Leo and Tom, Harry met Gerald Heard, a philosopher much influenced by Hindu mysticism. Heard was a gentle soul who in his later years became a guru in a Los Angeles ashram, but who at the time Harry met him lived, unaccountably, in Weybridge. Heard was sui generis. He suffered from persistent conjunctivitis, which required him to apply gentian violet to his eyelids, giving him the aspect of a cockeyed Theda Bara. He compounded this aura of eccentricity by adopting unusual habits of dress. Once he came to dinner at Joe Ackerley's parents' house wearing "purple suede shoes and a leather jacket with a leopardskin collar."

Harry returned the favor. He introduced Morgan to his circle of happy-go-lucky young men out of work and on the lookout for fun, petty thieves and gangsters and rough-faced working-class men, cheerful crooked boys with no money but plenty of Cockney charm, men who "scraped and pinched to buy gay clothes" and "stood about like peacocks, with empty pockets," who owned nothing more than the clothes on their backs. There were boxers and fitness buffs, pickpockets and scam artists, men with whom Daley broke bread and whom he occasionally had to lock up. There were no hard feelings on either side, since Daley's friends understood being arrested "as part of the excitement of their calling" and "were from families where such things are no disgrace." Besides, he was always willing to pass a cigarette to them through the bars.

Harry lived with ninety-nine other unmarried policemen in the Hammersmith Section House on Paddenswick Road, overlooking Ravenscroft Park. It was just blocks away from Joe's rooms on the river. The "big bare building" was essentially a barracks, with "a billiard room, a mess room and a kitchen on the ground floor, an old army hut in the yard, and lots of bathrooms and a hundred cubicles up the dingy stone stairs." Here—Harry deliciously relished the Metropolitan Police public relations slogan—*the finest body of men in the world* lived in the loose atmosphere of a workingmen's club. "In this cramped world of cubicles we lounged on one another's beds to talk and conduct our affectionate Platonic friendships . . . it was like camping out and it was heavenly."

The young men were supervised, if one could call it that, by a single exasperated sergeant who was universally loathed. He was a bully—which differentiated him from most of his subordinates—and cheerfully corrupt, which did not. It was commonplace for policemen to collect graft from small-time crooks and hustlers on their beat, and they made a habit of looking the other way when faced with minor infractions from friends and acquaintances.

At work Harry was openly gay. His fellow officers made a clear distinction between the behavior of one of their own and the "nancy boys" brought into the station on charges of soliciting. These men were routinely harassed and humiliated: their faces were rubbed with toilet paper to detect makeup; they were "laughed about as if [they were] not present," and subjected to searches in which the cops "always found the same sized tin of vaseline in [their] pocket[s]." But within the Section House, for the most part the men lived by the philosophy of laissez faire: "One policeman regularly hoisted his sweetheart over the gate on a rope, to spend the night with him in a bed on the gymnasium floor." A large, pudgy, and unprepossessing man, Harry was nevertheless capable of defending himself. He endured oblique slights:

a knothole in the main office wall was graffitied to look like an anus, and "love from 308"—Harry's badge number—was penciled below. But on the whole, Harry was let be.

Morgan was head over heels in love with the spirit of the place, which he slyly labeled "Erection Howze" in a letter to Sebastian. Harry took a photograph of Morgan standing on the roof, his little tonsure of gray hair flapping in the breeze. Often he would stay the night and join the men in the mess hall for a tremendous fry-up the next morning—"steak and eggs and bacon, tinned salmon, fruit, crusty new bread and lots of butter." On Harry's day off they would go to the theater—to see a Noel Coward play, or Patrick Hamilton's *Rope*, based on the Leopold and Loeb murder (and later adapted by Hitchcock), or to the bathhouse at Harry's workingmen's club. Morgan loved the texture of life in Harry's neck of the woods—walking the late-night beat beside his lover through streets deserted "except for a few coster's barrows," meeting the boxers, lorry drivers, fishermen, and gang leaders who frequented the neighborhood. The gangsters were especially dear to Morgan's heart—he felt they "spoke my language." He was delighted to read the written notice posted in the window of one café—"Nothing but the best margarine served"— wondering, "What on earth can they have been accused of serving?"

For privacy they met at Morgan's boîte at 27 Brunswick Square in Bloomsbury, an upstairs suite of rooms carved out of a dilapidated Regency townhouse that was later destroyed in the Blitz. His choice of décor was a deliberate rebuke to the sober Victorian good taste of Harnham. The sitting room wall boasted several handmade pictures of Indian ladies wearing brightly colored saris composed of the gaudy wrappers of Indian chocolate bars. The pied-à-terre was kitted out with all the necessities of London bachelor life— a gas ring for primitive cooking, a hot water bottle, and special black soap for killing crab lice. Here Morgan hosted Harry on many a night, and here he also juggled the various assignations of his new, comparatively rich sex life. Reg Palmer also stayed here when he could get away from Bess: though Morgan had vowed to break it off, telling Joe, "It is not my policy to break up homes," the two men continued to find time for private sex and friendship.

Here Morgan also stayed chastely with Frank Vicary, the young man whom he had befriended years before at the Montazah Hospital in Alexandria. The men resumed their friendship upon Morgan's return from India. Being near Vicary demanded a good deal of self-restraint. Morgan found Frank charming and attractive, was intrigued by his intellectual curiosity and quickness, but he dared not stray toward expressing appreciation. To Florence Barger, Morgan lamented, "Vicary cannot take M[ohammed]'s place, because there's a whole side of my nature remains ungratified and undiscussed." Morgan listened to Frank's woes—and he had plenty of them—and always believed the best about his friend's motives. Time and again Frank would quit a job, or get laid off; he traveled to Canada and the United States in search of work. but came home with his tail between his legs. His marriage, Frank claimed, was unhappy and sexless; his sister committed suicide, killing her child with her; and his beloved eldest son, to whom he was devoted, died in a hideous accident, having been scalded in the bath.

Morgan could not resist helping Frank through all his travails. He sponsored Vicary in numerous entrepreneurial ventures, even going so far as to buy him a small pig farm in Gloucestershire. In turn, Vicary named his second son Edward Morgan—thereby scandalizing Lily—and penned effusive letters to an unrequited Morgan. Morgan wrote Joe ruefully that visiting Vicary's farm was "heavenly . . . if heaven can be just sexless."

And to the Brunswick Square flat, like some sort of parcel, Sebastian Sprott sent Charles Lovett, his acquiescent lover from the slums of Nottingham. Lovett was a sweet, rather lumbering young man who adoringly did what was asked of him. He was genuinely fond of Morgan, and happy to be companionable. They established a routine. Morgan would pay Charles's train fare. Spending a weekend or a long day in London, Charles was treated to a nice meal and the theater. The sex was rather sedate—usually mutual masturbation. Then Charles would return to Sebastian and Nottingham with a small gift, such as new pocket handkerchiefs, for his trouble. Though Lovett was literate, the arrangements were always made between Morgan and Sebastian, with Morgan micromanaging the affair:

> "Don't let anyone 'spoil' Charles . . . though he seems perfectly sensible and resistant . . . And he shouldn't, for his comfort and others, talk more than he needs about my being a prominent writer . . ." "Tell Charles to arrive at 4.30 as planned and if I am not there to meet him . . . to go to Brunswick Square where he will find a note from me . . . on the mantelpiece . . ." "I have written to Charles and asked him for the 9th instead. You may kindly see I get a reply as soon as may be." "Do see that C. goes . . . through with his [false] teeth."

Lovett's reliability was his chief virtue—in his diary Morgan called their relationship an "elderly man's love."

Having a separate flat made Morgan feel "solid" and "independent of mother." But soon Morgan found that scheduling assignations there became exhaustingly complex. He juggled his own plans with requests for the key from Joe and Sebastian, or his old friend Francis Bennett. Occasionally he would bring Lily from Weybridge for an enervating day of London shopping or a musicale. One evening in 1928 he was startled to find "an enormous boy" in the flat when he arrived; he admonished Sebastian not to double-book.

Morgan's new friends offered a refreshing outlook, but they distracted him from intellectual work. He was publishing frequent reviews and incidental essays, but his life as a writer of fiction was stalled—and he admitted that he alone was largely responsible for his creative lassitude. His friend and translator Charles Mauron urged him to take up a new novel, but Morgan demurred, citing a temperamental weakness: "not to feel intact, not to [be] able to expose oneself to certain contacts because of self consciousness—that really is an aweful [sic] nuisance, and I spend a good deal of time now with people who are (vaguely speaking) my inferiors, and to whom I can very easily be kind."

It was hard to tell if Morgan's attitude revealed complacency or anxiety. Certainly it was seductive to surround oneself with people like Reg, who teased him by saying, "O, [the] celebrated author." But Morgan sometimes wished that his friendships "could have an intellectual basis." With the exception of Harry Daley, none of Morgan's working-class friends gave him much to *think* about. In consequence some of Morgan's friends suspected that he enjoyed the feeling of superiority. Leo Charlton noted, "Morgan's friends hushed their voices, as people do in cathedrals, when talking of him."

In truth, Morgan's attitude toward his social inferiors was complicated. More than many men of his class, Morgan saw how working-class people were slighted, treated as nearly invisible. In *Maurice* he had deliberately made Alec Scudder "loom up on the reader gradually," reflecting Maurice Hall's obtuse habit of looking through the servants until the "masculine blur" of the gamekeeper develops into a full-blown human being "who gives and takes love." He was disgusted by the senseless class strictures in his own daily life, railing in his diary at "the knowledge that I couldn't have Frank, e.g. to stay" with him at King's without causing a stir.

Morgan had long resented the middle-class shibboleth of avoiding the topic of money. His novels are filled with occasions when a heartfelt offer of generosity is rebuffed as *not the done thing*. When Philip Herriton offers Agnes and Gerald some of his inheritance so that they may forgo a long engagement (in *The Longest Journey*), the lovers treat his generosity as a rebuke. And Henry Wilcox is mystified by the Schlegels' willingness to discuss their financial status openly, or to try to help Leonard Bast. It was all very well to develop an unorthodox view of social class, but "only connect" remained a difficult proposition when Morgan consistently had more money than his friends. Disparity of income lent even the most ordinary generosity the odor of condescension. To counter this, in life as in art, Morgan insisted on being *patent* about money. From Mohammed he had learned that the poorer partner *wanted* to pay for things, as a matter of pride. Morgan was careful to mind economic reciprocity—and by inclination quite humble in his tastes. He was perfectly at home eating in a canteen or café, or watching a play from the nosebleed seats.

Morgan's generosity was exceptionally deep and thoughtful. He delicately ascertained the perfect needful thing, and made it occur with a minimum of fuss. Throughout his life he bestowed practical gifts with deft delicacy: he paid Joe Ackerley's expenses for a long-needed holiday, sent Sebastian Sprott small gifts of money, and took on the full cost of private medical care when Harry Daley's mother needed surgery. All told, the fees amounted to more than a hundred pounds—a sum so extravagant that he felt obliged to hide it from Lily, telling her he had contributed only half that amount.

Though he wore his generosity lightly, Morgan could not resist lecturing Harry on economies: "Those tickets cost 4/9 each I believe—well you mustn't ever spend so much on me again. Make 2/6 the limit, either for theatre or a meal. Will you agree? Isn't this common sense—given your present salary? And is anything in it contrary to friendship? I don't think so."

For his part Harry was happy enough to take Morgan's money, but resentful about being *managed*. After Morgan offered to foot the bill for his mother's medical care, Harry wrote one letter to Morgan, thanking him effusively, and a second to his mother, reassuring her, "Don't worry, old Morgan's got plenty of money." Then he inadvertently switched the envelopes and mailed the two letters in the same post. Morgan was terribly offended, but he stuck to his policy of preserving friendship—"Don't rebuke, don't arguefy, don't apologise."

He examined his own motives rather carefully. He was acutely aware that he viewed life through a veil of middle-class assumptions, that the virtues of thrift, forbearance, and courtesy that were the bedrock of his way of living might be qualities his poorer friends could ill-afford. So Morgan pondered whether the disappointing behavior of Harry and Reg and Frank Vicary was singular or social—"decayed morale or the natural morality of the non-bourgeois?" In Frank's case especially, he had reason to be appalled. In debt, perpetually out of work, increasingly feckless and prone to drink, Frank had mortgaged the little Gloucestershire farm and frittered the money away. Morgan's disappointment permanently punctured his romantic view of Vicary and their putative shared future. He ruefully told Joe that he had imagined himself toddling about the little farm "in old age, looked after by the robust and grateful lower classes."

Indeed, Morgan's ideal of intimacy consistently required a more delicate sensibility than his working-class friends could muster. His encounters with Reg were always physically satisfying, but asking for or expecting real conversation from him seemed hopelessly beside the point: after one session of lovemaking, Morgan wrote in his diary, "Coarseness and tenderness have kissed one another, but imaginative passion, love, doesn't exist in the lower classes." After another, he was more satisfied: "Lust + goodwill—is anything more wanted? . . . [I feel] not happiness, but proud to be alive." For his own part, he chastened himself, worrying that his own attitude reflected a "superficial itch for intimacy that makes for popularity and is misleading."

Joe Ackerley and Sebastian Sprott provided tutoring in the new practicalities of the double life. It was inevitable that in Morgan's hands subterfuge would sometimes descend into farce. In 1924 his Bunburying unraveled in spectacular style when he agreed to be part of a scheme to conceal Joe's whereabouts from his parents while he visited a lover in Italy. Morgan's first reaction was to ask rather reasonably, "Is a lie necessary?" But Joe insisted on an elaborate scheme. He told his parents he was at Harnham visiting Morgan, but his father had a sudden heart attack while Joe was en route to

Italy. Because Morgan didn't have a telephone in Weybridge, Mrs. Ackerley sent a domestic servant over in a rush to fetch her son, and Joe and Morgan's conspiracy was exposed. Parents were constantly making uncomfortable discoveries. A compromising and ribald telegram from Sebastian had to be elaborately explained away when Lily inadvertently opened and read it. So parcels and letters sent to West Hackhurst must be elaborately disguised. Morgan requested that Joe post a tube of ointment to treat crab lice—which Morgan charitably labeled "signs of fertility"—in a package disguised as a book.

By the mid-1920s, Morgan began to get the hang of the double life. In answer to a query from Joe, he totted up a full accounting of his sexual partners: eighteen to Joe's two hundred or so. Morgan celebrated their variety, if not their numbers. The list included "1 Scotchman, 1 Colonial and 1 Quaker." He managed to stay friendly with these men, in contrast to Joe, whose heart was broken several times a year, like clockwork. The secret, Morgan advised, was simple: "If you want a permanent relationship with . . . anyone, you must give up this idea of ownership, and even the idea of being owned."

Morgan became adept at using his network of friendly connections to discover or arrange sexy flings on trips abroad. Traveling to a conference in Copenhagen with George Barger, Morgan met up with a Danish boy named Aage, an acquaintance of Joe's; he took him to bed and—rather poetically— to see Elsinore Castle. On a voyage to visit Charles and Marie Mauron in France, he picked up a ship's stoker named Charlie Day, a big man with a sleepy flat face and a crooked smile. (Later, back in England, Charlie became a pest, making scenes and asking for money, and Morgan asked Joe to intervene and persuade him to desist.) If necessary, Morgan was perfectly happy to appear the stooge in these intrigues, so long as he was in on the joke. He began a casual and friendly love affair with a French sailor, an acquaintance of Joe's, named Achille Morgenroth. With Achille, Morgan acquiesced in a little charade, willingly posing as a dowdy "uncle in the clothes trade, long domiciled in England." Achille organized elaborate rules for these trysts, timing their exits from the hotel so as not to be seen together. These little bits of subterfuge to distract Achille's relatives amused Morgan.

Having adventures made him feel young. In the summer of 1929, coming back from a tour of South Africa with the Bargers, and starved for his secret life, Morgan wrote to Joe Ackerley, "I was 250 years old a fortnight back, and now you can knock off the nought." It was a testament to the success of his carefully crafted public persona during these years that even so close a friend as Virginia Woolf could thoroughly misread his situation. Writing to her sister, Vanessa Bell, Woolf lamented that Lily, with her iron-willed love, "is slowly dispatching him . . . he is limp and damp and milder than the breath of a cow." This was not so true as Virginia believed. Morgan's adventures would have shocked her.

The kind of fiction writing he wished to pursue cut him off from his audience, and he rechanneled his pen, writing for his own ear, for his friends, and for the more charitable future he had imagined in his dedication to *Maurice*. In contrast to the Rabelaisian fantasies he had destroyed when completing *A Passage to India*, the new stories were serious, thoughtful examinations of the psychological strain of being a gay Englishman. These were the short stories that Christopher Isherwood and John Lehmann would marvel over—and publish—after his death. "Dr. Woolacott," "Arthur Snatchfold," and "The Life to Come" were not strictly autobiographical—"The Life to Come" traced a fatal love affair between a missionary and a native chieftain, "Dr. Woolacott" the mental disintegration of a young veteran of the trenches—but the anxiety of their characters was informed by the tension of living in two worlds. There were very few people to whom he could trust the reading of this new fiction.

As he had done two years earlier, Morgan turned to T. E. Lawrence for literary advice. Lawrence had been sickened by the machine of celebrity, which propelled him into the public eye after the war. He achieved his goal of near-invisibility by reenlisting in the RAF; from his far-off posting in Karachi he wrote abject letters of admiration to Morgan. After months of this, Morgan was beginning to be irritated by Lawrence's alternating effusions and rebuffs. Lawrence had intellectual keenness, Morgan believed, but an evasive soul. "T. E. liked to meet people upon a platform of his own designing," Morgan decided—and in his own case, Morgan came to realize "I had to figure as a great artist" while he affected the role of "bungling amateur." Morgan renewed the offer to send T. E. the manuscript of *Maurice*, but his young friend cagily demurred:

> I wanted to read your long novel, & was afraid to. It was like your last keep, I felt: and if I read it I had you: and supposing I hadn't

liked it? I'm so funnily made up, sexually. At present you are in all respects right, in my eyes: that's because you reserve so very much, as I do. If you knew all about me (perhaps you do: your subtlety is very great: shall I put it "if I knew that you knew . . ."?) you'd think very little of me.

Morgan had correctly understood that being "an awful tease" was Lawrence's calculated emotional defense. Literally and figuratively Lawrence "did not like being touched," Morgan realized, and after this exchange he "touched him as seldom as possible."

That this bright young man, so attractive, so intelligent, was merely another iteration of the kind of charming, unknowable intellectual siren that Frank Vicary had become both vexed and saddened Morgan. He told Florence Barger that Lawrence was incapable of friendship—though he did not speculate on the psychological source of this handicap. Privately he believed that the effects of Lawrence's sexual abuse had somehow unhinged his character.

Despite his disappointment. Morgan decided to dedicate a "forthcoming volume of stories" to Lawrence. The stories in *The Eternal Moment* had all been published before. He took the occasion to tell a small sharp truth, writing Lawrence that he had settled on the epigraph "'To T. E. *in the absence of anything else*': The dedication can be given a wrong meaning, which you will enjoy doing, and I shall like to think of you doing it. The matter is decided therefore." The collection "promises to be [my] last created word that will ever find public utterance"; he warned Lawrence, "If you ever inscribe anything to me, good bad or indifferent, I shall be a lot annoyed."

He mailed the letter to Karachi from West Hackhurst, "the frail house of old women," admonishing that both he and Lawrence had been wrong to "hanker at all after a notion of escaping" such a world. It was far too resilient, Morgan understood: "a twig from the elm tree would shatter it, yet it preserves its relative strength internally. My mother still keeps the maids in order."

Silenced as a writer of publishable fiction, Morgan recast his public voice, banking on the eminence he had established with the publication of *A Passage to India* in 1924. In the spring of 1926 he was invited to deliver the Clark Lectures at Trinity College, Cambridge—a distinguished series on any topic in English literature after Chaucer. Morgan chose to take in hand the poetics of the novel form itself, from the perspective of a creative practitioner rather than an academician. Not so much a history of the novel form than an early version of narratology—how the novel does what it does, from characterization to emplotment, to how realism is conveyed—the lectures received mixed reviews, along familiar lines. Those in the audience who identified themselves as "common readers," following Dr. Johnson's dictum—taken up by Virginia Woolf in her essays of the same name—found them irreverent, refreshing, and commonsensical. The learned authorities on English literature who were beginning feel their oats as a profession at Cambridge found Morgan's literary criticism less persuasive: F. R. Leavis pronounced the lectures "intellectually null." The venerable A. E. Housman, whom Morgan had long admired and written to from the smoke-filled pub in Shropshire decades before, was a Fellow of Trinity. But the second encounter between the two authors went even worse than the first. Housman felt obscurely snubbed by Morgan's failure to attend formal supper in the college's Hall during the spring, and responded to a letter of praise from Morgan so vilely that Morgan burned the letter and never mentioned it again. The most significant response to the lectures came from the Fellows of King's, who offered Morgan a three-year fellowship, with the expectation that he would be in residence six weeks a year.

In the summer of 1928 his old and dear friend Leonard Woolf approached Morgan to join a cause. A mannish lesbian writer named Radclyffe Hall had just published a controversial new novel. *The Well of Loneliness* courted danger with its sexual subject matter: and now the author and publisher were drawn into a legal fight over its prosecution on charges of criminal obscenity. Hall's novel was a coming-of-age story of lesbian love. Much like *Maurice*, its protagonist (a tortured young woman named Stephen Gordon) struggles to understand her identity and find love, if not acceptance, in the modern world. But Hall's story ends tragically: Stephen's family rejects her, and her lover. Mary, leaves her for a man. The novel ends with Stephen Gordon's prayer, "Give us also the right to our existence!"

Almost immediately after the novel's publication, the editor of the conservative *Sunday Express* began a public campaign to suppress it on moral grounds. In a searing editorial, James Douglas called on Hall's publisher to withdraw all copies from circulation; failing that, he urged the home secretary to undertake prosecution against the book's publisher and distributor on the grounds of criminal obscenity. The *Express* explicitly rejected Hall's cry for tolerance of "inverts," arguing that "[the novel] is a seductive and insidious piece of special pleading designed to display perverted decadence as a martyrdom inflicted on these outcasts by a cruel society."

The home secretary, William Joynson-Hicks, was addicted to purity campaigns. He had already cracked down on gambling and nightclubs and all sorts of sin in the city; within days he took the newspaper's bait. Though the publisher, Jonathan Cape, did withdraw the book, "Jix" nevertheless instructed the director of public prosecutions to begin lining up witnesses who could attest to its nefarious influence on young people, anticipating that the "defendants have it in mind to procure a number of men of literary eminence to testify as to the innocuousness of the book." *Procure* indeed. So Morgan found himself in the low-ceilinged sitting room at Monk's House outside the little Sussex village of Rodmell, getting drunk with Virginia and Leonard Woolf, talking of "sodomy & sapphism, with emotion" and planning a counterattack.

"Soon we were telephoning and interviewing and collecting signatures," Virginia Woolf wrote her lover, Vita Sackville-West. The threatened suppression of the book and prosecution of its publisher quickly persuaded other famous writers—Arnold Bennett, G. B. Shaw, H. G. Wells, Lytton Strachey, T. S. Eliot, and Vera Brittain—to sign on. Leonard determined that Morgan would be the best emissary to approach the author herself. Hall was a formidable figure—wearing a full pinstriped man's suit, and a daunting black-rimmed monocle—and during their meeting Morgan let slip that while he found the novel to be courageous, he had not thought it particularly well written. Virginia described the debacle of Morgan's retreat:

> Radclyffe scolds him like a fishwife, and says that she wont [*sic*] have any letter written about her book unless it mentions the fact that it is a work of artistic merit—even genius. And no one has read her book; or can read it: and now we have to explain this to all the great signed names . . . So our ardour in the cause of freedom of speech gradually cools, and instead of offering to reprint the masterpiece, we are already beginning to wish it unwritten.

Morgan had been willing to defend the "meritorious dull book" on principle. But back at Monk's House, tipsy and scalded by Hall's tongue-lashing, he confided to Leonard and Virginia that he found lesbians "disgusting: partly from conventions, partly because he disliked that women should be independent of men." Hall's book embraced the modern psychological theories that claimed "inversion" to be a congenital condition—and the three writers' conversation turned to whether homosexuality could be "cured." Morgan told the Woolfs he had learned of a prominent neurologist's boast that he could "convert the sodomites" through an aversion cure—much as Dr. Lasker-Jones had proposed to do to Maurice. "Would you like to be converted?" Leonard asked him, genuinely curious. "'No' said Morgan, quite definitely." In the end Virginia and Morgan composed a rather tame "comic little letter" decrying that social opprobrium such as the Hall case would cause artists to suppress "creative impulses" and "shun anything original." By October, Morgan found himself sitting on a hard bench at the Bow Street Magistrates Court, alongside forty eminent scientists, theologians, and men of letters waiting to testify on behalf of Hall's defense. After a long peroration the chief magistrate concluded that as a matter of law he could determine whether the book was obscene without inviting any expert testimony, and summarily—and anticlimactically—dismissed the assembled crowd.

The real drama occurred in Morgan's life alone. His public and private personae collided with ironic force the very week of the *Well of Loneliness* trial. He told the story to Sebastian, gamely playing up the comedy of the occasion: "What with being blackmailed on Wednesday and Bow Street on Friday, life has really been quite a whirl." This single sentence embodies the tension between Forster's secret and his carefully cultivated public life. The attempted blackmail came through an elliptical approach. The wife of one of Morgan's casual sex partners discovered her husband had slept with Morgan, and confronted him. She assured him he would not be bothered further if he paid cash.

Morgan had been quite lucky in his adventures before this moment. With Bess Palmer he had played the part of a befuddled middle-aged man, with no designs on her husband besides hearty friendship. He even managed the delicate feat of remaining her husband's lover without her knowledge for the rest of his life. But this occasion was a little different. The proof of its sting is revealed by the paucity of records. Morgan destroyed all but the barest shreds of the record of this trauma—and these come elliptically in coded references to a few of his closest friends. "She swears I shan't be worried or even spoken to," Morgan wrote to Joe.

It might seem that Morgan would be ill-prepared to address the practicalities of blackmail. But, characteristically, he had imagined something similar to it more than a decade earlier, even before he had first touched the soldier on the beach in Alexandria. The scene in which Alec threatens Maurice with blackmail in the British Museum predated his own experience. Now he showed the blackmail letter to Gerald Heard. But Heard, sad to say, had been won over by *fiction*. His praise for this section of *Maurice* had been so effusive that it was Gerald whom Morgan first "summoned for advice and sympathy." Soft-hearted Gerald was too influenced by the example of *Maurice*, as Morgan himself came to recognize. Having "read the wrong book," Gerald "would do nothing but advise . . . sympathize with the blackmailers," Morgan wryly told Sprott, concluding that when he thought on it, the episode was not so frightening, since "the mailer indeed had only the faintest tinge of black."

The tantalizing reference to a not-very-dark blackmailer suggests that Morgan's partner, like Reg, was a dark-skinned man. The larger lesson was not to take too serious a view of such setbacks. They were all in a day's flirtation, it seemed. Quickly the scare blew over—"I calmed down rather quickly and am now O. K." In public and in private, Morgan was temperamentally unsuited to martyrdom. He paid off the blackmailer, laughed off his anxiety, and dusted off his dignity.

But Morgan's relations with Harry Daley began to deteriorate in the months after the *Well of Loneliness* affair. Harry had always been prickly, prone to take slights and to harbor grudges. But the veneer of Harry's freshness wore away quite quickly, exposing a man of reckless, even dangerous, self-regard. Morgan tried as tactfully as he could to make Harry see the consequences of his penchant for celebrity and bitchy gossip. Harry understood that his words had power, but he reveled in the fact that Morgan "was always frightened by what I would say next." In his memoir published decades later, Harry made it clear that he could not view Morgan's caution as entirely solicitous:

> "Love" seems hardly the right word to describe the spite and backbiting it all involved. People in love must never be crossed or disappointed, it seemed, and all that was asked was that I should give up all my former friends, acquaintances, hobbies and interests, and sit waiting at home until my lovers found time to call—and on no condition tell anyone I knew them.

Gradually Morgan came to understand that Harry had no internal governor; he told Joe, "I feel sickish over Harry's behaviour to you, and again have got the feeling that he will have us all in the dock before he is done."

It was really painful for Morgan to sever his friendship with Harry, but he did so, utterly. By mutual agreement the two men burned all their correspondence—only a tiny forgotten cache survived, tucked away in several of Harry's books. By the end of the decade Morgan had finished with counseling patience. He advised Joe, too, to cut off his friendship with Harry altogether, writing, "I don't blame you over Harry at all. He gets wrong with everyone sooner or later I think." Analyzing his former lover as if he were a character, Morgan wrote to Joe,

On Harry it is as easy to report on the position of a windmill sail. He is tragically unhappy, he has a cold, and speaking parentally, he is spoilt: a year's attention and treatings have made him less considerate of other people's comfort. His absence of self control the other day made me feel him scarcely human and this acted as an anti-aphrodisiac. I wish such an effect could be general.

Ending the affair with Harry allowed Morgan to assess the pleasures and dangers of the whole of the Hammersmith circle. He had been, he felt, too gullible about the virtues of the working class. Romance, it seemed, had degenerated into bitchiness and backbiting. Harry accused Morgan and Joe of acting like pimps, and there was some truth to this charge, though he had been a willing enough pawn. Singly Morgan's new friends could be entertaining and charming, but collectively they were becoming exhausting: "Hammersmith is a complete goose when audible *en masse*, loveable and valuable though the individual feathers may be." He was happy to keep at a slight remove, physically and metaphysically. "I am so glad you are not coming to Leo's this evening," he wrote to Joe. "I have got a kind of cat-ring feeling— so many Dicks, so many Toms . . . I suppose there is something secretive about me, unless I am growing old and I don't secrete enough." Perhaps he had outgrown this younger set, he concluded. Carrington, always an acute observer, wrote Sprott that she found Morgan to be "rather unhappy" at this point in his life. "He seemed as if he was trying to hide his feelings and to be gay in spite of an ache in his heart." Morgan found that Bloomsbury and his Bloomsbury friends offered a respite from the "cat-ring" of Hammersmith. In January 1930, when his lease on the flat expired, he moved next door to 26 Brunswick Square, where he would remain until the Blitz.

Joe's Hammersmith terrace house remained a perfect place for a gathering. Priding himself on his polyglot taste in friends, Joe used the occasion of the annual Oxford-Cambridge Boat Race on the Thames to host a party. The atmosphere was exaggerated radical chic. Mixing elements of society in a deliberately provocative way, Ackerley invited new friends from the BBC (where he was now working at the Talks Department), his lover du jour—usually a Guardsman or a cheerful scoundrel who might bring along his wife—artists and actors and local toughs, and his surviving family: his eccentric mother (a glamorous former vaudeville star who was a master of the gaudy hat), his aunt Bunny, who had "something of . . . Mae West in her character" and "an extraordinarily infectious chesty laugh," and his sister, Nancy—bony, regal in mien, unhappy in a sharp, patrician way. Morgan came too, and so did Anwar and Akbar, Masood's teenage sons, who had been sent to study in England as their parents' marriage disintegrated into divorce. Joe laid on magnums of champagne for the Cambridge crowd and bottles of beer for the cops—both camps becoming more raucous as the day wore on, each gawking at the beautiful young men rowing on the river, all embraced in a warm haze of alcohol and companionship. The party was like an Agatha Christie novel run amok.

On the cool, dull Saturday morning of April 12, 1930, Morgan struck up a conversation at Joe's Boat Race party with a burly young policeman whom Harry had brought from the Section House. He looked vaguely familiar to Morgan, with his dark hair parted in the center and slicked down, and his wide, open face, which broke into a ready smile. The young man was in his mid-twenties. He was affable, earnest, and at first tried to impress Morgan by expounding on the slight fib that he had been reading Dostoyevsky. In reality he was more expert in the manly, outdoorsy arts. He had been an amateur boxer, picking up a few bob here and there, and he had the broad mashed nose to prove his bona fides. The young man warmed up in conversation. He liked rowing for exercise, and knew a good bit about boats and the river. He had a wide smile. It turned out that his name was Bob Buckingham, and he would become the greatest love of Morgan's life.

10

"A Little Like Being Married"

Like Harry Daley, Bob Buckingham worked out of the Hammersmith Section House, and like Harry he had grown up in deep poverty and effectively fatherless. At a young age Bob had begun supporting his mother and many siblings while his feckless father disappeared for months at a time. The family lived in Somerstown, in the slums squeezed between St. Pancras and Euston stations. Like so many young men in the twenties, Bob scraped by on occasional work and lived through spells of unemployment. He was dexterous and enterprising: he could dismantle and fix small motors, knew his way around a bit of carpentry, and, strong-backed, he had worked on the docks and hauled parcels as a deliveryman before joining the police force. On the beat he was affable, but firm. He derived authority from his ample square-built frame and his booming bass voice. Harry, who took credit for introducing Bob to Morgan, channeled his envy at the success of their friendship into criticism of his rival. He consoled himself by believing that Bob was rather dim, "not really a reading man," pompous, and a bit of a lickspittle. Bob's bourgeois staidness was the real goad to Harry. He refused to see Harry as a threat, treating his machinations with "amused protective kindness." For Morgan, especially after Daley's tempestuous presence, Bob's loyalty and calm were a tonic.

Their relationship began, like so many of Morgan's affairs, with a delicate dance just shy of overt seduction. Morgan invited Bob to the movies, to the theater, to dinner, to stay the weekend at the Brunswick Square flat. After each treat, Bob sent a polite thank-you note in model penmanship, suggesting the next time he would be free to meet. Morgan took charge of Bob's education, lending him books and querying him earnestly on what he learned from them. From the earliest moments of their friendship, Morgan found a kindred spirit in Bob, projecting onto his new friend's calm a vulnerability not discerned by others in the Hammersmith set. Joe Ackerley was amused to watch Morgan shield the sturdy young man from gossip and intrigue. But Morgan was set on preserving Bob's reputation, adjuring Joe, "I must re-emphasise the need of silence about Bob."

Morgan proceeded with delicacy, he told Sprott, because "I am quite sure that [Bob's] feeling for me is something he has never had before." Bob was comfortable in the company of men, but had slept only with women; in the summer of 1931 Morgan reported that Bob had "fallen very violently in liking" with him. Morgan proudly told Lytton Strachey that he had achieved "a complete success" in an "affair" with his new young man, a description of sexual conquest that the more experienced Lytton found "fayish" and "delightful." To Sebastian, Morgan described his sex life with Bob as "a spiritual feeling which has extended to my physique." He was careful to allow Bob the freedom to pursue affairs with women, taking a lesson from the contretemps with Reg and Bess Palmer. Occasionally he even offered Bob the keys to the Brunswick Square flat for assignations with a woman he had met on the rebound from an earlier affair, a bright, practically minded young nurse in training named May Hockey. May was unthreatening, with a good sense of humor and a comfortable sense of herself. She resolutely resisted the cult of femininity. She didn't wear makeup, dressed sensibly, and had no room for religion or sentimentality.

As he grew comfortable in their love affair Morgan brought Bob to West Hackhurst, ostensibly to make small repairs around the house. Lily, almost eighty, was still alert enough to suspect that something was up. Rather waspishly she began a campaign to test Morgan's affections, remarking on how *ugly* his new friend was—with his broad, flattened nose—and how *common*. She obtusely refused to hear Bob's name correctly, referring to the end of her days to "Mr. Bucknam." Morgan, as usual, took the path of least resistance with her, acquiescing to her criticisms without standing up for Bob. At the same time he introduced Bob to his closest female friends—to Florence Barger, who set about befriending him warmly, and to Carrington, who "found Policeman Bob very charming and attractive to look at & 'easy to get on with', as they say."

It was Bob's very *ordinariness* that made him so attractive to Morgan. There was much to admire. He had found a profession by hard work and perseverance; despite a Dickensian past he engaged the world with cheerful curiosity. Like the eponymous protagonist of *Maurice*, Bob was a man "completely unlike" Morgan himself—"someone handsome, healthy, bodily attractive . . ."; and like Alec Scudder, Maurice's lover, Bob was working-class and exceptionally loyal. For his part, Bob was entranced by Morgan's adoration, keen to experience the world of culture Morgan opened to him, and touched by the warmth and acceptance of Morgan's friends. He worked eagerly to improve himself intellectually, striving to advance in the force in part because his success would bring pleasure to Morgan. Even Harry grudgingly admitted that temperamentally they were a well-balanced pair: "Bob was the man for Morgan, much more suitable than me, and I am glad that's how it ended."

Morgan began to fall deeply in love, and to his delight and surprise discovered that once Bob was committed to their relationship, once they had slept together, Bob exacted a pledge of fidelity in return. This intense loyalty was something Morgan had never dared to dream of, and he came to regard his new "lover and beloved" as a friend of a different order than he had known before. At this time, by a stroke of felicity, Morgan came across a key that he had misplaced for three years—the key that opened the hasp of the Locked Diary, which he had begun using in 1909. Unlocking the book again, and rereading his record, Morgan considered afresh the trajectory of his life's arc. In a superstitious way, he interpreted finding the key as a renaissance, and he set about self-consciously revising his diary. First he culled passages from small diaries he had begun in the interim, copying out impressions from the early days with Bob, and burning the discarded originals. Then Morgan did something wholly unusual. He began to inscribe Bob Buckingham into his life story.

Since he began keeping records in it, Morgan had written only on the rectos in the big bound book. Now turning back to its earliest pages, he began to pen addenda on the versos. Imitating the practice of Plutarch's parallel lives—the great classical biography—Morgan reconstructed the diary as a dialogue between his own life and Bob's up to the point of their meeting. While Morgan was agonizing over the suicide of Ernest Merz in 1909: "Bob, aged 5 goes to the infant school at Winchester St." In 1915, opposite a totting-up of the names of acquaintances among the war dead: "Bob, aged 10, goes to the Hugh Middleton school." The twenty-three-year difference in their ages shrank into insignificance. They were two halves of a platonic soul. The whole of the past became a prologue to this fateful moment.

At about the same time Morgan began a new address book, which he kept until his death. It reflected Morgan's young and widening world: A was for Ackerley and for the young poet Wystan (a.k.a. W. H.) Auden, with his gigantic ears and his long horsy face. B was for Buckingham and D for Daley and P for William Plomer, a young South African novelist, with his owlish spectacles and his hyperdiscreet bearing. Plomer seemed buttoned-up and correct, but was subject to outrageous spells of silliness. He was incredibly quick with words. A notorious punster, he cherished spoonerisms and peculiar names, always referring to the grandiose statue of Clive of India on the Thames Embankment as "Olive"; he managed to look innocent while delivering sharp observations that left his dinner companions gasping with laughter. Morgan himself found this sort of humor infectious, once remarking that he had caught William in an "unguardeed moment." Virginia and Leonard Woolf had been impressd with Plomer's first novel, *Turbott Wolfe*, a tragic depiction of an interracial love story set in South Africa. In 1931, their Hogarth Press published his second novel, *Sado*, set in Japan and loosely based on Plomer's love affair with a Japanese boy. Virginia found Plomer to be witty company, but this didn't prevent her from penning waspish sketches of him in her letters and diary.

Many of Morgan's young friends had moved to Maida Vale, a once-genteel and now down-at-heels quarter of London tucked behind Paddington Station. Joe Ackerley had joined them there, forced to decamp from the delicious house on the river in Hammersmith when his father died. To the world, and to his son, Roger Ackerley had been the picture of a well-to-do and robust family man; but when his will was opened this persona turned out to be more alarmingly true than Joe had supposed. Instead of inheriting an ample fortune, Joe discovered that his father had been an active bigamist who left strict instructions that his son should support his secret family as well as Joe's mother and sister, Nancy. But Roger left no money and his scandalized firm refused to pay out the life insurance. Joe's devil-may-care life collapsed. He took a job at the BBC, eventually rising to be literary editor of *The Listener*, where he worked for the rest of his life.

In Maida Vale, Joe could live for less than half the cost. In this shabby venue he joined a circle of young friends buoyed by their connection to the Woolfs. There was the poet Stephen Spender, looking at twenty-four more like a teenager than a young Turk, and Johnny Simpson, a peculiar young man whose veiled homosexual novel *Saturday Night at the Greyhound* was published under the pen name of John Hampson by the Hogarth Press. And through John Lehmann, who had been the Hogarth Press's typesetter, editorial assistant, and dogsbody, Morgan first met Christopher Isherwood. "John Lehmann is back from Vienna with a dumbelle, Christopher Isherwood, whom I like best of all that lot." Virginia in her diary did not hide her distaste for these "Lilies of the Valley"—"At Duncan [Grant]'s show, we met the Bugger boys, Joe, Morgan, William; & savoured the usual queer scent."

In the summer of 1932, facing prostate surgery, Goldsworthy Lowes Dickinson met Morgan in London to give him a packet of important papers: the autobiography he had just completed, and letters to be given to his two surviving sisters in the event of his death. This was a sober brief, to be sure, but Goldie seemed his same essential self—gentle and whimsical, serious of mind, as ever, philosophical. In July he held a dinner for a number of his friends at a restaurant in Soho, offering a toast at the conclusion of the evening. No one could quite recall what he said, but the tone was familiar: despite Goldie's "youthful interest in everything . . . he felt more and more that all human creatures were somehow equally important or unimportant in the scheme of things as we know it now." The surgery took place at Guy's Hospital in London on Monday, August 1. It was a major operation, but Goldie came through swimmingly; he was weak but cheerful and lucid when Morgan sat by his bedside the next day. He planned to recuperate at the home of his old friend and Apostle George Trevelyan. But the next evening Morgan received the "unreal" news that Goldie was dead.

He had slipped out of life just before dawn, "chiefly occupied in saving us trouble and sparing our feelings." But Goldie had always kept a very small footprint on the corporeal earth. There were just a few worldly goods— papers and letters and books, on one of which rested the threadbare Chinese silk cap he wore while writing. Morgan hastily wrote a tribute for *The Spectator*, duly praising the accomplishments of Dickinson as a scholar and policymaker, a shaper of the zeitgeist and an influential public man. But he reserved the greatest compliment for a letter to his old friend Malcolm Darling, who had known Goldie since their undergraduate days. "Mrs. Newman his bedmaker said 'he was the best man who ever lived,' and I would write that on his tomb, if he needed one." Stunned and heartbroken, Morgan helped to arrange the memorial service in the magnificent Gothic chapel across the courtyard from the window of Goldie's set of rooms. The service took place on Saturday, August 6, which would have been Goldie's seventieth birthday.

In the pews of the chapel sat dignitaries from the university, friends from King's over the generations, former students, Apostles, acolytes who came up from London to mark the ending of a life that was both important and ineffable. Morgan attended almost literally propped up by Bob, his frail frame leaning against the younger man's broad shoulder. But as the crowd filtered out to the dying strains of the organ, Bob turned to him quietly and confidentially. He spoke plainly. May was pregnant, he told Morgan. They would have to marry, and soon, by the end of the month. It was a matter of finding a day off, and booking the civil ceremony at the registry office. Bob asked Morgan to be his witness.

So on a muggy, hot, overcast afternoon, on the last day of August 1932, five people gathered at the civil registry: the clerk, the bride and groom, and two witnesses. Morgan stood beside Bob and May and stated that there was no impediment to their marriage. The plan was to repair to a local restaurant for a celebratory toast, but Morgan was too heartsick. He begged off, feeling unwell.

As summer turned to autumn after Bob and May's marriage, Morgan found it increasingly difficult to follow the sort of advice he had offered to friends on such occasions. He couldn't *let go*, couldn't resign himself. He thought of suicide, threatened to leave the country, and briefly believed he was going out of his mind, telling Joe after Bob canceled a planned date, "If he fails me again I *feel* I shall smash." Morgan vilified May, accusing her on scant evidence of being a "domineering, sly, and *knowing* woman." And he belittled Bob: "He must be made to see that there can't be a menage à trois, which I think is his dream, and, for the moment, possibly hers too; but he should easily see this when told." In a primitive way, Morgan imagined that he could simply assert his desires and everyone would acquiesce. But Bob treated Morgan's outbursts with aplomb, merely telling him, "We've got to go without pleasures for a bit." Not satisfied, Morgan fumed at a perceived inequity: "Yesterday when I went to tea at the S[ection] H[ouse] by arrangement, [I] was turned away at once . . . *May* can be seen, of course."

Consumed by anxiety and jealousy, equally disgusted by his behavior and his inability to control himself, Morgan consulted with Sebastian Sprott, as much as a psychologist as a friend.

> When I cannot "get what I want" I have tempers like collar-burning Charles. these came on last night, they are canny & calculating & non-suicidal and I hate them. and even if Bob gets the woman under control when his seed comes out of her next year—shall I be in a state to profit? . . . Perhaps I behave like this because of my week end at Cambridge in Goldie's rooms—but that seemed just sadness, which one always bears, it is the addition to sadness that's unmanageable.

Morgan was in a raw state of anxiety. The titanic struggle with May Buckingham was really a projection, a terror of *loss*. In truth, Goldie's death had been an "addition to sadness" in itself, the last in a series of deaths that even before Bob's marriage had shaken Morgan to the core. In January, six months before Goldie's death, Lytton Strachey had died horribly of stomach cancer; two months later Carrington, desperate with grief and unable to live without Lytton, had shot herself. Morgan recorded the twin tragedies in his diary, forgiving Carrington her suicide but wishing she had been able to hold on to life.

And eighteen months before, in the summer of 1929, the ancient Edward Carpenter had died too, bereft at having outlived his beloved younger partner, George Merrill. Goldie had visited Carpenter in the last months of his life; he told Morgan that during this sad final encounter the old man had insisted on walking to the cemetery. Goldie had stood mute while Carpenter stood over Merrill's grave sobbing, gasping out that his lover had been put in the cold, cold ground.

Even the irascible vibrant D. H. Lawrence was gone. Only forty-four, he had finally succumbed to tuberculosis on March 2, 1930. Despite their uneasy friendship. Morgan had believed Lawrence to be "the greatest imaginative novelist of our generation." and he publicly defended Lawrence against a hostile obituary in *The Times*. In private, to Lawrence's widow, Frieda, Morgan wrote a simple letter. dated two days after Lawrence's death:

> I have had such a shock over D.H.L. He was always in my heart, and I think too of the books he would still have written.

I have been thinking about you too, and wondering how you are, and what you will do. It's difficult to write, and please don't answer this. I wish I could help you.

E. M. Forster

In the wake of Bob's marriage, the death of these dear friends felt like an extinction. Morgan set to work dutifully on a project of recuperation: he decided to write a biography of Goldie's life. Surrounded by stacks of books and papers, picking through mountains of letters in Goldie's impenetrable hand, Morgan settled down in his friend's rooms, with their great half-circle window unblinkingly gazing at the golden flank of the chapel across the courtyard. Most of Goldie's correspondence proved banal in the extreme. Morgan wrote Joe, "I continue to read Goldie's letters to [his sister] May, which are even poorer than most of his letters, with placidity, and to hear him saying 'Really my dear Morgan that you should have to do this!'"

But almost imperceptibly, writing the biography began to give Morgan joy. He told Virginia Woolf that the process made him love Goldie all the more, and was going much more quickly than he had foretold. And the idea of a biography as a filial act got him thinking about his own posthumous legacy: "I wish I could get one written about me after I die," Morgan told Joe, "but I should want every thing told, everything, and there's so far so little. Goldie, because one's condemned to omissions, looms larger."

These "omissions" stemmed from Goldie's injunction against writing about his homosexuality. The "Recollections" he had given to Morgan were explicitly constructed as variations on a single theme: the effect of fifty years of failed or sublimated love affairs with men. He had recorded them frankly "in the hope that what I am writing, if it should ever see the light, may bring some help and encouragement to others who have the same temperament; or may contribute to enlighten and humanise public opinion on a point as to which, especially in England, it is singularly irrational and cruel."

But he had also tied Morgan's hands.

My present feeling is that if anything were published (as to which I have no judgement) the sex part should be omitted. One can't trust people yet (nor perhaps ever) to be decent about those things, and anyhow my relations are still alive. Remember that my sisters have not seen this autobiography and I don't wish them to, except in a safely bowdlerised form.

In writing the biography, Morgan faced the reality that Goldie's had been an *undramatic* life. Certainly Dickinson had been cerebral, and certainly the events of his life followed the serene plot of an academic story. But the greater narrative problem was that Goldie's life had been distorted both by sexual sublimation and sexual renunciation—and the cause of this tension within him could not be disclosed in the biography.

So Morgan shaped an entirely new genre, a biography that was truthful, if not exactly honest. In his writing, as in his dealings with Bob and May, he began to use creative silence to tell a story that would have been utterly destroyed by being labeled or named. Just as Adela Quested had felt diminished when she acquiesced in becoming Ronnie's *wife*—"Unlike the green bird, or the hairy animal, she was labelled now." In composing *Goldsworthy Lowes Dickinson*, Morgan left room for his "sensitive" readers to discover the source of his friend's unhappiness.

Working within the constraints established by Dickinson himself, Morgan was actually quite forthright. He painted a picture of a subject who lived entirely in a world of men, who had passionate male friendships and never thought of marriage. "Although he was never drawn to women in the passionate sense, all his deepest emotions being towards men, his life would have been empty and comfortless without them." Or, "Devoted to [Ferdinand] Schiller, but constantly parted from him, and doubtful whether his devotion was returned, Dickinson suffered for many years from a sense of frustration which the sensitive will understand."

Morgan also quoted Goldie directly: "I have seldom been out of love, if the word love may be used of a feeling continually thwarted on the physical side. That question I leave to casuists and medical men, though without much expectation they will have anything important to say about it." And "I think that few young men ever got less out of Paris than I did. For to get anything out of it, it seems essential to approach it by the route of women and that was no route for me."

To complete his very odd biography, Morgan wrote a curious afterword, adopting a Dickinsonian form: a Socratic dialogue between himself as a biographer and the voice of Mephistopheles. The devil demands he defend his choice to record such an inconsequential and *inward* life. The terms of Mephistopheles' objection make it clear that what was at stake for Morgan was personal—it was the threat of the utter extinction of homosexual lives.

> Mephistopheles . . . puts his head out at this point and asks me to set all personal feelings aside and state objectively why a memoir of . . . Dickinson need be written. If I say "Because I want to," the answer is "Who are you?" If I say "My friend was beloved, affection- ate, unselfish, . . ." the devil will reply "Yes, but that is neither here nor there, or rather it was there but it is no longer here. I have your word and the word of others that this was once so, but is there nothing which will survive when all of you also have vanished?"

Morgan had invoked this conceit before, in a short eulogy for Edward Carpenter. There he argued that Carpenter would likely be forgotten. He contrasted two types of fame—the sort that arose from "managing to adver- tise" oneself to the history books, and the kind that Carpenter evinced, which "rested on the constancy and intensity of his affection" for his friends. There was no doubt that the latter, while precious, could be easily extinguished. Morgan told Virginia Woolf, when she struggled with her own biography of their friend Roger Fry, that biographies as a genre would not "interest . . . the next generation."

The next generation was already a reality. On April 21, 1933, Morgan recorded in the Locked Diary: "Bob's son born at 5.0 am . . . Nice baby and like him, colour squashed raspberries." May and Bob named their only child Robert Morgan. To differentiate him from his father, they called him Robin. He was the third child named in honor of Morgan, and he was the center of the universe for his doting parents and for his secular godfather as well.

The birth of this baby, like the birth of the child of Helen Schlegel and Leonard Bast who inherits Howards End, set Morgan to thinking incredu- lously about the passage of time and his hopes for the future. When Robin was six weeks old, Morgan wrote to "my ever dear Bob,"

> I nearly dropped in for tea this afternoon but wasn't sure it would be convenient . . . I walked on Clapham Common instead and I found the house where I used to stop with my great-aunt [Marianne Thorn- ton] when I was a little boy. She was born in 1798! It seems incredi-

ble. Here is your baby, who is in a little way mine, because he bears my name, and he is born in 1933: one hundred and thirty five years later, and I have lived to see them both.

During this summer Morgan convinced Bob to accompany him on a driving tour of the West Country, in part to give May some rest, in part to reclaim Bob's affections. Harry Daley, true to form, took the opportunity of Bob's absence to visit May and stir up trouble. He broadly suggested that the friendship between Morgan and her husband was untoward, and did his best to undermine her confidence in Bob's love for her. But in the face of this May held firm without being rigid. She refused to begin a power struggle with Morgan, believing that Bob's loyalties, while divided, were more stable if he was with a man and not with other women. Harry's malign influence sometimes rattled Bob—"Harry . . . is always yapping back into Hammersmith on three legs and setting off Bob Barkingham"—but he couldn't fluster May.

So, in the first months after Robin's birth, the three worked out a détente—an unusual kinship that looked from the outside like a completely traditional marriage. It relied on leaving the unspoken unexplored, and on conventional ideas about May's absolute sway in domestic matters. But gingerly the arrangement grew into a kind of grace, a complex and undefined kinship that depended on Morgan and May's reciprocal love and admiration. With masterful aplomb, after Morgan's death May described the "stormy passages" of her relationship with him:

> I now know that he was in love with Robert and therefore critical and jealous of me and our early years were very stormy, mostly because he had not the faintest idea of the pattern of our lives and was determined that Robert should not be engulfed in domesticity. Over the years he changed us both and he and I came to love one another, able to share the joys and sorrows that came.

May did not ask, and she did not tell.

If Morgan resisted Bob becoming "engulfed in domesticity" with May, it was because he himself desired to set up housekeeping with his beloved. Morgan began to savor a domestic happiness with Bob at the Brunswick Square flat. It was the sort of quiet life between two men that he had hoped for since he wrote *Maurice*. He wrote Bob, "The happiest hours of my life will always be the short hours we can spend together in the flat." In the summer after Robin was born, Morgan amplified these domestic interludes into a monumental story, telling Florence Barger gleefully,

> Bob met me at 8.30 A.M. Liverpool Street, having already got breakfast ready in the flat. I suppose it must feel a little like being married, this sort of thing! Anyhow it is very pleasant and I have never experienced it before . . . I appreciate so much your reception of Bob. It isn't easy, at 53, to take a new important person into one's life, the doors should by ordinary rules have shut, but those whom I love, and Bob himself, have done their best to make it easy. I don't find it much use bothering about age—one is timeless until the end comes, and the years have only bound you and me together because they provided me with precious experience, which we have shared.

He would create a kind of marriage of his own, outside of ordinary rules, a marriage composed of real patience and joy with an admixture of magical thinking. Partly this meant devaluing the meaning of Bob's love for May as if it were some habit of working-class men in general; Morgan told Christopher Isherwood that he was considering revising the manuscript of *Maurice*: "I have sometime thought of Alec [Scudder] marrying."

In a real sense Morgan was rewriting his own life as he composed Goldie's biography. This was the life that Goldie, with his foot set solidly in the Victorian world, could never have. But watching Robin grow, and feeling the baby knit him and the Buckinghams together, Morgan began to take pleasure in being modern. Virginia Woolf noticed with interest how delighted Morgan seemed while writing Goldie's biography. Perhaps in homage to the tenor of Goldie's memoirs, Morgan began a separate section of his diary labeled "Sex," recording his own earliest memories of erotic desire. And in his "Commonplace Book" he wrote a little rebuttal to the note of caution Goldie had left him, imagining that this love for Bob might offer a lesson of hope for others.

HAPPINESS

I have been happy for two years . . . Happiness can come in one's natural growth and not queerly, as religious people think. From 51 to 53 I have been happy, and I would like to remind others that their turns can come too. It is the only message worth giving.

It was a curious thing that Morgan's interior world became so enchanted at the moment when the outer world—the world Margaret Schlegel had called the world of "telegrams and anger"—grew more malignant. From his beat, Bob reported to Morgan that trouble was brewing even on the streets of London. Oswald Mosley rented out Olympia, the huge Edwardian convention hall, to exhort a mob of English Fascists; Mosley's blackshirts spilled out onto the streets of Hammersmith, spewing hateful slogans about Communists and Jews. Bob was on duty to keep the peace at an enormous rally of blackshirts in Hyde Park; at Morgan's request, he took notes on the scene.

The political situation seemed dark for homosexuals as well as Jews. When Bob and Morgan visited Isherwood in Amsterdam, they were shadowed on the street by mysterious men, probably secret police. Morgan rebuffed Christopher's entreaty to consider publishing *Maurice*. Berlin, at least Berlin before Hitler, had seemed to the young man to embody the spirit of Freedom. But Morgan, with a longer view, was more cautious:

> Yes, if the pendulum keeps swinging in its present direction it might get published in time. But the more one meets decent & sensible people, of whom there are now a good few, the more does one forget the millions of beasts and idiots who still prowl in the darkness, ready to gibber and devour. I think I had a truer vision of civilisation thirty years ago, when I regarded myself as hiding a fatal secret.

The personal peril of Christopher and his German lover, Heinz Neddermeyer, weighed heavily on Morgan, who sent them money as they pursued peregrinations to keep Heinz from being conscripted into the German army. After Hitler's election the noose had tightened: Heinz's entry permit was denied by British immigration officials, who looked askance on his pretext of arriving as a domestic worker, and he was "put on the next boat back to Germany." The two men fled for respite to Tenerife in the Canary Islands. Their desperate situation—Heinz was eventually caught at the Trier near the Luxembourg border and forcibly conscripted—made Morgan anxious, both for them and on his own behalf. It was absurd to think that nationality meant anything at all! More than ever Morgan relied on the old Apostles' ethic of personal relationships.

The young homosexual men in Isherwood's circle worked out a creative way to apply Apostolic virtues to these exigent times: they married. Erika Mann, the lesbian daughter of Thomas Mann, approached Christopher in early 1935, asking if he would marry her so she could procure a British passport as a means of escape from Germany. The political cabaret she had founded with the actress Therese Giehse—Brecht's first Mother Courage— made her a target of the Nazis. Isherwood was too entangled with Heinz to agree to this arrangement, but he happily passed Mann along to Wystan Auden, who cabled back the single word "Delighted!" He and Mann married in June 1935—and remained companionable friends, and legally husband and wife, all their lives.

The next conscript was the novelist Johnny Simpson. (An odd-looking man with a huge chin, whose long face looked like the curve of a new moon, Simpson had known Wystan and Morgan since the early thirties.) Now Therese Giehse was in danger—not only for her political actions, but because she was a Jew. Auden approached Simpson with "irresistible" logic, asking, "What are buggers for?" In May 1936, the peculiar wedding party appeared at the registry office in Solihull, a posh suburb of Birmingham where Simpson lived—the bride, who spoke not a word of English, clutching a tiny bouquet. Auden, dolled up in full morning suit with striped trousers, grandly orchestrated the event as master of ceremonies. The married couple and their handful of guests repaired to a local pub, where they racked up a huge bar tab. Auden announced in stentorian voice that it was all right—"It's on Thomas Mann."

But not all weddings were fodder for comedy. In November 1933 Morgan was surprised to read the announcement of Siegfried Sassoon's engagement in *The Times*. Having lent a sympathetic ear both to Sassoon and to his theatrical but dear-hearted lover Stephen Tennant for the best part of a decade, Morgan was understandably dubious. Moreover he was hurt by learning the news by such impersonal means. He wrote Sassoon "a line of affection and good wishes and (in a sense) of farewell." In two senses, actually. It seemed clear that Sassoon, whose aspirations toward the condition of landed gentry had always amused Morgan, had succumbed to convention. And he had betrayed their friendship as well.

But Sassoon wrote back immediately, explaining that something sudden and mysterious had happened: he was in love with Hester Gatty. There was no accounting for it, but it was true. Morgan replied simply, "Your news, though I accept it as good news, startles me. (Not a question to be answered.)"

But he determined to be fair and not to treat Siegfried as a defector or Hester as an enemy.

In the waning days of 1935 Morgan faced an ironic recapitulation of his encounter with Goldie's life: his doctor diagnosed prostate trouble, and recommended the same surgery that Dickinson had undergone. The attitude of his doctor, who ascribed the condition to excessive masturbation, compounded the humiliating disease itself: "he seemed quite genuine in his disgust, and added that this sort of thing isn't natural and that nature takes it out of you somehow if you go against her. If he wants my reactions to shock he'll get them all right." Visiting the Woolfs, Morgan took Leonard aside and spoke to him gravely. After the two men's "little private talk" Virginia recorded in her diary, "I think he feels he may die."

Lily, not knowing the cause but grasping the context, began to panic and fear the worst. Even at fifty-six, Morgan had not resolved how to counter her machinations, and he repaired to the London flat in preparation for the surgery, but mainly as a temporary escape from West Hackhurst. Just days before the operation, he wrestled with his tone in composing letters to her: "You must try to treat me less like a small boy when I get back! You sometimes say that I am bored at home—I am not at all, but I do get depressed [with] so much supervision . . ." "I felt it was no good talking it over with you [buying a new divan], since although you want me to be comfortable you don't like change." Whereupon, ratifying his own worst excesses, he ended the letter childishly: "Will now have some cocoa or an orange (not sure which!) and then go to bedy-by."

The operation took place on December 18. Two nights before he went under the knife, Morgan composed a valedictory letter to Bob, telling him bravely, "I have an open mind whether I shall get through or not. I don't feel afraid of anything, and it is your love that has made me like this." But the procedure, the first of two, was a success; he rallied quickly, and quite soon forgot that he had worried over suffering Goldie's fate. Instead, as he recuperated slowly in a private nursing home, Morgan focused on the indignity of being cut off from the man he loved most dearly, complaining to Joe, "I don't expect mother has quite conveyed the position here. They have stopped Bob coming because I am fond of him . . ."

Even when in some pain, he retained his sense of humor, writing to Joe,

I was thinking yesterday of the prick with some detachment, probably rather like the Maharajah did. The maddening delight mine has so often given me and a knowledge of other people which no other part of my body could have given. And now it stands—or rather flops—for wet flannel trousers and changes of plans. No wonder they garlanded it with marigold and bedewed it with ghee. But to the Westerner such specialisation must always seem silly.

11

"The Last Englishman"

Marooned with Lily at the rambling Victorian pile of West Hackhurst, Morgan recovered from surgery. His mother was eighty-one, stout, crotchety, and "terribly authoritarian"; Morgan had just turned fifty-seven. Together, in this place, they seemed suspended in the past like bees in amber. They shared the sprawling house with two live-in servants: Agnes Dowland, the "last parlourmaid in England," and Henry Bone, the gardener, each almost as old as Lily and almost as infirm. Coal had to be carried to the grates, and ashes to the garden. There was no proper plumbing, no electricity, and no telephone. If they wanted to bathe, Agnes heated water atop the kitchen stove and painfully hauled it upstairs in brass cans. The mile-long path to the village trailed through a field of brambles.

Morgan's friends back at Hammersmith Section House may have regarded the Forsters as country gentry, but Lily had served as a governess to the children at Abinger Hall sixty years earlier, and even after decades of respectable widowhood she was sensitive to her precarious social standing. Both Forsters keenly understood their dependence on the Farrers of Abinger Hall, who had allowed their friend Laura Forster to build the house but refused her the freehold of the land under it. Since Aunt Laura's death, Morgan and Lily clung to the murky assumption that Lord Farrer would not enforce the terms of the lease. Now it was due to expire in months, just a short sixty years after Eddie Forster had drawn up the designs for the house. As the date loomed Morgan delicately bruited the question. The answer disquieted. Lord Farrer did not wish to tie his heirs' hands by voiding the original terms. Through skirmishes of hyperformal correspondence with his landlord, Morgan bargained for an extension of the lease for his lifetime, but he was forced to settle for a vague agreement for the presumably shorter term of Lily's lifetime instead. In the dozen years they lived at West Hackhurst, they had never been asked to dine at the "big house." Occasionally, in a burst of spite, they would instruct Agnes to turn on the tap in the kitchen to diminish the water pressure at the Hall.

Recuperating at the Buckinghams was out of the question. They, too, had been suffering health woes. Diagnosed with tuberculosis, May was sent to a sanatorium at Pinewood for the better part of a year. Little Robin, just two, had been packed off to live with an aunt and uncle, as Bob, exhausted, balanced his police rota with visits to May, to Robin, and to Morgan. When the little boy failed to recognize May on a hospital visit, his parents were heartbroken. The strain on his new family awoke a tenderness in Morgan; he sent May a stream of encouraging letters, books, and little gifts, regaling her with humorous stories about Robin, and reassuring her that all would be healed in time. He was especially solicitous that Bob and May must have time to rebuild their family life, advising her firmly, "You and R. and Robin will need to be alone together for quite a long time at first, if only to get accustomed to home life again, and you'll have to have in a woman at moments to do work which is too much for you."

Morgan's epistolary and practical support endeared him to May. In turn, he admired her pluck and loyalty during her long recuperation. Visiting her in the hospital was a stilted affair; a residue of Morgan's prickly possessiveness remained. But writing to her was different: being in control of words allowed him to articulate his love and admiration for her. It was as if by first becoming a character in Morgan's hands May Buckingham gradually transformed into a person in his consciousness. During her illness May became an individual, a "very decent sort," a "friend in her own right."

After she returned home, relations between Morgan and the couple adjusted very subtly into a stable triangle that would sustain all three of them in different ways for the next thirty-five years. The terms of this innovative family structure were never codified, nor were the boundaries tested. In an understated English way, each of them exercised restraint, each traded shared silence for a steady equanimity. Between them, Morgan and May deftly carved out an intimate space for their respective "marriages" to their beloved Bob, with the long weekends for May and the short weekends for Morgan. At the little brick house standing opposite a pocket-sized park in Shepherd's Bush, May ruled domestic life absolutely. Morgan fiercely claimed the flat at Brunswick Square, where Bob would fix an omelet on the gas ring. And wherever Morgan traveled, Bob accompanied Morgan in a cavalcade of male camaraderie, from Cerne Abbas (with its huge Neolithic chalk-figure of a man with a massive phallus) to Paris, to Amsterdam.

Bob and May decided not to have more children, and they sustained an amorous marriage. For his part, throughout the thirties Morgan continued to have the occasional fling, often reassuring Bob that he had kept vigilant against sexual infection. He acknowledged that the Buckinghams' robust sex life gave both of them pleasure and intimacy he could not share, but refused to accept that this diminished the legitimacy of his special bond with Bob. Only once did Bob rub Morgan's nose in the supremacy of his conjugal relations with May, which prompted a heartfelt rejoinder:

> I felt a bit sad at some of the things you said yesterday, not that you meant to make me sad, but you made me think of my limitations whereas generally you make me forget them. I believe that you are right—that particular experiences which I can't ever have *might* make the two people who share it feel they are in touch with the universe through each other. What a pity all (normal) people don't get it

The friendship between T. E. Lawrence and Morgan had settled into a fitful correspondence. Several times Morgan had visited Clouds Hill, the Spartan little cottage on the verge of the RAF camp at Bovington in Dorset, delighting in the raucous male company of Lawrence's working-class enlisted mates. To mitigate the cooling of their friendship over his strange response to Morgan's homosexual stories, Lawrence had revealed the manuscript of his next book, *The Mint*. It was an uncensored recounting of barracks life, full of foul language and homosocial camaraderie; Lawrence decided, ruefully, that it was unpublishable.

Lawrence's official work since he had returned from Karachi was all very hush-hush. Though he professed to be uneasy about the public image of himself as the icon of British manhood—debonair, reckless, patriotic, humble—Lawrence alternately stoked the public fantasy and retreated from it. One month he would be testing speedboats in the Solent on some top-secret orders from Winston Churchill himself; the next he would hole up in the whitewashed cottage and listen to music on the gramophone with the huge white bell. Morgan accepted an invitation to visit Lawrence there, sensing that he might need company after he was discharged from service. The conditions would be little better than camping: no toilet, and only the sparest bath in a lean-to, two sleeping bags, embroidered "Meum" and "Teum"—the guest on a little leather banquette, while Lawrence spread out on the floor. The lane to the cottage was so remote that Lawrence assured Morgan he would place a whitewashed stone in a newly built wall to mark the place. In early April 1935, just weeks after he had been severed from the RAF, Lawrence worked with a friend to make ready for Morgan's arrival.

On the very day that Morgan was to arrive, he learned that Lawrence had been hideously injured in a motorcycle accident just down the road from the white stone in the wall. Restless and despondent, Lawrence had become careless—overtaking two boys on bicycles, he lost control and crashed. Instead of the company of Lawrence, the sleeping bag, and the Victrola, Morgan found himself attending Lawrence's funeral in the little village. He stood beside a sobbing Winston Churchill as they laid Lawrence in the ground. Lawrence's brother approached Morgan to compile a memorial edition of Lawrence's letters. Despite his ambivalence about stoking the Lawrence myth, Morgan took on the task. Encouraged by William Plomer, he had begun assembling a collection of his own occasional essays, dating all the way back to the Alexandrian pieces. These meditations on the English character he would call *Abinger Harvest*; during the year after Lawrence's death, he toiled on both projects simultaneously.

Late on a Friday evening in June 1935, in a blistering heatwave, almost three thousand people packed into the *salle* of the Art Deco Palais de la Mutualité in the Latin Quarter of Paris to hear Morgan deliver the first speech at the International Congress of Writers. He had come to this unlikely moment, and into the public eye, urged on by desperation. The whole world seemed to have become a world of "telegrams and anger." For six years economic depression had staggered Britain, Germany, and the United States; the summer before, Hitler—now führer—began to rearm Germany in defiance of the Treaty of Versailles; Mussolini's invasion of Ethiopia was imminent; and six months before, General Franco had killed striking miners by the thousands. Morgan wrestled with a terrible sense of déjà vu as he watched the long, slow "dégringolade" of European civilization for the second time in a generation.

When André Malraux invited him to come to Paris to speak in "defense of culture," Morgan had few illusions about the power of writers to shape political events. But he felt he must stand up. He urged Virginia Woolf to join him—"I don't suppose the conference is of any use—things have gone too far. But I have no doubt as to the importance of people like ourselves *inside* the conference. We represent the last utterances of the civilised." Woolf demurred; so Morgan led the British delegation, alongside Aldous Huxley.

The congress's brief was deliberately amorphous so as to attract all stripes of left-leaning and antifascist thinkers. The roster included some of Europe's greatest writers—Bertolt Brecht, Gustav Regler, and Heinrich Mann in exile from Hitler's Germany, Boris Pasternak and Isaak Babel from the Soviet Union, René Crevel and André Breton from France. But its organizers—Henri Barbusse and Malraux—were entranced by communism. Together they embraced the peculiarly French belief that only public intellectuals could rescue the world from political disaster. At the epicenter stood Malraux's old friend André Gide, a recent convert, who traced the enlightenment from Diderot and Rousseau to Soviet communism, the "condition of society which would permit the fullest development of each man, the bringing forth and application of all his potentialities."

As always, Morgan stood in the uncomfortable position of seeing things a bit too clearly to be categorical. Fascism horrified him—it was an ideology that "does evil that evil may come." To communism he was willing to grant good intentions, though it "does many things which I think evil." Though pacifism was a ubiquitous position of the left—the Oxford Union having voted, 275 to 153, that it would "not take up arms for king or country under any circumstances"—Morgan found refusal to join a war rather beside the point. The prospect of another war seemed simultaneously inevitable and unthinkable. Preparing for the conference, he confessed to Christopher Isherwood.

> I don't think anyone could possess social nerves today, unless he was a fool or a communist, and I am too intelligent to be the first, and too old to be the second. All that I can do is to work out a private ethic which, in the outbreak of a war, might be helpful to me. The individual is more than ever the goods . . . I am O. K. personally, as we call it.

Personally was the watchword. Morgan attended the congress because it seemed like the last moment when it might be possible to speak as an individual to individuals whom he admired. By "next year," he wrote John Lehmann, "every one may know their own minds."

Standing behind the lectern in the immense hall, wearing a rumpled tweed suit, Morgan was almost obscured by a microphone as big as a plate. He looked out on row upon row of men in shirtsleeves, collars pulled off and cuffs popped open—intellectuals indistinguishable from their proletarian brothers in a democracy of sweltering. He spoke to them about the British tradition of free speech.

Morgan's address was a triumph of nuance and utterly ill-suited to its audience. To the young people drunk on ideology it was a tepid, bourgeois, provincial affair. Morgan began by parsing the limits of English liberty: "It means freedom for the Englishman, but not for the subject-races of his Empire." But in describing freedom, Morgan acknowledged, he was less concerned with politics than with insidious self-censorship. He told the intellectuals who sat before him, who for four days extolled their solidarity with the workingman, that the whole thrust of their congress was irrelevant: "The hungry and the homeless don't care about liberty any more than they care about cultural heritage." In his very English way, he focused on the spread of the dictatorial spirit within a culture, the creeping "national need for secrecy." His prime text was the Sedition Act, a recent law passed in the defense of national security, which criminalized the dissemination of Communist or pacifist writing to British soldiers. Not only did the law restrict liberties by impeding the moral education of soldiers; it also subjected citizens to general warrants (on a person rather than for a specific crime) for the first time in almost two hundred years. The law, he warned, "encourages the informer."

Too polite or too circumspect to draw attention to these same tactics as they reinforced Communist orthodoxy at the congress itself, Morgan ended with an example from his own heart—the suppression of a writer's work because of its content. James Hanley's homosexual novel *Boy* had been published in 1931 to good reviews—but just three months before the congress and four years after its initial publication, it was retroactively condemned as obscene and its publisher fined. As president of the newly formed National Council for Civil Liberties, Morgan had campaigned publicly against the Sedition Bill, and protested Hanley's prosecution; he viewed the congress as a vehicle for publicizing the backlash on civil rights in his own country. But he concluded by acknowledging that to his present audience this sort of issue might be very small beer.

> My colleagues . . . may feel it is a waste of time to talk about freedom and tradition when the economic structure of society is unsatisfactory. They may say that if there is another war writers of the individualistic and liberalising type, like myself . . . will be swept away. I am sure that we shall be swept away, and I think . . . that there may be another war. [I]f nations keep on amassing armaments, they can no more help discharging their filth than an animal which keeps on eating can stop itself from excreting. This being so, my job . . . is an interim job. We have just to go on tinkering with our old tools until the crash comes . . . After it—if there is an after—the task of civilisation will be carried on by people whose training has been different from my own.

Watching from the center of the hall, Katherine Anne Porter found the "slender little man with a large forehead and a small chin" speaking to be a pathetic sight. It was not only his tone; his delivery was hopelessly out of touch.

> [Forster] paid no attention to the microphone, but wove back and forth, and from side to side, gently, and every time his face passed the mouthpiece I caught a high-voiced syllable or two, never a whole word, only a thin recurring sound like the wind down a chimney . . . Then, surprisingly, once he came to a moment's pause before the instrument and there sounded into the hall clearly but wistfully a complete sentence: "I DO believe in liberty!"

After this curious display, Morgan's friend Charles Mauron firmly read his French translation. As the audience gathered the meaning of his words—so *antique*, so *bourgeois*, so *English*—they broke out in a "pantomime of malignant ridicule. Mr. Forster and all his kind were already as extinct as a dodo."

But they did not fully know who "his kind" were. For Morgan had also come to the congress to meet André Gide: Gide the sexual hero; Gide the implacable voice who had published *Corydon*, a defense of homosexuality cast in the form of a Socratic dialogue; Gide whose frank memoir *Si le grain ne meurt* chronicled his cruising for boys with Oscar Wilde in Morocco. (This was the Gide whom Joe Ackerley had held up as an example when Morgan resisted Joe's request that he should publish *Maurice*. Morgan had replied tartly, "But Gide hasn't got a mother!") It was in part to this Gide, who introduced him at the congress's opening, that Morgan was speaking when he lamented, "In England, more than anywhere else, [writers'] creative work is hampered because they can't write freely about sex, and I want it recognized that sex is a subject for serious treatment . . ."

It was this Gide in whom Morgan hoped to confide. He was thrilled to be invited to luncheon with Gide and Malraux, and brought along Bob Buckingham as his guest—a genuine solidarity of intellectuals and the working class. But Bob, stolid and handsome, spoke not a word of French, and the two great Frenchmen were absorbed in congress politics throughout the meal. Instead of his idealized Gide, Morgan was faced with a more self-satisfied figure, of reptilian face and arch demeanor. This Gide was "slippery as a trout." He spoke barely a word to Morgan and did not acknowledge Bob at all. At the conclusion of the meal, immediately upon putting down their demitasses and before Morgan even had a chance to clear his throat, the two Andrés disappeared, presenting him only with the spectacle of their "distinguished backs." The rest of the congress devolved into political theater: "many eulogies of Soviet culture . . . [where] the name of Karl Marx detonate[d] again and again like a well-placed charge . . . draw[ing] after it the falling masonry of applause." (Gide was to repudiate communism—well before some of his peers—after a visit to Stalin's Soviet Union the following year.)

Morgan returned to England, convinced both of the emptiness of the exercise and the necessity of performing it. A decade before, his old friend and adversary D. H. Lawrence (who had left England in a long, restless pursuit of freedom) diagnosed Morgan's admixture of insight and impotence perfectly. He was "[s]ad as ever," Lawrence told him, "like a lost soul calling Ichabod. But I prefer the sadness to [ironic] Stracheyism. To me you are the last Englishman. And I am the one after that."

In London, too, there were Philistines aplenty. The 1936 edition of *Abinger Harvest* had to be recalled and pulped because of a libel action. Morgan had unwittingly blundered into a dispute between two British civil servants who disagreed profoundly on the source of the Nile. The dispute had been played for comedy in Morgan's essay "A Flood in the Office," when he originally published it in 1919; but in the interim one party described had sued and won for libel; the reprinting repeated the libel, and the injured party sought to exact a heavy penalty on Morgan and Edward Arnold, his publishers. Five hundred pounds and a reprinting later, Morgan was justifiably jumpy. Looking over the T. E. Lawrence letters, Morgan decided that their frankness, Lawrence's ambiguous sexuality, and his politics all spelled trouble. More in sorrow than in anger he resigned as editor of the project, feeling wounded and cowardly.

He was disgusted by British exceptionalism, by the celebration of *Mrs. Miniver*, whose middle-class smugness and stoicism could be "exploited for their . . . factitious value . . . by rival government gangs." Just as twenty years earlier, self-styled decadence brigades patrolled the streets looking for nancy boys, in this moment Morgan recognized the "old herd instinct," the familiar specious tug of war between "the decadent" and "the civilised." But he had come a long way from the timid young man who condemned "the brassy rattle of civilisation" quietly. Now, in public, he sought to redefine the term—to claim the mantle of civilization for his own outlook. "The people I admire most are those who are sensitive and want to create something or discover something, and do not see life in terms of power," he wrote. He refused to consider human history to be synonymous with brute force: "Some people call its absences 'decadence'; I call them 'civilisation' and find in such interludes the chief justification for the human experiment. Whether this is due to courage or to cowardice in my own case I cannot be sure."

On the eve of the Munich Crisis, Morgan met up with Isherwood, just back from his "journey to a war" in China and about to emigrate to the New World. The prospect of war was horrifying: Morgan confessed that he was haunted by a vision of himself as if seen from above, "going mad—of suddenly turning and running away from people in the street." But Christopher discerned strength in Morgan's emotional clarity. In his diary, he wrote,

[Morgan] is as anxious and afraid as any of us, and never for an instant pretends not to be . . . But, actually, he's the last person who would ever go mad: he's far saner than anyone else I know. And immensely, superhumanly strong. He's strong because he doesn't try to be a stiff-lipped stoic, so he'll never crack. He's absolutely flexible. He lives by love, not by will . . . my "England" is E. M.; the anti-heroic hero, with his straggly straw mustache, his light, gay, baby blue eyes and his elderly stoop.

Christopher's friend Wystan Auden praised Forster's lonely voice in a sonnet he dedicated to him.

> *Though Italy and King's are far away*
> *And Truth a subject only bombs discuss,*
> *Our ears unfriendly, still you speak to us,*
> *Insisting that the inner life can pay.*

In the years between the writers' congress and the onset of war, Morgan learned how best to use a microphone. Hilda Matheson, the head of the Talks Department at the nascent BBC, invited Morgan (along with many famous writers of the day) to write and deliver occasional broadcasts. Sequestered in a booth soundproofed by quilted blankets, the microphone before him perched atop a tiny table covered in baize, Morgan felt much more at home than he had been at the Palais. He spoke deliberately, softly but clearly, into the instrument as if he were speaking into a single listener's ear. His voice was a measured, slightly wiry tenor; his accent suburban, much less plummy than the Received Pronunciation that the BBC director, Sir John Reith, dictated. (Reith's subordinates called him "Mussolini" behind his back.)

There was no getting around the intimacy of Morgan's distinctive voice. It was of a piece with his argument. In choosing to broadcast one man's views, to be an individual and to invite dissent, Morgan's approach was a deliberate rebuttal to Goebbels's plan for broadcasting. In Germany it was illegal to listen to the wireless with the windows closed; the radio became the perfect instrument to foster national conformity—*one people, one Reich, one Führer.* For Morgan, the microphone was not a megaphone but a humbler device. He had long been a student of the English national temperament, and now he brought to bear all that he had learned as a connoisseur of caution, speaking with utter honesty about the limits of what one man could do. It was the only kind of authority he could wield in good conscience—a still, small voice speaking his truth in public. Quoting Shakespeare's *Richard II*, he told his audience "I've been studying how I may compare 'This prison where I live unto the world.' I've been wondering where liberty ends and restraint begins in contemporary society. I suppose we're free."

In his BBC talks he returned, in a different register, to the old questions that Goldie and G. E. Moore had first posed to him by the coal grate in his rooms at King's—how to be *oneself* and how to be *good*. Without explicitly stating so, he made the ethics of his conflicted identity the subject itself. Though he thought himself a coward, in their unstinting observation of power and powerlessness the talks displayed their own sinewy courage. Powerlessness became the point. He told a friend, "All I can do is to 'behave well'. . . with the full knowledge that my behaviour cannot alter the course of events."

But he could change people's *minds*. Morgan's great gift was the ability to see life at a slant; in his radio addresses, he slyly invited his audience to consider unsettling comparisons. He warned against the willing sacrifice of domestic civil liberties in the name of national security. On the tercentenary of the *Areopagitica*, Milton's classic call for political freedom, Morgan remarked, "We are willing enough to praise freedom when she is safely tucked in the past and cannot be a nuisance," he wrote. "In the present, amidst dangers whose outcome we cannot foresee, we get nervous about her, and admit censorship."

And he discerned in the celebration of British national identity a "racial exercise" in its own right, disconcertingly similar to the Nazis' agenda. Homebred anti-Semitism was particularly familiar and frightening to him. In an essay on "Jew-Consciousness," he brilliantly and disarmingly argued that anyone could be subject to capricious cruelty.

Long, long ago, while Queen Victoria reigned, I attended two preparatory schools. At the first of these, it was held to be a disgrace to have a sister. Any little boy who possessed one was liable to get teased. The word would go round: "Oh, you men, have you seen the Picktoes' sister?" The men would then reel about with sideways motions, uttering cries of "sucks" and pretending to faint with horror . . .

I got through all right myself, because my conscience was clear . . . It was a very different story at my second school. Here, sisters were negligible, but it was a disgrace to have a mother. Crabbe's mother, Gob's mother, eeugh! . . . Those preparatory schools prepared me for life better than I realised, for having passed through two imbecile societies, a sister-conscious and a mother-conscious . . . I am now asked to consider whether the people I meet and talk about are or are not Jews . . . Having been a Gentile at my first preparatory school and a Jew at my second, I know what I am talking about.

The talks he reshaped into essays; these he would publish under the title *Two Cheers for Democracy* (he could not quite muster three) after the war.

In 1938, Morgan told William Plomer he was "trying to construct a philosophy." It was built out of the bricolage of the "liberalism crumbling beneath him." Too secular to be a credo, the essay was titled "What I Believe." It began startlingly.

> I do not believe in Belief. But this is an age of faith, and there are so many militant creeds that, in self-defence, one has to formulate a creed of one's own. Tolerance, good temper and sympathy are no longer enough in a world which is rent by religious and racial persecution, in a world where ignorance rules, and science, who ought to have ruled, plays the subservient pimp.

The essay was tough and clearheaded. It was a repudiation of machismo— and foreign policy as machismo—that utterly rejected public politics and national "causes." One famous line had a special bite. Morgan wrote, "I hate the idea of causes, and if I had to choose between betraying my country and betraying my friend, I hope I should have the guts to betray my country."

He refused to betray his friends Christopher and Wystan, though they stood accused of abandoning Britain in her time of greatest need. In January 1939, to loud opprobrium, the two young writers departed for the United States. But Morgan saw their situation differently. He alone saw them off at Waterloo Station. Their job, he told them, was "to keep away" and "see us sink from a distance." His job was to bear a different kind of witness: "I have myself to face a world which is tragic without becoming tragic myself."

When war was announced over the radio, he was in the parlor at West Hackhurst. He quietly wept alone for a few minutes, and then went to comfort Lily. Putting his emotional keel down, he determined to work his way sequentially through all the Beethoven piano sonatas. "Whatever one does is wrong," he told Christopher on the day war was declared, "so do not come back here, that is the wrongest." He sent off letters to his friend at implausible American addresses—the El Kanan Hotel in Santa Monica (nicknamed the "El K-Y"), the Vedanta Center in Hollywood where Christopher studied with the swami, and finally the eponymous Rustic Road. Morgan wrote his return address simply: "London, the Olde World."

In the spirit of wartime privation, Morgan let go his flat at Brunswick Square, moving west to a tiny aerie in Chiswick overlooking Turnham Green. It was half the cost and closer to Bob. The flat perched atop a postwar mansion block—it could be reached only by taking a rickety lift to the top floor, and then picking one's way across a sort of catwalk on the roof to the entrance. It was bone-cold in winter, and the pipes often froze, but it offered an unsurpassed view of the burning city. The pied-à-terre proved providential, for in May 1941 Joe Ackerley's flat in Maida Vale was virtually demolished in the Blitz; he escaped death, having gone around the corner to see how William Plomer was faring at the instant the bomb hit. Throughout the bombing, both men kept their sangfroid. Plomer drily described near-misses as "demi-vierges." Farther east, in Mecklenburg Square, just meters from Morgan's old Bloomsbury flat, the Woolfs' huge library was destroyed by fire. The couple retrenched to the Sussex countryside, Virginia desperately depressed.

Walking through the streets of London, Morgan observed how the scars of war opened unexpected vistas: "*What a wildness* south of St. Paul's! I stood (Feb. '43) by St. Augustine's—a tiny Wren—and saw the tower of St. Nicholas Cole rising from the plain . . . The sun had set, coldish . . . Full of my own desolation, I thought 'It will never get straightened out', also 'Here is beauty.' Oh I long for public mourning in the sense of recognition of what has happened." He promised Bob—whose job of patrolling the streets of London during the Blitz put him in mortal danger—that he would "look after Robin and May. Love does a good deal to cancel what seems unbearable." "Truly we live in strange times," Morgan told him, "and the only thing which is really real in them is love."

London was chock-a-block with beautiful young men in uniform. But spies were everywhere, and Morgan's natural reticence sharpened into anxiety as his friends fell into danger. Plomer left his job as a reader for Jonathan Cape to do some hush-hush intelligence work for the Admiralty, and just then published his autobiography *Double Lives*—a perhaps unconscious reference to his sharply compartmentalized public and private lives. He was hyperdiscreet about his naval work, but careless in his cruising. Early in 1943, Plomer was arrested for soliciting a soldier near Paddington Station;

he would have lost his job and his liberty but for the intervention of a nimble young coworker named Ian Fleming. (After the war Plomer returned the favor by recommending that Cape publish Fleming's novel about a dashing British agent named James Bond.) Terrified, Plomer burned his letters from Ackerley, Spender, Isherwood, and Lehmann. He carefully culled all of Morgan's letters that might hint of homosexuality, and urged him to do the same. Thereafter his letters lost their humor and tang—even in private, he felt watched.

Joe Ackerley's sexual escapades became increasingly reckless, and more and more often he called on Morgan to mop up the mess. Joe had taken a summer cottage in Dover just before the war; a stream of dashing young sailors and petty thieves eventually caught the attention even of his elderly landladies, and Morgan—who was their age and appeared respectable—was dispatched to make amends. He was willing to do so, but remonstrated: "What does concern me is that you won't face up to the fact that, to the average person, this sort of thing is disgusting, especially when it obtrudes its creaks-and-sheets end first upon their notice. No doubt it oughtn't to disgust. But it does."

In vain Morgan had tried to counsel Joe against his attraction to venal guardsmen, thieves, and opportunists whom he routinely tried to "rescue": "Joe—, you must give up looking for gold in coal-mines—it merely prevents you from getting amusement out of a nice piece of coal." But in 1943 Joe got himself and his friends into real danger. Persuading himself he was in love, he criminally abetted the desertion of a feckless Guardsman, giving the young man money and sequestering him in a spare room. After the police became involved, Morgan became obsessed with the idea that his letters to Joe might be found, and that both he and Bob might be implicated in a serious crime.

Morgan enlisted John Morris, an ex-army man and head of the BBC Far Eastern Service, to try to talk some sense into Joe. Morris was a friend of Plomer, the kind of bluff, frank, but reliably discreet homosexual who could make clear what was at stake. But Joe had "altered"—Morgan read his maddening narcissism as "indifference" to the capacity for real friendship. "I love and have loved you," Morgan wrote to Joe. "But none of that means anything to you, I'm afraid." He asked that Joe return all his letters. "I must seem selfish and timorous over this, but it is the only corner of a very large affair which I feel competent to touch." But the letters were precious to Joe;

he moved them to his office at the BBC for safekeeping, ducking the request. The friendship—and the letters—survived the war, but for a time things did not go smoothly.

In early April 1941 Morgan was shocked to read Virginia Woolf's obituary in *The Times*. Feeling helpless and miserable, unwilling to burden Leonard with a long spell of madness, she had drowned herself in the river behind their house in Rodmell. Morgan wrote to Leonard immediately upon hearing the news. The shock of her death made him ill for months—"turned my shit pale green and almost scentless"—and he deliberated whether her suicide was "the best course for a pure artist." He visited Leonard in Sussex, and delivered the Rede lecture in the Senate House in Cambridge the month after Virginia's death. He called it, simply, "Virginia Woolf." With the wound still raw, he dispelled the "legend of the Invalid Lady of Bloomsbury," calling her "tough but sensitive." "Like all her friends, I miss her greatly . . . But . . . I am sure there is no case for lamentation . . . Virginia Woolf got through an immense amount of work, she gave acute pleasure in new ways, she pushed the light of the English language a little further against darkness. Those are facts." Even a year later, he told Christopher, she "always seems in the next room. I can never get clear in my mind whether she was right or wrong to go."

But Morgan, not so pure an artist by his own account, knew that he must stay. West Hackhurst, at the far western margin of the metropolis, escaped the worst of the bombings. To this country refuge came a stream of ancient family members and friends displaced by the war: his cousin Percy Whichelo—recently retired from the Ecclesiastical Commission—and his wife, Dutchie; his uncle Philip Whichelo (in his mid-seventies); Lily's old friend Mrs. Mawe; and finally Florence Barger, who had been suddenly widowed just before the war, and whose house in Hampstead had been destroyed. Without much regret on either side, Morgan and Florence had outgrown the intimacy forged three decades before during his affair with Mohammed. In Abinger she proved to be of practical help and a good friend to Lily, and stayed on serenely for almost two years. The other visitors left after a few months, tempers frayed all around.

Morgan tried to see the humor in his new ménage. "It is part of the psychology of this war that everyone, sooner or later, will come to feel provincial," he wrote Christopher; he counseled himself to "be wary of melancholy as a sort of rage." In part to amuse himself, in part to add to the recorded history of his "race," he began to compose a canon of homosexual literature on a commercial tablet of lined paper. There was a certain reverence in setting aside a notebook for this purpose; paper was so scarce that Morgan had begun to cannibalize books from his library for letter paper. But there was irreverence, too. The notebook's cover was a World War I propaganda poster depicting four naval gunners on the deck of a warship, loading a huge phallic artillery shell into the mouth of a cannon. Across the top, Morgan wrote "Lest We Forget Him!" in a spidery hand, deftly appropriating Kipling's patriotic piety (from his 1897 poem "Recessional") into a different key. In it he carefully transcribed passages by Donne and Whitman and Symonds, a selection from an ancient Chinese pillow book translated by his friend Arthur Waley, and snippets of writing by young homosexual writers—Denton Welch, Desmond Stewart, and Roger Gellert. He would not forget them.

He titled the notebook with tongue in cheek, but it was designed with an eye to extinction. Cut off from the people whom he most loved, Morgan felt like "the last of my race." In case he should be killed, Morgan recorded a valedictory list of pals and lovers: "Johnny, Reg, Charles Lovett, Charlie Day, Harry Digby, George Dowsing, Achille, Mohammed and Bob himself . . ." The war put him in a contemplative, melancholy state of mind: "I have violent longings for fragments of my past . . . and I reconstruct partings which I hadn't at the time known would be for so long." The worst was the feeling that he had abandoned his old friend Charles Mauron in occupied France. Morgan could not shake the memory of himself—heedless—scrambling onto a little mountain train the summer before the war, leaving Charles, "already almost blind," his eyes tearing up behind the dark spectacles he wore to shield them, forlornly waving from the station platform.

In Greenwich Village the young painter Paul Cadmus read "What I Believe" in *The Nation* and was buoyed by Forster's singular vision. He sent Morgan a fan letter, enclosing photographs of two paintings inspired by his writing. In the essay Forster had argued for "not an aristocracy of power, based on rank and influence, but an aristocracy of the sensitive, the considerate and the plucky. Its members are to be found in all nations and classes, and all through the ages, and there is a secret understanding between them when they meet. They represent the true human tradition, the one permanent victory of our queer race over cruelty and chaos." It was clear from Cadmus's response that he took the phrase "queer race" to speak directly to him. Cadmus had always proudly called himself "queer."

The "secret understanding" that Forster, too, was homosexual was known to Cadmus through talk amounting to gossip that originated with Isherwood. But the passion with which Cadmus and his young friends responded to Forster's beliefs was serious and heartfelt. Without ever having met him, Cadmus wrote Morgan of

> the admiration and devotion I feel towards your works—and through them, towards you. "What I Believe" is so much what I believe too that I always read it to potential friends. I do it with so much conviction and emotion that I and they forget that it is not I speaking. They almost give me the credit. Once, it even caused me to be loved, I think: at least it was a strong, contributing factor. It was really You, not I who won the love and deserved it; and I am afraid I was not able to live up to it, nor to you.

The writer's warmth and intelligence struck a chord, and the old man and the painter thirty years his junior became epistolary friends. In turn, Cadmus widened the circle of friendship. Soon the painter Jared French, who shared Cadmus's studio on St. Luke's Place—and his bed—and French's wife, Margaret (also an artist), were sending letters to Morgan. Along with the letters came much-welcomed packages of food. All manner of unavailable luxuries found their way across the Atlantic in a swell of generosity.

The countertide of good cheer from sympathetic Americans came at an opportune time for Morgan. These foreigners awoke in him a sense of relevance, and—unknown to him at the time—a connection to the next generation of homosexual men. From the West Coast, Christopher orchestrated pilgrimages of friends and acquaintances traveling to England. One "present" came in the form of an exceptionally handsome young actor who was touring with Irving Berlin's patriotic revue *This Is the Army*. Before he was drafted, Bill Roerick had known Christopher in Hollywood. Tall, handsome, well-read, and a perfect disciple, he arrived on Morgan's doorstep with a charming entrée, a letter from Christopher that read in its entirety:

Dearest Morgan,

If this ever reaches you, it will be by the hand of Bill [Roerick], who needs no other introduction because you will like him, too.

As always,
your loving C.

Bill was bright, talkative, fun to be around. They "quickly became attached" in a platonic adulatory friendship. Though Bill was extravagantly generous, Morgan sensed that "something solid" lay beneath his considerable charm. Morgan detailed a list of his gifts for Plomer to savor: "200 cigarettes, 2 pks chocolate, 1 bottle lemon-essence, 1 guinea ticket for [the show], 2 modern American books, 2 acorns brought from the New World for plantation here." Morgan wryly admitted, "I quite like being pelted by such a storm." Reciprocating, Morgan concocted an odyssey to see Forrest Reid in Belfast and John Simpson in Birmingham. Bill became a young emissary of Morgan's goodwill, a kind of proxy younger self, much as Ackerley had been in India.

The new friendships were partial ballast against circumstances at home. A lot of his energy went to saying goodbyes. Morgan recorded in his diary each separation from Bob as if it might be the last: "Bob twice k'd me on Waterloo entrance No. 3 platform, 8 p.m., then walked away firmly, his broad shoulders in bluish sports coat last seen." In 1943, Bob set aside his pacifism to volunteer for a nearly suicidal bomber detail. Morgan and May were both in agonies of fear, but to their great relief Bob was rejected on account of poor eyesight. He worked night and day for the police force; they saw very little of one another.

By the spring of 1945, age and war exhaustion had thoroughly depleted Lily. A series of falls transformed her to a shade of herself. Though he had often blamed her for stunting his life, Morgan's compassion bloomed for her as his mother weakened. He found her "beautiful" in extreme old age. He began to rethink his resentments, and to take more responsibility for their sometimes stifling interdependence. A decade before, he had tempered Joe's accusation that Lily had ruined his life: "Although my mother has been intermittently tiresome for the last thirty years, cramped and warped my genius, hindered my career, blocked and buggered up my house, and boycotted my beloved, I have to admit that she has provided a sort of rich subsoil where I have been able to rest and grow." After her death, Morgan was more empathetic:

Now I am older I understand her depression better . . . I often think of my mistakes with mother, or rather the wrongness of an attitude that may have been inevitable. I considered her much too much in a niggling way, and did not become the authoritative male who might have quietened her and cheered her up. When I look at the beauty of her face, even when old, I see that something different should have been done. We were a classic case.

Lily died on March 11, 1945, at the age of ninety. The last night she lived, Morgan lay curled up on a blanket in the passageway outside her bedroom, listening for her breathing. In her intelligent, plainspoken way she accepted death, telling her only child that she could not last long. "No," he replied tenderly, "but your love will." In the early afternoon of a cool spring Sunday, as Morgan was feeding her some broth like a baby, Lily looked at him and died.

In the days after the funeral, Florence Barger and Agnes tended to him. For sixty-six years he had been psychically inseparable from Lily, and he felt so still, telling Christopher, "I partly died when my mother did, and must smell sometimes of the grave." The immediate burden was to sort out her effects. Every room of the vast house, and the carriage house, too, was crammed with *things*—"masses of rubbish from straw fans to wardrobes which are in many cases not absolute rubbish and have a semi-life which complicates their fate." And there was so much paper: brittle, ancient willow baskets stuffed with letters, wooden boxes and bound books of family accounts going back to Aunt Monie's father, Henry Thornton, and his busy, frugal Clapham friends. Morgan kept a record of what he burned on the bonfire, dragging out "destroying things—150 years of letters mostly from women to women"; "hundreds of letters in which one woman writes to another about the ill health of a third." Beyond this sorting out, he told Christopher, he was at a loss, "What I shall do is beyond me, as it is beyond the world."

Each time he "broke down" he totted it up in his diary. The most ordinary activity—standing on the railway platform in Dorking—could dissolve him. May and Robin, on holiday from his Quaker school in Saffron Walden, came to visit and cheered him immensely. It lifted his spirits somewhat to see Lily's possessions go out into the households of his friends. When William Plomer came to keep him company, Morgan gave him a beautiful gold-and-white tea service. To Florence he gave Lily's stout silver teapot and sugar bowl.

To distract him and diminish his depression, friends urged him to accept an invitation to the All-India PEN conference in Jaipur. He decided he could use the change of scene, knowing there would be no faces of friends there to greet him. Masood and His Highness had died within six months of each other in 1937—each, in his own way, a tragic ending. Masood, whose grandiosity always swirled before him, enveloping all his friends, had been stripped of his position at the university his grandfather had so proudly founded in Aligarh. His last years were spent in melancholy exile, and he had died at the young age of forty-seven.

Bapu Sahib, too, had outlived the India of grandeur—a place of his capacious imagination. Malcolm Darling had seen him in the final years of his unraveling, before he absconded from his throne, leaving the state's accounts in a shambles; when the old friends met, Bapu Sahib put his head in Darling's lap and sobbed. The *Times* obituary for His Highness blamed his downfall on "ungovernable temper and self-indulgence," but Morgan had written a protesting letter, celebrating the maharajah's imagination, hospitality, and tolerance.

And so Morgan set out on a tour of India as a public figure. cosseted and accompanied, but very much alone in his memory. It was a welcome distraction. "I feel like a sponge which has been dropped back into an ocean whose existence it had forgotten. I have a swelling soul," he wrote to Bob. Caravans and caves and camels and sticky cakes—two months of being fêted made him feel that he had been living on the surface of his visit. "With dissatisfaction," he recorded in his travel diary the evening he began his return, "I look back on myself in India, humorous, conciliatory, an old dear, whose lavish gestures gave away very little . . . The only first class thing about me now is my grief."

There would come more sorrow, and quickly. On his first morning back in London he learned from Bob that the lease was up at West Hackhurst. The landlords were claiming the house for a relative. Morgan broke the news to Christopher: "I returned to more worry and sadness, for I have been given notice to leave this house—it is not mine to sell." In his "Commonplace

Book," he made a careful map of the kitchen garden (as he had almost sixty years before for Rooksnest), this time dating it to "the year I was driven out and after it had been cultivated for 70 years."

It was less that he felt uprooted than that the soil of his life had washed away. Again and again in his letters to friends, he emphasized this sense of extinction. "I see myself as a historic figure," he told Plomer, "if not a very important one: the last survivor, the last possessor of a particular tradition." To Isherwood he confided, "My mother's death has been much more awful than I expected. I am glad that no one will miss me like that." But in the second wave of destruction, as he planned to leave the house forever, he began, perhaps unconsciously, to shape his own afterlife, to supplant the history of Lily and Aunt Monie's matriarchy with a new story, more androcentric, centered on his private life. He obliterated almost all of his family records, but he preserved the "great unrecorded history" of his personal sexual journey. All but a handful of photographs and letters were in ashes, but he saved his diaries, his photographs, his memoirs of el Adl, and every scrap and shard of his life with the most ordinary working-class men.

Just then, the sort of magical turn on which so many of his plots depended suddenly occurred in his life. Just as he was forced to decamp from West Hackhurst, he was offered a resident fellowship at King's. In college, he would be down to (literally) a room of his own—a single large sitting room in Staircase A just inside the gates. It was an unusual offer, since it came with no expectation of teaching. The room was bright and airy, its Gothic windows looking onto a little courtyard. (He would also retain a sitting room and bedroom nearby in Trumpington Street, at the home of the young classicist Patrick Wilkinson and his wife, Sydney.) Leaving Abinger, he peeled off some of the most precious flotsam to take with him to King's—an ornate mantelpiece his father had designed, the old nursery table from Aunt Monie's now-demolished mansion on Clapham Common, the table at which he had so earnestly read the etiquette book titled *Don't!*. At a farewell party in Abinger, the residents presented him with a book signed by every person in the village. Henry Bone stayed on to work the garden, and Agnes Dowland found belated retirement at the home of her niece. Packing up his library, two Victorian mahogany bookcases, some etchings and landscapes, in late October Morgan paused to observe his raggedy old cat, Toma, hop up on his lap to "honour" him— purring contentedly. He could not bring the canker-eared fellow with him. The next day Toma would—"rubbishy word"—be put to sleep.

In the autumn of 1947, Morgan moved to Cambridge, where he would live for the rest of his life. It took some time for his inner life to catch up. During the war he had had a strange, violent dream after revisiting Rooksnest. In it the Postons had been forced to move away from the house of his "childhood and safety . . . It was death and humiliation. The house was altered, and they were putting off the packing until I had left." Now he was plagued by dreams of similar intensity, but more horrifying—that Lily's coffin had gone to the little churchyard, but her body "had been left [at West Hackhurst] by mistake . . . and was going bad. I half looked at it lying on the bed where she died—hooked face. I woke up with 3 shrieks." From time to time, he was seized with the thought that "surely she will give up being dead now?"

As the days darkened, Morgan was cut adrift from the life he had known. But the tendrils of connection that he had spent a lifetime cultivating pushed up through the darkness. He discovered to his pleasure that his room in King's had belonged to his old undergraduate tutor, Nathaniel Wedd. At year's end he summed up simply, in gratitude. "O Bless Bob . . . Thank you Bob. I am there. Thank you O living and dead. Thus I end."

12

"My Dear America"

The trip to America came off after all. In mid-April 1947, he arrived at LaGuardia Field in New York. A boisterous Bill Roerick and his partner, Tom Coley, scooped him up and drove him along Flushing Bay toward the city. It was impossible not to feel New York's ebullient energy—the vertical thrust of the city, the traffic, the sea of hats as people poured along the sidewalk. It seemed that the whole of midtown Manhattan was being flattened to make way for skyscrapers. The two tallest—the Empire State Building and its glittering counterpart the Chrysler—were just fifteen years old. Times Square, bright as day when the theaters let out, dwarfed Piccadilly Circus.

Even in Bill and Tom's milieu of the theater, Morgan sensed the teeming variety of New York. They took him to new operas by Gian Carlo Menotti— *The Medium* and *The Telephone*—and to Irving Berlin's popular musical *Annie Get Your Gun*. Ethel Merman's ferocious portrayal of Annie Oakley seduced Morgan. He giddily spent the intermission imitating her singing "I'm an Indian too!" The Theater District was packed with new plays and full audiences. Just down the street from where Tom was acting in a "ratty little" melodrama, Marlon Brando rehearsed the new Tennessee Williams play, *A Streetcar Named Desire*. The city's creative energy radiated from Broadway all the way to London, where the most popular ticket that season was *Oklahoma!*, a transfer from New York.

The principal object of Morgan's three-month journey to America was to have universities pay him to visit his friends. A dispute between his publishers and the taxman had temporarily frozen Forster's royalties, and he was strapped for cash. He had accepted an invitation from Harvard to lecture at a symposium on music criticism, principally as a way of evading the endless unpacking in the move to King's. That speaking occasion was his anchor, and with Roerick's help and advice he fashioned a horseshoe-shaped itinerary that took him from New York to the West Coast and back again. Wherever possible, he financed a stay with friends with a nearby public reading. He continued to prospect even from New York, learning with disappointment that Berkeley's English department had run out of funds because it was so close to the end of term.

The continent was peppered with friends who begged him to visit. There were the émigrés Christopher Isherwood, Wystan Auden, Gerald Heard, and Florence Barger's son Harold, now a professor at Columbia, all eager to share their new lives in the New World. There were invitations from ordinary American and Canadian GIs who, like Roerick himself, Morgan and Bob had first encountered in London. Morgan also yearned to put faces to the cherished voices of epistolary friendships developed during the war—with Paul Cadmus and the Frenches, Edith Oliver, and the Roots of Hamilton College, who had all sent precious foodstuffs to Abinger. Also enticing was the promise of meeting the elusive ballet dancer Pete Martinez. Isherwood and Lincoln Kirstein had each been his lover, and they told fantastic tales.

Roerick was the ringleader of this circus of possibilities. In England, Morgan had warmed to Bill's generosity. On his home soil, Bill's courtesy was Byzantine. Like Dr. Aziz, he constantly downplayed his efforts. He paid for everything though he had very little money, abandoned his bedroom to make way for Morgan, worked tirelessly to make all his arrangements seem effortless. Years later, when he learned that Morgan was seriously ill, Bill sold a small Winslow Homer—the gem of his collection, which he had bought in a junk shop for a song—to pay for a flight to Cambridge. He never told his friend.

Morgan only vaguely sensed how deeply Bill and Tom had made a secular religion of his ideal of personal friendship. Morgan's books had changed their lives—had touched them and called out a transcendent humanity in them—and Bill and Tom revered him as a kind of guru. His arrival on their home territory was a chance to ratify their love for him and to affirm the values—fidelity, ideal friendship, and deep commitment to art—that all three shared. Without ever being bold enough to say so, Bill and Tom imagined themselves as part of the aristocracy of the "sensitive, the considerate and the plucky" souls whom Morgan celebrated in his essay "What I Believe."

That Bill and Tom had become actors was a great surprise to their half-bewildered, half-charmed middle-class families. They were both college men whose fathers aspired to financial success but died young. Bill's story was tragic. His father, he confided to Morgan, "worried because he was not a University man . . . went mad, first worrying over small points in his business, and finally tying his hands and feet and drowning himself in Bermuda." The young men, now both in their mid-thirties, had been groomed to succeed in business, not the itinerant, financially perilous life of a working actor. They were both voracious readers, pressing books on their fellow actors, attending lectures and keeping abreast of the arts and politics. One friend called them "true intellectuals."

That they had found each other at all was a twist of fate: they met in 1938, when they were cast in the small roles of the baseball players in the fledgling production of *Our Town*. The play was unprepossessingly simple, and cast and playwright alike were stunned when it won the Pulitzer Prize. The success of *Our Town* cemented their friendship and established their careers. First lovers and always best friends, Bill and Tom were together—separated only by war and work—for more than fifty years. They were both cautious men, formal in mien, uneasy about displays of affection, and reticent on the subject of sexuality. Even when they lived together, they always carefully preserved separate living quarters and separate bedrooms.

In negotiating the world, they were in perfect equipoise: Bill served as the worldly ambassador, Tom as the conscience and devastating wit. "I try never to make an unqualified superlative statement," Morgan once told them, "but is not Tom the funniest person in the world?" Gregarious and darkly handsome, Bill exuded a muscular charm. Tom was very tall, very shy, and very still. His authority derived from his powerful intelligence. A subtle, truthful actor, Tom had no stomach for self-promotion. He worked tirelessly in summer stock and regional theater, in small roles without complaint. Bill's personality brought more overt success: he had already been to Hollywood and made a musical film. A strong, sweet baritone had been his ticket from the infantry to a worldwide tour of Irving Berlin's musical *This Is the Army*. Tom had served in a more difficult theater of war. In the Pacific and in Alaska, he was a military policeman, rising to the rank of captain. Through five long years of service as soldiers in every part of the world they managed to miss each other at every turn. They were recently reunited and cleaved to each other.

In New York they forged a second family from a circle of intimates—
actors and writers, men and women—who had escaped to the city and loved
the arts. Their closest friend was Edith Oliver, the Off-Broadway drama
critic for *The New Yorker*, and already Morgan's benefactor. She hosted him
on his second night in America. Miss Oliver was tiny, sharp-eyed, and foul-
mouthed. She was tough in a city-dweller way, but uneasy about rural things.
She once agreed to meet her beloved great-niece's horse—named Oliver in
her honor—only if he were walked over to the car where she sat bolt upright
with the windows closed. Like all of Bill and Tom's close friends, Oliver
lived frugally and opened her heart to Morgan. On his second evening in
America, he found himself deep in conversation and deep in his cups from
drinking her homemade berry wine.

The visitor and his hosts settled into a humble and crowded encampment
reminiscent of West Hackhurst during the Blitz. Mrs. Roerick's apartment
was in Marble Hill, a middle-class enclave in the Bronx. It comprised the
top two floors of a house that had been subdivided during the war. Here she
lived with her son and Tom, Bill's sister and brother-in-law, and a skeptical
dachshund named Minky. They moved cots to the attic to give Morgan his
own room, where he piled the bed high with letters, newspapers, spectacles,
and fruit. They presented him with a key and he came and went as he wished.
Often he crept up the back stairs, appearing unexpectedly in the kitchen.
After so much privation, the city's ordinary abundance stunned him. Tom
and Bill found him outside a small greengrocer's shop on Third Avenue,
standing awestruck before row upon row of Italian oranges. "I think," Morgan said drily, "the English have taken the war as an excuse to indulge the
innate squalor of their palate."

The city was dazzling. But it was also legible, and map in hand he struck
out to explore it on foot, as he had done in Alexandria years before. The exercise gave him blessed anonymity and autonomy. He startled Robert Giroux,
the new editor in chief at Harcourt Brace, arriving unannounced at the reception desk and asking to see Mr. Brace, since retired, who had published
A Passage to India more than twenty years before. Though almost seventy,
Morgan seemed much younger. He was "an unprepossessing man . . . with a
gray mustache and wispy hair, wearing steel-rimmed glasses and a rumpled
gray suit." His only luggage—so light he forgot he was carrying it—was a
light blue knapsack, containing a toothbrush, a set of clean linens, and two
Penguin paperbacks.

Morgan had crammed for his travels by devising a whirlwind syllabus of American literature—Twain, Melville, and his beloved Whitman. He was so primed to encounter the exotic that he mistook the rumble of the trains beneath Park Avenue for an earthquake. Seeking out the house on East Twenty-sixth Street where Melville wrote *Billy Budd* and where he died, Morgan was disappointed to see that, like so much of New York, it had been razed to make way for a larger building. Then, spotting the curved verdigris roof of the nearby Regimental Armory, he remarked—melding Melville and *Hamlet*'s Osric—that it looked very like a whale. He delighted in navigating the subways. And he delighted in small human exchanges in the immense modern city. He bought an American schoolchild's notebook, with a speckled black-and-white cover and lined paper. In it he recorded that when he debarked at Marble Hill for the Roericks' apartment, the train conductor called after him softly, "Be good, sir."

He explored widely. One point of pilgrimage was St. Luke's Place. The part of Greenwich Village where Cadmus and the Frenches lived was already a mythic bohemian destination, albeit a belated one. It had been thirty years since Theodore Dreiser and Marianne Moore lived on the same small block. Moore had walked just a few steps across the street to the library branch where she worked. On the north side, a row of attached Victorian brownstones faced an empty yard surrounded by a chain-link fence—once a potter's field and now an asphalt playground. Before the First World War the anarchist John Reed had declared his Village apartment open to all, pinning a sign to the door that read simply "Property Is Theft." But after the war property became *property*—and expensive to boot. Two new subways bored into the enclave of low brick houses, and the Holland Tunnel opened traffic still further to occupants of the wider city. The Village was being gentrified by a new generation of young people who wanted that artistic feeling, but with a doorman and elevator. St. Luke's Place, Cadmus told Morgan, was now "on the fringe of the habitable sections of N.Y.," where, splitting the rent for the studio with Jared French, he could barely afford to live.

Getting off the subway at Sheridan Square, Morgan made his way south to Cadmus and French's studio. Twenty years later the square would be the site of the Stonewall riots, where gay men would fight back against police harassment at the Stonewall Inn, but even when Forster walked these streets this part of Greenwich Village was well-marked "queer" territory. As part of a WPA project in 1934, Cadmus had sketched a scene at Stewart's, a coffee shop on the square. In the picture a dozen men and women are crowded around a couple of small tables as the waiter squeezes by, his tray atilt. Sprawling, belching, stretching, leering couples of indeterminate sex talk and flirt. Are these "long haired men or short haired women" crammed around the small tables? It's hard to tell. But there's no mistaking the invitation from the beringed louche dandy at the mouth of the men's lavatory, who looks back over his shoulder at the viewer. *Follow me.*

Like Hogarth, Cadmus sketched the teeming city, but in his busy, ribald world gay life was part of the texture of everyday affairs. All his life Cadmus was open and unapologetic about his homosexuality. This idiosyncratic attitude had offended the authorities for some time. In 1934, an irate admiral had censored the exhibition of Cadmus's painting *The Fleet's In* on the grounds that it besmirched the reputation of the navy. The painting was a WPA project, and like Cadmus's other subjects, *Shore Leave* and *Y.M.C.A. Locker Room*, it was drawn directly from his observation of life in Manhattan.

Strongly horizontal, *The Fleet's In* depicted fourteen people (and a reluctant dog) perched on or standing in front of a low wall in Riverside Park near the piers on the Hudson where the navy ships anchored. Six of them are sailors on leave, flirting, leering, posturing, and grabbing flesh in the short time they are ashore. The small dog belongs to a sour-faced middle-aged woman—modeled on Cadmus's aunt—who disapproves of the spectacle. A sailor accepts a cigarette from an effeminate blond man who knowingly meets his gaze; three voluptuous young women cheerfully face down a pair of leering swabbies; a woman playfully pushes away a sailor who's wrapped his legs around her as he sits on the wall.

Sailors will be sailors, the painting told its audience cheerfully. But this depiction was too much for Admiral Henry Roosevelt, assistant secretary of the navy. He demanded that the painting be withdrawn from the Corcoran Gallery's WPA show as "an unwarranted insult" to enlisted men. Roosevelt accused Cadmus of having a "sordid, depraved imagination" and "no conception of actual conditions in our service." And so it was suppressed. But the admiral's moral rectitude did not prohibit him from appropriating the painting for his private club, charmingly named the Alibi Club. (There it stayed over the mantel for many years until a determined scholar pointed out that it had been purchased with taxpayer money.)

Six years later, when Cadmus appeared for his draft-board interview with work under his arm, one look at his subject matter made the military board summarily reject him as unfit for service. On the paperwork, he was classified as 4F because of a hernia.

By the time Cadmus completed his satirical portrait of Stewart's coffee shop, the greasy spoon was a destination not only for gay men and lesbians, but also for tourists who wanted to see "fairies," with their trademark marcelled hair, tweezed eyebrows, and red neckties. A popular song included the line "Fairyland's not far from Washington Square." To Morgan, who confided in a letter to Paul, "You can't imagine how stuffy we get here [in England]," both Cadmus's unequivocal approach to his homosexuality and the public presence of gay men and lesbians on the streets of the Village were immensely refreshing.

The glint of the Hudson was visible from Cadmus's stoop, and in the right wind it was possible to detect the weedy smell of the river. Walking up the brownstone steps that sunny April morning, Morgan surprised his hosts at work in their studio before they could "make suitable arrangements for entertaining the Great Writer." It was an auspicious blunder. The reverence of his American friends had begun to make him feel threadbare and inadequate. The faux pas of "busting in on them" humanized him. Paul and Jared ("Jerry") ran around the corner to the local delicatessen for "delicious prosciutto smoked salmon, wine . . ." and then all three picked their way down the creaky fire escape to the small, shady garden at the back of the house for an al fresco lunch. They peeled the meats off waxed paper, and drank and talked all afternoon, Forster volubly, and uncharacteristically, chattering away. He was quite at home. That afternoon he became, and would always remain, just Morgan to them.

Both his hosts and their environs were deeply "attractive" to Morgan. He noted with approval that "the flat is Bloomsbury and unsanitary . . ." The studio at number 5 was on the top floor of a shabby brownstone that had been divided into apartments by floor. The whole house retained battered but dignified remnants of Victorian elegance: a carved marble mantel on which Paul and Jerry photographed their friends nude, an oriel skylight in a lacy plaster frame, a dilapidated wrought-iron fence near the stoop. The walls were painted a greenish gray "that cleverly blends in with the dust." The two rooms at the outer edges of the apartment were commandeered for studios—Jerry's facing the sunny playground across the street, Paul's looking north toward the tiny overgrown garden and the back of the tenements beyond. Whenever it was warm enough Jerry painted naked, surrounded by a jumbled disorder: "large anatomy books, an Houdon écorché with muscles painted on, bottles of powdered pigments, dirty work clothes, paint rags with a slightly rotten egg smell, all piled anywhere: in the way of furniture, a drawing table, easel, etc and two pianos—a grand and an upright out of tune individually and with each other." In between was a pocket living room crammed with books and lit by a large skylight, with a daybed covered with a paisley shawl and assorted furniture so worm-eaten that it "might collapse with a bumptious guest." Before the lunch was finished, they offered Morgan the use of the place for the rest of his visit, and exacted a promise from him to visit them and Jerry's wife, Margaret, in their sprawling summer house in Provincetown.

From his correspondence, Morgan had imagined Paul Cadmus to be plump and unprepossessing; instead, to his relief, he found a tall, slender man with an angular bony face and hair cut "en brosse" in the most modern style. With his deep-set burning blue eyes, an aquiline nose, and a slight overbite, he looked like an amiable "sun burnt rodent," Morgan noted in his diary. Cadmus radiated benign sweetness. Jerry was shorter and a bit stocky, with a smoldering energy like a spring wound up. Paul captured Jerry's seductiveness, his powerful intelligence and charisma, in the 1931 work that he considered his first finished painting. The portrait showed Jerry lying in the disheveled sheets of the bed they shared. Naked to the waist, muscular and brooding, he looked as if he had been interrupted while reading the banned novel *Ulysses* just a second before—his fingers are still caressing the page, holding his place—to look up at his lover with a frank and steadfast gaze. This intensity *of looking* made Jerry sexy to everybody he met. He was utterly confident, sometimes to the point of belligerence. He knew what he wanted. He wanted Paul. And he wanted more than Paul.

Jerry was "the only true bisexual" man Paul had ever known. When the men returned from a two-year working idyll in the cheapest parts of Europe in 1933, Jerry fell in love and into bed with Margaret Hoening, a recent Smith graduate studying painting. They married in 1937. Margaret was enigmatic, brilliant, serene. Jerry painted a tiny tempera portrait of his wife, the size of a postcard, the expression in her huge, widely set blue eyes as flat as those of a kouros. Her eyes saw everything and seemed to judge nothing.

Margaret loved Paul dearly—who didn't? Both she and Cadmus had room for Jerry in their hearts and in their beds. They were both the sort of people, their friend Glenway Wescott noticed, who put others first: rising silently after a meal to wash the dishes together as Jerry held forth with the remnant of the guests. Margaret protected her husband fiercely and revered him—waiting patiently as he burned through love affairs. There was no mistaking Jerry's reciprocal love for her, or their physical passion after a decade of marriage: Margaret wrote letters to friends from their still-warm bed. And Jerry limned a life-size double portrait of them lazily lying in bed, half clothed and half asleep, knotted together in a loose embrace. Their friend George Platt Lynes embroidered the sketch into an enormous needlepoint cover for a daybed.

Jerry was magnetic, self-confident, proud, and driven to do his own thing, almost contemptuous of the art world and of passing fads. He could be cruel, "surly and morose." He had graduated from Amherst College and had worked at a white-glove financial firm, but he threw away the prospect of prosperity after taking classes at the Art Students League. Paul, Jerry, and Margaret blended their artistic lives together, in a melded partnership they called PAJAMA after the first syllables of their names. For years they took remarkable photographs of themselves and their friends on the beaches of Provincetown, Fire Island, and Nantucket, in the empty rooms of Margaret's childhood home in Hoboken, in the apartment below the studio at St. Luke's Place where Jerry and Margaret lived for a time. Sometimes the photos were studies for their paintings, archetypal arrangements of bodies in space that were either tranquil or stoical, modern or ancient, depending on the viewer's mood. The Frenches had a studied emotional flatness to their work. Paul's painting was much more animated—shot through with his irreverent sensibility, more corporeal and less cerebral.

Into this odd, contented, inseparable world of work and friendship came a fourth person at just around the time Morgan made his visit. The young painter George Tooker, recently separated from the Marines, became Paul's lover. Like Paul, he took up Jerry's painstaking method of tempera painting, passing the pliant yolk back and forth between his palms, pricking the membrane, and blending pigments, layering the milky unforgiving mixture as the medieval painters had done, slowly and carefully until a detailed painting appeared. Tooker had a wide-eyed innocence that translated into a remarkable artistic view. Like some mystical Pre-Raphaelite painter transposed to the modern world, he painted figures in urban landscapes, watching birds in Central Park, frozen in a tiled subway corridor, standing still in a waiting room or a soulless government office, encountering the world. Lynes photographed the three artists in the studio above St. Luke's Place in the summer of 1948 in receding perspective, each sitting at an easel, painting. The triple portrait was principally symbolic—Tooker never shared the studio with Paul and Jerry, though their methods and ideas influenced one another deeply. Gradually, for the most part amiably, the triangle of PAJAMA settled into two pairs.

Though Bloomsbury was Morgan's point of reference for understanding this domestic structure, it was actually an entirely new idiom of work and sexual expression to him. Cadmus had described it himself in a letter to Morgan: "I don't *look* like your Bohemian with a louse in his beard—in fact I dress almost elegantly with a tendency towards chi-chi in neckties—but I *live* almost as he might." Paul was a literal renaissance man: a draftsman as classical and beautifully precise as the Old Masters, a skilled self-taught pianist, a fine writer and cook, and a devoted friend. His figurative painting, like its ancient technique, was completely out of style in the art world of the day, but he remained steadily and serenely absorbed. His gentleness, his wicked grin, his love of life put him (usually happily) in the center of a swirling circle of young, free-spirited gay friends and ex-lovers. PAJAMA was like an idealized version of what Morgan had hoped his life with May and Bob could have been like, an indefinable kinship of blended platonic and sexual love. Though both Paul and Margaret were helpmeets to Jerry, Morgan identified with Cadmus. He worried about his endless accommodation of others' desires. He wrote in his diary, "Paul Cadmus must protect himself by retreating. Or he would lead no life of his own, nor be able to practice his accomplished art."

Somewhat wistfully Morgan left New York, which had "more blood and more allurement," for the isolation of Bill's rustic cabin in Tyringham, Massachusetts, to revise his Harvard address. When they arrived in late April it was snowing heavily, and Bill's tiny Colonial saltbox was snowbound and uninhabitable. Lost Farm—so named because it was deep in a thicket, down a disused dirt road—had no heat, electricity, toilets, or running water. For the first few days Morgan and Bill instead stayed nearby with the sympathetic family of Bill's college friend Robert Barnes Rudd. The Rudds were erudite people who lived in an enclave of buildings built and abandoned by the

Shakers early in the nineteenth century. Morgan cannily realized that this part of the Berkshires was "a charming place for rich Americans who do not want to seem so." He was "ravished . . . by the absence of bad taste in the buildings, widely spaced on both sides of the road." After a few days the weather tempered, and he and Bill set up together in the cozy house, lit by candles and heated by firelight. Morgan's room looked out toward a distant shoulder of mountains. Lost Farm reminded Morgan of T. E. Lawrence's Clouds Hill, a "sketchy, uncomfortable, but somehow comforting" male place. Like a platonic Alec and Maurice in a frozen greenwood, they worked together on the Harvard speech, which began as incomplete jottings. Morgan kneaded it into shape, but his imagination was not fired by the task. Instead, he focused on the view: "thousands and thousands of birch trees, their trunks whiter than the birch trees [in England], milk white, ghost white in the sharp sunshine . . ."

At Eliot House he was the guest of the master, the young classics scholar John H. Finley. Harvard's three-day music symposium was something of an extravaganza, with new pieces commissioned from Aaron Copland and Virgil Thomson, concerts every night and talks all day. The final night of the symposium unveiled a new Martha Graham ballet, which one reviewer described as "a highly refined stylized symbolized fertility rite, its sexuality as easily discernable as unobjectionable." In his journal Forster tartly compared the dance to a catheter.

Forster was the headline attraction, as a notable lover of music, but the atmosphere at Harvard was not encouraging. His speech, "The Raison d'Être of Criticism in the Arts," described the critic's mystic call to revere the place "where the artist worked." He described criticism, the proper understanding of a work of art, as "an unusual state" that "we can only enter . . . through love." His approach could hardly have been less congenial to the literary scholars in his audience. Academic critics after the war championed the humanities with scientific zeal, seeking to bring to the study of literature the same level of technical scrutiny, and the same esteem, as the sciences. T. S. Eliot, whose epic *The Waste Land* was accompanied by his copious footnotes, was their man and a Harvard alumnus to boot. The symposium was capped by a cocktail party with Forster and Eliot as the guests of honor. The two literary giants were parked on opposite sides of a massive ceremonial fireplace in the common room, and Morgan watched as acolytes circled around the poet like moths. The line to speak with Eliot grew longer and longer—students and faculty alike drawn into the fine points of the objective correlative, the meaning of *Four Quartets*, the best methods of properly dispassionate reading. Morgan was left in the good company of a single student with whom he chatted amiably about his plans to explore the western United States.

From Boston he made his way west to El Tovar Hotel at the mouth of the Grand Canyon. Flying over the desert, he discerned vast airfields of obsolete surplus materiel, thousands of airplanes that he learned were about to be destroyed. He was disheartened by the American "Spirit of Waste," the corollary to its vast abundance. Arriving at the Grand Canyon, he contemplated the descent to the canyon floor. It took several days to screw his courage to the sticking place, which turned out to be the back of a large slow mule named Monkey. From this vantage point he had a clear view of astonishing scenery: the "throbbing mad" Colorado river "between dark red precipices" and the back of a "lean cinematic cowboy" named James who zigzagged the pack down circuitous trails. At night by the campfire he heard music, "James or someone strumming a guitar and looking handsome no doubt."

Los Angeles and Berkeley followed Colorado. Ironically, having finally arrived in Southern California he missed Isherwood, who had traveled home to Cheshire to divest his ancestral properties to his younger brother. In Northern California he stayed for a week with Noel Voge, a young academic whom Bob had met on the banks of the Thames during the war, and Noel's new wife, Marietta. Noel took him to Yosemite and to the vast orchards of Los Gatos. It was a visit full of admiration and veiled lust, like his sojourns with Frank Vicary and his family. From California he traveled to Chicago through the Rockies on a long, spectacular train trip. He encountered wondrous sights: a young Mormon woman "Saint" reeling drunk down the street, the "gasper" of the final descent down the eastern face of the Rockies, Boulder Dam with its "vision of a transformed world." In Salt Lake City, Morgan was touched when a chambermaid rejected his tip, saying, "I don't like to take your money, brother, you need it more than I do."

Morgan wrote Sprott—who had by now reverted to merely "Jack"—that since his visit began he had been plagued with nightmares about being displaced from West Hackhurst. After a stay with Tom Coley's mother near Philadelphia, Morgan dreamed that Lily told him she was happy being dead. He recognized that he was "not correct psychically," concluding that "probably a little—*ahem* would help." In hopes of a brief sexual fling he wrote to Johnny Kennedy, a Canadian airman whom he had met in London, taking up his invitation to stay with him (and his wife and child) at his home near Niagara Falls. Telling Bob "I am just doing, in friendship's name, a slightly risky thing," Morgan braved immigration officials and possible humiliation to embark on a significant detour. But his hopes for sexual intimacy were not fulfilled, and he concluded—wrongly—that they would not be on this journey. He wrote in his notebook: "I have made an impression with my writing, music, genius, and modesty which saddens me not because it is undeserved but because no one impresses me comparably in return, and I shall leave the colonies insipidly without a heart-heat."

The long train ride gave him time to reflect on what he had learned of America over the weeks of his travels. The experience had given him much to think about. He was struck by the easy approachability of ordinary people. He told Joe Ackerley, "What a contrast to malnourished disgruntled England! One is never snubbed, and sometimes the contrary. I sat for half-an-hour in Arizona on a wall which a Mexican was cementing for his mother, and a correspondence has ensued."

Especially interesting to him were the glimpses of the way race relations were changing rapidly after the war. Though he had been in India and Egypt, Morgan had had only fleeting encounters with black people besides Reg Palmer. In Britain, the most pervasive image of people Morgan called "negroes" was a remnant of minstrelsy, the cartoonish figure of the golliwog on the Robinson's marmalade jar. The black street kids who played baseball on the asphalt across from Paul's studio held an exotic and erotic fascination for him, but he was intimidated by them, concluding defensively that "the negroes don't on the whole make a good impression—aggressive and rude." In the middle-class atmosphere of a long train journey, Morgan was more at ease to observe the worldliness and authority of black American GIs returned from service abroad. "I have had breakfast with a negro sergeant major from Japan, and have listened to the negro Pullman attendant ticking off a white G. I. for washing in too smart a lavatory. 'Gee, I'm surprised at you fellows.' The G.I. hung his spotty head." What a contrast to the stultifying, immutable British sense of social order. The second verse of "All Things Bright and Beautiful" was still warbled dutifully in England, though it has since been omitted from the hymnals:

> *The rich man in his castle,*
> *The poor man at his gate,*
> *He made them high or lowly,*
> *And ordered their estate.*

And Americans' easy, ribald sense of humor brought talk of sex out into the open. In 1935 Morgan had observed a flap at the BBC with distaste and incredulity: "All England convulsed since Saturday night because an improper joke was made on the wireless. Clapham and Dwyer the entertainers, who have delighted listeners for over nine years, came to grief. D said have you ever thought what comes out of the desert waste? C replied or out of a pretty girl's waist? D aghast, could not reply." American attitudes toward sex seemed so much more tolerant and good-humored. He jotted down a series of Burma Shave billboards "wittily spaced along the New York Philadelphia rd." as Isherwood and his lover Bill Caskey drove him from New York to a reading at Bryn Mawr College:

> *We know how much*
> *You love that gal*
> *But use both hands*
> *For driving, pal.*

The corollary to this friendliness was an undercurrent of menace that fascinated him and that he could not quite comprehend. He was appalled by the casual way his hosts and friends described the prevalence of crime in their lives. He took the temperature of each locale he visited, cautiously assessing the danger, contrasting Chicago, where his host had five locks on his door and "where clothes are stolen from bathers, keys extracted and flats gutted before the bathers can dress and return . . . ," with "Berkeley where the Voge house was left unlocked night and day."

The occasions that lingered most deeply in Morgan's imagination were attacks against men like himself, single writers and intellectuals, living alone. It is impossible to discern from the sketchy accounts in his diary whether the motives for the violence he recorded might have been homophobic, or whether all the victims he described were gay. But some of them were. In the winter of 1947 Monroe Wheeler and his partner, Glenway Wescott, had been pulled out of bed, beaten and robbed at gunpoint, then locked in a closet by a "trigger-happy bruiser" they knew slightly. They reported the robbery, but lived to regret doing so: the elevator man at Monroe's Park Avenue apartment told the police they sometimes lent the key to friends. Soon the robbery investigation became coercive. A detective came to Monroe's office at the Museum of Modern Art, trying to get the names and addresses of all his homosexual friends. Clearly Morgan's anxiety about crime in America was magnified by his sense of vulnerability as a gay man.

His return to the East Coast in mid-June 1947 turned out to be "very sympathetic." He took root in "deepest Greenwich Village" in Jerry and Paul's empty studio, which they had generously "cleaned . . . from side to side, filled the fridge with food and given me 8 bottles of booze." He urged Sprott to come over to New York the following year: "It is a charming place, and I am very high handed towards it with the whole of the West behind me, and do not allow myself to be overawed." But "the spectacle from the Staten Island Ferry" staggered him. A different spectacle was more disconcerting. Alone in the studio at night, Forster was unnerved by one of Jerry's paintings, *The Sea*. French had been reading Carl Jung, and the painting was an allegory of the mythic struggle of the anima. In it two stylized naked figures lay horizontally on a bright blue field of sea and sky, a light-skinned man swimming in an angular rictus, his head turned with wide eyes toward the viewer, and below him, also wide-eyed and with a hideous grin, a submerged dark gray figure floating, perhaps drowned. Morgan unfolded his cloth coat and hung it over the painting, unable to look at it. Word got out when a friend entered the studio and saw this comical tableau, and soon Jerry and Paul, and eventually Paul's sister Fidelma and her husband, Lincoln Kirstein, and the whole Provincetown crowd were quietly cackling at the power of Morgan's imagination. (They never told him.)

Also in the studio were some manuscripts by a young writer in Cadmus's circle, Donald Windham. His erotic short story "The Hitchhiker" and several others on homosexual themes warmed Forster. He thought Windham had real talent, and told him so when they met later in June, beginning a pattern of mixed friendship and literary promotion for the rest of his life. And back in New York he finally met the incomparable José Martinez. Known as Pete, Martinez was a Mexican dancer who after ten years as Lincoln Kirstein's lover had become "one of the great loves of his life." Pete lived on and off with Lincoln and was tolerated by Fidelma Kirstein. He was also a former lover and great confidant of Isherwood, who had worked with Pete at a pacifist hostel in Philadelphia before Martinez was drafted in 1942. Pete was gay in the oldest sense of the word, great fun to be around, camp and wickedly funny. In a somber Quaker meetinghouse, he had turned to Christopher and exclaimed "Darling . . . if you don't kiss me I shall *scream!*" With his "fluttering black eyelashes, flashing white teeth, ballet gestures and the scarf which he winds round his neck like a yashmak," Isherwood wrote with measured understatement, Pete was "an unusual figure for Haverford." He was considerably more at home in the Ramble of Central Park, a cruising spot so well established that by the twenties it was already called "the fruited plain." Late in June on the night before Morgan traveled to Provincetown, Martinez took Forster to the park for a glorious night of casual sex; whether with Pete or others, Morgan did not record. At the end of his journey, he reflected on "the kindness I receive from Bill, Paul Cadmus, etc." and "the graciousness of Pete."

The Frenches' rented house on Miller Hill Road kissed the beach. Morgan spent three nights there in the most congenial company of Tooker and Cadmus, and Jerry and Margaret French. They interrupted their usual habit of serious working holidays to make him the center of attention. He "felt to belong at Provincetown." He fumbled his way through piano duets with Paul, sat for a portrait by Jerry, was photographed laughing un-self-consciously in the dappled shade of the arbor covered with sea grapes that adjoined the rambling house. Jerry regaled him with stories of homoerotic fraternity rituals at Amherst. The PAJAMA trio gave him photographs of themselves and their friends, naked on the dunes, naked on a sunny bed, comically frolicking in a send-up of bodybuilders, arranged like Easter Island statues in the sand. One afternoon's walk became an allegory of bohemian utopia conquering the forces of convention.

> My diamond [insight] at Provincetown: walking out on the dunes with clear blue sky above, I looked into it, and it was radiant blue, coming back from the walk, we unwillingly scared the town crier, an elderly man with a nutcracker face who was foolishly decked out as a 17c puritan, and thought we were going to haze him. He scuttled off the path.

In Boston he missed an opportunity, falling "into the fat hands of a neurologist, Matthews, who commanded a destroyer during the war, and wanted to be hospitable. Spoke in disapproval of the sailorfied street through which we waddled and which I should like to have explored." He returned to New York after another short stay at Lost Farm to spend his last days "in this kindest of lands" in the happy company of Paul Cadmus and George Tooker.

Forster's presence was like rolling thunder: reports of his sympathetic visit to Provincetown brought invitations from an ever-widening circle of gay friends on the East Coast. Though he was delighted to have made a success of the trip, Morgan's time was running out. He declined an invitation from Glenway Wescott. As a sort of proxy, Wescott sent a mutual friend, the young artist Bernard Perlin, whom Morgan had met once before, in London during the war. At that first meeting Perlin was returning from service as an artist attached to the army, having documented the firebombing of Tokyo and the Germans' retreat from Syria. That day, to cleanse his visual palate, Morgan and Bernard toured the National Gallery, discussing "the pinchability of Rubens."

Now, in Cadmus's studio, Perlin sketched a quick silverpoint portrait while Cadmus and Tooker packed Morgan's bags as carefully as completing a jigsaw puzzle. Wescott claimed Perlin's portrait as a prize, since he had not yet met Morgan. For the time being, this memento would have to suffice.

13

"*I Favor Reciprocal Dishonesty*"

After all the excitement and adulation, Morgan returned to England's hum-drum rhythms—each week, back and forth from Chiswick to Cambridge, dinner with Bob, perhaps a play, an occasional visit with Reg Palmer, whose "present goodness warmth raffishness and affection" were still welcome. Christopher Isherwood tried to rev things up as he had by sending Bill Ro-erick, but his envoys disappointed: Tennessee Williams cocked up and missed the meeting, and Morgan "disliked" Gore Vidal "a lot."

By the autumn of 1948, the difference in age between Morgan and Bob began to signify. Morgan was weeks away from turning seventy, and Bob was only forty-five. Morgan worried about getting old, and being old, being bor-ing, and being taken for granted. He began to nurse wounded feelings and suspicions. Having spent a good deal of money to buy Bob and May a ter-raced row house in Shepherd's Bush a little more than a mile from his Chis-wick flat, he bristled that his generosity had only made Bob "boorish," entitled, and neglectful. "Bob's indifference to me and preoccupation with May fall unluckily in a year when I have bought them the house. He has seldom been gracious when I am there."

The dark, cold autumn amplified his alienation into something truly frightening. In early October, he turned to his diary:

After three miserable days in London I believed that I must address myself. For I cannot speak to others of my worst trouble, which is that I have got tired of people and personal relationships . . . Unless I can manage to settle down to some work this year, I may go wrong in my head. I feel so desolate and useless, and observant people see it in my face. A "red-Indian" slapped me on the arm in Tottenham Court Road saying "be cheerful". . . . I feel scared. If human beings have failed me, what is left?

For a short time he clung to the belief that neither Bob nor May could be counted in the ranks of "observant people." But over the winter invitations mounted and his anxiety slowly receded. He was included in the Buckinghams' Christmas plans and enjoyed a lavish seventieth birthday party organized by William Plomer and Joe Ackerley. He imagined that the reason "Bob changed suddenly" was that "the word has got round that I am old and must be spoilt. Kindness, consideration for all, also flattery for my fame. I am grateful and do not look too deep. Half-understanding the truest wisdom, at least in private matters . . ." "Half-understanding" had long been Lily's province. Now as he grew older Morgan made it his own. He was learning to modify his acute sensitivity, selectively to practice the art of the unexamined life.

Most of the ardor for friendship came from across the Atlantic. Morgan's visit to New York had inspired Paul Cadmus to begin an allegorical painting on sexual freedom. Paul was not merely working out an abstract idea of friendship and sexual desire. Before he met Morgan, the breakup of an affair and the delicate renegotiation of his relations with Jerry and Margaret French had been painful; more recently, his relationship with George Tooker had deepened. He was committed to remaining a friend to past lovers but under no illusions about the difficulties. He inched his way forward, using Forster's writing as a personal gospel. For months Paul worked on the painting, which he named *What I Believe* after the essay that had brought him friendship with Morgan. This was the project on his worktable when his friend the photographer George Platt Lynes climbed onto the rickety fire escape at St. Luke's Place with his camera to capture the three artists, Cadmus, Tooker, and Jerry French, together in the studio. When the painting was finished Paul sent a black-and-white photograph to Morgan.

Tolerance and sexual freedom were interlinked in Paul's mind. So he made *What I Believe* a paean to the polymorphous expression of desire. In the center of a vast field of naked humanity the figure of Forster presided— a naked Pan, smiling, his hair blown in the breeze like a dandelion gone to seed, his long thin hands palms up in a characteristic gesture both eloquent and awkward, between a shrug and a beatification. His counterpart, a ghastly figure of death, loomed from a recently dug grave. All around them were naked lovers and friends, lovers of every shape and color, lovers in a great tangle, grotesque or picturesque, enraptured, affectionate. Flesh, flesh, flesh.

And spirit. Partly influenced by Jerry's interest in Jung's dualities of the self, Paul painted several figures in the painting twice. There were two self-portraits: one Paul in the picture sat sketching intensely, embraced by Jerry while Margaret stood behind them, her arms encircling them both. The second Paul was more quizzical. He lay on his belly reading a chapter titled "Relationships" in a book labeled *What I Believe.* Cadmus painted his brother-in-law Lincoln Kirstein twice, the first comical, playing a panpipe, with a cat balanced on his head. The figure of Fidelma rested her head in his lap. The second Lincoln was tender, standing with his arms around Pete Martinez's neck. Forster, the gay paterfamilias to this extraordinary assemblage, wore nothing but a ribbon with the words "Love, the beloved republic" inscribed on it. In the far distance the tiny lighthouse of Pharos cast its enlightening beam. Forster was "charmed" to be the muse for this scene of sexual friendship, though he told Paul that he found his portrait too flattering, "for I *have* got so fat!" Still, to be the genius loci of a sexual utopia was a worthy immortality.

Paul was not the only younger artist who sought Morgan's approval. In the summer of 1948 the composer Benjamin Britten organized a music festival near his home in Aldeburgh on the Suffolk coast. He asked Morgan, "England's greatest novelist," to give a lecture. Morgan joined Britten and his partner, the tenor Peter Pears, sleeping several nights in the guest bedroom of Crag House, a stucco villa whose front garden touched the shingle of the North Sea. Late at night his hosts entertained him, Ben hunched over the grand piano while Pears stood, leaning on its cluttered closed lid. They made up little musical parodies and sang folk songs late into the night. Aldeburgh was "a bleak little place: not beautiful," Forster wrote. But he found the large sitting room congenial, and Ben and Peter to be "the sweetest people."

Britten and Pears had been inseparable partners, in love and work, for a decade. With his unruly cloud of curly hair and his sloping shoulders, Ben was slighter than the imposing Peter, whose craggy features amplified the expressiveness of his tenor voice. To the "shock" and consternation of some of their friends, the men brazenly shared a large bed in the main bedroom upstairs with a wide view of the sea. For the public they accommodated a more chaste cover story. The adjoining room with a spartan single bed (where Morgan slept) was labeled "Peter Pears' room" in a photo montage celebrating the nascent festival. During the visit, Britten proposed a future collaboration. When a commission for an opera for the Festival of Britain materialized, he invited Morgan to write the libretto. Together they would choose the subject.

Though Britten was only thirty-four at the time, he was already acknowledged as the greatest British composer of the century. He had met Morgan more than a decade before. Like so many of Morgan's younger friends, they were introduced by Christopher Isherwood. Then only twenty-three, Ben had written the incidental music for *The Ascent of F6*. Just after the play premiered Britten's mother died, and Morgan's sympathy and his musical sensitivity lingered in Ben's mind. Seven years later, in 1944, Morgan had come to London specially to hear Pears sing Britten's *Seven Sonnets of Michelangelo* in a J. A. Symonds translation.

The strong homoerotic ancestry of the work was unaccountably lost on most of the reviewers. But for these two artists so seasoned in the art of the unspoken, the song cycle became a kind of platonic dialogue, a connection to each other and to the unrecorded history hidden in plain sight. First Ben gave Morgan a copy of the score. Then—thoroughly moved by Pears's performance—Morgan bought the recording though he had no gramophone to play it on. When Ben heard of this, he bought Morgan a handsome record player. He inscribed Morgan's copy of *Albert Herring*—"For my dear Morgan / a very humble tribute to a very great man." Ben remembered that it was Morgan who had seen Christopher and Wystan off at Waterloo Station when they embarked for America, and Morgan alone of the old guard who had not sneered when, fueled by pacifism, he and Peter had followed their friends to America in 1939.

Britten and Pears's three-year sojourn in the United States had not been a success. Ben was a brittle, nervous man who needed settled conditions to work. He and Peter were obliged to tour to make money, and this restlessness made them unhappy and unproductive. In November 1940, they shared a row house in Brooklyn Heights with Auden; Thomas Mann's son Golo; Paul Bowles and his wife, Jane; the burlesque artist Gypsy Rose Lee; and Carson McCullers. But this bohemian ménage took its toll, and the pair fled west to California. There, in the summer of 1941, an encounter with Morgan's writing changed their lives. Homesick, cash-strapped, and unhappy, they discovered a copy of *The Listener*, and in it they read Morgan's radio talk on the forgotten poet George Crabbe and his character Peter Grimes, a "savage fisherman . . . who murdered his [three young] apprentices and was haunted by their ghosts."

Like Crabbe, Britten had grown up in the tiny provincial town of Aldeburgh in the Suffolk marshland. But both Crabbe's propinquity and his poetry were unknown to him. Reading Forster's essay gave Ben "such a feeling of nostalgia" that he and Peter combed the used bookstores of Los Angeles for a copy of Crabbe's *The Borough*, first published in 1810. They found one, and devoured the poems.

Nostalgia is a strange word for the feelings evoked by these sketches of folk life. Crabbe's poetry was, well, crabby. *The Borough* depicted the flinty, unhappy circumstance of poor rural people living in provincial isolation. Forster's essay began simply, "To talk about Crabbe is to talk about England." As a gay man Britten likely detected the ambivalence in these words. Morgan captured Crabbe's "uncomfortable mind," his "antipathy . . . connected with a profound attraction" toward the bleak, unforgiving landscape that shaped the townspeople of Aldeburgh, Crabbe, and his art. Morgan located the same "inner tension, the same desire for what repels" in both the poet and his unhappy fisherman. A similar tension may have surfaced in Britten, whose uneasy status as a homosexual and a conscientious objector complicated his desire to be canonized as a court composer. Reading Forster sharpened Ben's homesickness. Looking back on this moment, Britten wrote that Morgan's "revealing article" made him "suddenly realize . . . where I belonged and what I lacked." He and Peter decided to return to England. Morgan had led them home.

Britten spent the whole of 1944 in England, writing *Peter Grimes*. His adaptation was telling. Where Crabbe's Grimes killed his apprentices by neglect and privation, Britten and Pears imagined a character whose sexual desire for the boys is linked to his violence against them. In their preliminary sketch, Grimes replicated a cycle of violence—just as his father had beaten him, he beats the boys, thinking, "Would you rather I loved you? you are sweet, young etc.—but you must love me, why do you not love me? Love me darn you." Britten's librettist Montagu Slater took up this angle in the early drafts, emphasizing both Grimes's pederasty and the complicity of the villagers in looking the other way. (He quoted Crabbe directly: "some on hearing cries / Said calmly 'Grimes is at his exercise.'")

But in revision Britten and Pears thought better of their conception of Grimes's motives. They erased the hints of pedophilia, shaping a "liberal view" of an ambiguous misfit whose "behavior was excusable and understandable." Pears explicitly retreated from his original conception, writing to Britten, "The more I hear of it, the more I feel that the queerness is unimportant & doesn't really exist in the music (or at any rate obtrude) so it mustn't do so in words. P. G. is an introspective, an artist, a neurotic . . ." The completed libretto pitted Grimes as an Everyman against a hostile society. Britten changed the plot, introducing a sympathetic female champion of Grimes and making clear that the apprentices died by accident. Thus he created a complicated, closeted opera. One could read the plot as a grand allegory of good and evil. But viewers, if they wished, could find in both the villagers' ostracism and Grimes's behavior a dark story of homosexual guilt.

Morgan was pleased to have been an inspiration to Ben. He saw the chance to write with Britten as serious business. It made him feel vital to be at work again. As a skilled pianist and an accomplished music critic, Morgan found that "Music had a warmth and vitality which Life in Literature has lacked." Still aglow from the adulation of younger gay artists in America, Morgan imagined that his work with Britten would have some of the symbolic paternal relation that his friendship with Cadmus had achieved. But he was uneasy at undertaking a libretto without any experience of writing in the form, humbly accepting the help of Eric Crozier, Ben's experienced librettist and producer.

Almost immediately Ben and Morgan had the same "telepathic and simultaneous" thought—to adapt Herman Melville's novella *Billy Budd*. Crozier objected, thinking that an all-male opera with a homosexual subtext might be difficult if not dangerous to produce. But the chance to relish the physical beauty of an all-male cast, to "keep human beings and the smell of tar" was too compelling, and Ben and Morgan prevailed. In mid-January 1949, on their first morning of work, Morgan, Ben, and Eric outlined a list of characters and events, and made a rough sketch of the set—the man-of-war *The Indomitable* during the Napoleonic Wars. They also settled on a narrative frame. The story of Billy Budd, they decided, would be told as a long flashback through its sole survivor, Captain Edward Vere, "an old man who has experienced much." So they made Vere the same age as Morgan himself, and decided that Peter would sing the part.

Morgan thought *Billy Budd* had the dramatic intensity to be a grand opera. Its three central characters were impelled toward tragedy: Billy Budd, the innocent and beloved young seaman with a fateful stammer; the malevolent Petty Officer John Claggart, who falsely accuses Billy of mutiny, and is struck and killed by him when Billy, tongue-tied, cannot defend himself; and Captain Vere, who though he knows Billy is innocent invokes strict naval law and orders Billy hanged for manslaughter. But the tone of Melville's novella rankled Morgan. He told the critic Lionel Trilling that his job was "rescuing ... Vere from his creator." The man who wrote "What I Believe" could not celebrate Vere's sense of duty, could not even savor its tragedy. Morgan was repelled by Melville making Vere the hero of his tale. He wanted the hero to be Billy Budd himself.

Morgan reacted so strongly in part because, as he had done with Crabbe, he identified with the author's dilemma personally. The publication history of *Billy Budd* held uncanny parallels to his own long-suppressed *Maurice*. Like Forster, Melville had lain fallow as a fiction writer. After almost thirty years of silence, Melville wrote *Billy Budd* near the end of his life, finishing it just months before he died at age seventy-three, virtually the same age as Morgan now. For three decades after Melville's death in 1891 the manuscript languished. It was published for the first time—in London, in 1924—in the same year as *A Passage to India*.

As a redress, Morgan reconceived the story as a meditation on masculinity. To him the real tragedy was the story's blind machismo, the way all three protagonists were pressed into violence and moral inaction by unconscious rote notions of male duty. Placing the gorgeous, innocent figure of Billy at the center of the opera created an erotic triangle, with Billy as object of both Vere's benign and Claggart's malign love. ("N.B.," he wrote to Trilling, "Why is it Vere's touch on Billy's shoulder that precipitates the blow?") Melville had dwelt on Claggart's "natural depravity." To Morgan, this phrase unmistakably echoed the pseudo-scientific arguments that homosexuality was inherently sinful and perverse, the arguments so familiar from the early decades of his life. Instead he diagnosed Claggart's "depravity" as desire *thwarted*, desire corrupted into self-hatred. He criticized Ben's original music for Claggart's monologue in Act II as too tepid—"soggy depression or growling remorse." Instead he wanted Ben to depict Claggart's love for Billy as "*passion*—love constricted, perverted, poisoned ... a sexual discharge gone evil." He cautioned against constructing too pat a moral for the story, insisting to Ben that though Billy may be "our Saviour, yet he is Billy, not Christ." Morgan redirected Melville's tale into an allegory about the social experience of being a homosexual.

By March 1949 Eric Crozier and Morgan were "immersed in Billy Budd like two trappist monks," hammering out the libretto before Ben began to compose the score. The three men settled at Crag House for "sixteen remarkable Billy Budd days." Within a week, Crozier wrote his wife, they had mastered the "welter of technical [naval] terms" and allotted their writing duties—"Morgan is in charge of the drama, I am in command of the ship . . . It is going to be a stupendous opera." Crozier found Morgan to be humble and "typically generous . . . a most kind man," but even at this early moment in the process of composition there were cracks in the glaze. As a close friend of Britten, Crozier was cast in the role of go-between, finding "Ben . . . in a wretched state . . . He does not really want to do *Billy* as an opera but feels that he cannot withdraw . . . the long hours that Morgan and I are spending cloistered together seem almost to make him a little jealous." Britten told Crozier that he was "going through a period of revulsion against *Billy Budd*, from a misunderstanding about the purpose of the story, and he wanted to give the whole thing up." But Crozier smoothed his feathers—for the time being—and the project went on.

Enraptured by the work, Morgan was unaware of this behind-the-scenes drama. His creative energy translated into joy. Bob visited him at Aldeburgh, very affectionate. In his diary Morgan related his delight at their rapprochement: "The great goodness and love of Bob towers. I wonder why he was so short and harsh to me last year, don't think it was just his health." But Ben's response to creative difficulties was often evasion or flight. He suddenly accepted a recital tour abroad with Peter, leaving Morgan puzzled but unenlightened. In this gap, Morgan began to plan a second "American adventure," to introduce Bob to his new American friends. His work on the opera dictating that he "ought to be away from England for as short a period as possible," Morgan limited himself to two lucrative public events on the East Coast—the Blashfield lecture at the American Academy of Arts and Letters in New York City and an honorary degree at Bill Roerick's alma mater, Hamilton College.

He designed the journey to revisit the high points of two years before, viewing each destination vicariously through Bob's eyes—Lost Farm with Bill. Paul's studio, a short trip to Philadelphia to visit Tom Coley's mother.

The visit had a self-conscious, valedictory quality. Morgan began to feel enmeshed in time, as people do in late middle age—each event nestled in prenostalgia even before it is experienced. I have my health, people think. I am *enjoying* this. This is a golden moment, they think. In such a state of consciousness, even Bob began to seem older to Morgan. He told Paul, "I wish you could have [sketched] Bob as I first knew him 20 years ago . . ." It became impossible not to measure every moment against its un-self-conscious origins. "It was sad not seeing you in New York," he wrote to Paul, who was again away for the summer. "I often thought when I approached the house [at St. Luke's Place] of my first approach, and of my first meal there: every sort of cold delicacy and wine . . ."

Could things ever become different, or would they always be a continuation of the same? Wystan had happily emigrated, and Christopher, too. Might it be possible to transplant the whole Buckingham family to more amenable soil? Why not? Planning the visit, Morgan scouted for the answer to these questions, looking into his old love's eyes. For the time being, it was adventure enough to test how his American friends would respond to Bob, "Mr. Forster['s] lifelong beloved . . . policeman." The public honors were conspicuous and designed to impress Bob, who sat near General Omar Bradley at the luncheon fêting the Hamilton degree recipients. But too much pomp made Morgan irreverent: he filed away the sheepskin, but made special note of an informal citation, "'For being Morgan' Written by Bill Roerick on the reverse of a detached beer bottle label after some distinction or other had been conferred on me."

Inviting Morgan to give the lucrative Blashfield lecture was the brain-child of Glenway Wescott. Though he had been corresponding with Morgan since 1940, when he sent a copy of his new novel *The Pilgrim Hawk*, Glenway was the only person in his circle of friends who had not yet met Morgan, and he was envious of their proximity to the Great Writer. Newly elected to the academy, Glenway had the ear of its president, the poet Archibald MacLeish. He crowed to a friend that he had "killed cock robin" by persuading Morgan to come back to the States. Morgan accepted, and set to work finding "something to say which shall be profound but not disturbing" to earn his lecture fee.

Membership in the academy provided consolatory work for Glenway, who despite early precociousness as a writer had not achieved great literary fame. He had undeniable talent, and a knack for falling in with the right crowd. A willowy blond farm boy with a dreamy expression, Glenway had been just nineteen when he fled the Midwest with his lover Monroe Wheeler for Greenwich Village, then Paris, then southern France. By then Marianne Moore and William Carlos Williams had already published Wescott's poems. Monroe was a Chicago boy, two years older, compactly built, with saturnine good looks. The two young men were motivated more by an inchoate need for sexual freedom than by any specific vocation. Monroe cannily told Glenway, "In the American culture artists have privileges of freedom that are recognized . . . If you will be a poet and make a life of writing, they will let you alone." And so Glenway had begun to write quickly, publishing two novels and a collection of short stories. By his mid-twenties, he was a celebrity, his name mentioned in the same breath as Hemingway and Fitzgerald as a "prophet of a New America."

Hemingway in particular envied and reviled Glenway. He hated Wescott's polished sentences, the embellishment, the European air of his characters' exquisite sensibilities. He also resented Glenway's friendship with Gertrude Stein. Most of all, he detested the success of homosexual writers: "Glenway Wescott, Thornton Wilder and Julian Green have all gotten rich in a year in which I made less than I made as a newspaper correspondent—and I'm the only one with wives and children to support." He hated Glenway's speaking voice. Bitchily, he told Stein, "When you matriculate at the University of Chicago you write down just what accent you will have and they give it to you when you graduate." So much for Glenway being "let alone."

In the world he and Monroe made for themselves, they found sympathetic company. In France they made lifelong friends with an extraordinary array of artists: Katherine Anne Porter, Jean Cocteau, Marc Chagall, Willie Maugham, Thornton Wilder, the Sitwell siblings, and the novelist whom Osbert Sitwell called "Freud Madox Fraud." And they attracted friends back into Stein's circle. Just before they left New York, Monroe and Glenway had met a beautiful, restless, and painfully young son of an Episcopalian clergyman from the posh parts of New Jersey. George Platt Lynes was not quite twenty. He had gone to prep school with Lincoln Kirstein but lasted only a matter of weeks at Yale, bucking a family tradition. Lynes was preternaturally worldly: he offered the pair all sorts of entrées to the expatriate world of Paris, from which he had already returned.

George Platt Lynes was an aesthete with no settled métier, exasperating to his father, magnetic to his friends. He had opened an elegant little bookshop in Englewood, New Jersey, and sold it for a profit after six months. He knew books, theater, ballet, painting, photography, fashion, furniture. Bright, rakishly charming, hungry for life, fun, he was impossible to resist. Glenway wrote importuning him—"Dear Little George," "Sweet Boy," "Child New York"—to join him and Monroe in France. Dear Little George did, but not before seducing Glenway's resolutely heterosexual younger brother Lloyd, who had followed Glenway east to New York. Glenway was furious, Monroe philosophical. It was Glenway's "own fault" for introducing them. Then George followed directions. He arrived, like a comet, back in France in the summer of 1928.

Glenway had invited George, but George ended up chiefly in Monroe's bed. What might have been—for three more ordinary men—an impossible situation somehow settled, delicately and pleasurably, into a triangle in equipoise; all three found a clear way through into a kinship that—to the end of their lives—none of them ever bothered to label or define. It was deeply shared friendship with sex intermixed: passionate sex between George and Monroe; companionate, polite, less frequent sex between George and Glenway. Between Glenway and Monroe ardor had cooled slightly even before George had come to them, and they settled into a devoted sort of marriage, each comfortably taking on lovers for some months, all perfectly open and friendly.

George's eyes were hungry for beauty. As the three men traveled through Europe, he began to take pictures. The three of them together in perfect white linen suits, cut by the sharp shadow of a palm tree. A Roman-coiffed Gertrude Stein in profile, with the hills of Provence just a smudge in the distance. Cocteau, withdrawing from an opium habit, intensely facing the camera, all beaky nose, with a shock of curly hair shooting upward as if aflame. Man Ray took a striking portrait of George managing to look like a figure from a Greek myth, despite wearing a diaperlike loincloth. By the time the ménage was transplanted back to New York in 1934, George's aimless pursuit had focused into a vocation, as Glenway's had done. He became a fashion photographer.

When Morgan and Bob visited them in 1949, Glenway, Monroe, and George had their cleats into the city. The three men lived in "our household," a proper ménage à trois, until George, "spellbound, discontented with his life, dissatisfied with himself," left Glenway and Monroe together, the way they would stay for the next fifty years. All three traveled in a range of social worlds—Lincoln and the dancers of the New York City Ballet, Paul and his more bohemian friends, the rich patrons of the nascent Museum of Modern Art, where Monroe was director of publications. George attracted fashion models and a raffish crowd of young men—Pullman porters and rent boys and artistic types in advertising. Living in these worlds often meant depending on other people's money. Glenway enjoyed the patronage of his brother Lloyd and his wife, Barbara, who supported the whole family with her lavish inheritance. George, whether flush or in debt, "seemed to consider the world a gift that he bought and presented to his friends for his own pleasure." Monroe was like an impoverished aristocrat with brains and taste but little money. During his expatriate years, he had met Jean Renoir, Marc Chagall, and Pablo Picasso; and now, with these connections and a canny eye, he traveled frequently to Europe as one of the museum's most conspicuous emissaries. He was always impeccably and formally dressed. He had perfect manners. A portrait of him, looking casually suave, appeared in the November 1948 *Vogue*. This aura of "worldliness personified" was a necessary part of cultivating the museum's donors for Monroe, a Chicago boy with only a high school diploma.

They divided their time between urban and rural entertainments, and they swept Morgan and Bob along for both. The highlight of Wescott's plans was a dinner at Monroe's two nights before the lecture. Monroe's apartment was configured for show, with the large public rooms facing Park Avenue, while a tiny kitchen, truncated bedrooms, and bathroom faced the back. The drawing room and dining room could have been from an updated novel by Henry James—fitted with beautiful, expensive European furniture, bibelots, and fine books, many borrowed from Glenway's sister-in-law Barbara. A Courbet landscape hung over the mantelpiece.

Here George and his mother, Adelaide—an elegant and intelligent woman—joined the small company for cocktails. It was a disarming idea to start with George, like an amuse-bouche. He lingered just long enough to persuade Bob and Morgan to have their portraits taken the following week at his studio. Then the Lyneses evaporated. The six dinner guests—all men— had been carefully chosen to make the evening both provocative and welcoming. Monroe, who was serious about the closet, was "worried about it, hasn't warned EMF and keeps forbidding me to let the news item out, lest there be embarrassment about B.B.," Glenway wrote a friend. He had reason to be careful: each dinner party was organized around a theme, and the theme of this one, unbeknown to Morgan, was *sex.*

That the party would be fuel for news—and for local gossip—was inevitable. Morgan and Bob were the guests of honor. Glenway had also invited Joseph Campbell, whose work linking "ancient and primitive religions, especially the Hindu" with modern psychology had just earned him an American Academy grant. The history of world mythology was in Campbell's palm; he knew Sanskrit and shared a special love of India with Morgan. But the catalyst for controversy and conversation was the guest who had come to New York to research sex. Dr. Alfred Kinsey was the sixth man at the table. Monroe had penciled into his little leather daybook a full five hours on the following afternoon for Kinsey to take his sex history.

Dr. Kinsey wasn't a physician. A professor of zoology who had begun his career studying gall wasps, he had published his magisterial report *Sexual Behavior in the Human Male* just five months earlier. The tome was scientifically scrupulous and lucidly written by Kinsey himself. It presented the "actual behavior of people" based on more than twelve thousand firsthand interviews conducted by Kinsey and his handful of researchers at Indiana University in Bloomington.

In this urbane company, Kinsey came across as a Midwestern square. His hair was cut short on the sides to well above his ears, topped by a long bristle of thatch that he attempted to part in the middle. He wore, as always, a rumpled jacket, crisp white shirt, and bow tie. But his intense curiosity was beguiling. Like the Boy Scout he had once been, he was honest, hardworking, true and plain, kindhearted and utterly sincere. (He was also, unknown to himself and his dinner companions, on the edge of a dangerous decision. The night he met Morgan and Bob was the first night Kinsey met Glenway. Within a few months Glenway invited him to watch sex parties, and two summers later, Kinsey reciprocated, asking Glenway to come to Indiana to be filmed while masturbating. There they became sexual partners and close friends. Their secret would eventually endanger the project, and its funding, though it did not threaten Kinsey's very open marriage.)

Discovering the norms of sexual practice in America proved an irresistible impulse for many readers. Kinsey's book became an instant bestseller. He pursued a briskly American way of *measuring* sex: he counted orgasms. This emphasis was a bit *hydraulic.* Because it focused on behavior rather than psychology, all sorts of desire never counted in Kinsey's work. But just by closely observing and reporting, in *Sexual Behavior in the Human Male* Kinsey made an enormous impact. His survey proved supple enough to complicate the picture of human sexual expression.

Three observations about homosexuality in particular galvanized his readers. Thirty-seven percent of Kinsey's large sample of men reported homosexual experiences leading to orgasm. Ten percent of men were exclusively homosexual for at least three years between the ages of sixteen and sixty-five. And four percent of the men were "exclusively homosexual throughout their lives." Kinsey's sympathy to bisexuality may have deliberately shaped his method to "make there seem to be as much homosexual activity as possible." His coworkers later came to regret the three-year window of sexual activity as an indefensibly arbitrary measurement—but his reported figures were nonetheless transparent and incontrovertible.

To the gay men in Glenway's circle Kinsey's tireless work—and his unjudgmental air—made him something of a saint. He normalized their experience, and appealed to their narcissism. Only Lincoln Kirstein resisted the invitation to give his sexual history, telling Christopher Isherwood,

> all the staff of the Mus. Of Mod Art has been had by Dr. Kinsey; he is a disgusting old voyeur and his entire work is a scientific fraud, but he wants to talk to ARTISTS; he wants to know how Artists fuck and come; Glenway is his mentor . . . He has the greatest collection of dirty art in the world, which I long to see, but not at the price of telling him MY story.

Monroe had given Morgan no warning that Kinsey would be there, but the dinner, Glenway reported to Isherwood, "went like a charm. Indeed Mr. F. himself made it go. No reference or even identification while we drank cocktails—then the instant we were settled at table. Mr. F. turned + asked the first leading question, set the wonderful absurd ball rolling— + Dr. K. was so pleased. And how Mr. F. listens. now with the worried look, then with the chuckle—it makes one feel like a singer being accompanied on an inaudible piano."

They spoke of Kinsey's findings, and of the erotic friezes on the Hindu temples at Khajuraho, thousands of bodies connected in mutual pleasure, which both Campbell and Morgan had seen; of the differences Kinsey had found between the way women and men become sexually aroused; about "the cancer of unenforceable laws (worst of all sex laws) . . ." Kinsey drily noted that almost everyone he surveyed had broken a sex law of some sort, since premarital and extramarital intercourse, incest, miscegenation, sex outside of statutory age limits, homosexual activity, contact with prostitutes, sexual contact with animals, oral sex, sodomy, and even solitary masturbation were all restricted by law in one state or another. In this light, the stigma attached to particular occasions of homosexual activity—to urban queers, for example, but not as much to "lumbermen, cattlemen, prospectors, miners and hunters"—was clearly arbitrary, a matter of "social custom" rather than moral force.

Not knowing what to expect from Bob Buckingham, Glenway was "surprised" by his ease in the company, his "lively and approving interest at every point." Bob delightedly extended an invitation of his own to Dr. Kinsey to visit Scotland Yard's roomfuls of confiscated pornography on his next visit to England. There was much jolly, manly talk. But Morgan tendered no revelations about his own sex life. He offered only the cryptic phrase that Monroe recorded in his little datebook: "I favor reciprocal dishonesty." Whether the dishonesty in question was his own, Bob's, his readers', or society's was left, as always, to the imagination.

To Morgan, there was something refreshing about Kinsey's approach. He had so little in common with the European sexologists. He didn't, like Freud, feel the need to bore into the psyche and penetrate the mystery of desire— an impulse in Freud's work that both irritated and frightened Morgan. He didn't, like Hirschfeld and Krafft-Ebing, make "pigeonholes" for sexual desire. Most intriguing to Morgan was Kinsey's discovery that all men—gay and straight—responded sexually to "obscene" images and fantasies, while few women did. Imagination had long been the wellspring of lust for Morgan, and he cherished the power of his erotic dreams. He had always stoked his own lust, and satisfied it too, by writing erotic tableaux. The day after the dinner, while hiking with Bob and Glenway, Morgan walked ahead in silence for a few minutes, contemplating this nugget of truth. He stopped in his tracks. In a soft voice, he said, "I must say that it comforted me to be told this."

A second comfort was Kinsey's affirmation that homosexuals did not seem to be some intermediate sex, as the scientists of Morgan's youth— indeed even Edward Carpenter—had believed. Bob, in his conventional way, had missed this point. The next day in conversation, Bob quoted the

Bible verse "Male and female he created them" to affirm that Kinsey had identified "two divisions of humankind . . . half effeminate and half manly." But Morgan corrected him sharply. "'No, Bob no!' Forster protested. 'Effeminacy is only a manner. A homosexual man is as male as a heterosexual man. Only remember just one discovery that the good doctor told us: very few women take any interest in obscene things, whereas most men enjoy them and feel the need for them . . .'"

Two days after the dinner, an august collection of cultural figures from what Morgan teasingly called "fame's lower slopes" gathered in the grand hall of the academy on 155th Street to hear Morgan give a lecture, "Art for Art's Sake." It was an old-fashioned argument, and Morgan knew it.

> A writer . . . who chose "Art for Art's Sake" for his theme fifty years
> ago could be sure of being in the swim, and could feel so confident of
> success that he . . . dressed himself in esthetic costumes suitable to
> the occasion—in an embroidered dressing-gown . . . or a blue velvet
> suit with a Lord Fauntleroy collar . . . and carried a poppy or a lily
> or a long peacock's feather in his mediaeval hand. Times have
> changed.

But had they? Standing in a rumpled brown tweed suit rather than Wilde's ostentatious dress, Morgan told the assemblage of academics, newly inducted artists such as William Faulkner, John Steinbeck, Thomas Mann, and his friends Christopher, Wystan, and Glenway, that he, too, felt himself an outsider. It was exactly what he had written to Paul Cadmus several years earlier. They had been discussing whether painters revealed themselves in their art. Ingres was most mysterious, Morgan argued, "a painter's painter I should think," who "doesn't therefore reveal himself to the outsider." Morgan clearly identified with this position. He confided to Paul, "I am the outsidest of outsiders."

That afternoon at the academy Morgan embraced the idea, as he had in "What I Believe," that the artist must necessarily find himself out of favor and out of power. An artist would always be, he said, "the bohemian, the outsider, the parasite, the rat." So had Shelley been, and so were all great poet-prophets. He ended with a flourish: "I would sooner be a swimming rat than a sinking ship—at all events I can look around me for a little longer." It was a pessimism about the world he felt was justly earned. Then he collected his medal and his check and "beat it" to Glenway's farm in New Jersey.

Farm is probably the wrong word for the eighteenth-century house and grounds where Glenway's family lived. Mulhocaway Farm was, to use Alexander Pope's phrase, "nature to advantage dress'd." And Lloyd and Barbara Wescott were a modern American version of Pope's landed gentry. Cadmus had painted the couple in the style of Gainsborough grafted onto Thomas Hart Benton, in front of an opulent display of modern barns, machines, and artificially inseminated livestock, with a single almost invisible groomsman in the background. Lord of this queer manor, Lloyd Wescott stocked Mulhocaway Farm with prize heifers and horses, and eventually, piecemeal, with the whole of his dirt-poor Wisconsin clan—his mother and father, several of his sisters, and the triangle of aesthetes, George, Monroe, and Glenway. He provided them with an eighteenth-century stone farmhouse they called Stoneblossom, where Bob and Morgan slept in adjoining bedrooms at the top of the stairs while Glenway encamped in the paneled library below.

Living in this hothouse atmosphere, Glenway had developed the aura of a boy pressing his nose on the glass looking in at a party to which he had not been invited. His connoisseurship of dependence, and his acute sensitivity, made him an ideal host. He was determined insofar as he could to treat Bob Buckingham as a person in his own right for the duration of the visit. So they took Bob, who had an interest in police work in the United States, to a women's prison near the farm, where Lloyd knew the woman superintendent intimately. Bob commented, about arresting people, "I don't even use my truncheon. I use my fists. The poor devils resent it less."

At Mulhocaway, Glenway propelled Morgan and Bob into a scene of genuine, almost cartoonish familial conviviality. His sister played folk songs on the guitar as they settled around the fireplace after dinner. Glenway, in a gracious kind of reciprocal dishonesty, did not broach the question of *Maurice*—about which he had heard from Christopher—just as he did not broach the question of sleeping arrangements for Morgan and Bob, whose "duet of voices" could be heard laughing and teasing at the top of the stairs. Glenway quoted Morgan to himself: "Mutual secrecy being one of the conditions of life on the globe."

Notwithstanding this, the precise nature of the relationship between Morgan and Bob was intriguing to him, and the subject of intense speculation among Forster's American friends. Paul Cadmus believed Morgan and Bob were lovers, finding them to be temperamentally and otherwise "perfect for each other." From what he had seen on this trip, Glenway agreed. Lincoln found Bob to be "the toughest man I ever met. Let's face it," he told Christopher, "it's not by accident he is a cop, even though a very kind cop, and a wildly attractive one." In contrast, Bill Roerick was convinced that Bob was straight, and that Morgan was forced to walk gingerly at the edge of intimacy.

Even these very close friends found Morgan adept at "reject[ing] intimacy without impairing affection," to quote Morgan's own description of T. E. Lawrence. A strange moment of déjà vu between Monroe and Morgan on the way out to the farm underscored this point. They found a rural restaurant in which to eat supper. As they waited for the meal to arrive, Monroe snatched Morgan's "beclouded" glasses from his nose, and cleaned them. Pleased with himself, he asked Morgan, "Now, don't you see better?" Just as Mohammed had done when Morgan had touched his spectacles thirty years before, Morgan recoiled and looked around the room in mordant silence. Then he said, terribly politely, "Thank you Monroe. But if you don't mind my saying so, I'm not sure I want to see so much."

They were back at St. Luke's Place from Stoneblossom the Tuesday after Memorial Day. The next afternoon, Bob and Morgan dressed in their best bespoke suits, shaved and combed their hair, and took a cab to George Platt Lynes's midtown studio. It is hard to believe that the photographs from this session were taken only a day after the snapshots of a dowdy, middle-aged Bob sucking on a pipe at Stoneblossom. As he did for all his sitters, George made Bob and Morgan look wondrous.

Though he was only forty-two, Lynes had gone completely silver-maned. He was so striking that men and women stopped in their tracks to linger and look at him as he walked on the sidewalks of Manhattan. Entering his studio meant entering a seductive, charming, wholly artificial world. The workspace was essentially a stage, a large empty box with concrete walls and a scuffed cement floor. The skylight was painted over to deny all natural light. George devised complex and wildly inventive stage lighting that complemented the insight into character that was the hallmark of his portraits. He was already famous for his iconic photographs of Marianne Moore in her tricornered hat and Kirstein's New York City Ballet dancers enacting Greek myths. (He would be more famous still after his death at age forty-eight for his dazzling and provocative male nudes, which were a strong influence on Robert Mapplethorpe.)

In photographing Morgan, George had a real challenge because his subject was notoriously unphotogenic. His liquid moods played upon his face like a screen, but "[w]hen a camera approaches," Bill Roerick observed, "he looks at it, it looks at him, and they have nothing to say to each other. He produces an official silence, the camera produces an unlikeness." Only in occasional snapshots could Morgan "sometimes look . . . quite like himself." George had something even more ambitious in mind: to capture, with Morgan's cooperation, a chameleon variety of selves, the most beautiful best public and private selves his sitters could imagine.

To do this magic task, George worked stealthily. He used his physical beauty and his extraordinary charm to disarm his photographic subjects. He often worked shirtless while wearing dress trousers and a belt. He put sitters at ease with gentle wit. Most important, he created an aura of trust. It was clear that his only object in making a portrait was to bring out a self that resembled the sitter, but more perfectly. In his sessions, George avoided the gaze that would invite a sitter's self-consciousness by making it seem as though "the subject whom he was photographing appeared to be to him of the least concern." The actual moment that captured the likeness was disguised. Donald Windham noted, "When Lynes photographed me . . . I was waiting, listening to him telling his assistants to conceal a lamp behind a prop to adjust a spot or bowl, and wondering when he would get around to directing me beyond casually suggesting that I try looking right or left, when he announced that the sitting was over."

In a ninety-minute session, George took four sets of portraits, turning from one to another staged setup in his studio and relying on evocative props recycled from his commercial work in fashion photography: two of Morgan alone, a series of Bob alone, and a gay domestic portrait of the two men together. Pieced together, these prints reveal the dazzling balance of speed and spontaneity of Lynes's working method. George succeeded in fulfilling the fantasy that Morgan had confided in his letter to Paul: making Bob look as vital and seductive as he had when they met twenty years before. For this sequence, George used a mock-up of rough-hewn whitewashed wood, cleverly alluding to the boardwalk steps that descended to the beach at Fire Island that he, Paul, Jerry, and George Tooker frequented in the summers.

Leaning back against the crook of a railing, Bob was captured with a laugh fading from his lips, his formal dark suit in such contrast to the bright background that he almost seemed to loom out of a mist. Did Bob recognize the allusion? Did he collude in this portrait of himself as a gay man?

And Morgan was made to look eminent. George placed him on a mock-stone throne with his gold signet ring demonstratively visible. In several of the poses, he held his glasses cupped in his palm; in several others a piece of rolled-up paper. George did not ask Morgan to address the camera directly. Instead he captured Morgan's public self, lost in contemplation. The photo revealed a bit of Forster's gentleness; he could not help being both wistful and commanding. In the proofs, it's hard to ignore a startling cowlick.

Lynes reused the flat stone throne as a kind of plinth for the double portraits, printing the glass plate in such stark contrast that it appeared the two men were hovering alone in an empty white space. These photographs echoed the composition of a set of double portraits taken fifteen years earlier in London. Morgan had commissioned these portraits from Stephen Spender's brother Humphrey and Humphrey's lover, Bill Edmiston. Morgan showed scrupulous interest in retouching and refining them. (His notes to the photographers on retouching and printing remain in pencil on the back of the prints.) In both Spender's and Lynes's portraits, the physical position of the men—Bob looming above Morgan—spoke to some aspect of their psychic life together. Morgan willfully erased his status as a "great man" in Bob's company, becoming subordinate, sheltered by Bob's bulk, transparently the more emotionally vulnerable and weaker of the pair. In Lynes's dual portrait, their devotion and intimacy are palpable. Standing above the old man, his leg alongside Morgan's arm, his arm resting on his shoulder, Bob almost enveloped Morgan.

But George saved one final sequence that he never shared with Morgan. These two full-length portraits literally caught Morgan unawares, grasping the same piece of paper in his hand that he holds in several of the throne pictures, standing at the verge of the unadorned studio wall, like an actor waiting in the wings. His spectacles are on, and his left hand is in his trouser pocket. The photograph captured Morgan's owlishness and his vulnerability—the Morgan that Christopher Isherwood described as the sanest person he had ever known, alone, resolute, a tough humanist. Five years later, when George was destitute and dying of lung cancer, he bound up his most pre-

cious prints and sold them to Dr. Kinsey. There, hiding among the thousands
of photographs in what Lincoln sardonically labeled "the greatest collection
of dirty art in the world" at the Kinsey Institute was George's photograph of
Morgan, the lonely pioneer.

Less than a week later, Monroe saw Bob and Morgan off at LaGuardia Air-
port. Back in England, the ether of their fantastic journey wore off rather
quickly. Bob resumed his patrols in London, and Morgan repaired to King's.
Now Cambridge became a point of hegira for Morgan's American friends.
Monroe swung by when he traveled to London to collect paintings for the
museum; Donald Windham brought his new partner, Sandy Campbell—who
had once broken Paul Cadmus's heart—for a damp but pleasant three-day
stay. In the autumn of 1949, Morgan and Paul Cadmus managed a reunion
at King's. Returning from Italy with George Tooker, Paul stopped for a few
days to draw the promised portrait. To keep Morgan from stiffening into self-
consciousness they suggested he occupy himself in reading, and he obliged
in a familiar ritual, breaking out the typescript of *Maurice* and reading it
aloud to them as Paul completed the sketch. Isherwood found the portrait to
be unpersuasive, but Morgan loved it, and gave it to Bob and May.

The dream of emigration gradually retreated in the cool of common sense.
Morgan told Glenway that he retained "great affection for America, but, I
think, no sentimentality towards her." Looking back at his journey, his view
of American possibilities narrowed. "The American life would have proved
unendurable," Glenway wrote in a record of their conversation. Two years
after his return, he would look back to reflect that the moment of opportunity
had slipped by without a whisper. "Sometimes I wish," he told Monroe
Wheeler, "that I had led a more adventurous life, but the wish is followed by
a feeling of relief that I can't start living it now."

This fact was corporeally derived. Morgan's body seemed determined to
devise the most unhappy and humiliating reminders of old age. First, a suspected "cancer?" of "the arsehole" which turned out to be nothing terribly
malign; then he was forced to face the inevitability of a second prostate operation to stem a leaky bladder. It was scheduled for early January 1950, just
after his seventy-first birthday. Goldie's sudden death after just such a simple procedure haunted Morgan, and he made elaborate arrangements to be
properly looked after and even began to think practically on what should

happen if he should die. His greatest regret as he entered the private hospital in Sloane Square was that he might leave *Billy Budd* unfinished.

He was hurt but not surprised to learn that Bob—being no relation—would be barred from visiting him in the hospital. But May, trained as a nurse, volunteered to sit with him in the first few days after the surgery. Her wisdom and medical acumen saved his life. In the middle of the night she alerted the doctor that Morgan was becoming unresponsive. May's kindness and implacable compassion when he was most vulnerable subtly renewed their intimacy. He found himself sympathizing with her, imagining what it must be like to have always to share Bob, grateful for her quasi-maternal love.

In the immediate period of recuperation, Morgan stayed at Wendell Road in London with Bob, May, and sixteen-year-old Robin, who was apprenticing to be a plumber; but in the spring, as he regained his energy, he settled for a long stay in Aldeburgh with Peter and Ben to complete *Billy Budd*. The work went on well enough, but Morgan's hopes for a deepening friendship with Ben ran aground. As Britten composed the score for the libretto, both Crozier and Morgan became concerned that there was "a tendency to dry-dock feeling" in the music. In part, this cooling off was the inevitable consequence of Britten's creative method. He confessed to being "in a funny abstracted mood, rather selfish . . . demanding lots of treatment and extra consideration" as he wrote the opera. Ben routinely chewed up and spat out collaborators. Just before he began *Billy Budd* he spoke with Crozier, confessing rather heartlessly how abruptly he had dropped his previous librettist, Montagu Slater, even though he knew that Slater was terribly ill with cancer. With a mixture of savagery and regret, he told Crozier that he anticipated that he, too, one day would be "one of [my] corpses."

But Morgan had no intention of being dropped. Nonetheless, he was irritated by Ben's high-handedness, his pattern of taking on multiple commissions and jetting off to performances scheduled at the last minute. For Morgan, *Billy Budd* was the most pressing and important work he had done in a long while, and it wounded him to discover how quickly the mantle of affection had melted from his relations with Ben. He left Aldeburgh earlier than planned. Over the next months, the process of finishing the opera became painful for bystanders to watch. Billy Burrell, a young local fisherman who befriended Britten and attracted Morgan with his hearty good looks, "felt sorry for Morgan" when Ben began to discourage Morgan's visits as a distraction. Burrell said that Ben was unprepared for the logistics of dealing with the older man: "Morgan was slow . . . you'd have to fetch him from Cambridge . . . you'd have to take him back." The problem was compounded when Morgan slipped while climbing the steps of the bell tower at Aldeburgh and shattered his ankle. Burrell told Morgan, "We're only simple humble people, but you're quite welcome to . . . stay whenever you want." Thereafter, when Morgan came, he stayed with the fisherman and his wife. The demotion hurt Morgan, and the increasing creative tension between Ben and Morgan and Ben and Eric began to grow poisonous.

In late November 1950, about a year before the opera's scheduled premiere at Covent Garden, Ben and Eric came to Cambridge to iron out differences with Morgan. Ben's offhandedness catalyzed Morgan's simmering resentment. He exploded in rage. The even-handed Crozier was stunned by the virulence of Morgan's verbal attack: "To me, [Morgan] was chilly but polite. To Britten he was outrageous: he spoke to him like some low-class servant who deserves to be whipped." As he had done with the servant Kanaya, Morgan channeled the worst kind of snobbish savagery when he felt impotent and humiliated. He "berated [Ben] like a schoolboy." Then he stormed out of his rooms into the cold night.

In Morgan's mind, the contretemps blew over quickly. Totting up emotional accounts at the end of the year, he dismissed the incident's importance: "I am rather a fierce old man at the moment, and he is rather a spoilt boy, and certainly a busy one." But Ben became wary, and their friendship fizzled out.

By November 1951, rehearsals for the premiere were going well. The baritone Theodor Uppmann, all blond curls and muscles, made a handsome and impressive Billy—"gay young, strong charming, good voice and some acting power." Also, alas, resolutely heterosexual. Morgan wrote Tom Coley breathily: "Heavens the excitement in which we live. I adore it, and spend most of each day at rehearsals." Some hijinks leavened the tension: the orchestra burst into a surprise "Happy Birthday" instead of the prescribed music while Ben began conducting on his birthday. Joe Ackerley was banned from rehearsals because he was mooning around "like Dido" at the sailors. In early December 1951, *Billy Budd* opened to largely enthusiastic reviews of both the score and the libretto. Covent Garden had perhaps never held so many unlikely working-class operagoers. Morgan invited many of his closest friends. It was the first time Billy Burrell had ever worn evening dress.

Working on *Billy Budd*, Morgan came to realize, had been a way to "wrestle with the void." So much of his sense of self, of well-being was tethered to his aging body, to his hope that he could remain attractive or even lovable to Bob. As the glow of their New York adventure faded, Morgan had felt "gnawed by my failure to impress or interest Bob any more." But an unaccountable year-end burst of "randiness" in Bob distracted and warmed Morgan again. He assessed the texture of their long-lived love in his diary: "As for Bob, I do now know of the freshness and warmth of his love, not only of its reliability, and I hope I shall never again be fussed. I love him, I now know, more than any one else can, and he has helped me to care for living physically . . ."

For Morgan, lust had always been the green fuse of life and of imagination. He still felt it keenly, but what was it worth if this feeling could not connect to something *human*, if not physically, then at least metaphysically—as it had done at the Figsbury Rings when the spirit of Stephen Wonham appeared in the shepherd boy so many years before?

The back roads from Cambridge to Aldeburgh, which he had traveled so often in these last few years, took Morgan by a Suffolk crossroads near Moulton, where a primitive grave near the roadside was tended by local people who preserved a folk myth. Here, it was reported, lay the body of a young gypsy boy who had rashly killed himself when he could not account for all his herd of sheep. The story of this desperate outcast resonated with Morgan, "but not at an accessible layer of the mind." This figure—of Stephen Wonham, of Pan—conflated with the flotsam of newspaper clippings he had kept from decades before, of the boy who died of pneumonia on the road after being cast out of the school for loving his friend. The poignant feeling lingered like a "secret that has not been noticed."

When Morgan paused to visit the grave on one journey, he brought a talisman: he buried "a little polished shell" from the beach near Aldeburgh as a secret offering. The gypsy boy's tale stood somehow as "the wonder that has not been organized, the small thing I can cling to as proof of the void I feel in the modern world, which no reputable religion can fill." This "dark force" connected in Morgan's mind to the unrecorded history of his yearning, and all yearning. It recalled an image from the deep past:

> I remember—or think I remember—masturbating on a moonlight night in Zimbabwe in 1929 anyhow I went out there alone with masturbationary thoughts, and gained nothing. The ritual—like the phallic sea-shell I pressed into the boys' grave—is desirable but does not focus. It is as the <u>proof of the void</u> that all this is valuable.

14

"The Worm That Never Dies"

Morgan's fellowship at King's required no teaching or lecturing. He was simply *to be himself* in college. Each morning he picked his way down Trumpington Street, past the little shops opposite the imposing façade of the Fitzwilliam Museum, past Fitzbillies' bakery and the flinty tower of St. Botolph's, to the Gothic gatehouse, as if he were traveling back in time. Once in his room he settled into a William Morris chair, covered himself with a lap rug, and began to tackle the mountain of correspondence—letters from friends in Calcutta and California, invitations to lecture or to accept honorary degrees, drafts of radio talks for the BBC Indian Service (where Malcolm Darling was now a producer), earnest questions from graduate students about the symbolic meaning of his novels, requests from Joe Ackerley to review books for *The Listener*. He wryly accepted his new role, telling Joe, "I seem to be a Great Man." "My fame is much more of a pleasure than a nuisance," he noted in his diary, "but being an important person is almost a full-time job."

In 1949, Prime Minister Clement Atlee "offered a Knighthood," which Morgan, delighted, promptly but gently refused. To Bob he suggested that "the company"—two minor writers and a famous cricketer—was to blame; in truth, he feared "the nursing home [would] have just stuck the prices on." But on his birthday in 1953, he was pleased to accept the Companion of Honour, a civil award for contributions to literature. Benjamin Britten was his corecipient. In February 1953 Morgan went to the palace to receive the beribboned medal, knowing the occasion would impress both Bob and Agnes the parlormaid. He much relished his conversation with the Queen, whom he found entrancing; he told friends "if the Queen had been a boy he would have fallen in love with her." He made no friends among the servants at the palace, however. Examining the dazzling enameled medal, Morgan announced with relish, "Well, I got my little toy." This observation was met with a frosty reception. (Her Majesty may have been amused. In 1969, she selected Morgan to receive the Order of Merit, an honor only the monarch can bestow.)

About once a week he took the train and the tube to his London flat. Rail journeys offered blissful anonymity, the chance to chat up young strangers or to observe particular quirks of male beauty. There was the boy with "a tattoo on his fingers, which was the oddest I had ever seen—T, R, U, E on those of the one hand and L, O, V, E on the other . . . I occupied myself with inventing variants." He traveled light, carefully tucking a single egg and a pat of butter screwed into brown paper into his sock. In his Chiswick flat he met old friends, who crammed around the tiny table for dinner parties. He cooked simply, and a charwoman came to clean. There were the usual and the unusual domestic muddles: Bob tore the bedsheet with his sharp big toe; once, when there was a fire in the flat below, Morgan evacuated to the street, wearing only a wet bath towel, and clutching a decanter of brandy. To the very end of his life, this place welcomed the friends he had made in the thirties. The Weybridge bus driver Reg Palmer still came by to share comfort and sex. Their friendship was a "prank . . . I can think of nothing which has lasted so long and borne such odd fruit."

Daily life in King's had not changed much since his undergraduate days. At Evensong the low throb of the chapel organ rolled across the lawn; dinner in Hall; the clang of the bedmakers' mops and brooms in the morning; sherry in the Combination Room. In the middle courtyard, laborers were busy trying to dismantle the fountain erected in Goldie's memory. It was a useless water feature—never managing more than an intermittent trickle—but its wide basin was resilient and sturdy, so, unable to demolish it, they refashioned it into a huge planter instead. If he felt low, Morgan would trot around to Caius College, where his old friend Francis Bennett sympathetically listened to his woes. Attracted by the novelty of having such a famous personage across the landing, undergraduates were enchanted by Morgan's ability to cut across the decades and treat them simply as *people*. He had no condescension, and was especially welcoming to the now-less-rare young men from the north and from comprehensive schools, sons of miners and village teachers, who spoke in broad accents and stood forthrightly with their hands in their pockets.

Morgan picked up the old rhythms quickly, rejoining Apostles meetings. There in 1947 he met a brilliant young Fellow of Emmanuel College just back from service. Nick Furbank was a literature man, writing a biography of Samuel Butler. Like Morgan, he was a *listener*, fluent in French and widely read, a bit reticent, intellectually lithe. They shared the same sense of humor, the same cadence of laughter—a long pause followed by hapless, explosive giggles. Soon Nick had read the manuscript of *Maurice*, and was urging Morgan *not to burn anything*.

The displacement from West Hackhurst unearthed a good deal of long-forgotten writing. Lily had kept all his letters from the journey to India before the First War; unlike the faded silks he had brought back to her, they still sparkled. Morgan began to assemble these letters into a volume he would call *The Hill of Devi*. He dedicated it to his old friend Malcolm Darling. Encouraged by William Plomer, who had discovered and published a Victorian diary that became a bestseller, Morgan fished through a miscellany of family papers dating back to his Aunt Monie's childhood. They bore the fingerprints of generations of women, keepers of the family flame, the same women whom he had tried to erase in his exodus from Abinger.

Reading the family record, so carefully copied out in so many delicate hands, Morgan began to regret that he had burned so much. Marianne Thornton, Aunt Monie, had transcribed her estimable father's memoirs; Aunt Laura copied out Aunt Monie's letters; and his great-aunt had had dutifully prepared ten tiny leather volumes of family history for Morgan when he was born.

He began to think of his aunt's legacy as more than the money that had given him his freedom to write; and now, half in wonderment, half in expiation, he began *Marianne Thornton: A Domestic Biography*, dividing his aunt's life into her various roles: daughter, sister, aunt, and great-aunt. It was a wistful book as well as a whimsical one. When he published the biography in 1956, it was a commercial success. He felt happy to have written it.

In these two final books and in a sketch of West Hackhurst that he did not publish, Morgan recuperatively sifted through his past, in the process discharging some of the vitriol he felt at having been "deprived of a house," and saying a warm goodbye to his family. He dedicated *Marianne Thornton* to the memory of his mother.

The bouleversement of his library also revealed some more personal forgotten treasures: a cache of letters from Mohammed el Adl and the beginning of a novel inspired by Mohammed that Morgan had set aside almost forty years before. He shared the marvel with Nick Furbank:

> I assumed the letters would be nothing much, but gave a glance before destroying them and was amazed—all the things I most adore glimmering in them. [Mohammed] had gone underground in the interval, and there is no doubt that a little of him reemerged in Cocoa . . . I was an awful nuisance to one or two friends at the time, and no wonder. If I talk about him to you, you will anyhow not have to find him a job.

The Cocoa in question was a character from the long-discarded fragment. It, too, was intended for the scrap heap, but when Morgan showed it to Joe—a reliably exacting editor—he found the story to be coherent and intriguing. In December 1948 "Entrance to an Unwritten Novel," came out in *The Listener*, billed as Morgan's first new fiction since *A Passage to India*.

Now Morgan's pen picked up the scent of fiction writing. With Furbank's help in typing out the manuscript, he extended the fragment into a novella, a tragic love story between a young Englishman, Lionel March, and the half-caste boy he had met aboard ship as a child. In the first half of the story, the March family returns from India; in the second, Lionel encounters Cocoa a decade later, this time on the voyage out to take up imperial duties. Lionel's mother had excoriated Cocoa as a "silly idle useless unmanly little boy." But grown into a man, he seduces Lionel as his revenge. Lionel murders Cocoa in fear and shame, and kills himself by jumping into the ocean.

Morgan found that it was easier, and more honest, to shape the tangle of lust and guilt and racism into a tragedy. He told Furbank, "Two people made to destroy each other . . . was [a theme] more interesting than the theme of salvation, the rescuer from 'otherwhere,' the generic Alec [Scudder]. That was a fake." Dark, erotic, "The Other Boat" was one of the stories that Christopher Isherwood and John Lehmann would marvel over. It was published two years after Morgan's death.

As he worked over the story of Lionel and Cocoa, Morgan began to revise the *Maurice* manuscript one final time. He had never suitably determined the mechanics of the lovers reuniting at the novel's end. Over several months in 1958 and 1959, Morgan puzzled out the plot after Alec decides not to emigrate. He devised a fitting resolution with the lovers in each other's arms at the boathouse of Clive's ancestral home, Penge. The new plotting allowed him to discard the stiff and arbitrary epilogue that had troubled Isherwood when he read it twenty years before. It provided the double satisfaction of a happy ending for the lovers and a pointed retribution for Clive.

But a happy ending in life was not as easy after the Second World War as it might have been after the First. Things had not been conducive to homosexuals in England since, in Quentin Crisp's immortal words, "Peace Broke Out." Gone were the handsome young American soldiers, gone the protective cover of darkness on the streets of London. The lights were on everything in a blaze of family values, a march of modernity in pursuit of a New Jerusalem. There was a brand-new government, bursting with *order* and *sincerity*, New Towns sprouting up around London to house the bombed-out population in sprawling, shiny suburbs that ate up the village of Stevenage. Now Morgan's beloved childhood home, ramshackle Rooksnest, stood in a tiny patch of green just miles from row after row of low brick attached houses.

And now Bob and May lived in one of these too. Bob had reached the police retirement age, and after training to be a probation officer, was transferred to war-shattered Coventry. Their house in Shepherd's Bush, which Morgan had bought for the Buckinghams so near his Chiswick flat, was sold at a loss and replaced by a brick semidetached house, *all mod cons*, whose garden "forecasts an allotment in Hell: with the other gardens, it forms a huge quadrangle of despair overlooked from all sides." The vegetables grown there were to supplement a narrow diet of rationed meat, rationed butter, lard, margarine, eggs, rationed sugar, tea, cheese, jam, and chocolate. Even dish soap was rationed. Morgan stood awed by the sight of a "vast ham" Margaret French had sent to him from New York.

The social climate, too, had to be cleansed. Sir Theobald Mathews, the new puritanical director of public prosecutions, was appalled by the lax enforcement of the laws against indecent acts. The provinces were holding up their end, but London was a den of vice. Arrests for homosexual acts were duly reported in the newspapers euphemistically as "grave" offenses, "serious" offenses, crimes too horrible to name. But the tabloids echoed the lament of Viscount Samuel in the House of Lords, who decried the "insidious poisoning" of Britain's "moral state," complaining that juvenile crime and adultery were rampant, and "the vices of Sodom and Gomorrah, of the Cities of the Plain, appear to be rife among us." To curb this scourge, police agents provocateurs were sent out to entrap homosexuals through solicitation; a special division of the Metropolitan Police was formed solely to patrol public urinals.

The home secretary, Sir David Maxwell-Fyfe, had prosecuted Nazis at Nuremberg; now he undertook a crackdown on vice. The number of prosecutions for homosexual offenses skyrocketed. Even powerful and famous men were paraded as examples in the press—including the recently knighted actor Sir John Gielgud and the Labour MP William Field. In the most sensational case, three prominent men were charged with conspiring to commit indecency: the young peer Lord Montagu of Beaulieu, his second cousin Michael Pitt-Rivers, and Peter Wildeblood, chief diplomatic correspondent for the *Daily Mail*. The press was tipped and the timing of the arrests was orchestrated by the police so the story could appear prominently on the front pages of the Sunday newspapers. The evidence used to convict the men came from love letters—seized in kit searches of the RAF airmen who were their working-class lovers—and a warrantless search of Wildeblood's flat.

Newspapers were in a race to outdo one another in salacious reporting, spinning out contradictory stereotypes about sexual criminals with increasing certainty and fervor. In May 1952 the *Sunday Pictorial* devoted a full-page feature to ways to recognize these "Evil Men"; nine years later it helpfully explained "How to Spot a Homo." Readers could discern a homosexual by his sedate tweed jacket, suede shoes, and pipe, or alternately by his telltale effeminate manner and mincing step. These "exposés" reflected the anxieties born of the paradox that homosexuals, forced to live a double life, proved to be quite successful at it.

Popular explanations for the causes of homosexuality, in psychology books and newspapers, sermons and speeches, oscillated between the idea of an alien class of humans, diabolical and separate from normal people, or the natural and contagious consequence of men being in each other's company and kept away from the company of women. War service had brought on an epidemic of this problem. Or excess mother love. Or absent fathers. Morgan sent a copy of a letter he had published asking for "less social stigma" toward homosexuals to Lord Samuel, as a kind of catnip. The viscount took the bait. "Incomprehensible and utterly disgusting as [homosexuality] appears to all normal people," Lord Samuel replied to Morgan, "it seems to have the capacity to form a habit as potent as alcohol or narcotics."

The law that had sent Montagu and his friends to prison was the same law under which Oscar Wilde had been convicted in 1895. Goaded by concerns about public indecency on the streets, in 1954 the Home Office appointed a committee of mandarins—clergy and peers and respectable academics—to investigate the twin problems of female prostitution and male homosexuality. So it was that Sir John Wolfenden, former headmaster of a public school, now vice chancellor of Reading University, assembled a fifteen-person committee that would bear his name. In September 1957 the Wolfenden Report recommended that "homosexual activity between consenting adults over the age of twenty-one in private be no longer a criminal offense." It took a decade more to enact these recommendations into law—and even then the statute was "mild and aetiolated." It applied only to England and Wales, excepted members of the armed services, set the age of consent for homosexuals (at twenty-one) four years above that for heterosexuals, and denoted "private" space very narrowly. (Since anywhere a third person was likely to be present—whether present or not—was defined as *public* space, even the interior of one's own home was not always deemed private for the application of the law.) After the Sexual Offenses Act went into effect in 1967, prosecutions of homosexual acts soared. The vaunted milestone in homosexual rights was largely symbolic.

As he convened his committee members, Wolfenden apologized for the odious task, the "distasteful" subjects they were to face. To spare the three ladies on the committee (and the young women who compiled its deliberations), Sir John decided to use euphemisms—and so homosexuals and prostitutes were dutifully recorded in the committee minutes as Huntleys and Palmers, after the famous biscuits. Most of the expert testimony came from experts who had little basis for their conclusions, which gave the proceedings an air of Alice in Wonderland. One witness testified, "I think the only thing we can do is to give a firm opinion. That is the only thing we can do; there is no real evidence." A prominent clergyman solemnly informed the committee that homosexual behavior was "catching"; he had observed occasions where it "flared out enormously, involving a neighbourhood of boys and young men from just a tiny beginning."

Of course there *was* empirical evidence at hand, in the form of the recently published Kinsey reports. Alfred Kinsey himself met informally with committee members while visiting London for a lecture, but his data were rejected out of hand as the product of an aberrant American society. One committee member reasoned that Kinsey's numbers were not germane; he was convinced that America had many more homosexuals than Britain, on account of the many broken homes in the United States. The working presumption of Wolfenden and his colleagues was that no one on the committee actually *knew* a homosexual—a peculiar position since Sir John's eldest son, Jeremy, had explicitly announced his homosexuality to his father the previous year. Presumably Sir John's determination to be objective entailed forgetting this fact.

Only three of thirty-two days set aside to hear testimony were devoted to the experience of homosexuals under the law, and only three homosexual witnesses testified in person. The first was Peter Wildeblood, released from prison after his conviction in the Montagu trial, and pressing for a change in the law. The other two were "good homosexuals," respectable upper-middle-class professional men: Sir Patrick Trevor-Roper, a renowned eye surgeon, and Carl Winter, director of the Fitzwilliam Museum. Behind the scenes there was considerable informal lobbying. During the proceedings Morgan had a quiet luncheon with Sir John. He was only one of a "number of homosexuals anxious to discuss their problems." Morgan came away impressed, but not sanguine about the prospect of true reform. He understood the snail's pace of changing public opinion.

Meeting with Wolfenden was one of several small feints Morgan made in the direction of public advocacy. During the war, he and Joe Ackerley composed a letter (published under Joe's signature) protesting a horrifying case in Abergavenny, Wales, a purported "orgy of perversion" in a local cinema. (Twenty men were arrested; the convicted men were given sentences up to twelve years, one attempted suicide, and a nineteen-year-old walked in front of a train.)

Morgan served on the board of directors of the London Library, and there he observed a discussion that made him feel he was "in the vanguard of darkness." Dame Katherine Furse was writing a biography of her father,

John Addington Symonds. She asked to consult the papers her father had entrusted to the library in his will. One of these was the great memoir of his homosexual struggle and his unhappy marriage to her mother. Her request was denied; Morgan copied out the debate among the library's trustees verbatim in his diary.

As the Wolfenden Report languished and no law was forthcoming, Morgan composed a "Terminal Note" to the manuscript of *Maurice*.

HOMOSEXUALITY

Note in conclusion on a word hitherto unmentioned. Since *Maurice* was written there has been a change in the public attitude here: the change from ignorance and terror to familiarity and contempt. It is not the change towards which Edward Carpenter had worked . . . And I . . . less optimistic, had supposed that knowledge would bring understanding. We had not realised that what the public really loathes in homosexuality is not the thing itself but having to think about it. If it could be slipped into our midst unnoticed, legalised overnight by a decree in small print, there would be few protests. Unfortunately it can only be legalised by Parliament, and Members of Parliament are obliged to think or to appear to think. Consequently the Wolfenden recommendations will be indefinitely rejected, police prosecutions will continue, and Clive on the bench will continue to sentence Alec in the dock. Maurice may get off.

More and more publicly, Morgan began to take interest in real Alecs in the dock. In 1959 he wrote a letter to *The Times* protesting the treatment of a seventeen-year-old from Consett, Durham, suspected of homosexual offenses who committed suicide as he awaited trial. Though his family raised the money, he had been denied bail.

Morgan added a cautious voice to the chorus of liberal support for the Wolfenden Report. (He did not identify himself as homosexual, but defended the honor of the "married women" who urged Parliament to act.) He also donated five hundred pounds—a huge sum—to the Homosexual Law Reform Society, drily noting in his diary that he did not expect to see much return on his investment. When Harry Daley resurfaced briefly to announce that he planned to write his memoirs, he assured Morgan that he would be discreet. But Morgan casually told his estranged old lover to write what he wished. In his diary, Morgan reflected, "The older one grows, the less one values secrecy perhaps, anyhow there is very little of me that I feel worthwhile to lock up."

Sometimes the police crackdowns came very close to home. Through a friend Morgan met a young Bulgarian émigré, Mattei Radev, an art conservator whom he liked intensely. Radev confessed to Morgan that he had been arrested for cottaging. Shaken by "Mattei's disaster," Morgan decided that he must "speak for his character" in court proceedings. He worried about the situation for weeks, alternately appalled "that the police here are filthy as anywhere" and revved up at the prospect of defending his friend. He was eighty-five and stouthearted, but nonetheless a bit anxious. When the charges evaporated (Mattei paid only a small fine) Morgan wondered whether the threat of his testimony might have altered events. A second scare came on the heels of the first, when a police raid on a Soho club (fetchingly named the Mousehole) caused Joe Ackerley to caution Morgan against frequenting it until the scandal blew over. But Morgan reassured his younger friend that he was unafraid; in any case, he preferred Bobbie's—a tiny club with a working-class clientele on Dean Street. He told Joe protectively that Bobbie's "entrance arrangements were culpably slack," urging him to pass on the warning to its proprietors.

Indignant about the Mousehole raid, Morgan urged Joe to write a letter in protest; he cagily described an appropriate tone: "Be frisky, but not 'we homosexuals' nor so much about yourself. lest it humourlessly be brought against you. 'I have occasionally drawn a cup of coffee at the Mousehole myself little knowing of my peril, or that a policeman might be observing me and might demand my name and address because my taste in clothes differed from his'—is about the level."

At about the time of the Mousehole raid, the London press was transfixed by a libel trial. The American showman Liberace had made a great splash in his London appearances. His flamboyance attracted the invective of a columnist for the *Daily Mirror*, a moralist and gossip who published under the dire pen name Cassandra. In private Morgan mused over the curious phenomenon of Liberace's fans who "touched . . . his clothes as if they were the hem of Christ." But Cassandra *published* his pointed words:

[Liberace] is the summit of sex—Masculine, Feminine and Neuter. Everything that He, She and It can ever want . . . [T]his deadly, winking, sniggering, snuggling, chromium-plated, scent-impregnated, luminous, quivering. giggling, fruit-flavoured, mincing, ice-covered heap of mother love has had the biggest reception and impact on London since Charlie Chaplin arrived . . .

Like Oscar Wilde seventy years before, Liberace sued for libel; unlike Wilde, in the courtroom he chose to appear as the most sober version of himself. Setting aside the white tails and rhinestones for a gray flannel suit, Liberace testified that Cassandra's words had attacked his manhood and made his mother ill, and "cost me many years of my professional career by implying that I am a homosexual . . . It has caused untold agonies . . . and made me the subject of ridicule." On direct examination Liberace lied (as Wilde had done), saying he was not homosexual, nor had engaged in homosexual practices. He persuasively wrapped himself in the mantle of family values. He testified, "My feelings [about homosexuality] are the same as anybody else's. I am against the practice because it offends convention and offends society." The jury of ten men and two women determined that the flamboyant pianist had reason to believe that Cassandra's words implied he was a homosexual, and reason to fear they would harm his career. They awarded him the largest libel verdict to date—eight thousand pounds. Afterward, Liberace remarked that he had "laughed all the way to the bank."

The following year Morgan sat in the witness box at another civil trial. In 1928 he had been prepared to defend Radclyffe Hall's lesbian novel; thirty-two years later, he defended the literary merits of D. H. Lawrence's *Lady Chatterley's Lover*. The posthumously published novel became the next test case in Sir Theobald Mathews's latest purity campaign. Morgan's defense that *Lady Chatterley* had "very high literary merit" helped to win the day for the Penguin Press. Privately, he could not resist a bit of sardonic commentary: "By the way, did D. H. Lawrence ever do anything for anybody? Now that we have been sweating ourselves to help him, the idea occurs."

Neither trial was an unalloyed blow for sexual justice, but they clearly marked real changes in cultural attitudes about sex. In 1932 Morgan described the evolution of attitudes to homosexuality in a letter to the younger William Plomer:

I am very excited [about *Maurice*] . . . and thinking over the book again. Most people have thought it poignant and persuasive . . . but have thought it should have ended tragically. I shouldn't have felt it worth writing tragically. I was trying to escape from "a case" which was harder and tighter by a lot 20 years ago, and a little earlier still the only attitude available can have been a priestlike secrecy and a faith in the Cause and Subject.

Sex and homosexuality were less secret. *Lady Chatterley* may have seemed scandalous, but Morgan had read Roger Casement's Black Diaries, and *Ulysses*, *Lolita*, and *Giovanni's Room* in the interim years. And just down the street at the local cinema, Elvis Presley—"a handsome boy"—sang and danced "most provocatively" in *Jailhouse Rock*. Joe recommended it.

Morgan became inundated by the deaths of old friends. He told William Plomer, "I sometimes have the frightened feeling that people will now not stop dying." He reflected on the death of Frank Vicary, whom he had met decades before at Montazah Hospital in Alexandria:

> He was everything to me for about 20 years everything fading into nothing because he always needed help, never stuck to a job, and never did anything for me, despite romantic cries of affection. Florence [Barger] saw through him, to my annoyance, and condemned me for allowing him to depend on me. I see now that I was to blame, but he was a cunning trapper . . . He was a wonderful man, and perhaps would have been a failure, even had he not met me.

In 1960, at eighty-one, Florence Barger died in her sleep. Morgan (exactly her age) recorded her death in his diary, his handwriting terribly shaky from the news. He confided to Joe Ackerley:

> She has been as if dead for months, but these things are shocks. I have suddenly wanted to think or look at warm obscenities—this has happened to me when upset all my life, right back to Alexandria . . . I am rather prone to senile lechery just now—want to touch the right person in the right place, to shake off bodily loneliness . . . the loneliness is not total or tragic. Licentious scribblings help, and though they are probably fatuous I am never ashamed of them.

He chronicled the "very sad loss" of Charles Mauron; and another ghost—Hugh Meredith—HOM, his first love. Though they had drifted apart decades before, the death was a blow: "he was very beautiful at the beginning of the century."

He had expected to outlive old friends, but the early death of Robin Buckingham was the greatest tragedy of his life. Robin was Bob and May's only child, the little boy who had borne his name. Both Buckinghams and Morgan had not-so-secretly hoped that Robin, curious and bright and gentle, would abandon his working-class roots to attend King's. He grew tall and strong; he made it clear he would be entirely his own man. On a visit to London, Lincoln Kirstein described Robin—"seven feet tall with hands like hams and a dear smile . . . who is NOT under any circumstances going to Cambridge; he's going to be a plumber's assistant, he is, and that's wot."

In 1953, when he was twenty, Robin married a lovely young woman; soon they had two young sons. But a few years later he began to suffer from unexplained fevers and jaundice that led him and his extended family on a panicked roundelay of hospitals and specialists. There were exploratory surgeries, rest cures, and consultations—a seesaw of hope and fear and hope again. In 1961 he was diagnosed with terminal Hodgkin's disease.

As Robin grew pale and weak he took comfort in Morgan's gentle, silent company—"sitting side by side in peace our hands touching." But Morgan knew that the long, slow vigil over Robin's "perishing body" would change everything.

> Little Clive, held up by his grandfather—my Bob—waves from the end of the ward . . . Bob is the earth mourning, dense to hints and then stunned: he and I will not be together in one sense any more. Ahead looms deprivation as well as trouble. for "we seven" as May likes to put it, including the two noisy infants—were as I put it a symbiosis and had created a rhythm that worked perfectly. thanks largely to her.

On September 8, 1962. Robin died quietly. He was twenty-nine.

As Morgan had feared, Robin's death made Bob remote. Frozen in sorrow, he became impatient with Morgan's infirmities, shouting him down and bossing him about. But May, who had been with Robin when he died, wanted to talk openly. She and Morgan took great comfort in their shared disbelief in God or an afterlife; that Robin's cruel death was part of an indifferent universe made it much easier to bear. Robin's death had indeed altered the balance of affection among "we seven." It brought Morgan closer than ever to his beloved May.

That Christmas, perhaps sympathizing with May, Morgan reflected on "Jesus the nuisance" in his diary, narrating the story from Mary's point of view: "Dec. 25. Thinking of Mary's wretched life—Tidings of great joy indeed! When she never had sexual pleasure over him, he ran off to make trouble in the Temple, wandered away from home and neglected her, and finally she saw him killed. What did he bring her but sorrow? Were the younger and naturally-born children any comfort?"

Morgan's sage old friend Gerald Heard had told him, "As soon as a man ceases to be engrossed in the interest of sex he becomes concerned with the apprehension of death." After his second prostate operation in 1950, Morgan had thought himself to be completely impotent, but his aged body surprised him. At eighty-two he recorded an erection and orgasm, "the joyful resurgence which a lover can no longer provoke."

> The worm that never dies must have given its last wriggle this morning. Farewell and thanks. The pleasure, isolated by loneliness and old age, was more distinguished than ever before and distinct from anything attainable through the eye ear tongue, etc. Extraordinary that it came through a little bit of muscle whose daily occupation is pissing and changes its function by being handled skillfully. Nothing starts though, without appropriate thoughts, abandoned at the right moment. It is an art not realised as one until it dies. Previously it has been aiding or impairing human relationships.

He was equally curious about the sensation of death. He was "not the least afraid of dying, while reserving the right to be frightened at the time." He had dreams about the dead.

> I was told the Dead were upstairs, and found them in a couple of attics, lying in seedling boxes . . . and mostly in small pieces. There was no liquefaction, and the bones darkled rather than glittered. Skulls like pickled cabbages. They seemed to know I was there, and

I heard myself saying "I like the Dead,": to a pleased murmur . . . Walking away through them was a man in a red tarboosh who might be Mohammed, but just couldn't be, too long an interval had passed since we parted . . .

Two close calls in his eighties sent him to the hospital with serious anemia and a small stroke. From both he took the lesson of Bob's steadfast love. In his diary, under the heading of "Nearly Dying," he precisely detailed his sensations, which "convinced me that death is nothing if one can approach it as such. I was just a tiny night-light, suffocated in its own wax, and on the point of expiring."

No pain, no fear, no thoughts of eternity, infinity, fate, love, sin, humanity, or any of the usuals. Only weakness, and too weak to be aware of anything but the weakness . . . Bob's little finger pressed mine and pursued when it shifted. This I shall never forget.

A stroke [at the Buckinghams' house in Coventry.] Felt odd, and asked not to be driven to station . . . Recovering painless, except when I thrust my left arm under the pillow, found it hot, flung both arms round Bob, shrieked with pain, heard him say "Your *dear* Bob"—words ever to be remembered.

Though he sometimes felt muddled, losing a train of thought or forgetting a word, his imagination soared. At the age of eighty-two he began a final short story, "Little Imber," which he suspected might be good enough to "see the light of night after my death." The story was set in a futuristic world where almost all women are sterile; a few virile men are sent out to stud at the vast brood-farm nunneries set up in the countryside. But two men have eyes only for each other, and they wrestle themselves into orgasm. Miraculously, the "enigmatic mass" of their intermingled sperm begins to generate some kind of procreative life. (The story reads like a cross between D. H. Lawrence and Margaret Atwood's *The Handmaid's Tale*.) Morgan pronounced himself satisfied with the uncanny result.

• • •

The Wilkinsons left Trumpington Street. precipitating one last displacement. Morgan moved completely into King's, which found a spartan little bedroom for him near his sitting room. Visiting him here, a triumvirate of old friends helped him to sort out practical matters—Joe Ackerley up from Putney, Jack Sprott from Nottingham or his little villa on the Norfolk coast, and William Plomer, who had taken a devoted companion with him to a cottage in Sussex. They each took on a job: Joe served as a secretary, typing up letters and paying small bills; Jack accepted the duty of executor for Morgan's (eventual) estate; and William began gathering "autobiographicalia" for an authorized biography.

Talking with Plomer, Morgan set out two strong precepts for the book, to be published posthumously. The preeminent point was that "M. said he wanted it made clear that H[omosexuality] 'had worked.'" Second, Morgan told him "that none of his intimates had been eminent." These were the story of his life, the key to his unrecorded history. Morgan valued the company of unremarkable people on equal terms with his more celebrated friends. To him the ordinary was the human, the "routine" that the historian Eamon Duffy calls "the undocumented, invisible . . . texture of the past." The two principles were entwined for Morgan.

> I want to love a strong young man of the lower classes and be loved by him and even hurt by him. That is my ticket, and then I have wanted to write respectable novels. No wonder they have worked out rather queer. The "hurt by him" by the way ought to be written in fainter ink. Although it is on my ticket, it is not as vivid as "perfect union", and it is not underlined by the desire to be trodden on or shat on which characterizes extreme case. In the best love making I have known there has been a sort of laughter and the most violent embrace gets softened by it. That's to say my problem as a writer hasn't been as awful as some's. It is these lower class youths, rather than any special antic with them, that has bothered me. [N.B. I have never tried to turn a man into a girl, as Proust did with Albertine, for this seemed derogatory to me as a writer]
> [reread without much interest when I am almost 80]

So the principles of a thematic Life—to be brief and strongly written—were agreed on between Morgan and William.

It was harder and harder for anyone to remain friends with Joe. He had "disintegrated" into deafness and misanthropy. The treacherous lover-cum-deserter who had alienated Morgan from him during the war had left Joe with one precious thing—a beautiful Alsatian bitch named Queenie. She became the only female, and finally the only creature whom Joe could actually love. Over the years he became enthralled by her, and she—heartless and doggy—became his Belle Dame Sans Merci. She may have "loved him true," but she made life with other people impossible. Her barking drowned out conversation; her anxious possessiveness over Joe made her snarl and bite. Joe had (according to Harry Daley) "endless abusive exchanges with bus conductors . . . to say nothing of neighbours complaining and police calling with warnings," but he remained convinced that "he and his dog were the envy and admiration of the whole of Putney."

His love for Queenie—which he marvelously chronicled in his biography of her, *My Dog Tulip*—led Joe to declare, "Every one in the long run must decide for himself whether he is on the side of the human or the animal—one cannot serve both." He wrote endless letters to newspapers, decrying the treatment of animals; traveled to friends' houses to keep their cats company while they took a holiday; watched rats swimming in the Thames; lamented that it was unfair that wasps should get trapped indoors, or that birds should be shooed away from a mulberry tree. When Queenie died at a ripe age in 1961, Morgan paid for Joe to be sent on a long holiday to Japan to distract him from his heartbreak. (There he had one last and predictably disastrous love affair.) But Joe's bitterness and indifference to humans troubled Morgan, and they inexorably grew apart.

It was predictable in these circumstances that the system of "triangular correspondence" (among Plomer, Ackerley, and Sprott) should end up "weaving a pattern of remarkable complexity." The three old friends saw one another less and less often, and the communication among them raveled over time. Both Jack and Joe drank a good deal, and William Plomer, too, retreated in his own way, becoming religious and outwardly more punctiliously conventional as he grew older.

Seven years after the initial plan for Plomer to write the biography, Morgan wrote a letter, penned by Joe, asking Nick Furbank to undertake the project. Furbank accepted, wholly unaware that there was any previous agreement. Joe blamed the muddle on Morgan's failing memory, but William suspected nefarious doings. He was deeply hurt at being usurped, but graciously shared his notes with the new official biographer. For his part, Morgan seemed serenely oblivious to the tug-of-war over his legacy, which played out sometimes in the shadows and sometimes in the light. The truth was that all three of Morgan's friends were subject to the distorting conditions of having been in on the ground floor—so to speak—of the Great Man's career. To paraphrase Jane Austen, it became impossible to discern the mercenary from the prudent motive in the matter of Morgan's posthumous life.

Joe Ackerley began to feel rankled that the Buckinghams had received so much of Morgan's money—first the house and a car, then an allowance, and now ample money set aside for Robin's widow, and for her boys' education. Sprott, too, had been given an allowance in the past, and he stood to gain as executor. Joe felt very put-upon. His pension from the BBC was a pittance, and both an aged aunt and his neurotic sister were entirely dependent upon him—indeed lived with him for a time in his tiny flat. So he wrote to Morgan bluntly asking for money; in the return post, Morgan sent a thousand pounds, writing it was both "easy and pleasant" to do so. But Joe rightly suspected that Morgan had not given him more because he worried Joe might drink it away. Growing desperate, Joe wrote a long and moving tribute to Morgan, planned as an obituary. But when he shopped it to *The Times*, he discovered he had been beaten to the prize by William Plomer. He found a place for an abbreviated draft in *The Observer*. Finally he homed in on his only patrimony—almost eleven hundred letters from Morgan, written from 1922 to 1966. He sold the whole lot to the University of Texas for six thousand pounds. No one knows if Morgan ever learned of this. It would have broken his heart.

A widening gulf emerged as the friends considered the shape of Morgan's posthumous life and reputation, and how their own sex lives might be implicated by the revelations. All his life Plomer had mastered elliptical forms. The titles of his books can be read as coded commentary on his closeted life: *A Message in Code*, his edition of the diary of Richard Rumbold, a military man whose misery about being homosexual led him to suicide; the postwar book of poems *Borderline Ballads*; his memoir titled *Double Lives*—referring, of course, to his expatriate identity. (Morgan cannily critiqued the book, telling William that it "would have been balanced better if it had contained more about yourself.") Morgan's design for the biography threatened a different kind of border.

Whereas Plomer found "blatant homosexuality, like other forms of blatancy, can be tired and uncivilized," for his part Joe began to relish his new freedom as a writer. He had published the biography of Queenie with a chapter called "Liquids and Solids," and also a novel (*We Think the World of You*) chronicling the peculiar story of his craven lover, his wife, and their dog. Now he began a fiercely unsympathetic autobiography, *My Father and Myself*, which hinged on the twin secrets of his father's bigamy and his own homosexuality. (One version of the book began, "My father's penis was twelve inches long"; he settled for the published version, "I was born in 1896 and my parents were married in 1919.")

Both camps of friends invoked Morgan's approval in their approach to writing about private life, and each was right, because the old man's position veered. Like William, he felt that Joe Ackerley's memoir was sad, and should not have been published. "How I do agree with you about Joe's book— indeed more than agree with you . . . It is sad to leave such a recollection behind one—such a bother to write it out, I should have thought. However, he thought it worth while, and here is an addition to the literature." Morgan gave Nick Furbank all the erotic stories, which he knew William and Jack did not like, to protect and publish them after his death.

On June 4, 1967, at the age of seventy-one, Joe Ackerley died in his sleep. He had quit smoking with some fanfare the week before he died. Bob and May were with Morgan at the Aldeburgh Festival when they learned the news. They decided to wait until bedtime to tell Morgan, who absorbed the fact quietly. In some sense he may have felt that he had lost his friend already. The next morning, at breakfast, Morgan was very subdued and wept a little.

He culled over his papers, amending them with little editorial comments. On the manuscript of *Maurice* he wrote—"Publishable. But worth it?" In his unpublished diary, he remained cheerfully disgusted by public attitudes toward sex generally and homosexuality in particular: "I should have been a more famous writer if I had written or rather published more, but sex has prevented the latter . . ." Adding, "When I am 85 how *annoyed* I am with Society for wasting my time by making homosexuality criminal. The subterfuges, the self-consciousness that might have been avoided."

As he grew very old, more and more Morgan seemed to be quietly suspended in his imagination, closed in by increasing deafness and a habit of woolgathering. In a tribute to Morgan on his ninetieth birthday William Plomer wrote, "Let us pretend that Morgan's greatest novel is his life. It may have fictive elements . . . but it is stranger than fiction." This may have been a pointed commentary on Morgan's suppressed private life, but it was also a perceptive reading of the power of his creative will. All his life, Morgan's imagination had preceded and instructed his bodily experience; all his life his utopian belief in the human capacity to love one another had determined the limits of the possible. Nick Furbank put it beautifully: "He believed—literally, and as more than a sentimental cliché—that the true history of the human race was the history of human affection."

Plomer noted the corollary, that "it seemed perfectly right for a novelist to regard living persons as characters . . . Clearly he was a novelist peopling his life, as it were, with characters, and himself living, as in a novel, in a network of relationships with them."

In his old age, Morgan often discussed the fate of his characters as if they had lived on in the world. In 1958, on the fiftieth anniversary of *A Room with a View*, he wrote that Lucy Honeychurch "must now be in her late sixties." And her spurned fiancé, Cecil Vyse, had also reincarnated into life:

> With his integrity and intelligence he was destined for confidential work, and in 1914 he was seconded to Information or whatever the withholding of information was then entitled. I had an example of his propaganda, and a very welcome one, at Alexandria. A quiet little party was held . . . and someone wanted a little Beethoven. The hostess demurred. Hun music might compromise us. But a young officer spoke up. "No, it's all right," he said "a chap who knows about those things from the inside told me Beethoven's definitely Belgian."
>
> The chap in question must have been Cecil. That mixture of mischief and culture is unmistakable. Our hostess was reassured, the ban was lifted, and the Moonlight Sonata shimmered into the desert.

Even inanimate objects had a will and a life of their own. He was not so much superstitious as willing to listen to their inner call. Hearing coins drop out of his trouser pockets, he told Furbank half-comically, half-mournfully, "When they begin to sing, it's all over with them."

At eighty-five Morgan returned to the Figsbury Rings, the charmed land-

scape in Wiltshire that had inspired his favorite novel, *The Longest Journey.*
The writer William Golding drove him there. As the two men picked their
way up to the crest of the steep hill, Morgan's tonsure of white hair stood up
like a dandelion gone to seed. Sixty years after he had sketched the encounter with the lame shepherd boy, Morgan turned again to his diary, thinking
how strange it was that just at the moment he met the shepherd boy, his future lover Bob was "almost being born."

> It was a grey day which I do not mind in Wiltshire and we saw two
> blue butterflies which are everywhere else extinct. The second dis-
> played itself, open winged and heroically large at the entrance of the
> inner circle . . . The rings are heroically larger than I thought—I re-
> member them smaller and trimmer and perhaps turnipped. Their
> grass was tousled and sopping wet and through their wide entrance-
> gaps Wiltshire drifted into the invisible, which was not far off and
> included the spire of Salisbury.

Morgan did not confide in his host, whom he suspected would have "only
caught and condensed the homosexual whiff" of the moment. But the occasion grew outward, magically, into a fantasy of him leaving his corporeal life
and entering his imaginative one. He thought of Rickie Elliot's warm and
brusque brother Stephen Wonham at the end of *The Longest Journey,* lying
on his back looking up at the night sky, with his infant daughter tucked beside him in his coat: "The butterfly was a moving glint, and I shall lie in
Stephen's arms instead of his child. How I wish the book hadn't faults! But
they do not destroy it, and the gleam, the greatness, the grass remain. I don't
want any other coffin."

In late May 1970, at the age of ninety-one, Morgan had a final stroke in
his rooms in King's College. Nick Furbank, who had moved into the rooms
below, heard him fall and cry out. He and Mark Lancaster, who had watched
the moon landing with Morgan on the tiny television, carried him to bed.
Morgan's legs would not move. To be with Bob was all his desire. Hearing
that Bob could not come to fetch him for a few days, he murmured piteously
about what would become of him. But Bob did take him up to Coventry; ensconced in his special bedroom at the Buckinghams, Morgan rallied and
grew cheerful. Then he began to fade. In his final days he lay still and silent

while May continuously held his hand. If she tried to withdraw it, he half opened an eye in remonstration. On Sunday, June 7, he died in his sleep, surrounded by his beloved family.

The funeral service was just as he would have wished. There were no speeches and no hymns and no prayers, and very briefly—to the consternation of the undertaker and the presumed pleasure of the Indian gods—the hearse's engine refused to start. Morgan's ashes were scattered in the rose garden at the crematorium in Coventry.

In his will Morgan left a thousand pounds each to May and Bob Buckingham, two thousand for Robin's widow, Sylvia, to help raise the boys, and small bequests to several distant family members. To his bedmaker, who cleaned his rooms in King's, he bequeathed a hundred pounds. He left money to HOM's children and to Masood's boys, and a hundred pounds each to Charles Lovett and Reg Palmer, who had been faithful lovers and friends. The bulk of the estate went to Jack Sprott, who survived Forster by only a short time. Thereafter, Morgan's money and his papers went home to King's.

But as Morgan had feared, the revelation that he was homosexual made the Buckinghams uneasy. Christopher Isherwood took a benign view—"The poor Bucks, good souls really, are always on the grope for *terra firma*." They had cared for Morgan with great devotion, and Morgan had made them materially comfortable and their grandchildren secure, but they began to revise the history of "we seven" into something more conventional than it had been—domesticating Morgan into a kindly grandfather figure. After Morgan's stroke—the moment Morgan recorded as "Your *dear* Bob"—Bob Buckingham told May he was shocked that Morgan had embraced him and told him of his love.

After Morgan died, the new story hardened into a redoubtable myth. Much to the disgust of William Plomer and John Morris, the Buckinghams "reverted to the 'beautiful friendship' theory in the shock of the discovery in the last year of Morgan's life that he was homosexual." This was too much for Morris. "Had it not occurred to them, I could not bear from asking, that most of Morgan's friends were queer? Yes, it had. But never that Morgan shared the predilection. Well, well!"

After Bob's death, May came to accept the possibility that her husband and Morgan had been lovers. Bob might lie to himself, but she could not. She shared her reminiscences and all her family correspondence with Nick Furbank as he wrote the authorized biography published in 1977. She gave him a free hand. To Bill Roerick. who had known them all, she defended the legitimacy of her marriage and Bob's love. About these facts there was never any dispute.

The terms of the will also determined access to the unpublished writings, the "great unrecorded history" of his love for men that he had so carefully preserved. There were no restrictions placed on what readers could see, but Morgan forbade any sort of mechanical reproduction of manuscript materials. From the beautiful glass box of the Ransom Center at the University of Texas at Austin to a friend's sitting room in Hampstead, from the cool majesty of the Huntington Library in Southern California (where readers are exiled at the lunch hour into a fragrant rose garden) to the modern hush of the Beinecke Library at Yale. and especially in the serene little room in King's that looks out across the lawn to the great Gothic chapel, you must *touch* the letters and notebooks, the photographs, the ticket stub from Mohammed's trolley car, and the baby Morgan's wispy lock of hair. And you must *take the time*. Penetrating and puzzling out the difficult, dense penmanship, copying out the relevant scraps by hand, phrase by phrase, engenders a trance. a feeling of automatic writing, a fleeting fantasy of complete connection with Morgan's remarkable mind and heart. So great and honest a writer and so humane a man. whose "defence at any last Judgement would be 'I was trying to connect up and use all the fragments I was born with.'"

NOTES

BIBLIOGRAPHY

ACKNOWLEDGMENTS

INDEX

Notes

ABBREVIATIONS FOR LETTERS AND DIARIES

The Abinger edition of the works of E. M. Forster, published in twenty volumes between 1972 and 1988, comprises the most complete and authoritative text. Unless otherwise noted, all citations are from the Abinger edition.

ACF:	Alice Clara Forster	JRA:	J. R. Ackerley
BB:	Bob Buckingham	KCC:	King's College Modern Archives,
CI:	Christopher Isherwood		Cambridge University
DHL:	D. H. Lawrence	LK:	Lincoln Kirstein
EC:	Edward Carpenter	LS:	Lytton Strachey
EMF:	E. M. Forster	MEA:	Mohammed el Adl
FB:	Florence Barger	MT:	Marianne Thornton
GLD:	Goldsworthy Lowes Dickinson	PC:	Paul Cadmus
GW:	Glenway Wescott	TEL:	T. E. Lawrence
HOM:	Hugh Owen Meredith	VW:	Virginia Woolf
JL:	John Lehmann	WP:	William Plomer

PROLOGUE: "START WITH THE FACT THAT HE WAS HOMOSEXUAL"

3 *"impossible not to be drawn to him"*: Lehmann, *In My Own Time*, 120.

4 *"might have belonged to"*: Isherwood, *Christopher and His Kind*, 97.

4 *"pale narrowed quizzing eyes"*: Ibid.

4 *"the future of the English novel"*: *The Diaries of Virginia Woolf*, V:185, Nov. 1, 1938. Woolf records this comment by Somerset Maugham.

4 *Auden stayed in New York*: Isherwood, diary entry for Oct. 29, 1973. Quoted in "Introduction" to *Christopher Isherwood, Lost Years: A Memoir*, ed. Katherine Bucknell, xi.

5 *E. M. Forster, the "master"*: Isherwood, *Christopher and His Kind*, 105.

5 *"Instead of trying to screw"*: Isherwood, *Lions and Shadows*, 173–74.

5 *"possible to be friends"*: Forster, *A Passage to India*, 5.

5 *"so shy it makes"*: Spender to CI, *Letters to Christopher*, 57.

6 *"saner than anyone else"*: Isherwood, *Down There on a Visit*, 175.

6 *"weariness of the only subject"*: EMF, Locked Diary, June 16, 1911, KCC.

6 *With the mysterious package:* Lehmann, *Christopher Isherwood*, 121.

7 *"took [a] young boy and"*: Bachardy in *Chris and Don*, a film by Tina Mascara and Guido Santi, 2007.

7 *"unnerving habit of appearing"*: Wright, *John Lehmann: A Pagan Adventure*, 236.

7 *"very affectionate and gentle"*: Lehmann, *Christopher Isherwood*, 121.

7 *"a happy ending was imperative"*: Forster, "Notes on *Maurice*," in *Maurice*, 216.

8 *"handsome, healthy, bodily attractive"*: Ibid., 209.

8 *Alec dispels the suburban nonsense:* Isherwood, *Christopher and His Kind*, 127.

8 *"He knew what the call was"*: Forster, *Maurice*, 207.

8 *"Now we shan't be parted"*: Ibid.

8 *Christopher was gleeful:* Lehmann, *Christopher Isherwood*, 121.

9 *Only weeks before Morgan died:* Isherwood, *Christopher and His Kind*, 104–6.

9 *The March visit began:* Furbank, *E. M. Forster*, II:324; interview with Mark Lancaster, Jamestown, R.I., Feb. 24, 2007.

9 *"portraits of ladies in bonnets"*: Culme-Seymour, "Memories of E. M. Forster," in J. H. Stape, ed., *E. M. Forster: Interviews and Recollections*, 87.

9 *"stooped and feeble"*: Isherwood, *Christopher and His Kind*, 106.

9 *wily as a "raccoon"*: Interview with Don Bachardy, Santa Monica, Calif., Nov. 5, 2007.

9 *"as 'openly gay' as people were"*: Lancaster, "Artist in Residence," 16.

10 *"In the atmosphere of the Warhol Factory"*: Mark Lancaster, correspondence with author, March 10, 2007.

10 *"What do I have to do?"*: Interview with Mark Lancaster, Feb. 24, 2007.

11 *"was such a bore"*: Lancaster, "Artist in Residence," 16.

11 *"the man who comes"*: Plomer in Furbank, "The Personality of E. M. Forster," 61.

12 *"always makes me into a chatterbox"*: Sassoon, Diary, July 10, 1923, in Hart-Davis, ed., *Siegfried Sassoon Diaries*, 61.

12 *"false and tricky"*: Isherwood, *Christopher and His Kind*, 106.

12 *"startlingly shrewd look of"*: Rama Rau, "Remembering E. M. Forster," in J. H. Stape, ed., *E. M. Forster: Interviews and Recollections*, 133.

12 *"a baby who remembers"*: Isherwood, *Christopher and His Kind*, 106.

12 *"tip a sentence"*: Panter-Downes, "Kingsman," 62.

12 *"It's impossible to face facts"*: Forster to Josie Darling, 1914, in Furbank, *E. M. Forster*, II:2.

12 *"I will try to decide"*: Craft, "Tea in Cambridge," in J. H. Stape, ed., *E. M. Forster: Interviews and Recollections*, 25.

13 *"shuffled in, asked me"*: Lancaster, "Artist in Residence," 16; interview with Mark Lancaster, Feb. 24, 2007.

13 *When Christopher first met:* Isherwood, *Christopher and His Kind*, 105.

13 *"the key to the whole art"*: Ibid.

13 *"And so, one evening"*: Isherwood, *The Memorial*, 210.

14 *"I shall spend the entire morning"*: Isherwood, *Christopher and His Kind*, 104.

14 *"silly solemn old professor"*: Ibid., 17.

15 *"clasping this magic volume"*: Ibid., 106.

15 *His "lover and beloved," Bob Buckingham*: Lago and Furbank, eds., *Selected Letters of E. M. Forster*, II:112; EMF to Sprott, Oct. 4, 1932, KCC.

15 *Some homosexuals he knew:* Isherwood, *Christopher and His Kind*, 125.

15 *The truth was that to the younger man's ear:* Ibid., 126.

15 *"I have shared with Alec":* Forster, *Maurice*, 212.

16 *"imprisoned within the jungle":* Isherwood, *Christopher and His Kind*, 126.

16 *Apprehensively, he asked Christopher:* Ibid.

16 *"Eyes brimming with tears":* Ibid., 127.

16 *"bright-eyed little rat":* Parker. *Christopher Isherwood*, 277.

16 *"committed to wandering the world":* Ibid., 282.

16 *"I think what might happen":* EMF to CI, April 27, 1933, Huntington; Lago and Furbank. eds., *Selected Letters*, II:118–19.

17 *"I am ashamed at shirking":* EMF to CI, June 25, 1948, Huntington.

17 *"But Gide hasn't got a mother!":* Parker, *Ackerley*, 338.

17 *Then, after the war:* EMF to CI, Aug. 28, 1938, Huntington; Lago and Furbank, eds., *Selected Letters*, II:159

17 *"briefly and blazingly written":* EMF to CI, Aug. 28, 1938, Huntington; Lago and Furbank, eds., *Selected Letters*, II:159.

17 *But Morgan's earlier skepticism:* For thorough discussions of the homosexual prosecutions in the decades after World War II, see Higgins, *Heterosexual Dictatorship*, and Johnson, *The Lavender Scare*.

18 *Morgan jocularly called the packet:* EMF to Wheeler, Oct. 15, 1952, Beinecke.

18 *In Christopher's study:* Lehmann, *Christopher Isherwood*, 121.

18 *But the men shared a reverence:* Philip Gardner's editor's introduction to the Abinger edition of *Maurice* (1999) describes the peregrinations of the various *Maurice* manuscripts.

18 *"How annoyed I am":* EMF, Locked Diary, KCC. There is no specific date for this addendum, but Forster's notation that he was almost eighty-five gives it a rough date in the mid-1960s.

19 *"knowledge would bring understanding":* Forster, *Maurice*, 220.

19 *"can only be legalised":* Ibid.

20 *"writer so socially acceptable":* GW to CI, Sept. 20, 1971, Huntington.

20 *"there can be real love":* Isherwood, *Christopher and His Kind*, 126.

20 *"Of course all those books":* Lehmann, *Christopher Isherwood*, 121.

1: "A QUEER MOMENT"

25 *"I own, but not quite":* Marianne Thornton to ACF, quoted in Forster, *Marianne Thornton*, 285.

25 *While Lily rested at the hotel:* Ibid., 287.

26 *By the time they returned to London:* Ibid., 287.

26 *"months of languor and sickness":* Ibid., 289, 287.

26 *"she was accustomed to":* Ibid., 287.

26 *"fond of pleasure, generous":* Ibid., 278.

26 *"[S]he felt that her life":* Ibid., 288.

26 *"I wish tonight":* Forster, "Record of letters, books etc destroyed by me after my mother's death, 1945," KCC. ACF to Mamie Synnot, n.d., 1882.

27 *"a great heroine":* Furbank, *E. M. Forster*, I:3.

27 *"always had known best":* Forster, *Marianne Thornton*, 282.

27 *"a discipline and an institution":* Forster, "Henry Thornton," in *Two Cheers*, 194.

28 *"votive offerings of people":* Forster, *Howards End*, 346.

29 *"haze of elderly ladies"*: Furbank, *E. M. Forster*, I:28.

29 *"not wild like L[ily]"*: Mrs. Farrer to Laura Forster, Nov. 7, 1876, in Forster, "Record of letters," KCC.

29 *"won't be too old maidish"*: Forster, *Marianne Thornton*, 286.

29 *"the implication was obvious"*: Furbank, *E. M. Forster*, I:31.

29 *Aunt Monie had given Morgan:* Forster, *Marianne Thornton*, 289.

30 *"our usual game at Bézique"*: Furbank, *E. M. Forster*, I:21.

30 *"would much rather be"*: Ibid., I:20. The contents of the letters come from Forster's own transcription of letters he burned following the death of his mother in 1945. In Forster, "Record of letters," KCC.

30 *"half a girl"*: ACF to MT, in Furbank, *E. M. Forster*, I:23.

30 *"I'm a little boy"*: Ibid., I:19fn.

30 *"[t]iresome to be interrupted"*: Forster, *Marianne Thornton*, 300.

30 *Learning to read opened:* Forster, "Nottingham Lace (Unfinished Fragment)," in *Arctic Summer and Other Fiction*, 14.

30 *"It is not"*: Forster, "Notes on the English Character" (1926), in *Abinger Harvest and England's Pleasant Land*, 5.

31 *"Maurice had two dreams"*: Forster, *Maurice*, 12.

31 *"We built a little house"*: EMF, Sex Diary, KCC. The diary, a separate section in the Locked Diary, is marooned on its own. Internal references date the beginning of this sexual reminiscence to the mid-1930s, when Forster was in his mid-fifties.

31 *"[W]e all went to Bournemouth"*: Ibid.

31 *At Rooksnest he soon outstripped:* Forster, *Marianne Thornton*, 304.

32 *"I used to hang on the branches"*: EMF, Sex Diary, KCC.

32 *"Soon after Mr. Hervey came"*: Ibid.

32 *"presently . . . 'help me get rid'"*: Ibid.

32 *"Morgan never came out"*: Interview with Mollie Barger, Hampstead, July 24, 2001.

33 *"Felt deeply about boys in books"*: EMF, Sex Diary, KCC.

33 *"long serial stories"*: Ibid.

33 *"sleeping with naked black man"*: Ibid.

33 *Sexual issues began to ossify:* Weeks, *Coming Out*, 14–15.

34 *"A few more cases like Oscar Wilde's"*: Weeks, *Sex, Politics and Society*, 10.

34 *"I knew that [Aunt Monie] was ill"*: Forster, *Marianne Thornton*, 322.

34 *"Have you seen Forster's cock?"*: EMF, Sex Diary, KCC.

35 *"Having concluded he spoke to me"*: Ibid.

35 *"effect on [his] development"*: Ibid.

36 *"We know from the Bible"*: Ibid.

36 *The lesson of the pedophile:* To name just a few examples: There is the cowardice of Mr. Ducie, Maurice's headmaster, who gives the boy a frank facts-of-life speech, but (seeing ladies come near) rushes to erase his anatomical diagrams in the sand. In *A Passage to India* there is a British official who mistakes Dr. Aziz's missing collar stud as proof of the doctor's "slackness" and inability to dress properly because the doctor has lent it to his English friend Mr. Fielding—the real slacker. In *Howards End* there is Henry Wilcox's matter-of-fact response to the young clerk Leonard Bast's loss of his job, though Henry Wilcox is responsible—through bad business advice—for the young man's unemployment.

36 *"I made an entry in my Diary"*: EMF, Sex Diary, KCC.

37 *"Later in the term"*: Ibid.

37 *"Ladies and gentlemen, boys and bies"*: Forster, "Breaking Up," *The Spectator*. July 28, 1933.
38 *"Forster? The writer?"*: Furbank, *E. M. Forster*, I:42.
38 *"The position of a young man"*: Gosse to J. A. Symonds. March 5, 1890, in Bartlett, *Who Was That Man?*, 80.
39 *"Learnt that there was queer stuff"*: EMF, Sex Diary. KCC.

2: KINGS AND APOSTLES
40 *"silly and idle" fellow*: Forster, *Goldsworthy Lowes Dickinson*, 87.
40 *For more than four hundred years*: Wilkinson, *A Century of King's*, 1.
40 *"automatic and effortless advancement"*: Forster. *Goldsworthy Lowes Dickinson*, 23.
41 *"team work . . . and cricket"*: Ibid., 22.
41 *the "oddities and the crudities"*: Ibid., 23.
41 *"crept cold and friendless"*: Forster, *The Longest Journey*, 5.
42 *"could be seen rushing up"*: Forster, "Presidential Address to the Cambridge Humanists."
42 *To be listened to*: Furbank, *E. M. Forster*, I:51.
42 *Socially and academically*: Plomer, conversational notes toward Forster biography, Durham.
42 *"unsure of my clothes"*: Forster, Comments at Founder's Day, Dec. 2, 1952, KCC; EMF to ACF, late Nov. 1897, KCC; also in Lago and Furbank, eds., *Selected Letters*, I:16.
43 *"it is difficult for an inexperienced boy"*: Forster, *Goldsworthy Lowes Dickinson*, 22.
43 *In the spring of his first year*: EMF. Diary, May 1898, KCC.
43 *"shelter of the dell"*: Forster, *The Longest Journey*, 27.
43 *"Walked into old chalk pit"*: EMF, Diary, May 1898, KCC.
43 *"The green bank at the entrance"*: Forster, *The Longest Journey*, 27–28.
43 *"tell most things about"*: Ibid., 21.
44 *At the head of stairway W7*: Furbank, *E. M. Forster*, I:61.
44 *Within weeks of meeting Morgan*: Forster, "Presidential Address to the Cambridge Humanists."
44 *They sent a representative*: Wilkinson, *A Century of King's*, 47.
45 *"The idea of a god becoming"*: Forster, "Presidential Address to the Cambridge Humanists."
45 *"It so happened"*: Ibid.
45 *"no formula for unknown experience"*: Williams, *Culture and Society*, 334.
45 *"Athens in particular"*: Forster, *Goldsworthy Lowes Dickinson*, 106–107.
46 *"The love that dare not speak its name"*: Hyde, *The Trials of Oscar Wilde*, 236.
46 *"They attended the Dean's translation class"*: Forster, *Maurice*. 37–38.
46 *"saw in King's the material"*: Furbank, *E. M. Forster*, I:54.
47 *"soul-fingering"*: Wilkinson, *A Century of King's*, 19.
47 *"a deposit of radium"*: Forster, *Goldsworthy Lowes Dickinson*, 25.
47 *"a bully and a liar"*: Ibid., 24–25. The list is from Dickinson's memoir at King's.
47 *"Whatever his make up"*: Ibid., 25.
47 *"the hero of a lost play"*: Wilkinson, *A Century of King's*, 13. The quotation is from Nathaniel Wedd's memoirs at King's.
47 *"in his inner room"*: Forster, *Goldsworthy Lowes Dickinson*, 26. The words are Forster's direct quotation from Dickinson's then-unpublished memoirs.

47 *"Eton sacked OB":* Wilkinson, *A Century of King's,* 18.

48 *In the city, too, women:* Winstanley, *Later Victorian Cambridge,* 92. Winstanley served as a searcher alongside Forster in Alexandria during the First World War.

48 *In the 1890s Cambridge was:* Ibid., 121–43.

48 *"as usual the women":* EMF, Locked Diary, Sept. 19, 1910, KCC.

48 *"get a less superficial idea":* EMF, Diary, Dec. 31, 1904, KCC; quoted in Furbank, *E. M. Forster,* I:122.

49 *"could not make out why":* Furbank, *E. M. Forster,* I:171.

49 *"5 Nov. (Sunday) [1899]":* EMF, Diary, KCC.

49 *"To him more than to anyone":* Forster, *Goldsworthy Lowes Dickinson,* 61.

49 *As a King's undergraduate in 1882:* Wilkinson, *A Century of King's,* 24.

50 *As a don, Wedd remained:* Forster, *Goldsworthy Lowes Dickinson,* 61.

50 *"a desirable accomplishment":* Ibid.

50 *"gave all his time and energies":* Wilkinson, *A Century of King's,* 24.

50 *"wonderfully clever & amusing":* EMF to ACF, Nov. 5, 1899, KCC; Lago and Furbank, eds., *Selected Letters,* I:35.

50 *"advises me to think of journalistic work":* EMF to ACF, Sunday [Apr. 23, 1899], KCC.

51 *"While his pupil read out":* Wilkinson, *A Century of King's,* 12.

51 *"I came towards the end":* Forster, *Goldsworthy Lowes Dickinson,* 25.

51 *"in a lecture":* Forster, "My Books and I," ms., KCC.

51 *"He tells me that I might write":* Ibid.

52 *"What the public really loathes":* Forster, "Author's Note to *Maurice,*" *Maurice,* 220.

52 *"I'm an unspeakable of the Oscar Wilde sort":* Forster, *Maurice,* 134.

52 *"Rubbish, rubbish!":* Ibid.

53 *"associated with action":* Leonard Woolf, *Sowing,* 160. Here he is quoting Keynes.

53 *"We were at an age when":* Keynes, *My Early Beliefs,* 81.

53 *"Are crocodiles the best of animals?":* Beauman, *Morgan,* 85fn.

53 *"Is self-abuse bad as an end?":* Ibid., 85.

53 *"suddenly lifted an obscure accumulation":* Leonard Woolf, *Sowing,* 161.

53 *"We should have been very angry":* Keynes, *My Early Beliefs,* 86.

54 *"nicknamed him the Taupe":* Leonard Woolf, *Sowing,* 188.

54 *"the elusive colt of a dark horse":* Keynes, *My Early Beliefs,* 81.

54 *"He was strange, elusive, evasive":* Leonard Woolf, *Sowing,* 187.

54 *"a streak of queer humour":* Ibid.

54 *"Strachey issued [an] edict":* Keynes, *My Early Beliefs,* 84.

55 *"jockeying to procure [the] election":* Wilkinson, *A Century of King's,* 51.

55 *In Dickinson, Morgan:* Forster, "Author's Preface" to *Goldsworthy Lowes Dickinson,* xxii.

55 *"tended to inhabit the university":* E. M. Forster, *Goldsworthy Lowes Dickinson,* 28.

55 *"rope . . . people in to get ideas":* Ibid., 83.

56 *"a thin veil of melancholy":* Forster, "Author's Preface" to *Goldsworthy Lowes Dickinson,* xxi.

56 *"My sister has a bone to pick":* Forster, *Goldsworthy Lowes Dickinson,* 46.

56 *"the only man who could":* Furbank, *E. M. Forster,* I:79.

56 *a "maieutic" gift:* Forster, *Goldsworthy Lowes Dickinson,* 89.

56 *"teaching . . . could not be distinguished":* Ibid., 85.

3: "A MINORITY, NOT A SOLITARY"

58 *"Baedeker-bestarred Italy"*: EMF to Wedd, Dec. 1, 1901, KCC; quoted in editor's introduction to Forster, *A Room with a View*, ix.

58 *"Our life is where we sleep"*: EMF to GLD, March 25, 1902, KCC; quoted ibid.

58 *"the hotels are comfortable"*: EMF to Dent, Oct. 22, 1901, KCC; Lago and Furbank, eds., *Selected Letters*, I:46.

59 *"Philip could never read"*: Forster, *Where Angels Fear to Tread*, 12.

59 *"M is much quieter"*: ACF to Louisa Whichelo, May 19, 1902, KCC.

59 *"took her to buy butter dishes"*: Karen Arrandale to author, May 6, 2008.

59 *"never saw anybody so incapable"*: ACF to Louisa Whichelo, Nov. 3, 1901, KCC.

59 *"Now I am older I understand"*: EMF, Diary, Jan. 22, 1953, KCC.

59 *"I missed nothing"*: EMF, Diary, Oct. 10, 1901, KCC.

60 *"[C]herish the body"*: EMF, "Museo Kichneriano," ms., KCC.

60 *Even the tourist venues*: EMF, Diary, Oct. 20, 1901, KCC.

60 *"I've tried to invent realism"*: EMF to GLD, Dec. 15, 1901, KCC; Lago and Furbank, eds., *Selected Letters*, I:51.

60 *"Perugia would be nicer"*: Ibid.

60 *"Traveling does not conduce"*: EMF to GLD, March 25, 1902, KCC.

60 *"all females"*: EMF to Wedd, Dec. 1, 1901, KCC; quoted in editor's introduction to Forster, *A Room with a View*, x.

61 *"It is not what happens"*: Furbank, *E. M. Forster*, I:91.

61 *"Where all is obscure and unrealised"*: Forster, *Maurice*, 12.

61 *"I would bring some middle-class Britishers"*: Forster, "Three Countries," in *The Hill of Devi*, 290.

61 *"down on the theme"*: Forster, "Introduction to the 1947 edition of *Collected Short Stories*," in *The Machine Stops*, xv.

62 *"disquieting smile"*: Forster, "The Story of a Panic," in *The Machine Stops*, 8, 11, 15.

62 *"Then he showed Maynard"*: Forster, "My Books and I," ms., KCC. Transcribed in *The Longest Journey*, 300–306.

63 *"no thought of sex"*: Forster, "My Books and I," ms., KCC.

63 *"because he thinks"*: Ibid.

63 *"I watch my own inaction"*: EMF to Dent, Jan. 25, 1902, KCC.

63 *"Would you care"*: George Trevelyan to EMF, May 9, 1902, Trinity College, Cambridge. Quoted in Furbank, *E. M. Forster*, I:94.

64 *between the two "monsters"*: Forster, *Maurice*, 193.

64 *"I am afraid I enjoy"*: EMF to Dent, Oct. 30, 1902, KCC.

64 *"rational enjoyment and hard work"*: Davies, *The Working Men's College*, 30.

64 *"demanded more practical subjects"*: Fieldhouse, *A History of Modern British Adult Education*, 31.

65 *He remained a romantic*: *Week-Day Poems* was the title of Meredith's collection, published in 1911. He based his poems on the experiences of the men he taught in the Working Men's College, and on the streets of London. He wrote poems titled "The Motor-Bus," "The Bank Holiday," "Wages," "In the Parks," and "Seen in a Railway Station." The Poem "Ages of Man" begins:

> We children in our crowded home
> Had little food to eat,

Our breeding was the right to roam
And scavenge in the street;
My brothers died, my sister died,
And I grew all accurst,
With pigeon breast, with surly pride,
With hunger and with thirst.

65 *"a horror of people":* HOM to Bertrand Russell, July 1903, quoted in Furbank, *E. M. Forster*, l:140.

66 *"I've made my two discoveries":* EMF, Diary, Dec. 31, 1904, KCC.

66 *"I think I am dead":* HOM to Maynard Keynes, April 1906, quoted in Furbank, *E. M. Forster*, l:141.

66 *"something unimagined, indefinable":* Forster, "The Road from Colonus," *The Machine Stops*, 78.

66 *"depressing thing to look":* EMF to J. T. Sheppard, n.d., KCC; quoted in editor's introduction to Forster, *A Room with a View*, x.

67 *"to advocate sanity in":* Forster, *Goldsworthy Lowes Dickinson*, 96.

67 *"the woman of today":* Forster, "Pessimism in Literature," in Thomson, ed., *Albergo Empedocle*, 135.

67 *Lucy thinks she is safe:* EMF to Robert Trevelyan, Oct. 28, 1905, Lago and Furbank, eds., *Selected Letters*, I:83.

68 *"I do not resemble":* EMF, Diary, Dec. 13, 1907, KCC.

69 *"little bit of ivory":* Deirdre Le Faye, ed., *Jane Austen's Letters* (New York: Oxford University Press, 1997), 323.

69 *"question I am always discussing":* EMF to George Barger, July 27, 1899, Lago and Furbank, eds., *Selected Letters*, I:31.

70 *"Each time I see those Greek things":* EMF, Diary, March 13, 1904, KCC.

70 *"I'd better eat my soul":* EMF, Diary, March 21, 1904, KCC.

71 *He was not interested in being a "case study":* Grosskurth, *The Memoirs of John Addington Symonds*, 19.

71 *"an idea for an entire novel":* EMF, Diary, July 18, 1904, KCC.

72 *"the heart of our island":* Forster, *The Longest Journey*, 126.

72 *"The fibres of England":* Ibid.

72 *"gray and wiry" grasses:* Ibid., 125.

72 *As antiquities go:* Forster, "Author's Introduction" to *The Longest Journey* (1960), lxvii; *The Longest Journey*, 125.

72 *"the whole system":* Forster, "My Books and I," ms., KCC.

73 *Morgan called this feeling:* Ibid.

73 *"nothing—still one":* Forster, "Author's Introduction" to *The Longest Journey* (1960), lxvii.

73 *"pull at a pipe":* Ibid.

73 *"caught fire up on the Rings":* Ibid.

73 *"In that junction of mind":* Ibid., lxvi.

73 *"that the English can be":* EMF, Diary, Sept. 12, 1904, KCC.

74 *"I created, I received, I restored":* Forster, "Author's Introduction" to *The Longest Journey* (1960), lxvii.

74 *the Cambridge . . . "which I knew":* Ibid., lxviii.

74 *"Figsbury Rings became":* Ibid., lxvii.

74 *"I walked out* again": EMF, Diary, Sept. 12, 1904, KCC.

74 *"great wisdom":* Ibid.

75 *Twice more, on Monday:* Ibid.

75 *"Charles Sayle wipes his glasses":* Forster, "My Books and I," ms., KCC.

75 *With reluctance, years later:* Forster, "Author's Introduction" to *The Longest Journey* (1960), lxvii–lxviii.

76 *"because he would have been":* Forster, "My Books and I," ms., KCC.

4: "THE SPARK. THE DARKNESS ON THE WALK"

77 *"we have got a house":* EMF to Robert Trevelyan, Aug. 25, 1904, Lago and Furbank, eds., *Selected Letters*, I:61n.

77 *"small and somewhat suburban":* EMF to Dent, Oct. 1, 1904, KCC.

77 *"an inscription to the effect":* EMF to Robert Trevelyan, Aug. 25, 1904, Lago and Furbank, eds., *Selected Letters*, I:61n.

77 *"a field full of dropsical chickens":* Ibid.

78 *Like Adam in the garden:* EMF to Dent, Oct. 1, 1904, KCC.

78 *"quite pretty in some ways":* EMF to Robert Trevelyan, Aug. 25, 1904, Lago and Furbank, eds., *Selected Letters*, I:61n.

78 a *"sorry bit of twaddle":* Forster, "Three Countries," in *The Hill of Devi*, 291.

79 *"I knew not nor":* Forster, "My Books and I," ms., KCC.

79 *"almost with physical force":* Forster, "Three Countries," in *The Hill of Devi*, 290.

79 *"fundamental objection to the story":* Snow Wedgwood to Laura Forster, April 27, 1906, in "Editor's Introduction" to Forster, *Where Angels Fear to Tread*, xiii.

79 *"had not realised the solidity":* Gardner, ed., *Commonplace Book*, 15–16.

79 *"ability to expand or contract":* Ibid., 12–13.

79 *He defended the novel:* Robert Trevelyan to EMF, no date, quoted in *Where Angels Fear to Tread*, 150–51.

80 *"The object of the book":* EMF to Robert Trevelyan, Oct. 28, 1905, quoted ibid., 149.

80 *"My life is now straightening into":* EMF, Diary, Dec. 31, 1904, KCC; Furbank, *E. M. Forster*, I:121.

80 *"twenty-five is the boundary":* EMF, Diary, Dec. 31, 1904, KCC.

80 *"Growing old is an emotion":* Forster, "De Senectute," 15–16.

81 *To "keep the brutes":* EMF, Diary, Dec. 31, 1904, KCC; Furbank, *E. M. Forster*, I:122.

81 *His sojourn in Nassenheide:* EMF to ACF, April 4, 1905, KCC; Lago and Furbank, eds., *Selected Letters*, I:66–67.

82 *"indifferent false teeth & a society drawl":* Ibid., 67.

82 *"How d'ye do, Mr. Forster!":* Forster, "Nassenheide" in Jeffrey M. Heath, ed., *The Creator as Critic*, 207. The essay was written in 1954.

82 *"the country is unthinkably large":* EMF, Diary, April 8, 1905, KCC.

82 *"very clever, but most unattractive":* EMF to ACF, July 8, 1905, KCC; Lago and Furbank, eds., *Selected Letters*, I:81.

82 *"Fools rush in":* Alexander Pope, "Essay on Criticism," III:177.

82 *"settled into contentment":* EMF to Arthur Cole, July 7, 1905, Lago and Furbank, eds., *Selected Letters*, I:78. Cole, a musicologist, had been Malcolm Darling's best friend at King's.

83 *"Artists now realise that":* Forster, "Pessimism in the Novel," in Thomson, ed., *Albergo Empedocle*, 135; EMF, Diary, Feb. 27, 1906, KCC.

83 *"The writer who depicts":* Forster, "Pessimism in the Novel," in Thomson, ed., *Albergo Empedocle*, 144–45.

83 *"astonishing glass shade":* Forster, *Howards End* (Abinger), 171; EMF, Notebook Journal, Dec. 13, 1907, KCC.

83 *"To know and help":* EMF, Notebook Journal, June [n.d.], 1905, KCC.

84 *"I know I am not":* EMF to Robert Trevelyan, Oct. 28, 1905, Lago and Furbank, eds., *Selected Letters*, I:83.

84 *"I never was attached":* Shelley, *Epipsychidion* (1821), ll. 149–59.

85 *"owes something to my":* Forster, "Author's Introduction" to *The Longest Journey* (1960), xxvii.

85 *"just where he began":* Forster, *The Longest Journey*, 35.

85 *"foresee[s] the most appalling":* Ibid., 80.

85 *"You are not a person who":* Ibid., 81.

85 *"marriage is most certainly":* Forster, "Pessimism in the Novel," in Thomson, ed., *Albergo Empedocle*, 136.

86 *"Doubt whether the novel's":* EMF, Notebook Journal, March 26, 1906, KCC.

86 *From his very first drafts:* Forster, *The Longest Journey*, 141.

86 *The reviewers of* The Longest Journey*: Tribune*, April 22, 1907, in Gardner, *Critical Heritage*, 66; *Daily News*, May 3, 1907, in Gardner, *Critical Heritage*, 73; *Standard*, May 14, 1907, in Gardner, *Critical Heritage*, 83.

86 *"only students of the Master's Juvenilia":* EMF to Dent, no date, late April 1907, KCC; Lago and Furbank, eds., *Selected Letters*, I:87.

86 *"least popular of my . . . novels":* Forster, "Author's Introduction" to *The Longest Journey* (1960), lxvii.

87 *"cut off from HOM":* EMF, Notebook Journal, June 22, 1906, KCC.

87 *"the bodies of men":* Ibid.

87 *"you can hardly see":* EMF to ACF, Aug. 31, 1906, KCC.

87 *"There is a whole new street":* EMF to ACF, Aug. 29, 1906, KCC.

87 *"wearing a sweeping blue gown":* Ashby, *Forster Country*, 105.

87 *"no escape from Table d'hôte":* EMF to Dent, Oct. 3, 1906, KCC; Lago and Furbank, eds., *Selected Letters*, I:85.

88 *"pride and arrogance":* Sir Syed Ahmad Khan, quoted in Metcalf and Metcalf, *A Concise History of Modern India*, 100.

89 *"highest position a 'Native'":* Lelyveld, "Macaulay's Curse," 1.

89 *"wrapped up the shivering":* Furbank, *E. M. Forster*, II:329.

89 *"All that splendor":* Lelyveld, "Macaulay's Curse," 15.

90 *whom he regarded as "poor fellows":* Furbank, *E. M. Forster*, I:144.

90 *"sonorous and beautiful voice":* Ibid., 143.

90 *"the vast self-confidence":* Beauman, *Morgan*, 183–84.

90 *"Oh dear, I do":* Furbank, *E. M. Forster*, I:143.

90 *"Masood gives up duties":* EMF, Notebook Journal, Dec. 24, 1906, KCC.

90 *Their friendship seemed to:* See Kidwai, ed., *Forster-Masood Letters*.

90 *"Centuries may pass, years":* Masood to EMF, Nov. 22, 1908, in Kidwai, ed., *Forster-Masood Letters* [no page]. Also KCC.

90 *"measur[ing] out [his] emotions":* Forster, "Notes on the English Character," *Abinger Harvest*, 6.

91 *"There never was anyone":* Forster, "Syed Ross Masood," in *Two Cheers*, 292.

91 *"We like the like"*: EMF, Notebook Journal, Aug. 15, 1907, KCC.

91 *But his life remained:* EMF, Notebook Journal, Dec. 31, 1907, KCC.

91 *"pigging it"*: EMF to Dent, n.d., late April 1907, KCC.

91 *"The home-sickness and bed-sickness"*: EMF, "AE Housman," ms., KCC. This essay was composed around 1950.

91 *"unspoilt and alive"*: EMF, Notebook Journal, April 11, 1907, KCC.

91 *"I realized the poet"*: EMF, "AE Housman," ms., KCC.

92 *"Mr. Forster fastens himself"*: *Times Literary Supplement*, April 26, 1907, in Gardner, *Critical Heritage*, 67.

92 *"the sudden death rate"*: *Morning Post*, May 6, 1907, in Gardner, *Critical Heritage*, 79–80.

92 *"It was the Taupe"*: LS to Leonard Woolf, Jan. 26, 1906, in Levy, ed., *The Letters of Lytton Strachey*, 95.

92 *"The morals, the sentimentality"*: LS to Leonard Woolf, May 2. 1907, ibid., 126.

92 *"things in [your novel]"*: Furbank, *E. M. Forster*, I:150.

92 *"I have been looking"*: EMF to Robert Trevelyan, June 11, 1907, quoted in editor's introduction to *A Room with a View*, xiii.

92 *Five years had passed:* Stallybrass, ed., *The Lucy Novels*, 3.

93 *"Oh mercy to myself"*: EMF to Robert Trevelyan. Sept. 12, 1907, quoted in editor's introduction to *A Room with a View*, xii.

93 *"Sir, I hesitate to address you"*: EMF to Robert Trevelyan, postcard June 10. 1908, quoted ibid., xii.

93 *"Never heard of it"*: Forster, *A Room with a View*, 125.

93 *"I will escape from the sham"*: Forster, "Howard Overing Sturgis," in *Abinger Harvest and England's Pleasant Land*, 118.

94 *These Edwardian novels:* EMF, Diary, Dec. 31, 1907, KCC.

94 *In mid-January 1908:* EMF, Diary, Jan. 16, 1908, KCC.

94 *"a really first class person"*: EMF to Dent, Feb. 10, 1908, KCC; Lago and Furbank, eds., *Selected Letters*, I:92.

94 *"I felt all that the ordinary"*: Ibid.

94 *"effectively bald"*: EMF to ACF, Jan. 17, 1908, KCC.

95 *James would "know better"*: Ibid.

95 *"Your name's Moore"*: Forster, "Henry James and the Young Men" in *The Listener*, July 16, 1959.

95 *"More of a man"*: EMF, Diary, Jan. 16, 1908, KCC.

95 *The American transplant seemed:* Forster, *Aspects of the Novel*, 110.

95 *"pattern [is] woven"*: Gardner, ed., *Commonplace Book*, 14.

95 *"gutted of the common stuff"*: Forster, *Aspects of the Novel*, 110, 111.

95 *"merely declining to think"*: Gardner, ed., *Commonplace Book*, 18.

96 *"was not my own road"*: EMF, Diary, Jan. 16, 1908, KCC.

5: "ORDINARY AFFECTIONATE MEN"

98 *Working over the typescript:* EMF, Diary, May 1, 1908, KCC.

98 *"I opened Walt Whitman"*: EMF, Diary, June 16, 1908, KCC.

98 *"dissipate this entire show"*: Whitman, "In Paths Untrodden," in *Leaves of Grass* (1872 edition), 142. This edition, the first to include the Calamus poems in this form, was likely shown to Forster by Edward Carpenter, who was given his edition by Whitman himself.

98   *"no more fighting"*: EMF, Diary, June 16, 1908, KCC.

98   *"Passage to India!"*: Whitman, "Passage to India," in *Leaves of Grass*, ll. 31–36.

98   *"[i]dea for another novel"*: EMF, Diary, June 26, 1908, KCC.

99   *Morgan balanced two families:* Forster, *Howards End*, 25, 21.

99   *"the spiritual cleavage"*: EMF, Diary, June 26, 1908, KCC.

99   *"they desired that public life"*: Forster, *Howards End*, 25.

100 *"Your home at All Souls Place"*: EMF to GLD, March 17, 1931, KCC; quoted in "Introduction" to *Howards End*, ix.

100 *"to trust people is"*: EMF, Diary, Feb. 10, 1909, KCC.

100 *"a continual bubble"*: Dewey, *Anglo-Indian Attitudes*, 141.

101 *"[H]e left me, normal"*: EMF, Diary, July 13, 1909, KCC.

101 *"The more I think of it"*: EMF to Darling, July 16, 1909, HRC.

101 *Even as he sought:* Ibid.

101 *"I feel that I cannot feel"*: EMF, Diary, n.d., August 1909, KCC.

102 *"Going home, he wrote a letter"*: EMF, Diary, April 25, 1911, KCC.

102 *"disgraced the college and himself"*: Forster, *Arctic Summer and Other Fiction*, 189, 191.

102 *Was going to reflect sadly:* EMF, Locked Diary, Nov. 29, 1909, KCC.

102 *Just before Christmas:* Forster, "Notes on the English Character," in *Abinger Harvest and England's Pleasant Land*, 5.

102 *"Will [his love] ever be complete?"*: EMF, Locked Diary, Dec. 31, 1909, KCC.

102 *Back in London:* EMF, Locked Diary, Jan. 13, 1910, KCC.

103 *"From Forster, member of the Ruling Race"*: EMF to Masood, Jan. 14, 1910, KCC; Lago and Furbank, eds., *Selected Letters*, I:102.

103 *"o love, each time"*: EMF, Locked Diary, Dec. 31, 1909, KCC.

103 *His yearning for Masood:* EMF, Locked Diary, Jan. 29, 1910, KCC.

103 *"After lunch in the Savile"*: EMF, Locked Diary, July 28, 1910, KCC.

103 *"However gross my desires"*: EMF, Locked Diary, July 21, 1910, KCC.

103 *"joyful but inconclusive evening[s]"*: EMF, Locked Diary, Jan. 15, 1910, KCC.

103 *The crisis came:* EMF, Locked Diary, Dec. 29, 1910, KCC.

104 *"in an awful stew"*: EMF to Masood, Jan. 2, 1911, in Kidwai, *Forster-Masood Letters*, 62.

104 "Non respondit": EMF, Locked Diary, Dec. 31, 1910, KCC.

104 *"you devil!"*: EMF to Masood, Jan. 2, 1911, in Kidwai, *Forster-Masood Letters*, 62.

104 *"book to my own heart"*: EMF, Locked Diary, Aug. 3, 1910, KCC.

104 "Howards End *[is]* my best": Gardner, ed., *Commonplace Book*, 203.

104 *"There is no doubt about it"*: *Daily Telegraph*, Nov. 2, 1910, in Gardner, *Critical Heritage*, 130.

104 *"one of the handful"*: *Athenaeum*, Dec. 3, 1910, in Gardner, *Critical Heritage*, 151.

104 *"I go about saying"*: EMF to GLD, Nov. 21, 1910, KCC.

105 *"I am not vain"*: EMF, Locked Diary, Dec. 8, 1910, KCC.

105 *"is evidently deeply shocked"*: EMF, Locked Diary, June 16, 1911, KCC.

105 *"main causes of my sterility"*: EMF, Locked Diary, Sept. 19, 1910, KCC.

105 *"sorrow has altered her"*: EMF, Locked Diary, Dec. 31, 1911, KCC.

105 *"trivial and effeminate"*: EMF, Locked Diary, July 17, 1911, KCC.

105 *"just like his father"*: Furbank, *E. M. Forster*, I:218.

105 *"feared to tell mother"*: EMF, Locked Diary, July 26, 1911, KCC.

105 *"Satanic fit of rage"*: EMF, Locked Diary, Oct. 31, 1911, KCC.

106 *"mother does not think highly of me"*: EMF, Locked Diary, May 15, 1912, KCC; quoted in Furbank, *E. M. Forster*, I:218.

106 *"a bright healthy young man"*: EMF to FB, Dec. 24, 1911, KCC.

106 *"I say! Your son"*: Interview with Mollie Barger, London, July 24, 2001.

106 *"a honeymoon slightly off colour"*: Gardner, ed., *Commonplace Book*, 217; EMF, Locked Diary, Dec. 31, 1911, KCC.

106 *"is a photograph of us"*: Gardner, ed., *Commonplace Book*, 217.

106 *"'Out of the way brother'"*: EMF to ACF, Jan. 15, 1913, KCC.

107 a *"[v]ery great happiness"*: EMF, Locked Diary, Sept. 9, 1912, KCC.

107 *"Here smut postcard"*: EMF, Indian Diary, Oct. 11, 1912, in *The Hill of Devi*, 120.

107 *"a little nip of frost"*: Forster, *Goldsworthy Lowes Dickinson*, 113.

107 *"argued about the shape"*: Ibid., 117.

107 *"evanescent . . . shooting out little glints"*: Ibid., 113.

107 *"It's not a star"*: EMF, Indian Diary, Oct. 21, 1912, in *The Hill of Devi*, 125.

107 *"very intimate with the natives"*: EMF to FB, n.d., Oct. 1912, KCC. This letter was posted from S.S. *City of Birmingham* "off Perim."

107 *"perpetually in love"*: Proctor, ed., *The Autobiography of Goldsworthy Lowes Dickinson*, 178; EMF, Indian Diary, Oct. 15, 1912, in *The Hill of Devi*, 122.

107 *Morgan spent hours with him:* EMF, Indian Diary, Oct. 15, 1912, in *The Hill of Devi*, 122.

108 *"spread . . . out over the plain"*: EMF, Indian Diary, Oct. 25, 1912, in *The Hill of Devi*, 128.

108 *"superb in his uniform"*: Proctor, ed., *The Autobiography of Goldsworthy Lowes Dickinson*, 178.

108 *"fitted indifferently into official circles"*: Forster, *The Hill of Devi*, 26.

108 *"unconventional, ardent, fearless"*: Ibid.

108 *"The Darlings are ideal"*: EMF to ACF, Feb. 26, 1913, KCC; quoted in *The Hill of Devi*, 182.

109 *"I didn't go there to govern"*: Forster, "Three Countries," in *The Hill of Devi*, 296.

109 *"in a sort of starved omnibus"*: Forster, *The Hill of Devi*, 131.

109 *"I came out with no feeling"*: EMF, Indian Diary, Nov. 17, 1912, in *The Hill of Devi*, 145.

109 *"a cultivated man"*: EMF, Indian Diary, Jan. 4, 1913, in *The Hill of Devi*, 172.

109 *"so kind, but whatever"*: EMF to FB, Jan. 14, 1913, KCC.

109 *"winced with horror"*: Forster, *Goldsworthy Lowes Dickinson*, 115.

110 *"the oddest corner of the world"*: EMF to ACF, Dec. 16, 1912, KCC; Malcolm Darling to EMF, May 1907, quoted in *The Hill of Devi*, 17.

110 *"a waistcoat"*: Forster, *The Hill of Devi*, 8.

110 *"brown tennis-ball"*: Ibid., 9.

110 *At Chhatarpur, Goldie noted:* Proctor, ed., *The Autobiography of Goldsworthy Lowes Dickinson*, 180.

110 *"not even a little flirt"*: Forster, *The Hill of Devi*, 226, 223.

111 *"he who might be slipping away"*: EMF, Indian Diary, Nov. 18, 1912, KCC.

111 *"Long and sad day"*: EMF, Indian Diary, Jan. 13, 1913, KCC.

111 *Perhaps because of this:* EMF, Indian Diary, Nov. 18, 1912; March 14, 1913; Jan. 1913; March 14, 1913; March 25, 1913.

111 *"I am dried up"*: EMF to Forrest Reid, Feb. 2, 1913, KCC.

112 *"It's an awful pity"*: EMF to Masood, April 11, 1913, Lago and Furbank, eds., *Selected Letters*, I:201. This letter is not included in the published Forster-Masood letters, ed. Kidwai.

112 a *"radiant moment"*: EMF, "Mother," 1945, KCC.

112 *"modern life had absorbed"*: Dent, "Angel Wings," in Beith, ed., *Edward Carpenter,* 26–27.

112 *Carpenter was approaching seventy:* Edward Carpenter. *My Days and Dreams.* 147.

113 *"We're all in heaven here"*: Ibid., 163.

113 *For his part, Carpenter:* Ibid.

113 *"escap[ing] from culture by"*: Forster, "Some Memories," in Beith, ed., *Edward Carpenter,* 74–75.

113 *"candor about sex"*: Ibid., 75.

113 *"a creative spring"*: Forster, "Notes on *Maurice*," in *Maurice,* 215.

114 *"A happy ending was imperative"*: Ibid., 216.

114 *"unhappily, with a lad dangling"*: Ibid.

114 *"I was determined"*: Ibid.

114 *"I tried to create"*: Ibid., 209.

114 *The third figure:* Ibid., 217.

115 a *"ghastly old boy"*: EMF to FB, Aug. 10, 1915, KCC; Forster, "Notes on *Maurice*," in *Maurice,* 217; Lago and Furbank, eds., *Selected Letters,* I:229.

115 *"unfair on Clive"*: Forster, "Notes on *Maurice*," in *Maurice,* 217.

115 *"it bored him dumb"*: EMF to Forrest Reid, March 13, 1915 , KCC.

115 *"Hugh can't again"*: EMF to FB, Aug. 10, 1915, KCC.

115 *"I have talked to you so much"*: EMF to FB, June 29, 1914, KCC.

115 *"a new and painful world"*: EMF to FB, March 28, 1915. KCC; Lago and Furbank, eds., *Selected Letters,* I:223.

115 *"I am so happy that"*: EMF to FB, April 27, 1915, KCC.

116 *"beautiful . . . the best work"*: EMF to Dent, June 13, 1915, KCC.

116 *Morgan entrusted his most heartfelt discussion:* Ibid.

116 *"My smooth spurt is over"*: EMF, Locked Diary, Dec. 17, 1913, KCC.

116 *"3 unfinished novels"*: Ibid.

116 *"Forward rather than back"*: EMF, Locked Diary, Dec. 31, 1913, KCC.

116 *"the Scudder part"*: GLD to EMF, Dec. 11, 1914, KCC.

116 *"breaks my heart almost"*: Ibid.

116 *"are on a basis"*: EMF, Locked Diary, Dec. 31, 1914, KCC.

117 *"sublimated . . . sublime"*: Taylor, *The Green Avenue,* 104.

117 *"Dear Reid . . . My perspicacity"*: EMF to Forrest Reid, March 13, 1915, KCC.

118 *"To give these people a chance"*: Ibid.

119 *"I should have prophesied"*: LS to EMF, March 12, 1915, in Levy, ed., *The Letters of Lytton Strachey,* 246.

119 *"I really think the whole conception"*: Ibid.

119 *more than he "would have liked"*: EMF to LS, March 14, 1915, KCC.

119 *"No one ever breaks"*: EMF to LS, Nov. 1, 1913, KCC; Lago and Furbank, eds., *Selected Letters,* I:208.

119 *"You can scarcely imagine"*: EMF to Dent, March 6, 1915, KCC.

119 *"My work is all wrong"*: EMF, Locked Diary, Aug. 1, 1914, KCC.

120 *"[I] do not think"*: EMF, Locked Diary, Dec. 31. 1914, KCC.

120 *"a sandy haired passionate Nibelung"*: EMF to Forrest Reid, Jan. 23, 1915, KCC.

120 *it "is a beautiful book"*: Frieda Lawrence to EMF, Feb. 5, 1915, KCC.

120 *"you belied and betrayed"*: DHL to EMF, Jan. 28, 1915, KCC.

120 *"In [your] books"*: DHL to EMF, Wednesday [Feb. 3] 1915, KCC.

121 *It emerged that Lawrence's:* DHL to Bertrand Russell, Feb. 12, 1915, Boulton, Zytaruk, et al., eds., *Letters of D. H. Lawrence,* II:283.

121 *Lawrence told a friend:* DHL to Barbara Low, Feb. 11, 1915, ibid., II: 280.

121 *"which is beautiful"*: EMF to Dent, March 6, 1915, KCC.

121 *In his diary, Morgan:* EMF, Locked Diary, Sept. 9, 1915, KCC.

121 *"up till the last moment"*: Proctor, ed., *Autobiography of Goldsworthy Lowes Dickinson,* 189.

121 *"Don't say 'face facts'"*: Furbank, *E. M. Forster,* II:2.

122 *"What's to occupy me"*: EMF to GLD, Dec. 13, 1914, KCC.

122 *"I am leading the life"*: EMF to FB, Aug. 10, 1915, KCC.

6: "PARTING WITH RESPECTABILITY"

123 *"a very pale, delicately-built young man"*: Furbank, *E. M. Forster,* II:25. The speaker is the daughter of Aida Borchgrevink.

123 *Zealous self-described "brigades"*: Gullace, "White Feathers and Wounded Men," 178.

123 *He had rebuffed:* Furbank, *E. M. Forster,* II:19.

124 *"Who's for the khaki suit"*: Jessie Pope, 1915. *In Flanders Fields: Poetry of the First World War,* ed. George Walter. London: Allen Lane, 2004, 21.

124 *"khaki of sorts"*: Forster, "The Lost Guide," in *Alexandria,* 355.

124 *"My uniform is well received"*: Forster, "Incidents of War Notebook," KCC.

125 *found her "shrewish"*: EMF to ACF, Nov. 21, 1915, KCC.

125 *"mother was too much against it"*: EMF to FB, Aug. 10, 1915, KCC; Lago and Furbank, eds., *Selected Letters,* I:229.

125 *"All one can do"*: EMF to Masood, July 29, 1915; Lago and Furbank, eds., *Selected Letters,* I:224.

125 *"a vague scheme for a book"*: EMF to GLD, April 5, 1916, KCC.

126 *"This room contains nothing of beauty"*: Forster, *Alexandria,* 94, 95, 97.

126 *the "specimen is not even"*: Ibid., 121.

126 *"One can't dislike Alex"*: EMF to ACF, Nov. 21, 1915, KCC.

126 *From his "comfortable" room:* EMF to Masood, Dec. 29, 1915, KCC; Lago and Furbank, eds., *Selected Letters,* I:232.

127 *Forster was unaware:* See Dunne, "Sexuality and the Civilizing Process."

128 *It was "unthinkable"*: This was Judge A. C. McBarnet. See ibid., 191–92.

128 *The first friend:* EMF to EC, April 13, 1916 ("I knew [Furness] slightly" at King's), KCC.

128 *"I have long been a policeman"*: Robert Furness to Maynard Keynes, April 25, 1907, KCC.

128 *For Furness, the city:* Dunne notes in "Sexuality and the Civilizing Process," "In 1910, 786 boys and 1,477 girls had been intercepted at the Port, and they probably represented a small fraction of the sexual commerce in the town." 183.

128 *Like many British gentlemen:* EMF, Mohammed el Adl Notebook, KCC.

128 *"frugal, pungent" style:* Furness. Introductory Note, *Poems of Callimachus,* xii.

128 *The little vignettes:* Furness stayed in Egypt all his professional life. He was the head of the Egyptian Boy Scout League, and later a professor of literature at Fuad University in Cairo. Furness married in his sixties and had a daughter late in life, in England. He died in 1954.

129 *"what the inhabitants"*: Forster, *Alexandria*, 354.

129 *"I went to the Red Cross"*: Ibid., 355.

129 the *"ambitious and westernising Ottoman"*: Haag, *Alexandria*, 9.

129 *"a good deal of horse racing"*: Forster, *Alexandria*, 355.

129 *"the only buildings"*: Baedeker's *Egypt*, 16.

130 *"handsomely fitted up"*: Ibid., 9.

130 *"I . . . start out"*: EMF to Masood, Dec. 29, 1915, Lago and Furbank, eds., *Selected Letters*, I:232.

130 *"intense and unbelievable blue"*: Forster, *Alexandria*, 354.

130 *"coalesced into a set"*: Ibid., 355.

130 *"cerebral and ruffled heron"*: Grafftey-Smith, *Bright Levant*, 70.

130 *"discarding my uniform . . . [to] plunge"*: EMF to Masood, Dec. 29, 1915, Lago and Furbank, eds., *Selected Letters*, I:233.

130 *"symbolizes for me a mixture"*: Forster, *Alexandria*, 355–56.

131 *Anastassiades, a cotton broker*: EMF to Virginia Woolf, April 15, 1916, Lago and Furbank, eds., *Selected Letters*, I:234.

131 *"All that I cared for"*: EMF to Masood, Dec. 29, 1915, Lago and Furbank, eds., *Selected Letters*, I:233.

131 *"I imagine it is here"*: EMF to Virginia Woolf, Apr. 15, 1916, Lago and Furbank, eds., *Selected Letters*, I:234.

132 *"I came inclined"*: EMF to Malcolm Darling, Aug. 6, 1916, HRC; Lago and Furbank, eds., *Selected Letters*, I:238–39.

132 *"so pleasant and grateful"*: EMF to Masood, Dec. 29, 1915, Lago and Furbank, eds., *Selected Letters*, I:234.

132 *One young private*: Forster, "Incidents of War Notebook," KCC.

133 *"After giving careful evidence"*: Ibid.

133 *"'I'm awfully interested in ideas'"*: EMF to GLD, July 28, 1916, KCC; Lago and Furbank, eds., *Selected Letters*, I:237.

133 *"If one does get news"*: EMF to Masood, Dec. 29, 1915, Lago and Furbank, eds., *Selected Letters*, I:232.

134 *"little nameless unremembered acts"*: Wordsworth, "Tintern Abbey," ll. 34–35.

134 *The conscription that the Red Cross*: Four months after this initial call, the act was revised to include married men; by April 1917, it was expanded still further to include men discharged because of wounds or illness. Eventually, by April 1918, all men between the ages of seventeen and fifty-one were required to register for the draft. I am grateful to Laura Harbold for her research on conscription.

135 *Only his friends*: EMF to FB, July 2, 1916, KCC; Lago and Furbank, eds., *Selected Letters*, I:235.

135 *"I am quite shameless"*: EMF to ACF, July 10, 1916, KCC.

135 *"a splendid creature"*: EMF to FB, July 2, 1916, KCC; Lago and Furbank, eds., *Selected Letters*, I:235.

136 *"[w]e must have a numerous"*: Forster, "Incidents of War Notebook," KCC.

136 *"I was bathing myself"*: EMF to GLD, July 28, 1916, KCC; Lago and Furbank, eds., *Selected Letters*, I:237.

136 *"It's evidently not to be in our day"*: Ibid.

137 *"Come here Mustafa Pasha"*: Forster, "Gippo English," *Egyptian Mail*, Dec. 16, 1919, 2; quoted in Haag, *Alexandria*, 26.

137 *"I don't want to grouse"*: EMF to EC, April 12, 1916, KCC.

138 *"do the . . . brotherly" thing*: EMF to GLD, July 28, 1916, KCC.

138 *"No admission this way"*: Forster, "Gippo English," *Egyptian Mail*, Dec. 16, 1919, 2.

138 *An essay on the strangeness*: Forster, "Army English," *Egyptian Mail*, Jan. 12, 1919, 2.

139 *"We went up pitch black stairs"*: EMF to EC, May 18, 1916, KCC.

140 *"A few days after"*: EMF to Malcolm Darling, Aug. 6, 1916, HRC; Lago and Furbank, eds., *Selected Letters*, I:239.

140 *"sickened to the vitals"*: EMF to EC, April 13, 1916, KCC.

140 *A friend described him as*: Liddell, *Cavafy*, 180.

141 *"a literary evening"*: EMF to ACF, Aug. 24, 1916, KCC.

141 *a "Greek gentleman in a straw hat"*: Forster, "The Poetry of Cavafy," 13.

141 *"to give the impression"*: Liddell, *Cavafy*, 129–30.

141 *"Where could I live better?"*: Ibid., 180.

142 *"continuously adjusting the light"*: Ibid., 182.

142 *"his better furniture"*: Ibid., 181.

142 *"I am back from my work"*: Forster, "The Poetry of Cavafy," 40.

143 *"sensation that I love"*: Cavafy, "Come Back" (1904), trans. Keeley and Sherrard, 43.

143 *"How strong the scents were"*: Cavafy, "In the Evening," *The Complete Poems of Cavafy*, 73.

143 *Even more exciting*: Sherrard, "Cavafy's Sensual City: A Question," 96.

143 *For his nighttime self*: Liddell, *Cavafy*, 130.

144 *"expressions . . . that one might actually hear"*: Forster, "The Poetry of Cavafy," 14.

144 *"the world within"*: Ibid., 15.

144 *"burn . . . his fingers"*: The journal's editor was Stephen Pargas, who went by the pseudonym Nikos Zelitas. Haag, *Alexandria*, 68.

144 *"The best Alexandrian I know"*: EMF to GLD, Jan. 10, 1917, KCC.

144 *liked his own outrageous jokes*: Grafftey-Smith, *Bright Levant*, 36. Sometimes the joke would go too far. "When Johnny decided to raise a gale of laughter by going to a very English party with a mahogany girdle round his waist and a miniature gilt cistern over his head, pulling his little gilt plug-chain to spray his hostess with perfume, no one was amused."

145 *He was a peripatetic fellow*: See Claudel, "'De la part d'un ami sans visage.'"

145 *"To see a Sinadino again"*: Forster, untitled poem in the style of Cavafy, KCC.

146 *"It was not my knowledge"*: Forster, "The Poetry of Cavafy," 40.

146 *"All the times I wanted"*: John Chioles, translator. In Leontis et al., eds., *What These Ithakas Mean*, 68.

147 *"I wished you were here"*: EMF to GLD, July 28, 1916, KCC; Lago and Furbank, eds., *Selected Letters*, I:236–37.

147 *Finally, in mid-October*: Nicola Beauman gives a plausible reading of Morgan's sexual code in *Morgan*, 299.

148 *"Yesterday, for the first time"*: EMF to FB, Oct. 16, 1916, Lago and Furbank, eds., *Selected Letters*, I:243.

148 *"a decadent coward"*: Furbank, *E. M. Forster*, II:28. The correspondence, after the end of July 1916, is preserved in London in the India Records Office.

148 *"there is no foundation"*: O. V. B. Bosanquet, Agent to the Governor-General in Indore, to J. B. Wood, Political Secretary, Aug. 28, 1916; India Records Office, British Library.

148 *"I realise in the first place"*: EMF to FB, Oct. 16, 1916, KCC; Lago and Furbank, eds., *Selected Letters*, I:243.

149 *"Well, my dear,":* Ibid., I:244.

149 *"tighter and tinier and shinier":* EMF to Josie Darling, June 20, 1915, HRC.

149 *"To merge myself":* "Incidents of War Notebook," KCC; he repeated these phrases, probably copied from the notebook, in a letter to GLD, May 5, 1917; Lago and Furbank, eds., *Selected Letters,* I:251.

150 *"Montazah Sta.—":* Forster, *Alexandria,* 140–42.

7: "A GREAT UNRECORDED HISTORY"

151 *"unappetizing gloom":* EMF to Malcolm Darling, Dec. 1, 1916, HRC.

151 *"shifted about the sandy wastes":* Forster, "The Lost Guide," in *Alexandria,* 355.

152 *"Wherever she went":* Ibid.

152 *"charming and polite, I said yes":* EMF, Mohammed el Adl Notebook, c. August-September 1922, KCC. The small notebook Forster dedicated to Mohammed contains several separate manuscripts, accreted over fifty years. The first, the memoir of Mohammed's life and death, Forster began in the form of a letter addressed to his beloved on August 5, 1922, and concluded just after Christmas 1927; the other section, transcripts of letters from Mohammed and snatches of their conversation, which Forster labeled "words spoken," were transcribed in 1960.

152 *"'nice,' and the morning was":* Ibid.

152 *"Often as I let myself in at night":* Ibid.

152 *"that to be trusted":* EMF to FB, July 18, 1917, KCC.

152 *"I have plunged into":* EMF to FB, May 29, 1917, KCC.

153 *"c[a]me up into the swirl":* EMF, Mohammed el Adl Memoir, KCC.

153 *"God knows how many hours":* EMF to FB, Jan. 6, 1918, Lago and Furbank, eds., *Selected Letters,* I:281.

153 *Once Mohammed realized:* EMF, Mohammed el Adl Memoir, KCC.

153 *"a question about Mohammedans":* EMF to FB, Jan. 6, 1918, Lago and Furbank, eds., *Selected Letters,* I:281.

154 *"There's a Mosque":* EMF, Mohammed el Adl Memoir, KCC.

154 *"the reprehensible habit of joyrides":* EMF to FB, Jan. 6, 1918, KCC; Lago and Furbank, eds., *Selected Letters,* I:282.

154 *"I can only say":* Ibid.

154 *"It had blown away":* Ibid.

155 *"most sympathetic and helpful":* Furness's sexuality is a bit of a mystery. He had a passionate but platonic love for Aida, which may have been a psychological beard for them both. He remained a bachelor until he was almost sixty, marrying on his return to England. In his old age, he fathered a daughter, who survived him. His motives for displeasure don't necessarily preclude fear of exposure. But late in life Forster regretted imposing on him.

155 *"an awful nuisance":* EMF to Furbank, July 18, 1958, in Allott, introduction to Forster, *Alexandria,* xxxii.

155 *"the thing I am proudest of":* EMF to FB, Jan. 6, 1918, KCC.

155 *"sensuality . . . came violently":* EMF, Mohammed el Adl Memoir, KCC. The discovery that this is the wrong station stop I owe to Haag, *Alexandria,* 36.

156 *"Mazarita not Ramleh":* EMF, Mohammed el Adl Memoir, KCC.

156 *"dark and unfrequented":* EMF to FB, March 23, 1918, KCC.

156 *"look mediaeval by moonlight":* Forster, *Alexandria,* 130.

156 *"I do not care for cakes"*: EMF, Mohammed el Adl Memoir, KCC.

156 *"Would you like to see"*: EMF, "Words Spoken," transcriptions of Mohammed el Adl's sayings, in Mohammed el Adl Notebook, KCC.

157 *"showered everything in the room"*: EMF to FB, March 23, 1918 and July 18, 1917, KCC.

157 *"I have always ate apart"*: EMF, "Words Spoken," in Mohammed el Adl Notebook, KCC.

158 *"I have often thought of your sister"*: EMF to FB, May 29, 1917, KCC.

158 *It isn't* happiness: EMF to FB, June 17, 1917, KCC; Lago and Furbank, eds., *Selected Letters*, I:257–58.

158 *"One morning I woke up"*: Ibid.

158 *"I did not like Christianity"*: EMF, "Words Spoken," in Mohammed el Adl Notebook, KCC.

159 *"inroads on free thought"*: EMF to FB, July 31, 1917, KCC; Lago and Furbank, eds., *Selected Letters*, I:264.

159 *They talked a lot about sex:* EMF to FB, June 4, 1917, KCC.

159 *"We hadn't entirely"*: EMF to FB, July 31, 1917, KCC; Lago and Furbank, eds., *Selected Letters*, I:265.

159 *"Completely to part with Respectability"*: EMF to FB, Sept. 30, 1917, KCC; Lago and Furbank, eds., *Selected Letters*, I:272.

160 *"If we are to be"*: EMF, "Words Spoken," in Mohammed el Adl Notebook, KCC.

160 *"feared he was only externals"*: EMF to FB, Sept. 30, 1917, KCC; Lago and Furbank, eds., *Selected Letters*, I:272.

160 *"My damn prick stands up"*: EMF, Mohammed el Adl Notebook, KCC.

160 *For Forster, who had concluded:* EMF to FB, May 27, 1918, KCC. "A expects marriage and life among his own people, so far as he looks forward at all, and I scarcely look forward to anything different."

160 *made "a sinner"*: Rowson, "Vice Lists," 72–73. "[O]fficial morality restricted a man's penetrative options to his wife and female slaves, but if he chose to become 'profligate' he could expand these penetrative options . . ."

160 *"All have their foolishness"*: EMF, "Words Spoken," in Mohammed el Adl Notebook, KCC.

161 *his barely unexpressed desire to be penetrated:* Forster's diary reveals this was his desire, never realized. He writes: "While in India, I promised myself that on my return [to Egypt] I would get you to penetrate me behind, however much it hurt and although it must decrease your respect for me." (EMF, Mohammed el Adl Memoir, KCC.)

161 *Living after Freud and Foucault:* It's a mistake to think that the passage of time means progress. In *Why Marriage?* the gay historian George Chauncey cautions that "the major error of most post-Foucaultian histories of sexuality has been to assume the triumph of [the] modernist view of sexual identity." 187.

161 *"an understanding rather than an agreement"*: EMF to FB, July 18, 1917, KCC; Lago and Furbank, eds., *Selected Letters*, I:262.

161 *"Dearest Florence, R. Has been parted with"*: EMF to FB, Oct. 8, 1917, KCC; Lago and Furbank, eds., *Selected Letters*, I:274. The day of "parting with Respectability" was Oct 5.

161 *"The half moon,"*: EMF to FB, Aug. 25, 1917, KCC; Lago and Furbank, eds., *Selected Letters*, I:268–69.

162 *"would otherwise be ours"*: EMF to FB, Sept. 13, 1917, KCC.

162 *"It's absurd"*: EMF to FB, March 23, 1918, KCC.

162 *"to be a spy"*: EMF to FB, Oct. 8, 1917, KCC; Lago and Furbank, eds., *Selected Letters*, I:270.

162 *"Do you not think":* EMF to FB, Oct. 11, 1917, KCC; Lago and Furbank, eds., *Selected Letters*, I:274; "Words Spoken," in Mohammed el Adl Notebook, KCC.

163 *"it felt like the fall of a curtain":* EMF to FB, Oct. 11, 1917, KCC.

163 *"You called out my name":* EMF, Mohammed el Adl Notebook, KCC.

163 *"Everything seems breaking here":* EMF to FB, Sept. 30, 1917, KCC.

163 *His pool of friends:* EMF to FB, Aug. 25, 1917, KCC.

164 *"whatever that means":* EMF to FB, Oct. 8, 1917, KCC.

164 *"stupidity and deadness":* EMF to Lily, Nov. 26, 1917, KCC.

164 *"It is very sweet of you":* EMF to FB, Aug. 25, 1917, KCC.

164 *"reliability cleanliness, intellectual detachment":* EMF to GLD, Aug. 31, 1917, KCC.

164 *"Your good friend, Mrs. Barger":* EC to EMF, March 13, 1918, KCC.

165 *"I want to put a few things on record":* EMF to FB, Jan. 6, 1918, KCC; Lago and Furbank, eds., *Selected Letters*, I:280.

165 *"proof of something larger":* EMF to FB, misdated April 3, 1918 (probably May 3), KCC.

166 *"How does anything end?":* EMF to GLD, June 25, 1917, KCC.

166 *"nothing in my life":* EMF, Mohammed el Adl Notebook, KCC.

166 *And this view:* EMF to Plomer, Nov. 20, 1963, Durham.

166 *"I never did find":* EMF to GLD, Oct. 9, 1916, KCC.

166 *"He is unfortunately black":* EMF to FB, Sept. 13, 1917, KCC; Lago and Furbank, eds., *Selected Letters*, I:271. "His other . . . suit—besides his uniform—is a long and rather unpleasing nightgown over which you button a sort of frock coat: bare feet in clogs. Thus attired he may walk with me in the neighborhood of his room, but not elsewhere. He always wears a fez."

167 *"Taking me by the sleeve":* EMF to FB, Aug. 25, 1917, KCC; Lago and Furbank, eds., *Selected Letters*, I:268.

167 *"The whole ending of* Maurice*":* EMF to FB, Feb. 18, 1918, KCC; Lago and Furbank, eds., *Selected Letters*, I:287.

168 *"I have known in a way":* EMF to FB, Oct. 8, 1917, KCC; Lago and Furbank, eds., *Selected Letters*, I:274.

168 *"Oh Florence, what a mean":* EMF to FB, misdated April 3, 1918 (probably May 3), KCC.

168 *"he went to hospital":* EMF to FB, March [n.d.] 1918, KCC.

168 *"shovels [Egyptians] around like dirt":* EMF to FB, March 23, 1918, KCC; Lago and Furbank, eds., *Selected Letters*, I:288.

168 *"make an effort over A":* EMF to FB, March [n.d.] 1918, KCC.

168 *"obliged to tell him":* EMF to FB, May [n.d.] 1918, KCC.

169 *"as Maurice and Clive sat":* EMF to FB, May 14, 1918, KCC.

169 *"two days have passed":* EMF, "Words Spoken," in Mohammed el Adl Notebook, KCC.

169 *"some lovely cloud":* EMF to FB, May 14, 1918, KCC.

169 *"Your new arrangement isn't possible":* EMF to FB, May 27, 1918, KCC.

169 *"He strikes me as more fully attached":* EMF to FB, June 25, 1918, KCC.

169 *"chucked that infernal job":* EMF to GLD, May 31, 1918, KCC.

169 *"received a wire from Tanta":* MEA to EMF, June [n.d.] 1918, KCC.

169 *"Griefs never come":* MEA to EMF, June 27, 1918, KCC.

169 *"He was a good swimmer":* EMF to FB, July 16, 1918, KCC; Lago and Furbank, eds., *Selected Letters*, I:290.

170 *"seldom touched [the muddy floor]":* Ibid., I:290, 291.

170 *"Mr. Ganda and all":* MEA to EMF, July 23, 1918, KCC.

170 *"I am rather in favour"*: EMF to FB, July 16, 1918, KCC; Lago and Furbank, eds., *Selected Letters*, I:291.

170 *"I theorised to him"*: Ibid.

170 *"All is exceptions in men"*: EMF, "Words Spoken," in Mohammed el Adl Notebook. KCC.

170 *"Sick of" Mansourah*: MEA to EMF, July [n.d.] 1918, KCC.

171 *"bathing and sprawling"*: EMF to FB, Aug. 5, 1918, KCC.

171 *"more romantic"*: Ibid.

171 *"I think A's [Adl's] must be the saddest"*: EMF to FB, Oct. 2, 1918, KCC.

171 *"I have just been writing"*: EMF to FB, Oct. 7, 1918, KCC.

172 *"was scarcely in the world"*: EMF to FB, Oct. [n.d.] 1918, KCC.

172 *"She is like some tame"*: EMF to FB, Nov. [n.d.] 1918, KCC; Lago and Furbank, eds., *Selected Letters*, I:297.

172 *"Why not take them"*: Ibid.

8: "DO NOT FORGET YOUR EVER FRIEND"

177 *To Mohammed el Adl*: EMF, Mohammed el Adl Memoir, KCC.

177 *"I am sure that I could have lived"*: EMF to FB, Feb. 25, 1922, KCC; Lago and Furbank, eds., *Selected Letters*, II:23.

178 *"with my present freedom"*: EMF, Locked Diary, Dec. 31, 1919, KCC.

178 *"I see my middle age"*: EMF, Locked Diary, Aug. 12, 1919, KCC.

178 *"I don't see what it is"*: Ibid.

178 *"the outward nonsense of England"*: EMF to Seigfried Sassoon, March 28, 1919; Lago and Furbank, eds., *Selected Letters*, I:300.

178 *"[a] couple of sly references"*: EMF to FB, Jan. [n.d.] 1919, KCC.

178 *"very unwise as it puts me"*: EMF, Locked Diary, April 24, 1919, KCC.

179 *"The Trouble in Egypt"*: EMF, Letter to the Editor, *Manchester Guardian*, March 29, 1919.

179 *"I wish you was American"*: MEA to EMF, Oct. 3, 1919, KCC.

179 *"I found in my dictionary"*: MEA to EMF, Nov. 4, 1919, KCC.

179 *"In Egypt the native"*: EMF, Letter to the Editor, *Daily Herald*, May 30, 1919.

180 *"going as Prime minister"*: EMF to Forrest Reid, Feb. 17, 1921, KCC.

180 *Mohammed surprised him*: EMF to FB, March 17, 1921, KCC; Lago and Furbank, eds., *Selected Letters*, II:2.

180 *"a great coat and blue"*: EMF to FB, March 17, 1921, May 20, 1921, KCC; Lago and Furbank, eds., *Selected Letters*, II:7.

181 *"I wish he used"*: EMF to FB, May 20, 1921, KCC; Lago and Furbank, eds., *Selected Letters*, II:8.

181 *"He was a charming creature"*: Forster, "Three Countries," *The Hill of Devi*, 297.

181 *"finish it—it is stuck"*: EMF to ACF, March 19, 1916, KCC.

181 *"[P]anic and cruelty"*: Malcolm Darling to EMF, July 11, 1919, quoted in Furbank, *E. M. Forster*, II:61.

182 *"In his social life"*: EMF to FB, May 20, 1921, KCC.

182 *"You would weep at"*: EMF to ACF, April 1, 1921, KCC.

182 *"For acres around the soil"*: Ibid.

183 *"The least I can do"*: EMF, Kanaya ms., KCC. The Kanaya ms. has no date. It was typed much later by JRA; the original is likely dated to Forster's 1921 travels to India.

183 *"I think you know":* Ibid.

183 *Morgan recorded the conversation:* Ibid.

183 *"kind of saint":* Forster, "Three Countries," *The Hill of Devi,* 297.

184 *"I resumed sexual intercourse":* EMF, Kanaya ms., KCC.

184 *"It is difficult to find":* Ibid.

184 *"Do 'fondness' and 'love'":* EMF to GLD, Aug. 6, 1921, KCC; Lago and Furbank, eds., *Selected Letters,* II:10.

185 *"I was struck with the remoteness":* EMF to GLD, April 14, 1921, KCC; Lago and Furbank, eds., *Selected Letters,* II:4.

185 *"intelligent and forthcoming":* EMF to GLD, Sept. 17, 1921, KCC.

186 *"Today . . . began exquisitely":* EMF to GLD, Sept. 28, 1921, KCC.

186 *"across the slender sphinx":* EMF to GLD, Sept. 17, 1921, KCC.

186 *"Why can't we be friends":* Forster, *A Passage to India,* 312.

187 *"Mohammed collapsed under consumption":* EMF to FB, Jan. 28, 1922, KCC; Lago and Furbank, eds., *Selected Letters,* II:21.

187 *"an unhappy time":* Ibid.

187 *"all the traditional symptoms":* EMF to GLD, Jan. 28, 1922, KCC.

187 *"radiant spirits":* EMF to FB, Feb. 25, 1922, KCC; Lago and Furbank, eds., *Selected Letters,* II:23.

187 *"Mohammed was well enough":* Ibid.

188 *"depressed to the verge":* The Diaries of Virginia Woolf, II:171, March 12, 1922.

188 *"[t]he wrong channel":* EMF, Locked Diary, April 8, 1922, KCC.

189 *"although I know that":* EMF, Mohammed el Adl Memoir, KCC.

189 *"determined my life should":* EMF, Locked Diary, May 3, 1922, KCC.

189 *"Death destroys a man":* Forster, *Howards End,* 236.

189 *"The* mater *is a misfortune":* EMF to FB, June 17, 1922, KCC.

190 *"When I began the book":* EMF to Masood, Sept. 27, 1922, KCC; quoted in Furbank, "Introduction" to *A Passage to India* (Everyman's), xix–xx.

190 *"Pathos, piety, courage":* Forster, *A Passage to India,* 140.

190 *"the only person to whom":* EMF to Masood, May 23, 1923, KCC; quoted in Furbank, "Introduction" to *A Passage to India* (Everyman's), xix–xx.

191 *"he never possessed it":* Forster, "West Hackhurst: A Surrey Ramble," in Jeffrey M. Heath, ed., *Creator as Critic,* 111.

191 *"There was . . . no gas":* Ibid.

191 *"I have to visit":* EMF to Carrington, June 27, 1924, HRC.

192 *"The Hogarth Press are":* EMF to FB, July 7, 1922, KCC.

192 *"I have just written":* Ibid.

192 *"I may show it":* Ibid.

192 *"exactly what I want":* EMF to Sassoon, Dec. 12, 1923, quoted in Furbank, *E. M. Forster,* II:119.

193 *"among the elect":* TEL to EMF, Feb. 20, 1924, copy at KCC.

193 *"I'd very much like":* TEL to EMF, April 6, 1924, copy at KCC.

193 *"one of the funniest things":* TEL to EMF, April 30, 1924, copy at KCC.

193 *"I am glad you wrote":* EMF to TEL, May 3, 1924, KCC.

194 *"I've put the last words":* The Diaries of Virginia Woolf, II:289, Jan. 23, 1924.

194 *"Talking of Proust":* Ibid., II:269, Sept. 18, 1923.

194 *"In the best love making":* EMF, Sex Diary, n.d., c. 1935, KCC.

195 *"I don't see what"*: EMF, Locked Diary, Aug. 12, 1919, KCC.

195 *"I am not at all"*: *The Diaries of Virginia Woolf*, II:268, Sept. 18, 1923.

195 *Reviewers welcomed his novel*: Sylvia Lynd, "A Great Novel at Last," *Time and Tide*, June 20, 1924, in Gardner, *Critical Heritage*, 215.

195 *In India and in England*: EMF, Locked Diary, Aug. 31, 1934, KCC.

195 *"Famous wealthy, miserable"*: EMF, Locked Diary, Jan. 2, 1925, KCC.

9: "TOMS AND DICKS"

196 *"Hearing him yet"*: J. R. Ackerley, "Ghosts," quoted in Parker, *Ackerley*, 51. The poem was published in the *London Mercury* in April 1922.

196 *"the horror, beauty, depth"*: EMF to JRA, April 26. 1922; Lago and Furbank, eds., *Selected Letters*, II:24.

197 *Like many survivors*: Ackerley, *My Father and Myself*, 74.

197 *"guilty and frustrated"*: Ibid.

197 *"I don't quite like A."*: EMF, Locked Diary, Oct. 14, 1923, KCC.

198 *"It was like a return"*: EMF, Locked Diary, March 24, 1925, KCC.

198 *"No personal relationships"*: EMF, Locked Diary, May 23, 1923, KCC.

198 *"some black blood"*: EMF, Locked Diary, Oct. 2, 1924, KCC.

198 *"She was a very nice woman"*: EMF to FB, Oct. 24. 1924, KCC; Lago and Furbank, eds., *Selected Letters*, II:65.

199 *"he learned some strange"*: EMF to JRA, n.d., early 1925, HRC.

199 *"I had better have"*: EMF to FB, Oct. 2, 1924, KCC.

199 *"a queer ending"*: EMF to JRA, Jan. 19, 1925, HRC.

199 *"The visit was sticky"*: Ibid.

199 *"mere social behaving"*: EMF to JRA, n.d., early 1925, HRC.

199 *"Madame n'est pas sans soupçons"*: EMF to JRA, July 20,1925, HRC.

199 *"when the women went"*: Welty, "The Life to Come," 365.

200 *"tatty pubs in Soho"*: Ackerley, *My Father and Myself*, 134.

200 "Women have got out of hand": Gardner, ed., *Commonplace Book*, n.d.. c. 1930, 59–60.

200 *"I have just discovered"*: EMF to JRA, Oct. 17, 1924, HRC.

201 *Sprott was bright*: Carrington to Gerald Brenan, Dec. 18, 1921, in Garnett, ed., *Carrington*, 199.

201 *"voice shooting up"*: Furbank, *E. M. Forster*, II:118.

201 *"I knew you were"*: Parker, *Ackerley*, 109.

201 *"a dreary nowhere"*: EMF to Sprott, March 22, 1925, KCC.

202 *"a statue of a Greek"*: Parker, *Ackerley*, 103.

202 *"[I]n this négligé"*: Ackerley, *My Father and Myself*, 184.

202 *"I do not think"*: de Jongh, *Not in Front of the Audience*. 25.

202 *The problem play was*: Parker, *Ackerley*, 90.

203 *"You see! Incest as well"*: de Jongh, *Not in Front of the Audience*, 25.

203 *"start . . . upon a long quest"*: Ackerley, *My Father and Myself*, 123.

204 *"I think you are"*: EMF to JRA, Oct. 25, 1924, HRC.

204 *"Proust seems to think"*: EMF to JRA, Tuesday [n.d.], late Oct. 1924, HRC.

204 *"It is curious"*: EMF to JRA, n.d., early 1925, HRC.

204 *At the bottom*: Ibid.

204 *"Hammersmith Broadway was the pleasure"*: Daley, *This Small Cloud*, 92, 21.

204 *An aficionado, Harry had unusual:* Daley to Furbank, March 21, 1968.
205 *"made him wonderfully loveable":* Ibid.
205 *"gay and all embracing":* Daley, *This Small Cloud,* 135.
205 *"purple suede shoes":* Parker, *Ackerley,* 110.
205 *"scraped and pinched":* Daley, *This Small Cloud,* 114.
206 *"as part of the excitement":* Ibid., 131.
206 *"a billiard room":* Ibid., 86.
206 *"In this cramped world":* Ibid., 90–91.
206 *"laughed about as if [they were]":* Ibid., 101.
206 *"One policeman regularly hoisted":* Ibid., 90.
206 *A large, pudgy, and unprepossessing:* Ibid., 112.
207 *Morgan was head over heels:* EMF to Sprott, Aug. 21, year obscured, KCC.
207 *"steak and eggs and bacon":* Daley, *This Small Cloud,* 90.
207 *"except for a few coster's barrows":* Daley to Furbank, March 21, 1968.
207 *"spoke my language":* Ibid.
207 *"Nothing but the best":* Ibid.
207 *"It is not my policy":* EMF to JRA, Oct. 17, 1927, HRC.
208 *"Vicary cannot take":* EMF to FB, Sept. 19, 1924, KCC.
208 *"heavenly . . . if heaven can be":* EMF to JRA, June 4, 1926, HRC.
208 *"Don't let anyone 'spoil'":* EMF to JRA, Jan. 15, 1928, KCC.
208 *"Tell Charles to arrive":* EMF to Sprott, Feb. 28, 1928, KCC.
208 *"I have written to Charles":* EMF to Sprott, June 2, 1934, KCC.
208 *"Do see that C. goes":* EMF to Sprott, Oct. 14, 1929, KCC.
209 *"elderly man's love":* EMF, Locked Diary, Dec. 31, 1927, KCC.
209 *"solid" and "independent of mother":* EMF, Locked Diary, July 12, 1926, KCC.
209 *"an enormous boy":* EMF to Sprott, Sept. 15, 1928, KCC.
209 *"not to feel intact":* EMF to Charles Mauron, April 6, 1930; Lago and Furbank, eds., *Selected Letters,* II:91–92.
209 *"O, [the] celebrated author":* EMF to JRA, n.d., early 1925, HRC.
209 *"could have an intellectual basis":* Ibid.
209 *"Morgan's friends hushed their voices":* Daley to Furbank, date obscured, March–April 1968.
209 *"loom up on the reader":* Forster, "Notes on *Maurice,*" in *Maurice,* 218.
210 *"the knowledge that I couldn't":* EMF, Locked Diary, Dec. 31, 1927, KCC.
210 *"Those tickets cost 4/9":* EMF to Daley, July 18, 1926, quoted in Furbank, *E. M. Forster,* II:141.
210 *"Don't worry, old Morgan's got plenty":* Daley to EMF, quoted ibid., 143.
211 *"Don't rebuke, don't arguefy":* EMF to JRA, April 9, 1928, HRC.
211 *"decayed morale or the natural":* EMF, Locked Diary, Dec. 31, 1928, KCC.
211 *"in old age, looked after":* EMF to JRA, quoted in Furbank, *E. M. Forster,* II:159. The letter dates from 1929.
211 *"Coarseness and tenderness":* EMF, Locked Diary, March 24, 1925, KCC.
211 *"superficial itch for intimacy":* EMF, Locked Diary, Oct. 24, 1923, KCC.
211 *"Is a lie necessary?":* EMF to JRA, n.d., Monday [Nov. 1924], HRC.
212 *"signs of fertility":* EMF to JRA, June 22, 1926, HRC.
212 *"1 Scotchman, 1 Colonial":* EMF to JRA, Dec. 15, 1926, HRC.
212 *"If you want a permanent":* EMF to JRA, April 9, 1928, HRC.

212 *"uncle in the clothes trade"*: Furbank, *E. M. Forster*, II:186.

212 *"I was 250 years old"*: EMF to JRA, early Aug. 1929, HRC.

213 *"is slowly dispatching him"*: Virginia Woolf to Vanessa Bell, May 19, 1926; Nicholson and Trautmann, eds., *The Letters of Virginia Woolf*, 266.

213 *"T. E. liked to meet people"*: Forster, "T. E. Lawrence," in A. W. Lawrence, ed., *T. E. Lawrence by His Friends*, 247.

213 *"I wanted to read"*: TEL to EMF, Sept. 8, 1927, in Malcolm Brown, ed., *T. E. Lawrence: The Selected Letters*, 368.

214 *"an awful tease"*: Forster, "T. E. Lawrence," in A. W. Lawrence, ed., *T. E. Lawrence by His Friends*, 247.

214 *"did not like being touched"*: Ibid., 248.

214 *"forthcoming volume of stories"*: EMF to TEL, Dec. 16, 1927, KCC.

214 *"promises to be [my] last"*: Ibid.

214 *"the frail house of old"*: Ibid.

214 *"hanker at all after"*: Ibid.

215 *"intellectually null"*: F. R. Leavis to Oliver Stallybrass, quoted in Furbank, *E. M. Forster*, II:144.

215 *"Give us also the right"*: Hall, *The Well of Loneliness*, 506.

215 *"[the novel] is a seductive"*: *Sunday Express*, Aug. 19, 1928.

216 *"defendants have it in mind"*: Home Office to Sir Archibald Bodkin, Oct. 22, 1928, National Archives DPP 1/92.

216 *"sodomy & sapphism"*: *The Diaries of Virginia Woolf*, III:193, Aug. 31, 1928.

216 *"Soon we were telephoning"*: Virginia Woolf to Vita Sackville-West, Aug. 30, 1928; Nicholson and Trautmann, eds., *The Letters of Virginia Woolf*, III:520.

216 *"Radclyffe scolds him"*: Ibid.

216 *"meritorious dull book"*: *The Diaries of Virginia Woolf*, III:193, Aug. 31, 1928.

216 *"disgusting: partly from conventions"*: Ibid.

217 *Hall's book embraced:* Ibid.

217 *"Would you like to be converted"*: Ibid.

217 *"comic little letter"*: Virginia Woolf to Vita Sackville-West, Sept. 8, 1928; Nicholson and Trautmann, eds., *The Letters of Virginia Woolf*, III:530; Forster, "The New Censorship," *The Nation and Athenaeum*, Sept. 1, 1928.

217 *"What with being blackmailed"*: EMF to Sprott, n.d., Nov. 1928, KCC.

217 *"She swears I shan't be"*: EMF to JRA, Nov. 16, 1928, HRC.

218 *"summoned for advice and sympathy"*: EMF to Sprott, n.d., Nov. 1928, KCC.

218 *"read the wrong book"*: Ibid.

218 *"I calmed down rather quickly"*: Ibid.

218 *"was always frightened"*: Daley to Furbank, date obscured, 1968.

218 *"'Love' seems hardly the right"*: Daley, *This Small Cloud*, 135.

219 *"I feel sickish"*: EMF to JRA, Nov. 13, 1930, HRC.

219 *"I don't blame you"*: EMF to JRA, Feb. 14, 1931, HRC.

219 *"On Harry it is as easy"*: EMF to JRA, Jan. 3, 1928, HRC.

219 *"Hammersmith is a complete"*: EMF to JRA, Jan. 5, 1928, HRC.

219 *"I am so glad you are"*: EMF to JRA, n.d., August [?] 1926, HRC.

219 *"rather unhappy"*: Carrington to Sprott, early March 1929, in Garnett, ed., *Carrington*, 405.

220 *"something of . . . Mae West"*: Ackerley, *My Father and Myself*, 20.

10: "A LITTLE LIKE BEING MARRIED"

221   *"not really a reading man"*: Daley to Furbank, April 12, 1968.

221   *"amused protective kindness"*: Daley to Furbank, date obscured, late March 1968.

222   *"I must re-emphasise the need"*: EMF to JRA, Jan. 14, 1931, HRC.

222   *"I am quite sure"*: EMF to Sprott, July 16, 1931; Lago and Furbank, eds., *Selected Letters*, II:105.

222   *"fallen very violently"*: Ibid.

222   *"fayish"*: LS to Roger Senhouse, April 21, 1931; Levy, ed., *The Letters of Lytton Strachey*, 642.

222   *"a spiritual feeling"*: EMF to Sprott, July 16, 1931; Lago and Furbank, eds., *Selected Letters*, II:105.

222   *"Mr. Bucknam"*: Furbank, *E. M. Forster*, II:167.

222   *"found Policeman Bob"*: Carrington to Sprott, summer 1931, KCC.

223   *"completely unlike"*: Forster, "Notes on *Maurice*," in *Maurice*, 216.

223   *"Bob was the man"*: Daley to Furbank, March 21, 1968.

223   *"lover and beloved"*: EMF to Sprott, Oct. 4, 1932; Lago and Furbank, eds., *Selected Letters*, II:112.

223   *"Bob, aged 5"*: These entries, both from the Locked Diary, are undated, added to the verso sides of entries in 1909 and 1915.

224   *"Olive"*: Alexander, *William Plomer*, 231.

224   *"unguardeed moment"*: Furbank, *E. M. Forster*, II:178.

225   *"John Lehmann is back"*: EMF to Sprott, Sept. 21, 1933, KCC.

225   *"At Duncan [Grant]'s show"*: "Lilies," VW to Quentin Bell, Dec. 21, 1933; Nicholson and Trautmann, eds., *The Letters of Virginia Woolf*, V:262; "Bugger Boys," *The Diaries of Virginia Woolf*, V:120, Nov. 30, 1937.

225   *"youthful interest in everything"*: Forster, *Goldsworthy Lowes Dickinson* (Abinger), 196.

225   *"unreal"*: Ibid., 197.

225   *"chiefly occupied in saving"*: Ibid.

225   *"Mrs. Newman his bedmaker"*: EMF to Malcolm Darling, Aug. 24. 1932, HRC.

226   *"If he fails me"*: EMF to JRA, Nov. 10, 1932, HRC.

226   *"He must be made"*: EMF to Sprott, Oct. 4, 1932, Lago and Furbank, eds., *Selected Letters*, II:112; EMF to Sprott, July 16, 1931, Lago and Furbank, eds., *Selected Letters*, II:105.

226   *"We've got to go"*: EMF to Sprott, Oct. 11, 1932, KCC.

226   *"Yesterday when I went"*: Ibid.

227   *"When I cannot 'get'"*: EMF to Sprott, Oct. 4, 1932, Lago and Furbank, eds., *Selected Letters*, II:112.

227   *"the greatest imaginative novelist"*: Forster, "D. H. Lawrence," *Nation and Athenaeum*, March 29, 1930.

227   *"I have had such a shock"*: EMF to Frieda Lawrence, March 4, 1930, Lago and Furbank, eds., *Selected Letters*, II:91.

228   *"I continue to read"*: EMF to JRA, Feb. 12, 1933, HRC.

228   *"I wish I could"*: EMF to JRA, Jan. 10, 1933, HRC.

228   *"in the hope that"*: Proctor, ed., "Introduction" to *The Autobiography of Goldsworthy Lowes Dickinson*, 9.

228   *"My present feeling"*: GLD to EMF, July 10, 1932, KCC.

229   *"Unlike the green bird"*: Forster, *A Passage to India*, 85.

229 *"Although he was never"*: Forster, *Goldsworthy Lowes Dickinson*, 47.

229 *"Devoted to [Ferdinand] Schiller"*: Ibid., 63.

229 *"I have seldom been"*: Ibid., 56.

229 *"I think that few"*: Ibid., 58.

230 *"Mephistopheles . . . puts his head"*: Ibid., 199.

230 *"rested on the constancy"*: Forster on Carpenter, in Beith, ed., *Edward Carpenter*, 81.

230 *"interest . . . the next generation"*: *The Diaries of Virginia Woolf*, V:314, Sept. 2, 1940.

230 *"Bob's son born"*: EMF, Locked Diary, April 21, 1933, KCC.

230 *"I nearly dropped in"*: EMF to BB, Sunday [early June 1933], Lago and Furbank, eds., *Selected Letters*, II:117.

231 *"Harry . . . is always yapping"*: EMF, Locked Diary, Dec. 26, 1933, KCC.

231 *"I now know that"*: May Buckingham, "Some Reminiscences," reprinted in J. H. Stape, ed., *E. M. Forster: Interviews and Recollections*, 77.

231 *"The happiest hours"*: EMF to BB, Sunday [early June 1933], Lago and Furbank, eds., *Selected Letters*, II:117.

232 *"Bob met me"*: EMF to FB, July 4, 1932, KCC.

232 *"I have sometime thought"*: EMF to CI, Aug. 28, 1938, Huntington; Lago and Furbank, eds., *Selected Letters*, II:158.

232 *"I have been happy"*: Gardner, ed., *Commonplace Book* (1932), 94.

233 *"Yes, if the pendulum"*: EMF to CI, July 16, 1933, Huntington; Lago and Furbank, eds., *Selected Letters*, II:118-19.

233 *"put on the next"*: Parker, *Christopher Isherwood*, 277.

234 *"Delighted!"*: Humphrey Carpenter, *W. H. Auden*, 176.

234 *"What are buggers for?"*: Allen, *As I Walked Down New Grub Street*, 56.

234 *"It's on Thomas Mann"*: Ibid., 58.

234 *"a line of affection"*: EMF to Sassoon, Nov. 6, 1933, quoted in Furbank, *E. M. Forster*, II:181.

234 *"Your news, though I accept"*: EMF to Sassoon, Nov. 8, 1933, quoted ibid.

235 *"he seemed quite genuine"*: EMF to JRA, Dec. 1, 1933, HRC.

235 *"little private talk"*: *The Diaries of Virginia Woolf*, IV:357, Dec. 14, 1935.

235 *"You must try"*: EMF to ACF, Nov. 30, 1932, KCC.

235 *"I felt it was"*: EMF to ACF, Dec. 6, 1932, KCC.

235 *"Will now have some"*: Ibid.

235 *"I have an open"*: EMF to BB, Dec. 16, 1935, KCC.

235 *"I don't expect mother"*: EMF to JRA, March 17, 1936, HRC.

236 *"I was thinking yesterday"*: EMF to JRA, Feb. 19, 1936, HRC.

11: "THE LAST ENGLISHMAN"

237 *"terribly authoritarian"*: EMF to Forrest Reid, Sept. 4, 1942, quoted in Furbank, *E. M. Forster*, II:252.

237 *"last parlourmaid in England"*: Furbank, *E. M. Forster*, II:235.

238 *"big house"*: Forster, "West Hackhurst: A Surrey Ramble," KCC.

238 *"You and R."*: EMF to May Buckingham, June 16, 1935, KCC.

238 *"very decent sort"*: EMF to CI, Sept. 9, 1935, Huntington.

239 *"I felt a bit"*: EMF to BB, Sat. [Feb. 20, 1943], Lago and Furbank, eds., *Selected Letters*, II:201.

240 *"Meum"*: TEL to Francis Rodd, Nov. 23, 1934, in Malcolm Brown, ed., *T. E. Lawrence: The Selected Letters*, 500.

240 *"telegrams and anger"*: Forster, *Howards End*, 25.

241 *"dégringolade"*: Forster, "The Lost Guide," in *Alexandria*, 355.

241 *"I don't suppose"*: EMF to VW, June 6, 1935, in Furbank, *E. M. Forster*, II:193.

241 *"condition of society"*: Gide, quoted in Shattuck, *The Innocent Eye*, 23.

241 *"does evil that evil"*: Forster, "Liberty in England," *Abinger Harvest*, 61.

241 *"does many things"*: Ibid.

241 *"not take up arms"*: Shattuck, *The Innocent Eye*, 9.

241 *"I don't think anyone"*: EMF to CI, Feb. 17, 1934, in Parker, *Christopher Isherwood*, 281, and Huntington.

242 *"every one may know"*: EMF to JL, July 12, 1935, quoted in Furbank, *E. M. Forster*, II:196.

242 *"It means freedom"*: Forster, "Liberty in England," *Abinger Harvest*, 60.

242 *"The hungry and the homeless"*: Ibid., 61.

242 *Sedition Act:* Officially called the Incitement to Disaffection Act (1934).

242 *"encourages the informer"*: Ibid., 62.

243 *"My colleagues . . . may feel"*: Ibid., 65.

243 *"[Forster] paid no attention"*: Katherine Anne Porter, "Paris, 1935" in J. H. Stape, ed., *E. M. Forster: Interviews and Recollections*, 15–16.

243 *"pantomime of malignant ridicule"*: Ibid.

244 *"But Gide hasn't got"*: Parker, *Ackerley*, 338.

244 *"In England, more than anywhere"*: Forster, "Liberty in England," *Abinger Harvest*, 64.

244 *"distinguished backs"*: Forster, "Gide's Death," in *Two Cheers*, 232.

244 *"many eulogies of Soviet culture"*: Forster, quoted in Saunders, "What Have Intellectuals Ever Done for the World," 3.

244 *"[s]ad as ever"*: DHL to EMF, Feb. 19, 1924; Roberts et al., eds., *The Letters of D. H. Lawrence*, IV:584.

245 *"exploited for their . . . factitious"*: Forster, "Mrs. Miniver," in *Two Cheers*, 300.

245 *"the brassy rattle"*: EMF to FB, Aug. 25, 1917, KCC.

245 *"Some people call its absences"*: Forster, "What I Believe," in *Two Cheers*, 71.

245 *"going mad"*: Isherwood, *Down There on a Visit*, 162.

245 *"[Morgan] is as anxious"*: Isherwood, *Down There on a Visit*, 162, 175.

246 *"Though Italy and King's"*: Auden, "To E. M. Forster," preface to *Journey to a War*.

246 *"I've been studying"*: Forster, "Seven Days Hard," March 10, 1934, Lago et al., *The BBC Talks*, 124.

247 *"All I can do"*: Mitchison, *You May Well Ask*, 106.

247 *"We are willing enough"*: Forster, "The Tercentenary of the 'Areopagitica,'" in *Two Cheers*, 54.

247 *"Long, long ago"*: Forster, "Jew-Consciousness," in *Two Cheers*, 12–13.

248 *"liberalism crumbling beneath him"*: EMF to WP, Feb. 9, 1938, Durham; *Two Cheers*, 76.

248 *"I do not believe"*: Forster, "What I Believe," in *Two Cheers*, 67.

248 *"I hate the idea"*: Ibid., 68.

248 *"to keep away"*: EMF to CI, July 10, 1939, Huntington.

248 *"I have myself to face a world"*: EMF to WP, March 21, 1943, Durham.

248 *"Whatever one does"*: EMF to CI, Sept. 1, 1939, Huntington.

249 *"London, the Olde World"*: Parker, *Christopher Isherwood*, 578; EMF to CI, April 21, 1940, Huntington.

249 *"demi-vierges"*: Alexander, *William Plomer*, 233.

249 "What a wildness": Gardner, ed., *Commonplace Book*, 150.

249 would *"look after Robin and May"*: EMF to BB, April 21, 1939, KCC; Lago and Furbank, eds., *Selected Letters*, II:164.

249 *"Truly we live in strange times"*: EMF to BB, July 19, 1939, KCC; Lago and Furbank, eds., *Selected Letters*, II:167–68.

250 *"What does concern me"*: EMF to JRA, Saturday n.d. [late July 1938], HRC.

250 *"Joe—, you must give up looking"*: EMF to JRA, Aug. 18, 1939, HRC.

250 But Joe had *"altered"*: EMF to WP, June 12 and Sept. 25, 1943, Durham.

250 *"I love and have loved you"*: EMF to JRA, Sept. 25, 1943, HRC.

250 *"I must seem selfish"*: EMF to JRA, n.d. [c. Sept. 27, 1943], HRC.

251 The shock of her death: EMF to JRA, June 8, 1941, HRC; EMF to BB, April 4, 1941, KCC.

251 *"Like all her friends"*: Forster, "Virginia Woolf," in *Two Cheers*, 258.

251 she *"always seems in the next room"*: EMF to CI, July 25, 1942, Huntington.

251 *"be wary of melancholy"*: Ibid.

252 The notebook's cover: KCC, catalogue number xvi/5–C. The catalogue dates the contents page c. 1942, but a slightly later date is more likely, because Forster changed his habits to be less guarded after Lily's death. He unlocked his Locked Diary, for example. The date of the most recent published writing copied into the book is 1958. The artist who painted the "Lest We Forget Him!" poster was Cyrus Cuneo, 1879–1916. Cuneo was born in the United States, but emigrated to Britain in 1903. He made a good living as a commercial artist, publishing drawings in the *Illustrated London News*. His patriotic war paintings were very popular; several were auctioned to raise money for the war effort. A civilian, he died of septicemia after being accidentally jabbed by a hatpin.

252 *"the last of my race"*: EMF to CI, March 17, 1938, Huntington.

252 *"Johnny, Reg, Charles Lovett"*: EMF to JRA, Sept. 8, 1939, HRC.

252 *"I have violent longings"*: EMF to CI, June 8, 1942, Huntington.

252 *"already almost blind"*: Ibid.

252 *"not an aristocracy of power"*: Forster, "What I Believe," in *Two Cheers*, 73.

253 *"queer race"*: Cadmus was unapologetic about his sexuality, and always preferred to be known as a queer. Interview with Jon Anderson, Oct. 10, 2007, Westport, Conn.

253 *"the admiration and devotion"*: PC to EMF, Dec. 12, 1943, Jon Anderson. Copy in KCC.

254 *"Dearest Morgan, If this ever reaches you"*: CI to EMF, July 27, 1943, KCC. Isherwood spells Bill's surname as "Roehrick." He adopted Roerick as a stage name.

254 *"quickly became attached"*: EMF to CI, Feb. 10, 1944, Huntington.

254 *"I quite like being pelted"*: EMF to WP, "Weds" [1943], Durham.

254 *"Bob twice k'd me"*: EMF, Diary, Sept. 1939, KCC.

254 *"Although my mother has been"*: EMF to JRA, n.d. [1938], HRC.

255 *"Now I am older"*: EMF, Locked Diary, Jan. 22, 1953, KCC.

255 *"No," he replied tenderly*: Interview with P. N. Furbank, June 6, 2008, London.

255 *"I partly died"*: EMF to CI, Aug. 26, 1945, Huntington: quoted in Furbank, *E. M. Forster*, II:259.

255 *"masses of rubbish"*: EMF to CI, May 9, 1945, Huntington.

255 *"destroying things"*: Ibid.; EMF to WP, April 15, 1945, Durham.

255 *"What I shall do"*: EMF to CI, May 9, 1945, Huntington.

255 Each time he *"broke down"*: Ibid.

256 *"ungovernable temper"*: Quoted in Furbank, *E. M. Forster*, II:220.

256 *"I feel like a sponge"*: EMF to BB, Oct. 8, 1945, KCC; quoted ibid., II:260.

256 *"I look back on myself"*: EMF, Indian Diary, KCC.

256 *"I returned to more worry and sadness"*: EMF to CI, April 1, 1946, Huntington.

257 *"the year I was driven out"*: Gardner, ed., *Commonplace Book*, 169.

257 *"I see myself as a historic figure"*: EMF to WP, July 3, 1946, Durham.

257 *"My mother's death"*: EMF to CI, April 1, 1946, Huntington.

257 *"rubbishy word"*: EMF, Locked Diary, Oct. 22, 1946, KCC.

258 the house of his *"childhood and safety"*: EMF, Locked Diary, July 15, 1944, KCC.

258 *"had been left [at West Hackhurst]"*: EMF, Locked Diary, June 1, 1945, KCC.

258 *"surely she will give up being dead"*: EMF, Locked Diary, Sept. 6, 1945, KCC.

258 *"O Bless Bob"*: EMF, Locked Diary, Dec. 31, 1947, KCC.

12: "MY DEAR AMERICA"

259 a *"ratty little"* melodrama: Roerick, "Forster and America," in Oliver Stallybrass, ed., *Aspects of E. M. Forster*, 64.

260 *Bill and Tom revered him:* A student correspondent from the Hamilton College newspaper described Forster's visit in ecstatic terms: "E. M. Forster was here. But what can any person say about Percivale or Galahad or Bors . . . ? We did experience the holiness of the holiness of the real Forster through his art . . . So it is that we have been blessed by the sweetness of Harmony." *Here and There*, June 1949, 7.

261 *"worried because he was not a University man"*: EMF, American Journal, April 7, 1947, KCC. The journal, coincident with Forster's journey in the spring of 1947, does not routinely record dates. It is in a small, singular notebook.

261 *"true intellectuals"*: Interview with Mary Jackson, Hollywood, Aug. 6, 2002.

261 *"is not Tom the funniest person"*: The inscription is carved on the back of Tom Coley's tombstone in Tyringham, Massachusetts.

262 *She once agreed:* Correspondence with Heather Thompson, Aug. 31, 2007.

262 *"I think," Morgan said drily:* Roerick, "Forster and America," in Oliver Stallybrass, ed., *Aspects of E. M. Forster*.

262 *"an unprepossessing man"*: Giroux, "Meeting 'An Old and Valued Author,'" in J. H. Stape, ed., *E. M. Forster: Interviews and Recollections*, 91.

263 *it looked very like a whale:* Ibid., 95.

263 *"Be good, sir"*: EMF, American Journal, April 20, 1947, KCC.

263 *"on the fringe of the habitable sections"*: PC to EMF, May 7, 1944, copy in KCC.

264 *"long haired men"*: Chauncey, "Long Haired Men," in *Greenwich Village*, 153.

264 *"an unwarranted insult"*: *Time*, April 30, 1934; quoted in Kirstein, *Paul Cadmus*, 25.

265 *the greasy spoon was a destination:* Chauncey, *Gay New York*, 166f.

265 *"Fairyland's not far from"*: Chauncey, "Long Haired Men," 152.

265 *"You can't imagine how stuffy"*: EMF to PC, July 30, 1944, KCC.

265 *before they could make "suitable arrangements"*: EMF to BB, May 8, 1947, KCC.

265 *"delicious prosciutto"*: EMF, American Journal, April 20, 1947, KCC.

265 *"the flat is Bloomsbury"*: Ibid.

265 *"that cleverly blends in"*: PC to EMF, May 7, 1944, KCC.

266 *furniture so worm-eaten:* Ibid.

266 *an amiable "sun burnt rodent"*: EMF, American Journal, April 20, 1947, KCC.

266 *"the only true bisexual" man:* Interview with Jon Anderson, Oct. 10, 2007.

267 *"surly and morose"*: Duberman, *The Worlds of Lincoln Kirstein*, 414. Duberman's quote is from an interview with George Tooker.

268 *"I don't look like your Bohemian"*: PC to EMF, May 7, 1944, KCC.

268 *"Paul Cadmus must protect himself"*: EMF, American Journal, June 29, 1947, KCC.

268 *"more blood and more allurement"*: EMF to Sprott, May 24, 1947, KCC.

269 *"a charming place for rich Americans"*: EMF, American Journal, April 20, 1947, KCC; "The Raison d'Être of Criticism in the Arts," in *Two Cheers for Democracy*, 47.

269 a *"sketchy, uncomfortable, but somehow comforting" male place:* Roerick, "Forster and America," in Oliver Stallybrass, ed., *Aspects of E. M. Forster.*

269 *"thousands and thousands of birch trees"*: Forster, "The United States," in *Two Cheers*, 332.

269 *"a highly refined stylized symbolized fertility rite"*: Burkat, "Letter from America," 8.

269 *"an unusual state"*: Forster, *Two Cheers*, 118.

270 *"James or someone strumming"*: EMF to BB, May 15, 1947, KCC.

270 *He encountered wondrous sights:* EMF, American Journal, n.d., 1947; EMF to BB, June 5, 1947, KCC.

270 *"I don't like to take your money"*: Forster, "The United States," in *Two Cheers*, 334.

270 *"not correct psychically"*: EMF to Sprott, May 29, 1947, KCC.

271 *"I am just doing"*: EMF to BB, June 5, 1947, KCC.

271 *"I have made an impression"*: EMF, American Journal, June 7, 1947, KCC.

271 *"What a contrast"*: EMF to JRA, May 31, 1947, HRC; Lago and Furbank, eds., *Selected Letters*, II:224.

271 *"the negroes don't on the whole"*: EMF to Sprott, June 15, 1947, KCC.

271 *"I have had breakfast"*: EMF to JRA, May 31, 1947, HRC; Lago and Furbank, eds., *Selected Letters*, II:224.

271 *The second verse:* Correspondence with Mark Lancaster, March 10, 2007.

272 *"All England convulsed"*: EMF, Locked Diary, June 22, 1935, KCC.

272 *"We know how much"*: EMF, American Journal, May 19, 1947, KCC.

272 *"where clothes are stolen"*: Ibid.

273 a *"trigger-happy bruiser"*: Phelps, ed., *Continual Lessons*, 180.

273 in *"deepest Greenwich Village"*: EMF to JRA, May 31, 1947, HRC; Lago and Furbank, eds., *Selected Letters*, II:224.

273 *"It is a charming place"*: EMF to Sprott, June 15, 1947, KCC.

273 *cackling at the power of Morgan's imagination:* Interview with Bernard Perlin, Pound Ridge, N.Y., Sept. 30, 2001.

273 *"one of the great loves"*: Duberman, *The Worlds of Lincoln Kirstein*, 326.

274 With his *"fluttering black eyelashes"*: Bucknell, ed., *Christopher Isherwood: Diaries,* I:210.

274 *"the fruited plain"*: Chauncey, *Gay New York*, 182.

274 he reflected on *"the kindness"*: EMF, American Journal, June 27, 1947, KCC.

274 He *"felt to belong"*: Ibid.

274 *"My diamond [insight]"*: EMF, American Journal, July, 14, 1947.

275   *"into the fat hands"*: EMF, American Journal, June 29, 1947.

275   *"in this kindest of lands"*: EMF, American Journal, July 12, 1947.

275   *"the pinchability of Rubens"*: EMF to Monroe Wheeler, Oct. 2, 1945, Beinecke.

13: "I FAVOR RECIPROCAL DISHONESTY"

276   *"present goodness warmth"*: EMF to JRA, April 11, 1951, HRC.

276   *Morgan "disliked" Gore Vidal:* EMF to CI, June 25, 1948, Huntington.

276   *"Bob's indifference to me"*: EMF, Locked Diary, Oct. 8, 1948, KCC.

276   *"After three miserable days"*: Ibid.; quoted in Furbank, *E. M. Forster*, II:282.

277   *He imagined that the reason:* EMF, Locked Diary, Dec. 27, 1948, KCC.

278   *"I* have *got so fat"*: EMF to PC, April 21, 1949, KCC.

278   *He asked Morgan:* Britten to Henriette Bösmans, March 18, 1949; Mitchell et al., eds., *Letters from a Life*, 499.

278   *"a bleak little place"*: Forster, "George Crabbe: The Poet and the Man," in Brett, *Benjamin Britten: Peter Grimes*, 3.

278   *"the sweetest people"*: EMF to WP; Furbank, *E. M. Forster*, II:282.

279   *The adjoining room:* Humphrey Carpenter, *Benjamin Britten*, 257.

279   *"For my dear Morgan"*: Mitchell et al., eds., *Letters from a Life*, 363.

280   *a "savage fisherman"*: Forster, "George Crabbe: The Poet and the Man," in Brett, *Benjamin Britten: Peter Grimes*, 4.

280   *"such a feeling of nostalgia"*: Brett, *Benjamin Britten: Peter Grimes*, 148.

280   *"To talk about Crabbe"*: Forster, "George Crabbe: The Poet and the Man," ibid., 3.

280   *Crabbe's "uncomfortable mind"*: Ibid., 10, 11.

280   *the same "inner tension"*: Ibid., 18.

280   *Morgan's "revealing article"*: Britten, "On Receiving the First Aspen Award" (1964), in Humphrey Carpenter, *Benjamin Britten*, 156.

280   *"Would you rather I loved"*: Pears's Grimes monologue, quoted in Philip Brett, "Peter Grimes in Progress" in Brett, *Benjamin Britten: Peter Grimes*, 50.

280   *He quoted Crabbe directly:* Forster, "George Crabbe and Peter Grimes," in *Two Cheers*, 177.

281   *whose "behavior was excusable"*: Pears, quoted in Brett, *Benjamin Britten: Peter Grimes*, 57.

281   *"The more I hear of it"*: Pears to Britten, letter 1189, Mitchell et al., eds., *Letters from a Life*, 1.

281   *a complicated, closeted opera:* Matthias, "The Haunting of Benjamin Britten," 4.

281   *"Music had a warmth"*: EMF, Diary, Nov. 5, 1963, KCC.

281   *the same "telepathic and simultaneous" thought:* Britten quoted in Humphrey Carpenter, *Benjamin Britten*, 270.

281   *to "keep human beings"*: EMF to Britten, Dec. 20, 1948, Lago and Furbank, eds., *Selected Letters*, II:235.

281   *"an old man who has experienced much"*: Forster, Crozier, and Britten, *Billy Budd*, 7.

282   *his job was "rescuing . . . Vere"*: EMF to Lionel Trilling, April 16, 1949, Columbia; Lago and Furbank, eds., *Selected Letters*, II:237.

282   *Placing the gorgeous, innocent figure of Billy:* EMF to WP, March 10, 1949, Durham.

282   *"Why is it Vere's touch"*: EMF to Lionel Trilling, April 16, 1949, Columbia; Lago and Furbank, eds., *Selected Letters*, II:237.

282   *"soggy depression or growling remorse"*: EMF to Britten, early Dec. 1950, Lago and Furbank, eds., *Selected Letters*, II:242.

283 *"yet he is Billy, not Christ"*: EMF to Britten, Dec. 20, 1948, Lago and Furbank, eds., *Selected Letters*, II:235.

283 *"immersed in Billy Budd"*: Crozier to Nancy Evans, March 4, 1949, Mitchell et al., eds., *Letters from a Life*, 497.

283 *"sixteen remarkable Billy Budd days"*: EMF, Diary, April 12, 1949, KCC.

283 *the "welter of technical [naval] terms"*: Crozier to Nancy Evans, Fri. [March 11, 1949], Mitchell et al., eds., *Letters from a Life*, 498.

283 *"typically generous"*: Crozier to Nancy Evans, March 4, 1949, quoted in Humphrey Carpenter, *Benjamin Britten*, 282.

283 *"going through a period of revulsion"*: Crozier to Nancy Evans, March 6, 1949, quoted ibid.

283 *"The great goodness and love of Bob"*: EMF, Diary, April 12, 1949, KCC.

283 *Morgan began to plan:* Ibid.

283 *"ought to be away from England"*: EMF to PC, Feb. 21, 1949, copy at KCC.

284 *"I wish you could have [sketched] Bob"*: EMF to PC, April 21, 1949, copy at KCC.

284 *"It was sad not seeing you"*: EMF to PC, June 18, 1949, KCC.

284 *"Mr. Forster['s] lifelong beloved"*: GW to Bernard Perlin, April 20, 1949, Beinecke.

284 *"'For being Morgan'"*: EMF, American Journal, 1949, KCC.

284 *He crowed to a friend:* GW to Bernard Perlin, April 20, 1949, Beinecke.

284 *"profound but not disturbing"*: EMF to GW, Feb. 28, 1949, Beinecke.

285 *"In the American culture"*: Rosco, *Glenway Wescott*, 19.

285 *a "prophet of a New America"*: Ibid., 46. This is the headline of a review in the *Boston Evening Transcript*.

285 *"Glenway Wescott, Thornton Wilder and Julian Green"*: Ibid., 41.

285 *"When you matriculate at the University of Chicago"*: Stein, *The Autobiography of Alice B. Toklas*, 200.

285 *"Freud Madox Fraud"*: Rosco, *Glenway Wescott*, 24.

286 *"Dear Little George"*: Phelps, ed., Lynes, Wheeler correspondence, 1927–29, Beinecke.

286 *It was Glenway's "own fault"*: GW to George Platt Lynes, June 24, 1927, Beinecke.

286 *The three men lived:* Phelps, ed., *Continual Lessons*, 107. This is from a letter to Lloyd and Barbara Wescott, Feb. 26, 1943.

287 *"seemed to consider the world a gift"*: Windham, *Tanaquil*, 84. *Tanaquil* is a novel, and this phrase describes Page, a photographer modeled on George Platt Lynes.

287 *"worldliness personified"*: Wescott, ms. of "A Dinner, a Walk, a Talk . . . ," Beinecke.

287 *was "worried about it"*: GW to Bernard Perlin, June 1, 1949, Beinecke.

288 *linking "ancient and primitive religions"*: Program, The American Academy of Arts and Letters and the National Institute of Arts and Letters Ceremonial Program, May 27, 1949.

288 *It presented the "actual behavior of people"*: Kinsey et al., *Sexual Behavior in the Human Male*, 3; quoted in Gathorne-Hardy, *Sex the Measure of All Things*, 259.

289 *four percent of the men:* Kinsey et al., *Sexual Behavior*, 651.

289 *may have deliberately shaped his method:* Gathorne-Hardy, *Sex the Measure of All Things*, 259.

289 *"all the staff"*: LK to CI, "Aug. last, 1949," Huntington.

289 *"went like a charm"*: GW to CI, May 16, 1949, Huntington.

290 *"the cancer of unenforceable laws"*: Wescott, ms. of "A Dinner, a Walk, a Talk . . . ," Beinecke.

290 *not as much to "lumbermen, cattlemen, prospectors, miners and hunters"*: Kinsey et al., *Sexual Behavior*, 631, 633.

290 *Glenway was "surprised"*: GW to CI, May 16, 1949, Huntington.

290 *"I favor reciprocal dishonesty"*: Monroe Wheeler datebook, Aug. 1949, Beinecke.

290 *"I must say that it comforted me"*: Wescott, "A Dinner, a Walk, a Talk . . . ," in J. H. Stape, ed., *E. M. Forster: Interviews and Recollections*, 107.

291 *"Effeminacy is only a manner"*: GW to CI, Sept. 20, 1971. Despite the date of the letter, GW makes it clear that the quotations are taken from contemporaneous notes on Forster's conversation.

291 *"A writer . . . who chose"*: Forster, "Art for Art's Sake," in *Two Cheers*, 88.

291 *"I am the outsidest of outsiders"*: EMF to PC, Oct. 31, 1943. He is referring both to his limitation as a visual observer and his status as an artist.

291 *"I would sooner be a swimming rat"*: Forster, *Two Cheers*, 93–94.

292 *"beat it" to Glenway's farm*: GW to EMF, Feb. 20, 1949, Beinecke.

292 *"nature to advantage dress'd"*: Alexander Pope, "Essay on Criticism," II:297–98.

292 *"I don't even use my truncheon"*: Wescott, "A Dinner, A Walk, a Talk . . . ," in J. H. Stape, ed., *E. M. Forster: Interviews and Recollections*, 105.

292 *"Mutual secrecy"*: Forster, *Aspects of the Novel*, 47.

293 *"perfect for each other"*: Interview with Jon Anderson, Oct. 10, 2007.

293 *"the toughest man"*: LK to CI, April 26, 1950, Huntington.

293 *"reject[ing] intimacy without impairing affection"*: Forster, "T. E. Lawrence," in A. W. Lawrence, ed., *T. E. Lawrence by His Friends*, 285.

293 *"Now, don't you see better?"*: Wescott, "A Dinner, A Walk, a Talk . . . ," in J. H. Stape, ed., *E. M. Forster: Interviews and Recollections*, 106.

294 *"[w]hen a camera approaches"*: Roerick, "Forster and America," in Oliver Stallybrass, ed., *Aspects of E. M. Forster*, 62.

294 *"the subject whom he was photographing"*: Windham, "Which Urges," 27.

294 *"When Lynes photographed me"*: Ibid.

296 *"the greatest collection of dirty art in the world"*: LK to CI, "Aug. last, 1949," Huntington.

296 *"great affection for America"*: EMF to GW, Nov. 22, 1951, Beinecke.

296 *"The American life would have proved unendurable"*: Wescott, ms. of "A Dinner, a Walk, a Talk . . . ," Beinecke. Though GW refers to "someone" telling him this, Kirstein, Cadmus, and Isherwood were likely his sources.

296 *"Sometimes I wish"*: EMF to Monroe Wheeler, Jan. 1951, Beinecke.

296 *a suspected "cancer?"*: EMF, Diary, Dec. 27, 1948, KCC.

297 *"a tendency to dry-dock feeling"*: Eric Crozier quoted in Humphrey Carpenter, *Benjamin Britten*, 287.

297 *"in a funny abstracted mood"*: Britten to Erwin Stein, quoted ibid., 297.

297 *"one of [my] corpses"*: Mitchell et al., eds., *Letters from a Life*, 521. Letter from Crozier to Nancy Evans, July [n.d.] 1949.

298 *"Morgan was slow"*: Burrell, quoted in Humphrey Carpenter, *Benjamin Britten*, 290.

298 *"To me, [Morgan] was chilly but polite"*: Crozier quoted ibid., 290.

298 *"berated [Ben] like a schoolboy"*: Crozier to Furbank, in Furbank, *E. M. Forster*, II:285.

298 *"I am rather a fierce old man"*: EMF, Diary, Dec. 31, 1950, KCC.

298 *"Heavens the excitement"*: EMF to Tom Coley, Nov. 21, 1951.

299 *a way to "wrestle with the void"*: EMF, Diary, June 29, 1950, KCC.

299 *"gnawed by my failure"*: Ibid.
299 *"As for Bob,"*: EMF, Diary, Dec. 31, 1950, KCC.
299 *"but not at an accessible layer"*: Ibid.
299 *"a little polished shell"*: Ibid.

14: "THE WORM THAT NEVER DIES"
301 *"offered a Knighthood"*: EMF to JRA, Dec. 2, 1949, HRC. Morgan told Ackerley that he was surprised to have been approached, since Benjamin Britten had a theory that the king would not offer a knighthood to a homosexual.
301 *"the nursing home"*: EMF to BB, Dec. 2, 1949, KCC.
301 *"I seem to be a Great Man"*: Ackerley, *E. M. Forster*, 3.
301 *"My fame is much more of a pleasure"*: EMF, Locked Diary, Jan. 10, 1949, KCC.
302 *"if the Queen had been a boy"*: Furbank, *E. M. Forster*, II:289.
302 *"Well, I got my little toy"*: Quoted ibid.
302 *the boy with "a tattoo on his fingers"*: EMF to WP, n.d., Durham.
302 *Their friendship was a "prank"*: EMF, Locked Diary, May 11, 1966, KCC.
303 *"deprived of a house"*: Forster, *Marianne Thornton*, 205.
304 *"I assumed the letters would be nothing much"*: EMF to Furbank, July 16, 1958. Lago and Furbank, eds., *Selected Letters*, II:271.
304 *a "silly idle useless unmanly little boy"*: Forster, "The Other Boat," in *The Life to Come*, 170.
304 *"Two people made to destroy each other"*: Furbank, *E. M. Forster*, II:303. This entry is from Furbank's diary, dated Oct. 25, 1958.
305 *"Peace Broke Out"*: Crisp, *The Naked Civil Servant*, 167.
305 *"forecasts an allotment in Hell"*: EMF to WP, March 27, 1954, Durham.
305 *a "vast ham"*: EMF, Locked Diary, Dec. 27, 1948.
306 *"the vices of Sodom and Gomorrah"*: November 4, 1953, quoted in Furbank, *E. M. Forster*, II:335, 334.
306 *Newspapers were in a race*: Higgins, *Heterosexual Dictatorship*, 288–90. Higgins includes a facsimile of the article; Weeks, *Coming Out*, 163.
307 *"Incomprehensible and utterly disgusting"*: Forster, "Society and the Homosexual: A Magistrate's Figures," *The New Statesman*, Oct. 31, 1953; Lord Samuels to EMF, Nov. 29, 1953, quoted in Furbank, *E. M. Forster*, II:335.
307 *The Wolfenden Report recommended*: Higgins, *Heterosexual Dictatorship*, 115. The recommendation was number one of nine.
307 *"mild and aetiolated"*: Weeks, *Coming Out*, 156.
307 *the "distasteful" subjects*: Wolfenden, June 20, 1955, in Higgins, *Heterosexual Dictatorship*, 15.
307 *"I think the only thing we can do"*: Dr. Eustace Chesser, quoted ibid., 19.
308 *homosexual behavior was "catching"*: Rev. Dr. Holland, quoted ibid., 26.
308 *He was only one of a "number of homosexuals"*: Houlbrook, *Queer London*, 254. This is from an undated memo of the committee in the Public Records office.
308 *a purported "orgy of perversion"*: Parker, *Ackerley*, 228–29. Coverage, including JRA's letter, in *The Spectator*, Nov. (20 and 27) and Dec. (4 and 18), 1942.
308 *"in the vanguard of darkness"*: EMF, Locked Diary, Oct. 12, 1939, KCC.
309 *"Note in conclusion"*: Forster, *Maurice*, 220.

309 *he wrote a letter to* The Times: The letter was printed in *The Times*, Dec. 11, 1959.
309 *defended the honor of the "married women":* EMF, Letter to *The Times*, May 9, 1958.
310 *"The older one grows":* EMF, Locked Diary, Oct. 27, 1958, KCC.
310 *"the police here are filthy as anywhere":* EMF, Locked Diary, July 11 to 17, 1964, KCC.
310 *Bobbie's "entrance arrangements were culpably slack":* EMF to JRA, Jan. 7, 1958, HRC.
310 *"Be frisky":* EMF to JRA, n.d., Jan. 1958, HRC; quoted in Parker, *Ackerley*, 338.
310 *"touched . . . his clothes":* EMF, "Notes on the Future of Civilisation," undated ms., KCC.
310 *"[Liberace] is the summit of sex":* The Times, June 12, 1959.
311 *"cost me many years":* Pyron, *Liberace*, 228.
311 *"My feelings [about homosexuality]":* New York Times, June 9, 1959, 43.
311 *he had "laughed all the way to the bank":* Pyron, *Liberace*, 168. The first instance of Liberace using this phrase is a letter dated to 1954. But he repeated it as a laugh line in his performances after the Cassandra case.
311 *"very high literary merit":* EMF, quoted in Furbank, *E. M. Forster*, II:312.
311 *"did D. H. Lawrence":* EMF to JRA, Dec. 4, 1960, HRC.
311 *"I am very excited":* EMF to WP, Dec. 4, 1932, Durham.
312 *"a handsome boy":* JRA to EMF, n.d. [c. 1958], quoted in Parker, *Ackerley*, 402.
312 *"I sometimes have the frightened feeling":* EMF to WP, Jan. 4, 1956, Durham.
312 *"He was everything to me":* EMF, Locked Diary, Dec. 31, 1955, KCC.
312 *"She has been as if dead":* EMF to JRA, Thurs. [March 10, 1960], Lago and Furbank, eds., *Selected Letters*, II:276; n.d., winter 1960–61, HRC; EMF to JRA, Oct. 16, 1961; quoted in Furbank, *E. M. Forster*, II:317.
313 *the "very sad loss":* EMF, Locked Diary, Dec. 1966, KCC; EMF to JRA, Aug. 4, 1960, HRC.
313 *"seven feet tall":* LK to CI, April 26, 1950, Huntington.
313 *"sitting side by side":* EMF, Locked Diary, April 14, 1962, KCC.
313 *"Little Clive":* EMF, Locked Diary, Jan. 16, 1962, KCC.
314 *"Dec. 25. Thinking of Mary's wretched life":* EMF, Locked Diary, Dec. 25, 1962, KCC.
314 *"As soon as a man":* EMF, Locked Diary, Jan. 16, 1962, KCC.
314 *"the joyful resurgence":* EMF, Locked Diary, Jan. 7, 1963, KCC.
314 *"The worm that never dies":* EMF, Locked Diary, April 21, 1962, KCC.
314 *"not the least afraid of dying":* EMF to Eric Fletcher, Sept. 24, 1951, KCC.
314 *"I was told the Dead were upstairs":* Gardner, ed., *Commonplace Book*, 227.
315 *"convinced me that death is nothing":* Ibid., 231.
315 *"No pain, no fear":* Ibid.
315 *"A stroke":* Ibid., 256.
315 *to "see the light of night":* EMF, Locked Diary, Dec. 1, 1961, KCC.
315 *the "enigmatic mass":* Forster, "Little Imber" ms., KCC.
316 *William began gathering "autobiographicalia":* Plomer, "Notes Toward a Biography," Plomer archive, Durham.
316 *"M. said he wanted it made clear":* Ibid.
316 *"the undocumented, invisible":* Duffy, *Voices of Morebath*, 67.
316 *"I want to love a strong young man":* EMF, Sex Diary [c. 1935, emended 1959], KCC.
317 *He had "disintegrated":* EMF, Locked Diary, Dec. 1, 1961, KCC.
317 *"endless abusive exchanges with bus conductors":* Daley to Furbank, Nov. 24, 1968.
317 *"Every one in the long run":* Ibid.
317 *"triangular correspondence ":* Parker, *Ackerley*, 424.

318 *"easy and pleasant"*: EMF to JRA, Nov. 14, 1966, HRC; quoted in Parker, *Ackerley*, 427.

318 it *"would have been balanced better"*: EMF to WP, April 4, 1943, Durham.

319 *One version of the book*: Parker, *Ackerley*, 316, 317.

319 *"How I do agree with you"*: EMF to WP, Oct. 29, 1968, Durham; the book was published after Ackerley's death, in Sept. 1968.

319 *"I should have been a more famous writer"*: EMF, Sex Diary [n.d., c. 1965], KCC.

320 *"Let us pretend"*: Plomer, "Forster as a Friend," in Oliver Stallybrass, ed., *Aspects of E. M. Forster*, 104.

320 *"He believed—literally"*: Furbank, *E. M. Forster*, II:295.

320 *"it seemed perfectly right"*: Plomer, "Forster as a Friend," in Oliver Stallybrass, ed., *Aspects of E. M. Forster*, 101–2.

320 *"With his integrity and intelligence"*: Forster, "A View Without a Room" in *A Room with a View*, 212.

320 *"When they begin to sing"*: Furbank, *E. M. Forster*, II:297.

321 *"It was a grey day"*: EMF, Locked Diary, June 26, 1964, KCC.

321 *"The butterfly was a moving glint"*: Ibid.

322 *"The poor Bucks"*: CI to WP, May 6, 1967, Durham.

322 *"reverted to the 'beautiful friendship' theory"*: John Morris to WP, Aug. 23, 1972, Durham.

322 *"Had it not occurred to them"*: Ibid.

323 whose *"defence at any last Judgement"*: EMF to Forrest Reid, March 13, 1915, KCC.

Bibliography

ARCHIVES

Beinecke: Beinecke Rare Book and Manuscript Library, Yale University (Lynes, Wescott, Wheeler)

Columbia: Columbia University Archives (Trilling)

Durham: Durham University Archives (Plomer and Morris)

HRC: Harry Ransom Center for the Humanities, University of Texas at Austin (Ackerley, British Society for Sex Psychology, Darling)

Huntington: Christopher Isherwood Collection, Huntington Library, San Marino, California

KCC: King's College Modern Archives, Cambridge University (Buckinghams, Dickinson, Forster, Sprott, Strachey)

New York Public Library for the Performing Arts at Lincoln Center, Lincoln Kirstein Papers (Kirstein and Martinez)

Smithsonian Institution, Archives of American Art

PRIVATE COLLECTIONS

David Adkins (Roerick and Coley)

Gwyneth Barger (Harold Barger)

Mollie Barger (Florence Barger, Evert Barger, Mollie Barger)

P. N. Furbank (Daley)

PUBLICATIONS

Ackerley, J. R. *E. M. Forster: A Portrait*. London: Ian McKelvie, 1970.

———, ed. *Escapers All*. London: Bodley Head, 1932.

———. *Hindoo Holiday*. New York: Viking, 1932.

———. *My Dog Tulip*. New York: Poseidon Press, 1965.

———. *My Father and Myself*. New York: Harcourt Brace, 1968.

———. *Prisoners*. London: Chatto and Windus, 1925.

———. *We Think the World of You* (1960). New York: Simon and Schuster, 1988.

Adams, Phoebe. "Prisoner of the Perverse." *Atlantic Monthly*, September 1964, 122–23.

Aldrich, Robert. *Colonialism and Homosexuality*. New York: Routledge, 2002.

Alexander, Peter F. *William Plomer: A Biography*. Oxford: Oxford University Press, 1989.

Allen, Walter Ernest. *As I Walked Down New Grub Street: Memories of a Writing Life*. Chicago: University of Chicago Press, 1981.

Annan, Noel. *The Dons: Mentors, Eccentrics and Geniuses*. London: HarperCollins, 2000.

———. *Our Age: English Intellectuals Between the World Wars, a Group Portrait*. New York: Random House, 1990.

———. "Preface," in Dennis Proctor, ed., *The Autobiography of Goldsworthy Lowes Dickinson*.

Anstruther, Ian. *Oscar Browning: A Biography*. London: John Murray, 1983.

Arlott, John. "Forster and Broadcasting," in Oliver Stallybrass, ed., *Aspects of E. M. Forster: Essays and Recollections Written for His Ninetieth Birthday, Jan. 1, 1969*, 87–93.

Armstrong, James. "The Publication, Prosecution, and Re-Publication of James Hanley's *Boy* (1931)." *Library* 19:4 (1997), 351–62.

Arran, Lord. "The Sexual Offenses Act." *Encounter*, March 1972, 3–9.

Ashby, Margaret. *Forster Country*. Stevenage, UK: Flaunden, 1991.

Auden, W. H. "Forward," in Forster, *Goldsworthy Lowes Dickinson*, ed. Oliver Stallybrass.

———. "Introduction" in Cavafy, *The Complete Poems of Cavafy*, trans. Rae Dalven. New York: Harcourt Brace Jovanovich, 1976.

———. "Papa Was a Wise Old Sly-Boots." *New York Review of Books*, March 27, 1969, 34.

Auden, W. H., and Christopher Isherwood. *Journey to a War*. New York: Random House, 1939.

Avery, Todd. *Radio Modernism: Literature, Ethics and the BBC, 1922–1938*. Burlington, Vt.: Ashgate, 2006.

Bachardy, Don. *One Hundred Drawings*. Los Angeles: Twelvetrees Press, 1983.

———. *Stars in My Eyes*. Madison: University of Wisconsin Press, 2000.

Bachardy, Don, and James P. White, eds. *Where Joy Resides: A Christopher Isherwood Reader*. New York: Michael di Capua, 1989.

Baedeker's Egypt. Leipzig: Karl Baedeker, 1914.

Bakshi, Parminder Kaur. "Homosexuality and Orientalism: Edward Carpenter's Journey to the East," in Tony Brown, ed., *Edward Carpenter and Late Victorian Radicalism*, 151–77.

Banerjee, Jacqueline. *Literary Surrey*. Headley Down, Hampshire, UK: John Owen Smith, 2005.

Barger, Evert. "Memories of Morgan." *New York Times Book Review*, Aug. 16, 1970.

Barnes, Clive. "Theatre: A Passage to E. M. Forster." *New York Times*, Oct. 28, 1970, 57.

Bartlett, Neil. *Who Was That Man: A Present for Mr. Oscar Wilde*. London: Serpent's Tail, 1988.

Bawer, Bruce. "Glenway Wescott: 1901–1987." *New Criterion*, May 1987, 36–45.

Baxter, Walter. *Look Down in Mercy*. London: Reader's Union, 1953.

Bayley, John. "Sex and the City." *New York Review of Books*, March 25, 2004, 17–18.

Beard, Rick, and Leslie Cohen Berlowitz, eds. *Greenwich Village: Culture and Counter Culture*. New Brunswick, N.J.: Rutgers University Press, 1993.

Beauman, Nicola. *Morgan: A Biography of E. M. Forster*. London: Sceptre, 1993.

Beaver, Harold. "Homosexual Signs." *Critical Inquiry* 8:1 (1981), 99–119.

Bedford, Sybille. "Poor Old Chap! Review of Isherwood's *A Single Man*." *The Spectator*, Sept. 11, 1964, 343.

Beith, Gilbert, ed. *Edward Carpenter: In Appreciation*. London: George Allen and Unwin, 1931.

Belshaw, Patrick. *A Kind of Private Magic*. London: Andre Deutsch, 1994.

Benson, E. F. *As We Were: A Victorian Peep Show*. New York: Blue Ribbon, 1930.

Bergman, David. "J. R. Ackerley and the Ideal Friend," in Peter F. Murphy, ed., *Fictions of Masculinity*, 255–67.

Bien, Peter. "Cavafy's Homosexuality and His Reputation Outside Greece." *Journal of Modern Greek Studies* 8 (1990), 197–211.

———. *Constantine Cavafy*. Columbia Essays on Modern Writers. New York: Columbia University Press, 1964.

Bland, Lucy, and Laura Doan, eds. *Sexology in Culture: Labeling Bodies and Desires*. Chicago: University of Chicago Press, 1998.

Blyth, John A. *English University Adult Education, 1908–1958: The Unique Tradition*. Dover, N.H.: Manchester University Press, 1983.

Boone, Joseph Allen. *Libidinal Currents: Sexuality and the Shaping of Modernism*. Chicago: University of Chicago Press, 1998.

Boulton, George J., James T. Zytaruk, et al., eds. *The Letters of D. H. Lawrence*. 8 vols. Cambridge: Cambridge University Press, 1979–2000.

Boyle, Richard J., Hilton Brown, and Richard Newman, eds. *Milk and Eggs: The American Revival of Tempera Painting, 1930–1950*. Chadds Ford, Pa.: Brandywine Museum, 2002.

Braybrooke, Neville, ed. *The Ackerley Letters*. New York: Harcourt Brace Jovanovich, 1975.

Brett, Philip. "The Authority of Difference." *Musical Times*, 1993, 633–36.

———. *Benjamin Britten: Peter Grimes*. Cambridge Opera Handbooks. Cambridge: Cambridge University Press, 1983.

———. "Britten and Grimes." *Musical Times*, December 1977, 111–24.

———. *Music and Sexuality in Britten: Selected Essays*, ed. George E. Haggerty. Berkeley: University of California Press, 2006.

Bristow, Joseph. *Effeminate England: Homoerotic Writing after 1885*. New York: Columbia University Press, 1995.

———, ed. *Sexual Sameness: Textual Differences in Lesbian and Gay Writing*. New York: Routledge, 1992.

Brown, Malcolm, ed. *T. E. Lawrence: The Selected Letters*. New York: Norton, 1989.

Brown, Tony, ed. *Edward Carpenter and Late Victorian Radicalism*. London: Frank Cass, 1990.

Browning, Frank. *The Culture of Desire: Paradox and Perversity in Gay Lives Today*. New York: Vintage, 1994.

———. *A Queer Geography: Journeys Toward a Sexual Self*. New York: Crown, 1996.

Buckingham, May. "Some Reminiscences," in G. K. Das and John Beer, eds., *E. M. Forster: A Human Exploration: Centenary Essays*, 183–85.

Bucknell, Katherine, ed. *Christopher Isherwood: Diaries. Volume One. 1939–1960*. London: Vintage, 1996.

———, ed. *Christopher Isherwood, Lost Years: A Memoir. 1945–1951*. New York: HarperCollins, 2000.

Bullough, Vern L., ed. *Before Stonewall: Activists for Gay and Lesbian Rights in Historical Context*. New York: Harrington Park Press, 2002.

Burkat, Leonard. "Letter from America." *Tempo* 4 (Summer 1947), 7–9.

Burnett, A. D. "A Literary Ghost: William Plomer's Proposed Biographical Account of E. M. Forster." *Review of English Studies* XLVII:185 (1996), 53–59.

Burton, Peter. *Talking To ... Peter Burton in Conversation with Writers Writing on Gay Themes*. London: Third House, 1991.

Bush, Russell. *Affectionate Men: A Photographic History of a Century of Male Couples*. New York: St. Martin's Press, 1998.

Cadmus, Paul. "Interview" (1988). Archives of American Art, Smithsonian Institution.

Calisher, Hortense. "A Heart Laid Bare." *Washington Post*, Jan. 13, 1991, I5.

Capote, Truman. *Music for Chameleons*. New York: Random House, 1980.

Carpenter, Edward. *Days with Walt Whitman with Some Notes on His Life*. New York: Macmillan, 1906.

———. *Edward Carpenter: Selected Writings, Volume One: Sex*. London: GMP, 1984.

———. *Homogenic Love and Its Place in a Free Society*. Manchester: Labour Press Society, 1894.

———. *Iolaus: An Anthology of Friendship*. London: Swan Sonnenschein, 1902.

———. *Love's Coming of Age*. New York: Mitchell Kennerley, 1922.

———. *My Days and Dreams*. London: George Allen and Unwin, 1916.

———. *Narcissus and Other Poems*. London: Henry S. King, 1873.

———. *Towards Democracy*. London: George Allen and Unwin, 1883.

Carpenter, Humphrey. *Benjamin Britten: A Biography*. London: Faber and Faber, 1992.

———. *W. H. Auden: A Biography*. Boston: Houghton Mifflin, 1981.

Carter, Miranda. *Anthony Blunt: His Lives*. New York: Farrar, Straus and Giroux, 2001.

Cavafy, C. P. *The Complete Poems of Cavafy* (1961). Trans. Rae Dalven. New York: Harcourt Brace Jovanovich, 1976.

Chapman, R. W., ed. *Jane Austen: Selected Letters* (1955). Oxford: Oxford University Press, 1985.

Charlton, Lionel Evelyn Oswald. *More Charlton*. London: Longmans, Green and Co., 1940.

Chauncey, George. "Christian Brotherhood or Sexual Perversion? Homosexual Identities and the Construction of Sexual Boundaries in the World War I Era," in Martin Bauml Duberman et al., eds., *Hidden from History: Reclaiming the Gay and Lesbian Past*, 294–317.

———. *Gay New York: Gender, Urban Culture, and the Making of the Gay Male World, 1890–1940*. New York: Basic Books, 1994.

———. "Long Haired Men and Short Haired Women: Building a Gay World in the Heart of Bohemia," in Rick Beard and Leslie Cohen Berlowitz, eds., *Greenwich Village: Culture and Counter Culture*, 151–65.

———. "The Policed: Gay Men's Strategies of Everyday Resistance," in William R. Taylor, ed., *Inventing Times Square*, 315–328.

———. *Why Marriage? The History Shaping Today's Debate over Gay Equality*. New York: Basic Books, 2004.

Childs, Peter, ed. *E. M. Forster's A Passage to India*. London: Routledge, 2002.

Claudel, Paul-André. "'De la part d'un ami sans visage': Agostino J. Sinadino, 1876–1956, un poète sans profil: Correspondance inédite avec André Gide." *Studi Francesi* 147 (2005), 565–98.

Cocks, H. G. *Nameless Offences: Homosexual Desire in the Nineteenth Century*. London: I. B. Tauris, 2003.

Coley, Thomas. *Our Town Remembered*. New York: Hudson Rudd, 1982.

Coley, Thomas, and William Roerick. "A Passage to E. M. Forster." Unpublished play, David Adkins.

Cooke, Mervyn. *The Cambridge Companion to Benjamin Britten.* Cambridge: Cambridge University Press, 1999.

Cooper, Emmanuel. *Fully Exposed: The Male Nude in Photography.* New York: Routledge, 1995.

Cooper, John M., ed. *Plato: Complete Works.* Indianapolis: Hackett Publishing, 1997.

Cozzolino, Robert Marshall, N. Price, and M. Melissa Wolfe, eds. *George Tooker.* London: Merrell, 2008.

Craft, Robert. "Tea in Cambridge," in J. H. Stape, ed., *E. M. Forster: Interviews and Recollections,* 24–26.

Crisp, Quentin. *The Naked Civil Servant.* New York: Penguin Classics, 1997.

Crozier, Eric, ed. *Benjamin Britten: Peter Grimes, Vol. 3.* London: Sadlers Wells Opera Books, 1946.

Crozier, Ivan. "Becoming a Sexologist: Norman Haire, the 1929 London World League for Sexual Reform Congress, and Organizing Medical Knowledge About Sex in Interwar England." *History of Science* XXXIX (2001): 299–329.

Crump, James. *George Platt Lynes: Photographs from the Kinsey Institute.* New York: Little Brown, 1993.

Culme-Seymour, Mary. "Memories of E. M. Forster," in J. H. Stape, ed., *E. M. Forster: Interviews and Recollections,* 80–89.

Cummings, Dave. "'Now with My Hand I Cover Africa': A Love Poem Sent by Stephen Spender to William Plomer." *Journal of European Studies* 32:2–3 (2002), 223–33.

Curley, Daniel. "The Reality of Love: Review of Isherwood's *A Single Man.*" *New Leader* 18 (Jan. 1965), 22–23.

Daiches, David. "Life Without Jim." *New York Times Book Review,* Aug. 30, 1964, 5, 16.

Daley, Harry. *This Small Cloud.* London: Weidenfeld and Nicolson, 1986.

Das, G. K. *E. M. Forster's India.* Totowa, N.J.: Rowman and Littlefield, 1977.

Das, G. K., and John Beer, eds. *E. M. Forster: A Human Exploration: Centenary Essays.* New York: New York University Press, 1979.

Davenport, Guy. *The Drawings of Paul Cadmus.* New York: Rizzoli International, 1989.

David, Hugh. *On Queer Street: A Social History of British Homosexuality, 1895–1995.* London: HarperCollins, 1997.

Davidson, Michael. *The World, the Flesh and Myself* (1962). London: GMP, 1985.

Davies, John Llewellyn. *The Working Men's College, 1854–1954.* London: Routledge, 1954.

Deitcher, David. *Dear Friends: American Photographs of Men Together, 1840–1918.* New York: Harry Abrams, 2001.

de Jongh, Nicholas. *Not in Front of the Audience: Homosexuality on Stage.* London: Routledge, 1992.

Delavenay, Emile. *D. H. Lawrence and Edward Carpenter: A Study in Edwardian Transition.* London: Heinemann, 1971.

Dellamora, Richard. "Textual Politics/Sexual Politics." *Modern Language Quarterly* 54:1 (1993), 155–64.

Dent, Edward. "Angel Wings," in Gilbert Beith, ed., *Edward Carpenter: In Appreciation.*

Deslandes, Paul R., ed. *Oxbridge Men: British Masculinity and the Undergraduate Experience, 1850–1920.* Bloomington: Indiana University Press, 2005.

Dewey, Clive. *Anglo-Indian Attitudes: The Mind of the Indian Civil Service.* London: Hambledon Press, 1993.

Dickinson, Goldsworthy Lowes. *Appearances: Being Notes of Travel.* London: Dent and Sons, 1914.

———. *The Choice before Us.* London: George Allen and Unwin, 1917.

———. *The Greek View of Life.* London: Methuen, 1989.

———. *Proposals for the Avoidance of War.* N.p., 1915.

———. *Sex Life in Greece and Rome.* Little Blue Book No. 163. Girard, Kans.: Haldeman-Julius, 1924.

Doan, Laura, and Jay Prosser, eds. *Palatable Poison: Critical Perspectives* on The Well of Loneliness. New York: Columbia University Press, 2001.

Doctor, Jenny. "Afterword," in Philip Brett, *Music and Sexuality in Britten: Selected Essays*, 225–46.

Dowling, Linda. *Hellenism and Homosexuality in Victorian England.* Ithaca, N.Y.: Cornell University Press, 1994.

Driberg, Tom. *Ruling Passions.* Briarcliff Manor, N.Y.: Stein and Day, 1979.

Duberman, Martin. *About Time: Exploring the Gay Past.* New York: Penguin, 1986.

———. *Cures: A Gay Man's Odyssey.* Boulder: Westview Press, 2002.

———. *The Worlds of Lincoln Kirstein.* New York: Knopf, 2007.

Duberman, Martin Bauml, Martha Vicinus, and George Chauncey, Jr., eds. *Hidden from History: Reclaiming the Gay and Lesbian Past.* New York: Penguin New American Library, 1989.

Duffy, Eamon. *The Voices of Morebath: Reformation and Rebellion in an English Village.* New Haven: Yale University Press, 2001.

Dunne, Bruce W. "French Regulation of Prostitution in Nineteenth-Century Colonial Algeria." *Arab Studies Journal* 2:1 (1994), 24–30.

———. "Power and Sexuality in the Middle East." *Middle East Report*, Spring 1998, 8–11.

———. "Sexuality and the Civilizing Process." Ph.D. diss., Georgetown University, 1996.

Dyhouse, Carol. *Students: A Gendered History.* New York: Routledge, 2006.

Egremont, Max. *Siegfried Sassoon: A Biography.* London: Picador, 2005.

Ehenrenstein, David. *Open Secret: Gay Hollywood, 1928–2000.* New York: HarperCollins, 2000.

Elia, John P. "History, Etymology and Fallacy: Attitudes Toward Male Masturbation in the Ancient Western World." *Journal of Homosexuality* 14:3/4 (1987), 1–19.

Eliasoph, Philip. *Paul Cadmus: Yesterday & Today.* Oxford, Ohio: Miami University Press, 1981.

Ellem, Elizabeth. "E. M. Forster's Arctic Summer." *Times Literary Supplement*, Sept. 21, 1973, 1087–89.

———. "E. M. Forster: The Lucy and the New Lucy Novels." *Times Literary Supplement*, May 28, 1971, 623–24.

Ellenzweig, Allen. *The Homoerotic Photograph: Male Images from Durieu/Delacroix to Mapplethorpe.* New York: Columbia University Press, 1992.

Ellimann, Michael, and Frederick Roll, eds. *The Pink Plaque Guide to London.* London: GMP, 1986.

Ellis, Havelock. *My Life.* New York: Houghton Mifflin, 1939.

———. *Studies in the Psychology of Sex.* 2 vols. New York: Random House, 1936.

———. *The Task of Social Hygiene.* London: Constable, 1912.

Epstein, Joseph. "Maurice, by E. M. Forster." *New York Times Book Review*, Oct. 10, 1971, 1.

Faulks, Sebastian. *The Fatal Englishman: Three Short Lives.* New York: Vintage, 1996.

Fieldhouse, Roger. *A History of Modern British Adult Education.* Leicester, U.K.: National Institute of Adult Continuing Education, 1996.

Finney, Brian. *Christopher Isherwood: A Critical Biography*. New York: Oxford University Press, 1979.

Fletcher, John. "Forster's Self-Erasure: Maurice and the Scene of Masculine Love," in Joseph Bristow, ed., *Sexual Sameness: Textual Differences in Lesbian and Gay Writing*, 64–90.

Forster, E. M. *Abinger Harvest*. New York: Harcourt Brace, 1936.

———. *Abinger Harvest and England's Pleasant Land*. Abinger Edition, ed. Elizabeth Heine. London: Andre Deutsch, 1996.

———. *Alexandria: A History and a Guide* and *Pharos and Pharillon*. Abinger Edition, ed. Miriam Farris Allott. London: Andre Deutsch, 2004.

———. *Anonymity: An Enquiry*. London: Hogarth Press, 1925.

———. *Arctic Summer and Other Fiction*. Abinger Edition, ed. Elizabeth Heine and Oliver Stallybrass. London: Edward Arnold, 1981.

———. "Army English." *Egyptian Mail*, Jan. 12, 1919, 2.

———. *Aspects of the Novel* (1927). Abinger Edition, ed. Oliver Stallybrass. London: Edward Arnold, 1974.

———. *The Celestial Omnibus and Other Stories*. New York: Knopf, 1923.

———. "Charlie Day." Unpublished ms., King's College, Cambridge.

———. "De Senectute." *London Magazine* 4:11 (1957), 15–18.

———. "D. H. Lawrence." *The Listener*, Apr. 30, 1930, 753–56.

———. *The Eternal Moment and Other Stories*. New York: Harcourt Brace, 1928.

———. "Gippo English." *Egyptian Mail*, Dec. 16, 1919, 2.

———. *Goldsworthy Lowes Dickinson*. New York: Harcourt Brace, 1934.

———. *Goldsworthy Lowes Dickinson* (1934). Abinger Edition, ed. Oliver Stallybrass. London: Edward Arnold, 1973.

———. *The Government of Egypt: Recommendations*. London: Labour Research Department, 1921.

———. "Henry James and the Young Men." *The Listener*, July 16, 1959, 103.

———. *The Hill of Devi*. New York: Harcourt Brace, 1953.

———. *The Hill of Devi and Other Indian Writings*. Abinger Edition, ed. Elizabeth Heine. London: Edward Arnold, 1983.

———. *Howards End*. New York: G. P. Putnam's Sons, 1910.

———. *Howards End*. Abinger Edition. London: Edward Arnold, 1973.

———. "Incidents of War Notebook." King's College Modern Archives, 1915–1919.

———. *The Life to Come and Other Stories*. Abinger Edition, ed. Oliver Stallybrass. London: Edward Arnold, 1972.

———. *The Longest Journey* (1905). Abinger Edition, ed. Elizabeth Heine. New York: Holmes and Meier, 1984.

———. *The Machine Stops and Other Stories*. Abinger Edition, ed. Rod Mengham. London: Andre Deutsch, 1997.

———. "A Magistrate's Figures." *The New Statesman and Nation*, Oct. 31, 1953, 508–9.

———. *Marianne Thornton: A Domestic Biography*. New York: Harcourt Brace, 1956.

———. *Maurice: A Novel* (1971). Abinger Edition, ed. Philip Gardner. London: Andre Deutsch, 1999.

———. "The National Council for Civil Liberties." *Time and Tide*, July 5, 1941, 560–61.

———. "The New Censorship." *The Nation and Athenaeum*, Sept. 1, 1928, 696.

———. "Obituary for E.K. (Francis) Bennett." *The Caian* 55:3 (1959), 123–27.

———. *A Passage to India*. New York: Harcourt Brace, 1924.

————. *A Passage to India.* Abinger Edition, ed. Oliver Stallybrass. London: Edward Arnold, 1978.

————. *Pharos and Pharillon.* London: Hogarth Press, 1923.

————. "The Poetry of Cavafy," in Denise Harvey, ed., *The Mind and Art of C. P. Cavafy,* 13–18.

————. "Presidential Address to the Cambridge Humanists," Summer 1959, King's College, Cambridge.

————. "Prosecutions of Publishers." *The Spectator,* April 25, 1935, 696.

————. "The Psychology of Monarchy." *The New Statesman and Nation,* Feb. 11, 1936, 260.

————. *A Room with a View* (1908). Abinger Edition, ed. Oliver Stallybrass. London: Edward Arnold, 1977.

————. "A Room Without a View," in *A Room with a View,* Abinger Edition.

————. "Still the Sedition Bill!" *Time and Tide,* Oct. 27, 1934.

————. "Three Countries," in *The Hill of Devi and Other Indian Writings.*

————. "The Torque: An Unpublished Story." *Encounter,* July 1972, 3–11.

————. "Two Cheers for Democracy." *The Nation,* 1938, 65–66.

————. *Two Cheers for Democracy.* New York: Harcourt Brace, 1951.

————. *Where Angels Fear to Tread* (1907). Abinger Edition, ed. Oliver Stallybrass. London: Edward Arnold, 1975.

Forster, E. M., Eric Crozier, and Benjamin Britten. *Billy Budd.* London: Boosey and Hawkes, 1951.

Foucault, Michel. *A History of Sexuality.* 3 vols. New York: Pantheon, 1978.

Francis, Richard. *Mark Lancaster, Paintings.* Cambridge and New York: Walker Gallery, 1973.

Freud, Sigmund. *New Introductory Lectures on Psycho-Analysis,* trans. W. H. J. Sprott. London: L. and V. Woolf at the Hogarth Press, 1937.

Furbank, P. N. *E. M. Forster: A Life.* 2 vols. New York: Harcourt Brace Jovanovich, 1977.

————. "Introduction," in E. M. Forster, *A Passage to India.* New York: Everyman's Library, Knopf, 1991.

————. "Introduction," in J. R. Ackerley, ed., *We Think the World of You.* New York: Simon and Schuster, 1988.

————, ed. *The New Collected Stories of E. M. Forster.* London: Sidgwick and Jackson, 1985.

————. "The Personality of E. M. Forster." *Encounter,* Nov. 1970, 61–68.

Furbank, P. N., and F. J. H. Haskell. "E. M. Forster," in *Writers at Work: The Paris Interviews,* ed. George Plimpton. New York: Penguin, 1958, 24–35.

Furness, Robert Allason. *Poems of Callimachus.* London: Jonathan Cape, 1931.

Gardiner, James. *A Class Apart: The Private Pictures of Montague Glover.* London: Serpent's Tail, 1992.

————. *Who's a Pretty Boy Then? One Hundred Fifty Years of Gay Life in Pictures.* London: Serpent's Tail, 1996.

Gardner, Philip, ed. *E. M. Forster: Commonplace Book.* Stanford: Stanford University Press, 1985.

————. *E. M. Forster: The Critical Heritage.* London: Routledge and Kegan Paul, 1973.

————. "The Evolution of E. M. Forster's *Maurice,*" in Judith Scherer Herz and Robert K. Martin, eds., *E. M. Forster: Centenary Revaluations,* 204–24.

Garnett, David, ed. *Carrington: Letters and Extracts from Her Diary.* New York: Holt Rinehart & Winston, 1971.

Garver, Thomas H. *George Tooker.* San Francisco: Pomegranate Artbooks, 1992.

Gathorne-Hardy, Jonathan. *Sex the Measure of All Things: Alfred C. Kinsey, A Biography.* London: Pimlico, 1999.

Gellert, Roger. *Quaint Honour.* Gay Plays. Vol. II. Methuen: London, 1985.

Ghoussoub, Mai, and Emma Sinclair-Webb, eds. *Imagined Masculinities: Male Identity and Culture in the Modern Middle East.* London: Saqi, 2000.

Gilder, Cornelia Brook. *Views of the Valley: Tyringham 1739–1989.* Tyringham, Mass.: Hop Brook Community Club, 1989.

Giroux, Robert. "Meeting 'An Old and Valued Author,'" in J. H. Stape, ed., *E. M. Forster: Interviews and Recollections,* 91–98.

Gittings, Christopher E., ed. *Imperialism and Gender: Representations of Masculinity.* Hebden Bridge, U.K.: Dangaroo Press, 1996.

Goldman, Paul, and Brian Taylor, eds. *Retrospective Adventures: Forrest Reid, Author and Collector.* Oxford: Scolar Press, Ashmolean Museum, 1998.

Goodyear, Sara Suleri. *The Rhetoric of English India.* Chicago: University of Chicago Press, 1992.

Gorer, Geoffrey. "English Ideas About Sex." *Encounter,* Dec. 1953, 45–56.

———. *Exploring English Character.* New York: Criterion, 1955.

Grafftey-Smith, Laurence. *Bright Levant.* London: John Murray, 1970.

Grant Duff, Shiela. *The Parting of Ways: A Personal Account of the Thirties.* London: Peter Owen, 1982.

Green, W. C. *Memories of Eton and King's.* Eton College, U.K.: Spottiswoode and Co., 1905.

Grimes, Nancy. *Jared French's Myths.* San Francisco: Pomegranate Artbooks, 1993.

Grosskurth, Phyllis. *Havelock Ellis: A Biography.* London: Allen Lane, 1980.

———, ed. *The Memoirs of John Addington Symonds: The Secret Homosexual Life of a Leading 19th-Century Man of Letters.* New York: Random House, 1984.

———. *The Woeful Victorian: A Biography of John Addington Symonds.* New York: Holt Rinehart and Winston, 1964.

Gullace, Nicoletta F. "White Feathers and Wounded Men: Female Patriotism and the Memory of the Great War." *Journal of British Studies* 36:2 (1997), 178–206.

Haag, Michael. *Alexandria: City of Memory.* New Haven: Yale University Press, 2004.

Hall, Lesley A. "'Disinterested Enthusiasm for Sexual Misconduct': The British Society for the Study of Sex Psychology, 1913–1947." *Journal of Contemporary History* 30:4 (1995), 665–86.

———. "'The English Have Hot-Water Bottles': The Morganatic Marriage Between Sexology and Medicine in Britain since William Acton," in Roy Porter and Mikuláš Teich, eds., *Sexual Knowledge, Sexual Science.* Cambridge: Cambridge University Press, 1994, 350–66.

Hall, Radclyffe. *The Well of Loneliness.* New York: Blue Ribbon Books, 1928.

Haller, Gary. *Private Realisms: American Paintings, 1934–1949.* New Haven: Master's House, Jonathan Edwards College, Yale University, 2000.

Halperin, David. *Before Sexuality: The Construction of Erotic Experience in the Ancient Greek World.* Princeton, N.J.: Princeton University Press, 1990.

————. "Forgetting Foucault: Acts, Identities and the History of Sexuality," in Martha Nussbaum and Juha Sihvola, eds., *The Sleep of Reason: Erotic Experience and Sexual Ethics in Ancient Greece and Rome*, 21–55.

————. *How to Do the History of Homosexuality*. Chicago: Chicago University Press, 2002.

————. *One Hundred Years of Homosexuality and Other Essays on Greek Love*. London: Routledge, 1990.

Hammond, Toby [pseud.]. "Paedikion: A Paiderastic Manuscript." *International Journal of Greek Love* 1:2 (1966), 28–37.

Hanquart, Evelyne. "'Dearest my Joe': une Lecture des lettres de E. M. Forster à J. R. Ackerley (1922–1966)." *Cahiers d'Études & de Recherches Victoriennes et Édouardiennes* (1977), 100–111.

Hardwick, Elizabeth. "Sex and the Single Man." *New York Review of Books*, Aug. 20, 1964, 4.

Hart-Davis, Rupert, ed. *Siegfried Sassoon Diaries, 1920–1922*. London: Faber, 1985.

Harvey, Denise, ed. *The Mind and Art of C. P. Cavafy: Essays on His Life and Work*. Athens: Denise Harvey, 1983.

Hauser, Katherine. "George Tooker, Surveillance, and Cold War Sexual Politics." *GLQ: A Journal of Lesbian and Gay Studies* 11:3 (2005), 391–425.

Headington, Christopher. *Britten*. London: Holmes and Meier, 1982.

————. *Peter Pears: A Biography*. London: Faber and Faber, 1992.

Heath, Chris. "Pete Townshend: The Rolling Stone Interview." *Rolling Stone*, July 19, 2002.

Heath, Jeffrey M., ed. *The Creator as Critic and Other Writings by E. M. Forster*. Toronto: Dundern Press, 2008.

Heidt, Sarah. "'Let J A S Words Stand': Publishing John Addington Symonds's Desires." *Victorian Studies* 46:1 (2003), 7–31.

Henry, George. *Sex Variants: A Study of Homosexual Patterns*. Vol. II. New York: Paul Hoeber, 1941.

Herz, Judith Scherer. "E. M. Forster and the Biography of the Self." *Prose Studies* 5:2 (1982), 326–35.

————. "Forster's Three Experiments in Autobiographical Biography." *Studies in the Literary Imagination* 13:1 (1980), 51–67.

Herz, Judith Scherer, and Robert K. Martin, eds. *E. M. Forster: Centenary Revaluations*. London: Macmillan, 1982.

————. *The Short Narratives of E. M. Forster*. London: Macmillan, 1988.

Higgins, Patrick. *Heterosexual Dictatorship: Male Homosexuality in Postwar Britain*. London: Fourth Estate, 1996.

Higham, Charles. *Charles Laughton: An Intimate Biography*. Garden City, N.Y.: Doubleday, 1976.

Hoberman, Ruth. *Modernizing Lives: Experiments in English Biography, 1918–1939*. Carbondale: Southern Illinois University Press, 1987.

Hodges, Andrew, and David Hutter. *With Downcast Gays: Aspects of Homosexual Self-Oppression*. Toronto: Pink Triangle Press, 1979.

Holland, Merlin. *The Real Trial of Oscar Wilde: The First Uncensored Manuscript of the Trial of Oscar Wilde vs. John Douglas, Marquess of Queensbury, 1895*. New York: Fourth Estate, 2003.

Horne, Peter, and Reina Lewis, eds. *Outlooks: Lesbian and Gay Sexualities and Visual Cultures*. New York: Routledge, 1996.

Houlbrook, Matt. *Queer London: Perils and Pleasures in the Sexual Metropolis, 1918–1957.* Chicago: University of Chicago Press, 2005.

Howgate, Sarah, and Barbara Stern Shapiro. *David Hockney: Portraits.* New Haven: Yale University Press, 2006.

Husein, Iqbal, ed. *Justice Syed Mahmood Papers.* Aligarh, India: Aligarh Muslim University, 2005.

Hyde, H. Montgomery, ed. *The Trials of Oscar Wilde: Regina v. Queensbury; Regina v. Wilde and Taylor.* London: William Hodge and Company, 1952.

Hynes, Samuel Lynn. "The Old Man at King's: Forster at 85," in *Edwardian Occasions: Essays on English Writing in the Early Twentieth Century.* New York: Oxford University Press, 1972, 114–22.

Ibson, John. *Picturing Men: A Century of Male Relationships in Everyday American Photography.* Washington, D.C.: Smithsonian Institution Press, 2002.

Isherwood, Christopher. *Christopher and His Kind.* New York: Methuen, 1977.

———. *Down There on a Visit.* New York: Simon and Schuster, 1962.

———. *Exhumations: Stories; Articles; Verses.* London: Methuen, 1966.

———. *Lions and Shadows.* London: Hogarth Press, 1938.

———. *The Memorial* (1932). New York: Avon, 1974.

———. *A Single Man* (1964). Minneapolis: University of Minnesota Press, 2001.

Ives, [C.] George. *The Continued Extension of the Criminal Law.* London: J. B. Francis, 1922.

Jeffrey-Poulter, Stephen. *Peers, Queers and Commons: The Struggle for Gay Law Reform from 1950 to the Present.* London: Routledge, 1991.

Jeffreys, Peter. "Cavafy, Forster, and the Eastern Question." *Journal of Modern Greek Studies* 19 (2001), 61–87.

Jenkins, Nicholas, ed. *By with to & from: A Lincoln Kirstein Reader.* New York: Farrar, Straus and Giroux, 1991.

Johnson, David K. *The Lavender Scare: The Cold War Persecution of Gays and Lesbians in the Federal Government.* Chicago: University of Chicago Press, 2004.

Jones, James H. *Alfred C. Kinsey: A Public/Private Life.* New York: Norton, 1997.

Jusdanis, Gregory. *The Poetics of Cavafy: Textuality, Eroticism, History.* Princeton, N.J.: Princeton University Press, 1987.

Kauffman, Stanley. "Death in Venice, Cal." *The New Republic,* Sept. 5, 1964, 23–25.

Keeley, Edmund. *Cavafy's Alexandria.* Princeton, N.J.: Princeton University Press, 1996.

Keeley, Edmund, and Philip Sherrard, eds. *C. P. Cavafy: Collected Poems.* Princeton, N.J.: Princeton University Press, 1992.

Keynes, John Maynard. *Two Memoirs—"My Early Beliefs."* London: Rupert Hart-Davis, 1949.

Kidwai, Jalil Ahmad, ed. *Forster-Masood Letters.* Karachi: Education and Culture Society of Pakistan, 1984.

King, Francis. *Christopher Isherwood.* London: Longman, 1976.

———. *A Domestic Animal.* London: Longman, 1970.

———. *E. M. Forster and His World.* London: Thames and Hudson, 1978.

———, ed. *My Sister and Myself: The Diaries of J. R. Ackerley.* Oxford: Oxford University Press, 1990.

———. *Yesterday Came Suddenly.* London: Constable, 1993.

Kinsey, Alfred C., Wardell Baxter Pomeroy, and Clyde E. Martin. *Sexual Behavior in the Human Male.* Philadelphia: W. B. Saunders, 1948.

Kirkup, James. *A Poet Could Not but Be Gay: An Uninhibited Biography.* London: Peter Owen, 1991.

Kirstein, Lincoln. *Paul Cadmus.* New York: Chameleon Press, 1996.

———. *Quarry: A Collection in Lieu of Memoirs.* Pasadena: Twelvetrees Press, 1986.

Kynaston, David. *Austerity Britain, 1945–1951.* New York: Walker & Company, 2008.

Lago, Mary. *A Calendar of the Letters of E. M. Forster.* London: Mansell, 1985.

———. *E. M. Forster: A Literary Life.* London: Macmillan, 1995.

———. "E. M. Forster and the BBC." *Yearbook of English Studies* 20 (1990), 132–51.

Lago, Mary, and P. N. Furbank, eds. *Selected Letters of E. M. Forster.* 2 vols. Cambridge, Mass: Harvard: Belknap Press, 1985.

Lago, Mary, Linda K. Hughes, and Elizabeth MacLeod Walls, eds. *The BBC Talks of E. M. Forster, 1929–1960: A Selected Edition.* Columbia: University of Missouri Press, 2008.

Lagrange, Frederic. "Male Homosexuality in Modern Arabic Literature," in Mai Ghoussoub and Emma Sinclair-Webb, eds., *Imagined Masculinities: Male Identity and Culture in the Modern Middle East,* 169–99.

Lancaster, Mark. "Artist in Residence." *King's Parade* (2006), 16–17.

Lane, Christopher. *The Ruling Passion: British Colonial Allegory and the Paradox of Homosexual Desire.* Durham, N.C.: Duke University Press, 1995.

Law, Joe, and Linda K. Hughes, eds. *Biographical Passages: Essays on Victorian and Modernist Biography.* Columbia: University of Missouri, 2000.

Lawrence, A. W., ed. *T. E. Lawrence by His Friends.* London: Jonathan Cape, 1937.

Lawrence, T. E. *The Mint: A Day Book of the R.A.F. Depot Between August and December 1922, with Later Notes.* London: Jonathan Cape, 1955.

Leavitt, David. *The Man Who Knew Too Much: Alan Turing and the Invention of the Computer.* New York: Norton, 2005.

Leavitt, David, and Mark Mitchell, eds. *Pages Passed from Hand to Hand: The Hidden Tradition of Homosexual Literature in English from 1748 to 1914.* New York: Houghton Mifflin, 1997.

Leddick, David. *Intimate Companions: A Triography of George Platt Lynes, Paul Cadmus, Lincoln Kirstein and Their Circle.* New York: St. Martin's Press, 2000.

———. *Naked Men: Pioneering Male Nudes, 1935–1955.* New York: Universe Publishing, 1997.

Leedham-Green, Elisabeth. *A Concise History of the University of Cambridge.* Cambridge: Cambridge University Press, 1996.

Lehmann, John. *Christopher Isherwood: A Personal Memoir.* New York: Henry Holt, 1988.

———. *In My Own Time.* Boston: Little, Brown & Co., 1969.

———. *In the Purely Pagan Sense* (1976). London: GMP, 1985.

———. *The Whispering Gallery: Autobiography I.* New York: Harcourt Brace, 1955.

Lelyveld, David. *Aligarh's First Generation: Muslim Solidarity in British India.* Princeton, N.J.: Princeton University Press, 1978.

———. "Macaulay's Curse: Sir Syed and Syed Mahmood." Unpublished paper.

Leontis, Artemis, Lauren E. Talalay, and Keith Taylor, eds. *What These Ithakas Mean: Readings in Cavafy.* Athens: Hellenic Literary and Historical Archive, 2002.

Levine, June Perry. "The Tame in Pursuit of the Savage: The Posthumous Fiction of E. M. Forster." *PMLA* 85:1 (1970), 284–94.

Levine, Philippa. *Prostitution, Race, and Politics: Policing Venereal Disease in the British Empire.* London: Routledge, 2003.

Levy, Paul, ed. *The Letters of Lytton Strachey*. New York: Farrar, Straus and Giroux, 2005.

Lewis, Anthony. "E. M. Forster Homosexual Novel Due." *New York Times*, Nov. 11, 1970, 1.

Lewis, Edward. *Edward Carpenter: An Exposition and an Appreciation*. New York: Macmillan, 1915.

Liddell, Robert. *Cavafy*. New York: Simon and Schuster, 1974.

———. *Unreal City* (1953). London: Peter Owen, 1995.

Livingstone, Marco, David Hockney, and Kay Heymer. *Hockney's Portraits and People*. London: Thames and Hudson, 2003.

Ludden, David. *India and South Asia: A Short History*. Oxford: Oneworld Publications, 2002.

Mahmud, S. F. *A Concise History of Indo-Pakistan*. Karachi: Oxford University Press, 1988.

Malik, Hafeez. *Sir Sayyid Ahmad Khan and Muslim Modernization in India and Pakistan*. New York: Columbia University Press, 1980.

Mandler, Peter. "New Towns for Old: The Fate of the Town Centre," in Frank Mort et al., eds., *Moments of Modernity: Reconstructing Britain, 1945–1964*, 208–27.

Mannin, Ethel. *Confessions and Impressions*. London: Jarrolds, 1930.

Martin, Kingsley. "The Abominable Crime." *The New Statesman and Nation*, Oct. 31, 1953, 508.

Martin, Robert K. "Appeals from Across Some Frontier: The Novels of John Lehmann," in A. T. Tolley, ed., *John Lehmann: A Tribute*. Ottawa: Carleton University Press, 1987, 6–67.

———. "Edward Carpenter and the Double Structure of *Maurice*." *Journal of Homosexuality* 8:3/4 (1983), 35–46.

———. "The Paterian Mode in Forster's Fiction: *The Longest Journey* to *Pharos and Pharillon*," in Judith Scherer Herz and Robert K. Martin, eds., *E. M. Forster: Centenary Revaluations*, 99–112.

———. "Whitman and the Politics of Identity," in Ed Folsom, ed., *Walt Whitman: The Centennial Essays*. Iowa City: University of Iowa Press, 1994, 172–81.

Martin, Robert K., and George Piggford, eds. *Queer Forster*. Chicago: Chicago University Press, 1997.

Mascara, Tina, and Guido Santi, directors. *Chris and Don: A Love Story*. 2007.

Matthews, Geoffrey, and Kelvin Everest, eds. *The Poems of Shelley*. London: Longman, 1989.

Matthews, Kenneth. *Aleko*. London: Peter Davies, 1934.

Matthias, John. "The Haunting of Benjamin Britten: A Review of Humphrey Carpenter's *Benjamin Britten: A Biography*." www.electronicbookreview.com/thread/electropoetics/prodigal.

Matz, Jesse. "Maurice in Time." *Style* 34:2 (2000), 188–211.

McDowell, Frederick P. W. "E. M. Forster and Goldsworthy Lowes Dickinson." *Studies in the Novel* V:4 (1973), 441–57.

McGuiness, Ilona. "The Collaborative Rhetoric of E. M. Forster's *Goldsworthy Lowes Dickinson*." *a/b: Auto/Biography Studies* 6:2 (1991), 253–71.

Meredith, Hugh Owen. *Week-Day Poems*. London: Edward Arnold, 1911.

Metcalf, Barbara D., and Thomas R. Metcalf. *A Concise History of Modern India*. 2nd ed. Cambridge: Cambridge University Press, 2006.

Meyer, Richard. *Outlaw Representation: Censorship and Homosexuality in Twentieth-Century American Art*. Oxford: Oxford University Press, 2002.

Mitchell, Donald, Philip Reed, and Mervyn Cooke, eds. *Letters from a Life: Selected Letters of Benjamin Britten. Vol. 3: 1946–1951*. London: Faber and Faber, 2004.

Mitchison, Naomi. *You May Well Ask: A Memoir, 1920–1940.* London: Gollancz, 1979.

Moffat, Wendy. "*A Passage to India* and the Limits of Certainty." *Journal of Narrative Technique* 20:3 (1990), 331–41.

Lord Montagu of Beaulieu. *Wheels Within Wheels: An Unconventional Life.* London: Weidenfeld and Nicolson, 2000.

Moran, Leslie. *Homosexual(ity) of Law.* London: Routledge, 1993.

Morris, John. *Eating the Indian Air.* London: Hamilton, 1968.

———. *Hired to Kill: Some Chapters of Autobiography.* London: Rupert Hart-Davis, 1960.

———. "The Lawrence Enigma." *Encounter,* April 1955, 78–80.

Mort, Frank. "Mapping Sexual London: The Wolfenden Committee on Homosexual Offences and Prostitution, 1954–1957." *New Formations* 37 (1999), 92–113.

Mort, Frank, Betsy Conekin, and Chris Waters. *Moments of Modernity: Reconstructing Britain, 1945–1964.* London: Rivers Oram, 1999.

Munby, A. N. L., ed. *This Book Belongs to E. M. Forster—a Catalogue of Forster's Library.* Cambridge: W. Heffer and Sons, 1971.

Murals by Jared French. New York: Julien Levy Gallery, 1939.

Murphy, Peter F., ed. *Fictions of Masculinity.* New York: New York University Press, 1994.

Nadel, Ira B. "Moments in the Greenwood: Maurice in Context," in Judith Scherer Herz and Robert K. Martin, eds., *E. M. Forster: Centenary Revaluations,* 177–90.

New York Times, "William Roerick Obituary," Dec. 7, 1995, B18.

Nicholson, Nigel, and Joanne Trautmann, eds. *The Letters of Virginia Woolf.* 6 vols. New York: Harcourt Brace Jovanovich, 1975–80.

Nisetich, Frank (trans.). *The Poems of Callimachus.* Oxford: Oxford University Press, 2001.

Noble, R. W. "'Dearest Forster'—'Dearest Masood.'" *Encounter,* LVI:6 (1981), 61–72.

Nowell-Smith, Simon. "Postscript," in Nowell-Smith, ed., *The Autobiography of William Plomer.* London: Jonathan Cape, 1975, 424–48.

Nussbaum, Martha, and Juha Sihvola, eds. *The Sleep of Reason: Erotic Experience and Sexual Ethics in Ancient Greece and Rome.* Chicago: University of Chicago Press, 2002.

O'Brien, M. D. *Socialism and Infamy: The Homogenic Love Exposed.* Sheffield, U.K.: Dronenfield, 1909.

Panter-Downes, Mollie. "Kingsman." *New Yorker,* Sept. 19, 1959, 51–80.

Parker, Peter. *Ackerley: A Life of J. R. Ackerley.* London: Constable, 1989.

———. *Christopher Isherwood: A Life.* London: Picador, 2004.

Parkes, Adam. *Modernism and the Theater of Censorship.* New York: Oxford University Press, 1996.

Parris, Matthew. "'Heroic in Perversity.' A Review of Peter Wildeblood's *Against the Law* Reissue." *Times* (London), Nov. 20, 1999, 22.

Partridge, Frances. *Life Regained: Diaries, 1970–1972.* London: Phoenix, 1998.

———. *Other People: Diaries, 1963–1966.* New York: HarperCollins, 1993.

Peacock, John. "A Kiss from a Sailor." Unpublished BBC radio play.

Phelps, Robert, with Jerry Rosco, eds. *Continual Lessons: The Journals of Glenway Wescott, 1937–1955.* New York: Farrar, Straus and Giroux, 1990.

Pinchin, Jane Lagoudis. *Alexandria Still: Forster, Durrell, and Cavafy.* Princeton, N.J.: Princeton University Press, 1977.

Plato. "Phaedrus," in Alexander Nahamus and Paul Woodruff, eds., *Plato: Complete Works.* Indianapolis: Hackett Publishing, 1997.

Plomer, William. *At Home: Memoirs*. London: Jonathan Cape, 1958.

———. *Borderline Ballads*. New York: Noonday, 1955.

———. *Double Lives: An Autobiography*. London: Jonathan Cape, 1943.

———. "Forster as a Friend," in Oliver Stallybrass, ed., *Aspects of E. M. Forster: Essays and Recollections Written for His Ninetieth Birthday, Jan. 1, 1969*, 99–107.

———. *A Message in Code: The Diary of Richard Rumbold. 1932–1960*. London: Weidenfeld and Nicolson, 1964.

———. *Sado*. London: Hogarth Press, 1931.

———. *Turbott Wolfe*. London: Hogarth Press, 1925.

Plummer, Kenneth. "Intimate Citizenship and the Culture of Sexual Storytelling," in Jeffrey Weeks, Janet Holland, and Matthew Waites, eds., *Sexual Cultures: Communities, Values, and Intimacy*, 34–53.

———. *The Making of the Modern Homosexual*. Totowa, N.J.: Barnes and Noble, 1981.

Pohorilenko, Anatole, and James Crump, eds. *When We Were Three: The Travel Albums of George Platt Lynes, Monroe Wheeler, and Glenway Wescott*. New York: Arena, 1988.

Pomeroy, Wardell. *Dr. Kinsey and the Institute for Sex Research*. New York: Thomas Nelson, 1972.

Porter, Kevin, and Jeffrey Weeks, eds. *Between the Acts: Lives of Homosexual Men, 1885–1967*. London: Routledge, 1991.

Portrait: Photographs of George Platt Lynes, 1927–1955. Santa Fe: Twin Palms Press, 1994.

Price, Martin. *Forms of Life: Character and Moral Imagination in the Novel*. New Haven: Yale University Press, 1983.

Proctor, Dennis, ed. *The Autobiography of Goldsworthy Lowes Dickinson*. London: Duckworth, 1973.

Pyron, Darden Asbury. *Liberace: An American Boy*. Chicago: University of Chicago Press, 2000.

Rama Rau, Santha. "Remembering E. M. Forster," in J. H. Stape, ed., *E. M. Forster: Interviews and Recollections*, 132–53.

Rau, Petra. "John Lehmann (1907–1987)." *The Literary Encyclopedia*, Mar. 21, 2002. www .litencyc.com/php/speople.php?rec=true+UID=2681.

Reade, Brian, ed. *Sexual Heretics: Male Homosexuality in English Literature from 1850 to 1900: An Anthology*. London: Routledge and Kegan Paul, 1970.

The Rediscovery of Jared French. New York: Midtown Payson Galleries, 1992.

Reed, Philip. "Eric Crozier Obituary." *Guardian*. Sept. 8, 1994.

Rees, Jenny. *Looking for Mr. Nobody: The Secret Life of Goronwy Rees*. London: Weidenfeld and Nicolson, 1994.

Reid, Forrest. *The Garden God: A Tale of Two Boys*. London: Brilliance Books, 1986.

———. *Private Road*. London: Faber and Faber, 1940.

———. *Tom Barber*. New York: Pantheon, 1945.

———. *Young Tom, or Very Mixed Company*. London: Faber and Faber, 1944.

Reiss, Timothy. "Discourse, Politics and the Temptation of Enlightenment: Paris, 1935." *Annals of Scholarship* 8:1 (1991), 61-78.

Roberts, Warren, James T. Boulton, and Elizabeth Mansfield, eds. *The Letters of D. H. Lawrence: Vol. IV, June 1921–March 1924*. Cambridge: Cambridge University Press, 1987.

Robinson, Christopher. *C. P. Cavafy*. Bristol: Classical Press, 1988.

Robinson, Paul. *Gay Lives: Homosexual Autobiography from John Addington Symonds to Paul Monette*. Chicago: University of Chicago Press, 1999.

———. *The Modernization of Sex: Havelock Ellis, Alfred Kinsey, William Masters and Virginia Johnson*. Ithaca, N.Y.: Cornell University Press, 1989.

Roerick, William. *Collection on a Shoestring*. Root Art Center, Hamilton College, 1964.

———. "Forster and America," in Oliver Stallybrass, ed., *Aspects of E. M. Forster: Essays and Recollections Written for His Ninetieth Birthday, Jan. 1, 1969*, 61–73.

———. "The Frame Alone." Unpublished ms., David Adkins collection.

———. "Where Shall John Go? A Reply to Anthony Bourne." *Horizon* 9:1 (1944), 204–7.

Roerick, William, and Thomas Coley. *The Happiest Year: A Comedy in Three Acts*. London: Samuel French, 1948.

Rosco, Jerry. *Glenway Wescott, Personally*. Madison: University of Wisconsin Press, 2002.

Rothblatt, Sheldon. *The Revolution of the Dons: Cambridge and Society in Victorian England*. New York: Basic Books, 1969.

Roueché, Burton (uncredited). "Tourist." *New Yorker*, May 3, 1947, 27–28.

Rowbotham, Sheila. *Edward Carpenter: A Life of Liberty and Love*. London: Verso, 2008.

———. "In Search of Carpenter." *History Workshop* 3 (1977), 121–37.

Rowbotham, Sheila, and Jeffrey Weeks. *Socialism and the New Life: The Personal and Sexual Politics of Edward Carpenter and Havelock Ellis*. London: Pluto Press, 1977.

Rowson, Everett K. "The Categorization of Gender and Sexual Irregularity in Medieval Arabic Vice Lists," in Julia Epstein and Kristina Straub, eds., *Body Guards: The Cultural Politics of Gender Ambiguity*. New York: Routledge, 1991.

Rugg, Linda Haverty. *Picturing Ourselves: Photography & Autobiography*. Chicago: University of Chicago Press, 1997.

Saunders, Frances Stonor. "What Have Intellectuals Ever Done for the World?" *Observer*, Nov. 28, 2004.

Sayle, Charles. *Cambridge Fragments*. Cambridge: Cambridge University Press, 1913.

———. *Erotidia*. Rugby: George Over, 1889.

———. *Musa Consolatrix*. London: David Nutt, 1893.

Schlesinger, Peter. *Checkered Past: A Visual Diary of the '60s and '70s*. New York: Vendome, 2003.

Schuller, Herbert, and Robert L. Peters, eds. *The Letters of John Addington Symonds*. 3 vols. Detroit: Wayne State University Press, 1968.

Scott, Suzanne, and Lynne M. Constantine. "Bird Watchers (1948)/George Tooker (b. 1920)." *Journal of the American Pharmaceutical Association* 40:6 (2000), 880.

Scupham, Peter. "Shelf Lives 17: William Plomer." *PN [Poetry Nation] Review* 151, 36–39.

Sedgwick, Eve Kosofsky. *Between Men: English Literature and Male Homosocial Desire*. New York: Columbia University Press, 1985.

———. *Epistemology of the Closet*. Berkeley: University of California Press, 1990.

———. *Novel Gazing: Queer Readings in Fiction*. Durham, N.C.: Duke University Press, 1997.

———. *Touching Feeling: Affect, Pedagogy, Performativity*. Durham, N.C.: Duke University Press, 2003.

Selfe, David W., and Vincent Burke. *Perspectives on Sex, Crime and Society*. London: Cavendish, 1998.

Seymour, Anne. *Marks on a Canvas: Junge Engländer: Patrick Caulfield, Bernard Cohen, David Hockney, John Hoyland, Paul Huxley, Allen Jones, Mark Lancaster, Jeremy*

Moon, Bridget Riley, Richard Smith, John Walker. Hannover, Germany: Hannover Kunstverein, 1969.

Shattuck, Roger. *The Innocent Eye: On Modern Literature and the Arts.* New York: Farrar, Straus and Giroux, 1984.

Sherrard, Philip. "Cavafy's Sensual City: A Question," in Denise Harvey. ed., *The Mind and Art of C. P. Cavafy: Essays on His Life and Work.*

Sinfield, Alan. *Gay and After.* London: Serpent's Tail, 1999.

———. *The Wilde Century: Effeminacy, Oscar Wilde, and the Queer Moment.* New York: Columbia University Press, 1994.

Slater, Montagu. *Peter Grimes: Libretto.* London: Boosey & Hawkes, 1945.

———. "The Plot of 'Peter Grimes.'" *Tempo* 9 (1941), 10–11.

Smith, Timothy D'Arch. *Love in Earnest: Some Notes on the Lives and Writings of English "Uranian" Poets from 1889 to 1930.* London: Routledge and Kegan Paul, 1970.

Smith, Zadie. "E. M. Forster, Middle Manager." *New York Review of Books* (2008), 8–12.

Soffer, Reba N. *Discipline and Power: The University, History, and the Making of an English Elite, 1870–1930.* Stanford, Calif.: Stanford University Press, 1994.

Souhami, Diana. *The Trials of Radclyffe Hall.* New York: Doubleday, 1999.

Spender, Stephen. *Letters to Christopher: Stephen Spender's Letters to Christopher Isherwood, 1929–1939, with "The Line of the Branch"—Two Thirties Journals,* ed. Lee Bartlett. Santa Barbara: Black Sparrow, 1980.

———. *World Within World.* New York: St. Martin's Press, 1994.

Spivak, Gayatri Chakravorty. "Can the Subaltern Speak?" in Cary Nelson and Lawrence Grossberg, eds., *Marxism and the Interpretation of Culture,* Champaign: University of Illinois Press, 1988, 271–316.

Spring, Justin. *Paul Cadmus: The Male Nude.* New York: Universe, 2002.

Sprott, W. J. H. *Science and Social Action.* London: Watts and Company, 1954.

Stallybrass, Oliver, ed. *Aspects of E. M. Forster: Essays and Recollections Written for His Ninetieth Birthday, Jan. 1, 1969.* New York: Harcourt Brace, 1969.

———, ed. *The Lucy Novels: Early Sketches for a Room with a View.* London: Edward Arnold, 1977.

———, ed. *The Manuscripts of Howards End.* London: Edward Arnold, 1973.

Stape, J. H. *An E. M. Forster Chronology.* New York: Macmillan, 1993.

———, ed. *E. M. Forster: Interviews and Recollections.* New York: St. Martin's Press, 1993.

———. "Leonard's 'Fatal Forgotten Umbrella': Sex and the Manuscript Revision of Howards End." *Journal of Modern Literature* 9:1 (1981–82), 123–32.

Stein, Gertrude. *The Autobiography of Alice B. Toklas* (1933). New York: Random House, 1960.

Steward, Samuel M. *Chapters from an Autobiography.* San Francisco: Grey Fox, 1981.

———. "George Platt Lynes: The Man." *The Advocate,* Dec. 10, 1981, 22–24.

Swan, Tom. *Edward Carpenter: The Man and His Message.* London: Jonathan Cape, 1922.

Symbolic Realism in American Painting, 1940–1950. London: Institute of Contemporary Arts, 1950.

Symonds, John Addington. *A Problem in Greek Ethics: Being an Inquiry into the Phenomenon of Sexual Inversion Addressed Especially to Medical Psychologists and Jurists.* London: n.p., 1901.

Tambling, Jeremy. *Confession: Sexuality, Sin, the Subject.* Manchester: Manchester University Press, 1990.

————, ed. *E. M. Forster: New Casebook.* London: Macmillan, 1995.

Taylor, Brian. *The Green Avenue: The Life and Writings of Forrest Reid, 1875–1947.* Cambridge: Cambridge University Press, 1980.

Taylor, William R., ed. *Inventing Times Square.* New York: Russell Sage, 1991.

Thiele, Beverly. "Coming of Age: Edward Carpenter on Sex and Reproduction," in Tony Brown, ed., *Edward Carpenter and Late Victorian Radicalism,* 100–25.

Thomson, George, ed. *Albergo Empedocle and Other Writings by E. M. Forster.* New York: Liveright, 1971.

Tilby, Michael. "André Gide, E. M. Forster and G. Lowes Dickinson." *Modern Language Review* 80:4 (1985), 817–32.

Times Literary Supplement. "George and Jim." Sept. 10, 1964, 837.

Tippins, Sherrill. *February House.* Boston: Houghton Mifflin, 2005.

Trilling, Lionel. *E. M. Forster.* New York: New Directions, 1943.

Waley, Arthur. *Translations from the Chinese.* New York: Knopf, 1941.

Walter, George, ed. *In Flanders Fields: Poetry of the First World War.* London: Allen Lane, 2004.

Waters, Chris. "Disorders of the Mind, Disorders of the Body Social: Peter Wildeblood and the Making of the Modern Homosexual," in Frank Mort et al., eds., *Moments of Modernity: Reconstructing Britain, 1945–1964,* 134–51.

————. "Havelock Ellis, Sigmund Freud and the State: Discourses of Homosexual Identity in Interwar Britain," in Lucy Bland and Laura Doan, eds., *Sexology in Culture: Labelling Bodies and Desires,* 165–79.

Weeks, Jeffrey. *Coming Out: Homosexual Politics in Britain, from the Nineteenth Century to the Present.* London: Quartet, 1977.

————. *Invented Moralities: Sexual Values in an Age of Uncertainty.* New York: Columbia University Press, 1995.

————. *Sex, Politics and Society: The Regulation of Sexuality Since 1800.* London: Longman, 1981.

————. *Sexuality and Its Discontents: Meanings, Myths, and Modern Societies.* London: Routledge and Kegan Paul, 1985.

Weeks, Jeffrey, Janet Holland, and Matthew Waites, eds. *Sexual Cultures: Communities, Values, and Intimacy.* New York: St. Martin's Press, 1996.

Weinberg, Jonathan. "Boy Crazy: Carl Van Vechten's Queer Collection." *Yale Journal of Criticism* 7:2 (1994), 25–49.

————. *Speaking for Vice: Homosexuality in the Art of Charles Demuth, Marsden Hartley and the First American Avant-Garde.* New Haven: Yale University Press, 1993.

Weininger, Otto. *Sex and Character.* New York: G. P. Putnam's Sons, 1908.

Weintraub, Stanley. "Review of Isherwood's *A Single Man.*" *Books Abroad,* Summer 1965, 351.

Welch, Denton. *A Voice Through a Cloud* (1950). New York: E. P. Dutton, 1966.

Welty, Eudora. "The Life to Come." *New York Times Book Review,* May 13, 1973, 365.

Werth, Barry. *The Scarlet Professor: Newton Arvin—A Literary Life Shattered by Scandal.* New York: Random House, 2001.

Wescott, Glenway. "A Dinner, a Talk, a Walk with E. M. Forster," in J. H. Stape, ed., *E. M. Forster: Interviews and Recollections,* 104–12.

————. *The Babe's Bed.* Paris: Harrison, 1930.

————. *Images of Truth: Remembrances and Criticism.* London: Hamish Hamilton, 1963.

————. *The Pilgrim Hawk*. New York: Farrar, Straus and Giroux, 1940.

White, Chris. *Nineteenth Century Writings on Homosexuality: A Sourcebook*. London: Routledge, 1999.

Whitman, Walt. *Leaves of Grass; a Passage to India*. No publisher, 1872.

Wildeblood, Peter. *Against the Law* (Original American 1954 ed.). New York: Julian Messner, 1959.

Wilkinson, L. P. *A Century of King's, 1873-1972*. Cambridge: King's College, 1980.

————. "Forster and King's," in Oliver Stallybrass, ed., *Aspects of E. M. Forster: Essays and Recollections Written for His Ninetieth Birthday, Jan. 1, 1969*, 13–29.

————. *Kingsmen of a Century*. Cambridge: King's College, 1981.

Williams, Raymond. *Culture and Society: 1780–1950*. New York: Columbia University Press, 1958.

Willis, Deborah, ed. *Picturing Us: African American Identity in Photography*. New York: New Press, 1994.

Wilson, Jean Moorcroft. *Siegfried Sassoon: A Journey from the Trenches—a Biography*. Vol. II. New York: Routledge, 2003.

Windham, Donald. *The Dog Star*. Signet: New York, 1950.

————. *E. M. Forster's Letters to Donald Windham*. Verona: n.p., 1975.

————. "The Hitchhiker." Private printing.

————. *Tanaquil*. New York: Holt Rinehart, 1977.

————. *Two People*. New York: Coward-McCann, 1965.

————. *The Warm Country*. New York: Scribner and Sons, 1948.

————. "Which Urges and Reasonably So the Attraction of Some for Others." *Yale Review* 86:4 (1998), 18–31.

Winstanley, D. A. *Later Victorian Cambridge*. Cambridge: Cambridge University Press, 1947.

Wolfenden, John. *Report of the Committee on Homosexual Offences and Prostitution*. New York: Stein and Day, 1963.

————. *Turning Points: A Memoir*. London: Bodley Head, 1976.

Wolff, Charlotte. *Magnus Hirschfeld: A Portrait of a Pioneer in Sexology*. London: Quartet Books, 1986.

Woody, Jack, ed. *Collaboration: The Photographs of Paul Cadmus, Margaret French, and Jared French*. Santa Fe: Twelvetrees Press, 1992.

Woolf, Leonard. *Sowing: An Autobiography of the Years 1880 to 1904*. New York: Harcourt, Brace and Company, 1960.

Woolf, Virginia. *The Diaries of Virginia Woolf*, ed. Anne Olivier Bell. 5 vols. London: Hogarth Press, 1977–84.

————. *The Letters of Virginia Woolf*, ed. Nigel Nicolson and Joanne Trautmann Banks. 6 vols. New York: Harcourt Brace Jovanovich, 1975–1980.

Wright, Adrian. *John Lehmann: A Pagan Adventure*. London: Duckworth, 1998.

Yagoda, Ben. *About Town: The New Yorker and the World It Made*. New York: Da Capo Press, 2000.

Acknowledgments

Dickinson College has been my intellectual home for almost twenty-five years. It has also been the fount of most material support for this ten-year project. I would like to thank my colleagues on the Research and Development Committee and Provost Neil Weissman for money, time, and the chance to collaborate with students using Dana and Mellon funds. Dickinson students Jason Murray, Sara Hoover, and George Fitting provided valuable help and insight. Laura Harbold, now a colleague, checked quotations and obtained permissions with her usual intelligence and aplomb.

Sydelle Kramer, agent extraordinaire, saw in this project something greater than I imagined and helped me to show it to others. Jonathan Galassi has edited with the grace and patience of a Zen master. More than anyone, he has taught me how to write this book. Immeasurable care has been taken by Jesse Coleman, Jeff Seroy, and many others at Farrar, Straus and Giroux. Bill Swainson loves literature and lent me his impeccable ear.

Jeff Wood, the last independent bookseller in Cumberland County, has steered me in the right direction more times than I can count.

At Dickinson there are many people who have helped me to become a better teacher and writer. College librarians, especially Chris Bombaro and Tina Maresco, have performed many miracles. Thanks also to Rafael Alvarado, Greg Berrier, Dan Buchan, Ryan Burke, Andrew Connell, Amanda deLorenzo, Brenda Landis, Pat Pehlman, Andy Petrus, Tom Smith, Chuck Steel, Brenda Steely, and Jean Weaver for years of technical support.

I would like to thank my friends for rich and challenging conversations and the freedom to explore these problems through teaching. Kelly Winters-Fazio has supported me at every step. Susan Rose, Bob Winston, Carol Ann

Johnston, Bob Ness, and David Ball have encouraged and goaded me. Sharon O'Brien knew that I could write this book long before I believed I could. Dickinson's program at the University of East Anglia offered a home away from home in 1997 and 1998. Thanks to Jackie Fear-Segal and Allan Segal, Simon Middleton and Caroline Wade, Sophy Rickett and Robert Innes Hopkins, Margaret Homberger, Judy Homberger, and Eric Homberger (who charitably and thoughtfully read an early draft of the manuscript).

A monthlong fellowship at the Beinecke Rare Book and Manuscript Library at Yale in September 2007 afforded me access to the papers of many of Forster's American friends, the company of congenial scholars, and a generous stipend. During that time Liliane Greene graciously shared her home and heart.

I have followed in the steps of extraordinary biographers of Forster. Francis King spoke with me very early in the project. Nicola Beauman warmly reached out to me and offered useful advice. Nick Furbank shared his insight, unpublished correspondence, photographs, and audiotapes. I am grateful for their generosity.

I relied on the wise counsel of scholars and experts in a range of fields: Paul Armstrong, Karen Arrandale, Todd Avery, Michael Bernstein, Robert Caserio, George Chauncey, David Commins, Nicholas de Jongh, Ed DeLuca, Bruce Dunne, Max Egremont, Philip Eliasoph, Jay Grossman, Judith Scherer Herz, Lisa Hodermarsky, Hubert Kennedy, the late Mary Lago, Linda Leavell, David Lelyveld, Glen Leonard, Christofilis Maggidis, Jesse Matz, Ira Nadel, Peter Parker, Ted Pulcini, Jerry Rosco, S. P. Rosenbaum, Everett K. Rowson, Richard Shone, Justin Spring, Bill Thompson, Karen Van Dyck, Robyn Warhol, Jonathan Weinberg, and Glenn Willums. Betty Sams lent me a rare Baedeker. Sue Schweik lent me the talisman of Morgan's calling card, found by her father in the pages of a book. Now it can go home again.

Thanks to the following people who granted me interviews: David Adkins, Tyringham MA and NYC (June 30, 2002; Aug. 21, 2002; Dec. 6, 2002), Gwyneth Barger, Lenox MA (June 27, 2002), Mollie Barger, Hampstead (July 24, 2001; June 26, 2009), Gary Haller, New Haven CT (June 28, 2002), Eugenie Rudd Fawcett, John Fawcett, Donald Fawcett, and Jim Fawcett, Tyringham MA (June 29, 2002), the late Mary Jackson, Los Angeles (Aug. 6, 2002), Bruce Kellner, Lancaster PA (March 14, 2003), Mary D. Kierstead, Tyringham MA (June 29, 2002), Francis King, Kensington (July 20, 2001), Bernard Perlin, Ridgefield CT (Sept. 30, 2001; Sept. 23, 2007), George

Tooker, Hartland VT (Sept. 28, 2001), Mark Lancaster, Jamestown RI (Feb. 24, 2007), Ed DeLuca, NYC (Sept. 25, 2007), Jon Anderson and Philis Raskind, Weston CT (Oct. 10, 2007), John Connolly and Ivan Ashby, Rosemont NJ (Oct. 5, 2007), George Lynes II and Jane Lynes, NYC (Oct. 11, 2007), Angela Hederman, NYC (Oct. 12, 2007), Don Bachardy, Santa Monica (Nov. 5, 2007), Jensen Yow, Califon, NJ (Nov. 20, 2007), Nick Furbank, London (June 6, 2008, June 24, 2009). Correspondence with Norman Coates, Lord Kennet, the late Mattei Radev, Mark Lancaster, and Tim Leggatt was illuminating. Thanks, too, to Barbara Roe and Kevin Greenback at the Centre of South Asian Studies, Cambridge, for information about Malcolm and Josie Darling; to Karen Kukil and Barbara Blumenthal at the Mortimer Rare Book Room, Smith College; to Shan McAnena at the Naughton Gallery, Queen's University, Belfast; to Rick Frederick at the McNay Museum, San Antonio; to Wendy Hurlock Baker at the Smithsonian Institution's Archives of American Art; to Manuel Savidis at the Cavafy Archive; to Michael Spick at the Sheffield City Archives; and to Jeremy Megraw at the Photographic Collection of the Billy Rose Theater Division of the New York Public Library for the Performing Arts at Lincoln Center. Special thanks to Pat Belshaw, Mark Lancaster, and the Buckingham family, for sharing photos and private memories.

Archival research at the Beinecke Rare Book and Manuscript Library at Yale (Lynes, Wescott, Wheeler), Columbia University Archives (Trilling), Durham University Archives (Plomer and Morris), the Huntington Library (Isherwood), King's College Modern Archives (Buckinghams, Dickinson, Forster, Sprott, Strachey), and the New York Public Library for the Performing Arts at Lincoln Center (Kirstein, Martinez) and the Ransom Center for the Humanities at the University of Texas at Austin (Ackerley, British Society for Sex Psychology, Darling) was made immeasurably more pleasant by the help of the librarians and archivists, Timothy Young, Patricia Willis, Nancy Kuhl, Sue Hodson, Andrew Grey, Jacky Cox, Rosalind Moad, Charles Perrin, and Thomas Staley. Thanks to Brad Meade and Dr. Brad Goff for the chance to look at remarkable paintings. At King's Patricia McGuire knows everything and has done much more than she was asked to do. At crucial times Rachel Malkin, Lucy Kaufman, and Pat Fox were my eyes in archives afar; I thank them.

Thanks, too, for the assistance of staff at Amherst College, Bryn Mawr College, University of California at Berkeley, University of California at Los

Angeles, University of Chicago, Columbia University, University of Georgia, Hamilton College, University of Texas at Austin, Huntington Library, Washington and Lee University, and Yale. Also, Professors William Kelly Simpson and Gary Haller at Yale, Catherine Anne Johnson and the Kinsey Institute, John Stevenson, the Whitney Museum, DC Moore Gallery, Berkshire Historical Society, Berkshire Eagle, Tobin Gallery, Brandywine Museum, David Leddick, Cornelia Gilder, Alice Truax, Larry Simpson, James Seidel, Frank Lorenz, Bill Roberts, Andrew Patterson, Jay Satterfield, Peter Nelson, and Dennis Bitterlich. I am also grateful to Nicholas Jenkins, Lincoln Kirstein's literary executor, for permission to read the Lincoln Kirstein Papers.

I am indebted to so many people, not only for the help and kindness they showed me but also for the freedom they afforded me in telling what is, at least in part, their story too. I have endeavored to be accurate and to be true. For the paperback edition I have gratefully accepted the suggestions of my readers. Any errors in this book are my own.

A long time ago, three extraordinary teachers taught me to think and to write. This book belongs to the memory of Richard Sewall, to Martin Price, and especially to my mentor and friend Alice Miskimin.

Writing this life evolved in the circle of my large and loving family. Archie and Fritz have been good company. My brothers, Gabe and James, my sisters, Lynn and Catherine, and my sisters-in-law, Nancy and Molly, have been a great support. My grandmother Jean's presence is with me always, though she did not live to see this to the close. All the parents—my mother, Anne, my father and stepmother, Donald and Gwen, and my in-laws Barbara and Tracy—have looked forward to new chapters with the kind of eager anticipation that makes a writer want to keep going. I owe much of my sense of the texture of Forster's England to my dad. And one of the particular pleasures of this long journey has been to watch my daughters, Lucy and Emma, develop into beautiful writers, whose own passions and ideas have become enmeshed in my work. Donald Kaufman, to whom the book is dedicated, is the love of my life.

Index

Abinger (Surrey), 191, 204, 237, 257, 260; Lily's house in, *see* West Hackhurst

Abinger Harvest (Forster), 240, 244

Ackerley, J. R. ("Joe"), 196–200, 209, 225, 244, 254, 298, 310, 316–19; Buckingham and, 220, 222; correspondence of Forster and, 196, 199, 204, 207, 208, 211, 217, 219, 226, 228, 235–36, 250–51, 271, 312; Daley and, 204–206, 219; Forster's financial generosity to, 210, 317; *The Listener* edited by, 224, 301, 304; production of play by, 202–203; seventieth-birthday party for Forster organized by, 277; tutelage of Forster in homosexual affairs by, 198, 200, 211–12; during World War I, 197, 202; during World War II, 249–51, 308, 317

Ackerley, Nancy, 220, 224

Ackerley, Roger, 224

Adcock, F. E., 11

Adl, Mohammed el, 152–73, 183, 191–92, 208, 210, 251, 252, 293, 315, 323; correspondence of Forster and, 163, 166, 177–79, 188, 304; death of, 177, 188–90, 196; departure from Alexandria of, 163–65; Forster's memoir of, 257, 344n, 345n; illness of, 171, 187–88; initiation of Forster's sexual

relationship with, 255–63; marriage of, 170–73; Palmer's resemblance to, 198; photographs of, 167, 177; Port Said visit of Forster with, 180, 184

"Ages of Man" (Meredith), 333n

Agincourt, Battle of, 40

Ahmad Khan, Syed, 88, 108

Aida (Verdi), 131

Albany, The (magazine), 94

Albert Herring (Britten), 279

Aldeburgh (Suffolk), 280, 297, 299; music festival at, 278, 319

Alexander the Great, 125–27

Alexandria, 123–52, 178; Cavafy's salon in, 140–47; Forster's love affair with el Adl in, 152–73; Forster's sexual awakening in, 148–51; Red Cross hospital in, 124, 125, 129–30, 132–35, 140, 146, 152, 312; sexual climate of, 127–28, 136–40

Alexandria: A History and a Guide (Forster), 150

Ali, Mohammed, 129

Aligarh (India), 88–89, 108, 256

All-India PEN conference (Jaipur, 1946), 256

American Academy of Arts and Letters (New York), 283, 288, 291

Amherst College, 267, 274

Anastassiades, Pericles, 130–31, 140

Anglican Church, 33, 42, 58, 127, 129

PERMISSIONS ACKNOWLEDGMENTS

Grateful acknowledgment is made for permission to reprint excerpts from the following unpublished and previously published material:

Ackerley, J. R. *E. M. Forster—A Portrait*. Reprinted by permission of David Higham Associates Limited.

Alexander, Peter F. *William Plomer: A Biography*. Reprinted by permission of Oxford University Press.

Anderson, Jon F. Correspondence with author. Reprinted by permission of Jon F. Anderson, Executor of the Cadmus Estate.

Auden, W. H., and Christopher Isherwood. *Journey to a War*. Copyright © 1939 by W. H. Auden and Christopher Isherwood. Reprinted by permission of Curtis Brown Group Ltd., London, on behalf of the Estate of W. H. Auden and the Estate of Christopher Isherwood.

Bartlett, Neil. *Who Was That Man?* Reprinted by permission of Serpent's Tail.

Beauman, Nicola. *Morgan: A Biography of E. M. Forster*. Reprinted by permission of the author

Belshaw, Patrick. *A Kind of Private Magic*. Reprinted by permission of Andre Deutsch.

Berlowitz, Rick Beard, and Leslie Cohen, eds. *Greenwich Village: Culture and Counterculture*. Copyright © 1993 by the Museum of the City of New York. Reprinted by permission of Rutgers University Press.

Brett, Philip. *Benjamin Britten: Peter Grimes*. Reprinted with the permission of Cambridge University Press.

Brown, Malcolm, ed. *T. E. Lawrence: The Selected Letters*. Reprinted by permission of W. W. Norton & Company, Inc.

Bucknell, Katherine, ed. *Christopher Isherwood: Diaries, Vol. I, 1939–1960*. Copyright © 1996 by the Estate of Christopher Isherwood. Reprinted by permission of the Random House Group Ltd. (USA) and by permission of Curtis Brown Group Ltd., London, on behalf of the Estate of Christopher Isherwood (UK).

Burkat, Leonard. "Letter from America," *Tempo* (Summer 1947). Reprinted by permission of *Tempo*.

Correspondence by Paul Cadmus reprinted by permission of Jon F. Anderson, Executor of the Cadmus Estate.

Carpenter, Humphrey. *W. H. Auden: A Biography*. Copyright © 1981 by George Allen & Unwin (Publishers) Ltd. Copyright © 1981 by the Estate of W. H. Auden. Reprinted by permission of Houghton Mifflin Harcourt Publishing Company. All rights reserved.

Chauncey, George. *Gay New York*. Reprinted by permission of Perseus Books Group.

Crisp, Quentin. *The Naked Civil Servant*. Reprinted by permission of Penguin Group (USA) Inc.

Daley, Harry. *This Small Cloud*. Reprinted by permission of the Orion Publishing Group.

Duffy, Eamon. *The Voices of Morebath: Reformation and Rebellion in an English Village*. Reprinted by permission of Yale University Press.

Excerpt from "Friday 31 August" in *The Diary of Virginia Woolf, Volume III: 1925–1930* by Virginia Woolf, copyright © 1980 by Quentin Bell and Angelica Garnett, reprinted by permission of Houghton Mifflin Harcourt Publishing Company.

Excerpts from "May 19, 1926," "September 8, 1923," and "August 30, 1928" in *The Letters of Virginia Woolf, Volume III: 1923–1927*, copyright © 1977 by Quentin Bell and Angelica Garnett, reprinted by permission of Houghton Mifflin Harcourt Publishing Company.

Excerpts from "November 30, 1937," "November 1, 1938," and "September 2, 1940" in *The Letters of Virginia Woolf, Volume V: 1923–1927*, copyright © 1984 by Quentin Bell and Angelica Garnett, reprinted by permission of Houghton Mifflin Harcourt Publishing Company.

Excerpts from "Sunday 12 March 1922" and "Tuesday 11 September 1923" in *The Diary of Virginia Woolf, Volume II: 1920–1924*, copyright © 1978 by Quentin Bell and Angela Garnett, reprinted by permission of Houghton Mifflin Harcourt Publishing Company.

Excerpts from "Art for Art's Sake" in *Two Cheers for Democracy*, copyright 1949 by E. M. Forster and renewed 1977 by Donald Parry, reprinted by permission of Houghton Mifflin Harcourt Publishing Company.

Excerpts from "George Crabbe and Peter Grimes," "Henry Thornton," "Gide's Death," "Virginia Woolf," "Syed Ross Masood," "Mrs. Miniver," and "The United States" in *Two Cheers for Democracy*, copyright 1951 by E. M. Forster and renewed 1979 by Donald Parry, reprinted by permission of Houghton Mifflin Harcourt Publishing Company.

Leontis, Artemis, Lauren E. Talalay, and Keith Taylor, eds. *What These Ithakas Mean: Readings in Cavafy*. Reprinted by permission of Hellenic Literary and Historic Archive (ELIA).

Levy, Paul, ed. *The Letters of Lytton Strachey*. Reprinted by permission of Farrar, Straus and Giroux.

Liddell, Robert. *Cavafy*. Reprinted by permission of Gerald Duckworth & Co. Ltd.

Metcalf, Barbara, and Thomas Metcalf. *A Concise History of Modern India*. Reprinted by permission of Cambridge University Press.

Mitchell, Donald, Philip Reed, and Mervyn Cooke, eds. *Letters from a Life: The Selected Letters of Benjamin Britten, Vol. III, 1946–1951*. Reprinted by permission of University of California Press.

Plomer, William. Unpublished correspondence. The Plomer Collection, Durham University. Reprinted by permission of the William Plomer Trust.

Proctor, Dennis, ed. *The Autobiography of Goldsworthy Lowes Dickinson*. Reprinted by permission of Gerald Duckworth & Co. Ltd.

Roberts, Warren, James T. Boulton, and Elizabeth Mansfield, eds. *The Letters of D. H. Lawrence, Vol. IV, June 1921–March 1924*. Reproduced by permission of Pollinger Limited and the Estate of Frieda Lawrence Ravagli.

Rosco, Jerry. *Glenway Wescott, Personally*. Reprinted by permission of the University of Wisconsin Press.

Saunders, Frances. "What Have Intellectuals Ever Done for the World?" *The Observer*, November 28, 2004. Reprinted by permission of the author.

Stein, Gertrude. *The Autobiography of Alice B. Toklas*. Reprinted by permission of David Higham Associates Limited.

Taylor, Brian. *The Green Avenue*. Reprinted by permission of Cambridge University Press.

Weeks, Jeffrey. *Coming Out: Homosexual Politics in Britain, from the Nineteenth Century to the Present*. Reprinted by permission of Quartet Press.

Weeks, Jeffrey. *Sex, Politics and Society: The Regulation of Sexuality Since 1880*. Reprinted by permission of Pearson Education Ltd.

Welty, Eudora. "The Life to Come." *New York Times Book Review*, May 13, 1973. Reprinted by permission of the publisher.

Wescott, Glenway. Unpublished correspondence. Beinecke Rare Book and Manuscript Library, Yale University. Reprinted by permission of Harold Ober Associates, Inc.

Williams, Raymond. *Culture and Society*. Published by Chatto & Windus. Reprinted by permission of the Random House Group Ltd.

Windham, Donald. "Which Urges and Reasonably So the Attraction of Some for Others." *Yale Review* (1998). Reprinted by permission of the publisher.

Windham, Donald. *Tanaquil*. Reprinted by permission of Henry Holt and Company, LLC.

Winstanley, D. A. *Later Victorian Cambridge*. Reprinted by permission of Cambridge University Press.

Wright, Adrian. *John Lehmann: A Pagan Adventure*. Reprinted by permission of Gerald Duckworth & Co Ltd.

Made in the USA
Coppell, TX
23 September 2020